"This stunning collection of marriage contracts in many media, from paper cuts to fabric, accompanied by an accessible history, is a must-have for anyone who loves Jewish ritual art."

—JODI EICHLER-LEVINE, Berman Professor of Jewish Civilization at Lehigh University and author of *Painted Pomegranates and Needlepoint Rabbis: How Jews Craft Resilience and Create Community*

"Clear, well organized, and thoroughly researched, *Ketubah Renaissance* will make an outstanding gift to a couple soon to be married, providing ideas for the text and illustration of their own marriage contract as well as teaching about the history of ketubot. For rabbis, educators, and scholars as well, it's an exceptional addition to the existing volumes on historical ketubot."

—DORION LIEBGOTT, editor of *Art and Tradition: Treasures of Jewish Life*

"This comprehensive and accessible introduction to ketubot will aid couples in their ketubah decision-making process."

—RABBI MICHAEL STRASSFELD, coeditor of *The Jewish Catalog*

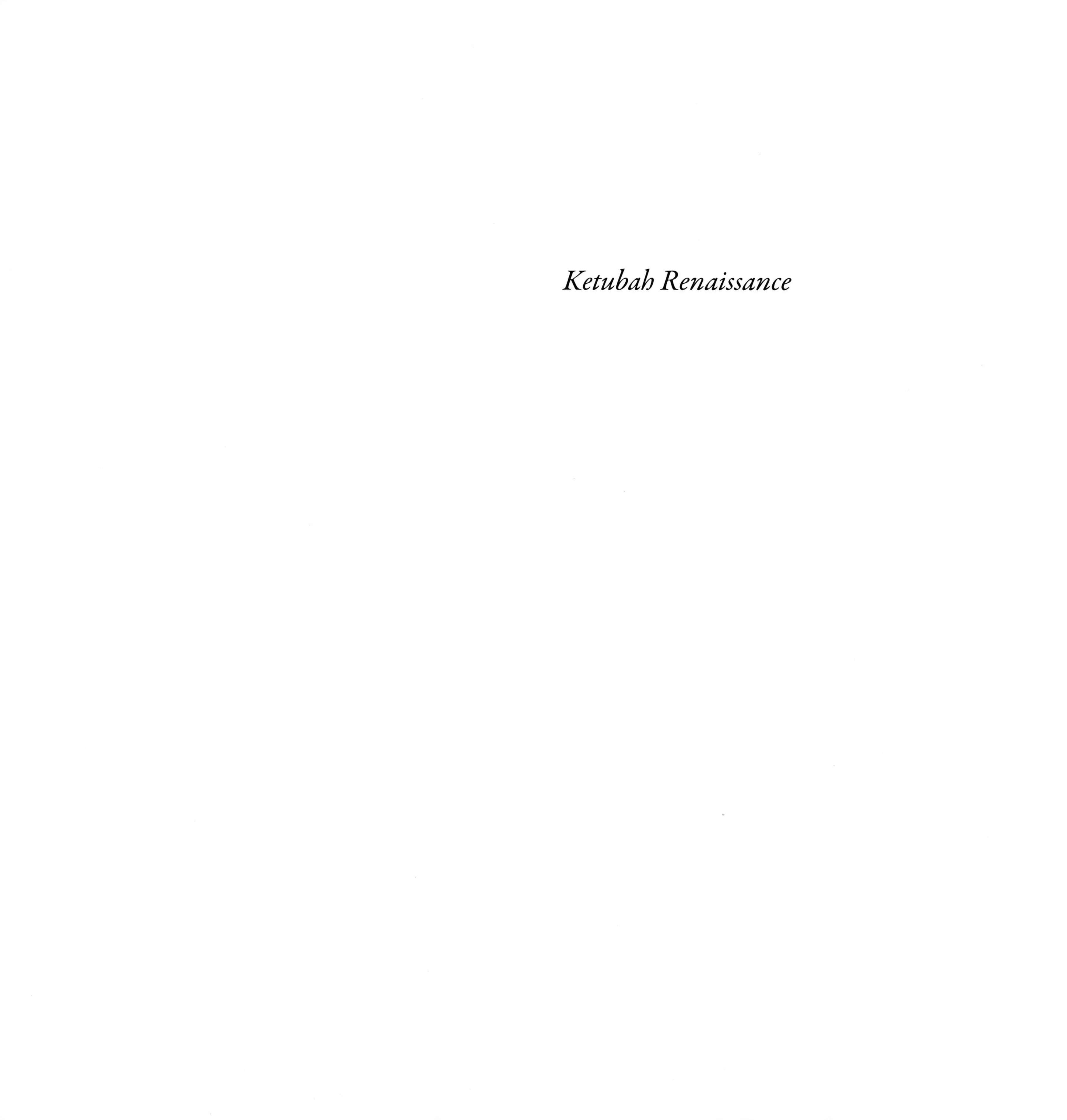

Ketubah Renaissance

Ketubah

University of Nebraska Press *Lincoln*

Renaissance

The Artful Modern Revival of the Jewish Marriage Contract

MICHAEL SHAPIRO

Foreword by SHALOM SABAR

Preface by JOANNA HOMRIGHAUSEN

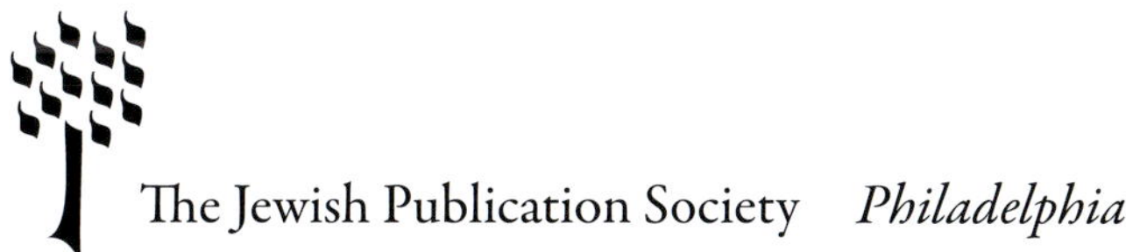
The Jewish Publication Society *Philadelphia*

 Published by the University of Nebraska Press as a Jewish Publication Society book. Manufactured in China.

Library of Congress Cataloging-in-Publication Data
Names: Shapiro, Michael, author. | Sabar, Shalom, 1951– writer of foreword.
Title: Ketubah renaissance: the artful modern revival of the Jewish marriage contract / Michael Shapiro; foreword by Shalom Sabar; preface by Joanna Homrighausen.
Description: Lincoln, Nebraska: University of Nebraska Press; Philadelphia: Jewish Publication Society, [2025] | Includes bibliographical references.
Identifiers: LCCN 2025004979
ISBN 9780827615625 (hardback)
ISBN 9780827619302 (pdf)
Subjects: LCSH: Ketubah—History. | Ketubah—Pictorial works. | BISAC: RELIGION / Judaism / Rituals & Practice | FAMILY & RELATIONSHIPS / Marriage & Long-Term Relationships
Classification: LCC BM713 .S474 2025 | DDC 296.4/4409—dc23/eng/20250403
LC record available at https://lccn.loc.gov/2025004979

Designed and set in Garamond Premier Pro by L. Welch.

TO ADDA, LYLA, AND EZRA

May you follow pursuits that light you up,
even when others haven't the faintest idea why.

And above all, remember that the meaning of life is to build a life as if it were a work of art.

ABRAHAM JOSHUA HESCHEL

Contents

Illustrations

Ketubah Plates

Following page 55

18. Robin Hall and Richard Sigberman, "Synagogue Ketubah," c. 1990
19. Jonathan Kremer, Untitled, 1991
20. Mordechai Rosenstein, Untitled, 1991
21. Ardyn Halter, "Seven Species," 1991
22. Avraham Cohen, "Flowers at Sunset," 1993
23. LSA (Artist Unknown), Untitled, 1995
24. Lee Loebman, "For Susan and Stephen's Rededication Ceremony," 1995
25. Betsy Platkin Teutsch, "Trees of Life," 1997
26. Stephanie Caplan, "Pomegranate," 1998
27. Archie Granot, "Jerusalem Ketubah," 1999
28. Amram Ebgi, Untitled, 2000
29. Tamar Messer, "Many Waters," 2001
30. Izzy Pludwinski, "Wildscript Roundel," 2002
31. Sandi Knell Tamny, "Ortman Gardberg Ketubah," 2002
32. Rachel Deitsch, "Trees Ketubah," 2004
33. Ian Kochberg, "Above All," 2004
34. Oded Ezer, Untitled, 2007
35. Amy Fagin, "Embrace," 2007
36. Diane Palley, "Hamsa Ketubah," 2007
37. Ruth Stern Warzecha, "Gefen Papercut—Charcoal," 2008
38. Dafna Jalon, "Growing Together," 2009
39. Judith Joseph, "Blue Forest," 2009
40. Jessica Carew Kraft, "Four Seasons," 2009
41. Jeanette Kuvin Oren, "Fabric Ketubah," 2009
42. Ruth Becker, "Revelry 18-Layer," 2010
43. Baruch Sienna, "Love, Period," 2010
44. Robert Saslow, "Love's Mosaic—Sapphire and Amethyst," 2011
45. Debra Band, "Intertwined," 2012
46. Aliza Boyer, "Canopy," 2012
47. Celia Lemonik, "Betrothed," 2012
48. Daniel Sroka, "Twin Tulips," 2013
49. Sivia Katz, "Creation in Three Languages," 2014
50. Nava Shoham, "Infinite Love," 2014
51. Danny Azoulay, "Azure," 2016
52. Amalya Nini, "Garden of Eden," 2017
53. Shell Rummel, "Adventure of a Lifetime II," 2017
54. Linda Frimer, "Summit Vista," 2019
55. Enya Keshet, "Sasson Papercut Luxe," 2019
56. Britt Yudell, "White & Gold Garden Embroidery," 2020
57. Jessica Tamar Deutsch, "Forest at Night," 2020
58. Rachel Ellison, "The Old Will Be Made New; The New Will Be Made Holy. The Phoenix Will Rise," 2020
59. Ayala Ophir, "Modern Nature," 2021
60. Hadass Mor Gerson, "Camp Harlam 60th Anniversary Ketubah," 2021

Foreword

The Joyous Art of the Ketubah

SHALOM SABAR

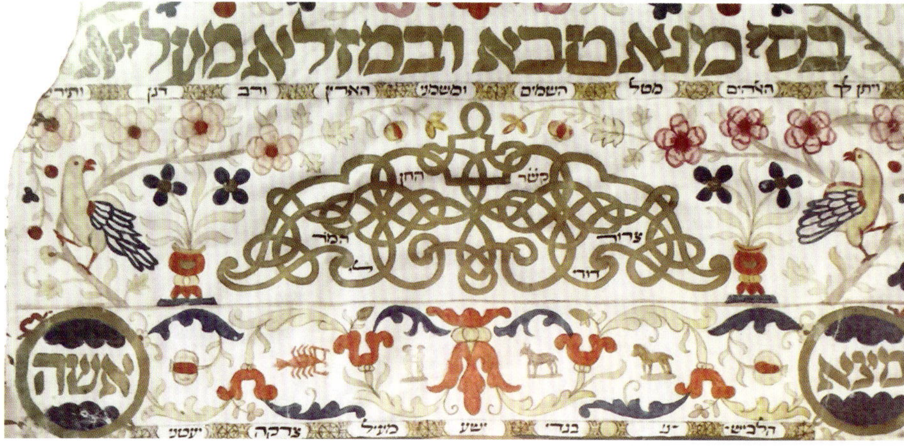

Fig. 1. Top portion of the Kesher Ha-Chen / Knot of Love ketubah, Venice, 1712. Courtesy of Shalom Sabar.

Over its long history traditional Jewish art has been created to celebrate life and enhance the observance of the commandments. Whether fabricating ceremonial art for the synagogue or ritual objects for the Sabbath, festivals, or multifaceted life cycle ceremonies, artists and craftspeople across the Diaspora have dedicated themselves to creating attractive items that "beautify the commandments" (*hiddur mitzvah*), appeal to the senses, and make the celebration more spiritually uplifting.

A primary example is the Torah scroll—though produced laboriously under strict and limiting rules, it is imaginatively and regally adorned. In Europe, it is "dressed" with highly detailed embroidered textiles and silver ornaments, including a majestic crown. In the lands of Islam, it is "housed" in a splendid cylindrical wooden case (*tik*), which in some communities (for example, Iraq, Kurdistan) is covered with richly ornamental embossed silver sheets, mounted by one or more impressive pairs of silver and gold finials (*rimonim* or *tapuḥim*), and delicately embellished with foliate and other motifs.

Marriage has always been considered one of the most important commandments in Judaism. The wedding, the most elaborate ritual in the Jewish life cycle, has called for the production of myriad ornate objects reflecting the status of the families involved. The lengthy preparations, which can last several years, have allowed for the meticulous creation of a wide range of items, from compelling bridal dresses and specially designed jewelry to highly decorated canopies (chuppahs) and luxurious gold and enamel wedding rings (sometimes in the shape of a magnificent tower).

Among all these sumptuous wedding items, one object undoubtedly stands out for its artistic achievements and great visual variety: the marriage contract, or ketubah.[1] Firm halakhic rules govern the wording of the traditional ketubah's basic text, which slightly recalls the sanctified Torah scroll, while allowing for some variations from one community to another. And yet, rabbinical authorities and community leaders from East to West commonly gave the folk artists who decorated the ketubah a free hand to showcase their creative talents through attractive images that contributed to the festivity and joy of the wedding ceremony.

But these artistic contributions only arrived much later in the history of the ketubah. The Bible does not mention a marriage contract (though a bill of divorce is referenced). Rather, the Rabbis of the Mishnah and Talmud developed this document, along with a list of the husband's obligations toward his wife in consequence of their marriage, to protect the wife's status and property in case of divorce or her husband's death. Primarily viewed as an essential and official legal document required for the marriage procedure, this document, like other parallel rabbinic documents, did not call for artistic enhancement.

This attitude changed around the late tenth to twelfth centuries, when the Jews of Egypt and Eretz Israel started to issue decorated ketubot, as evidenced by the fragments discovered in the famous Cairo Genizah (a synagogue chamber reserved for storing discarded items with sacred significance, found to be a treasure trove of over one thousand years of Jewish history). In this period, the wedding ritual among the dominant Jewish communities in the Islamic realm had become an increasingly elaborate festivity. Many members of the community were invited, and a substantial dowry of varied items (jewelry, clothing, bed linens, in some cases house furniture, kitchenware, and so forth, often taking several years to prepare) were publicly displayed and evaluated by special appraisers. Each item's value was also fully inscribed in the ketubah. Moreover, a new custom developed that is still followed to this day: reading aloud the contents of the marriage contract in front of all present. Many at the festive ritual also viewed the contract itself. A combination of these factors undoubtedly led to the desire to enrich the physical appearance of the marriage contract. The ketubot of the leading families became more elaborate in size, format, and decoration. Some ketubot included intricate micrography that required many hours of work by a talented scribe/artist; sometimes, specific names of the heads of the community/yeshivot were displayed in large square letters in the epithalamium decoratively inscribed at the top of the contract. Eventually the ketubah became a central artistic object of the wedding, and thereby also attested to the status of the bridal families.

From Egypt and Eretz Israel, the practice of decorating the marriage contract spread to medieval Europe. Though the earliest known figuratively illustrated contract was produced in an Ashkenazic community (Krems, Austria,

1391–92), this art form did not take root among the Jews of German-speaking lands, who predated by centuries most of those who settled in East Europe. By the time Jews came in increasing numbers to Poland from Germany, this tradition was no longer practiced in these lands. In these communities, the standardization of the text, including the financial obligations and dowry, reduced the importance of the physical document; thus, aside from first names and dates, medieval Ashkenazic ketubot show few variations. The Jews of medieval Spain, on the other hand, frequently added special conditions drawn between individual families to the main text, such as forbidding the husband-to-be to move his wife from one town/country to another against her will, or to take a second wife unless he divorced her first, paying her as specified in the ketubah and giving her a *get* (Jewish divorce document). There were also stipulations concerning inheritance laws, such as which part of the dowry she brought would be returned to her heirs if she died before him with no offspring (or one that didn't reach maturity). The stipulations changed from one document to another, and reflected local traditions agreed upon in the different communities. All in all, in Sephardic communities these ketubot helped protect the status and rights of Jewish women. By contrast, no such agreements appeared in standard-type Ashkenazic ketubot.

After the Jews' expulsion from Spain in 1492, they brought a richly illustrative ketubah tradition to their new lands across Northwestern, Central, and Southern Europe and the Middle East, where the visual tradition flourished for several hundred years. During the seventeenth and eighteenth centuries, Italy became the most creative center of this art form, which reached an artistic peak in leading Jewish communities such as Venice, Rome, Mantua, and Ancona.[2]

As we approach the modern era, the wonderful creative traditions of this unique Jewish art form were seemingly in danger of being abandoned and forgotten. Many centuries-old customs and traditional institutions lost their importance and place in daily Jewish life with the emancipation and liberation of Jews from ghettos across Europe. The production of illustrated ketubot declined significantly in the second half of the nineteenth century and early twentieth century. Lavishly designed and meticulously planned examples gave way to simpler, less ornate contracts, often created on smaller pieces of parchment or paper. In Islamic lands, where modernity followed a different trajectory and Jewish and Muslim traditions remained more intact, illustrated ketubot continued to be produced into the early decades of the twentieth century. However, even there, these works grew increasingly modest in design, a trend largely driven by the rise of printed ketubot. Eventually, printed contracts became so widespread that they entirely replaced hand-illustrated ketubot in some lands (for example, Iraq, Turkey, Eretz Israel). Furthermore, after the Jews from Islamic lands emigrated en masse to the Land of Israel in the 1940s through the 1960s, the practice of decorating a ketubah was reluctantly abandoned, along with many other such traditions that contrasted with the European-Ashkenazic dominant culture of the young State of Israel. In the following decades, the majority of Israelis regarded this document as a meaningless formality required by the Chief Rabbinate, with no real meaning for the wedding or married life.

Yet even before then, more than a generation before the creation of the State of Israel, some prominent twentieth-century artists in the Land of Israel and the United States, such as Ze'ev Raban and other artists from the Bezalel Academy of Arts and Design (established in Jerusalem in 1906 to create a new style of Jewish art in the spirit of Zionist ideology) created ketubot with innovative designs reflecting new styles in Jewish art. Still, the few original ketubot they created did not take root or motivate other couples to commission additional examples. This is perhaps not surprising, given the difficult conditions of life in the Land of Israel at a time when modesty and national ideals dominated the public sphere.

In the postwar period in North America, on the other hand, it wasn't until the late 1960s that the ketubah surged in interest among young American Jews in Jewish visual arts and traditions from different corners of the world. As will be elaborated in this book, the 1968 publication of the first bilingual volume with full-page color reproductions of ketubot from Europe and Islamic lands, David Davidovitch's *The Ketuba: Jewish Marriage Contracts Through the Ages*, followed by the richly illustrated popular *Encyclopedia Judaica* (1971–72), coincided with the initial stages of the ketubah renaissance and provided essential resources, both visual and textual, for inspiration. By the first decades of the twenty-first century, the phenomenon had become increasingly popular, reaching Israel and other countries such as Canada, Australia, England, France, Italy, Russia, and Belgium. And so, this is an especially appropriate time to showcase and analyze the resurgence of one of the most captivating Jewish art forms.

On a personal note, when as a graduate student in art history at the University of California, Los Angeles, I was invited to catalog the superb collection of ketubot in what is now known as the Skirball Cultural Center, I was certain it would be an easy task involving only "frozen text" and naïve decorations. To my great surprise, these contracts contained a wealth of information about bygone Jewish communities and their forgotten traditions, unknown or lost marriage customs, exquisite wedding poetry written by anonymous individuals, original and little-known blessings, and deep knowledge of rabbinic sources and Jewish law. The illustrations were by no means simple. They opened wide vistas to the decorative arts in many lands, hinted at the intriguing relationships with the culture and arts of the host societies, and featured inventive designs. The ketubot integrated powerful Jewish symbols and motifs, rich biblical and occasionally mythological episodes, striking wedding scenes, and curious visual references to the bridal couple and their families—and even displayed the families' hidden aspirations in the intricate decorative designs they selected and popularized in their respective communities. Furthermore, much of this invaluable and fascinating information was not available from other sources, and was nearly absent from the written sources historians customarily use to learn about the past. Therefore, it was puzzling to soon discover that, prior to my involvement in the field, only one scholarly essay had been written on the art of the ketubah (by the late German-Jewish art historian Franz Landsberger in 1955).[3]

The results of this initial project, followed by many others, were published in my first book on ketubot, a comprehensive study of every marriage contract in the Skirball Cultural Center collection (*Ketubbah: Jewish Marriage Contracts of the Hebrew Union College Skirball Museum and Klau Library*) that The Jewish Publication Society published in 1990. How fortunate are we that now, more than three decades later—after a significant period in which the academic study of Jewish art has been astoundingly expanded and commissioning an illustrated ketubah has become commonplace—JPS is publishing this wonderful new book that beautifully displays and elucidates the stunning ketubot reimagined in our contemporary era.

Preface

Between the Ketubah's Margins and Center

JOANNA HOMRIGHAUSEN

At first gaze, the colorful borders of this book's "Gallery of Ketubah Plates" (see p. 55) might seem to be no more than fun ornament. Not that there is anything wrong with beautification. In Jewish tradition, the principle of *hiddur mitzvah*, or beautifying a commandment, sanctifies the skill and time imbued into the full range of ritual objects in Jewish life, from Shabbat candle holders to the Torah scroll.[1] David Moss invoked it in his 1974 ketubah exhibit so crucial to the history recounted in this book, explaining, "The principle of *Hiddur Mitzvah* suggests that when a joyous commandment requires a physical object for its performance, that object should be a beautiful one if possible."[2] Through midrashic rereading, the Rabbis of the Talmud discover this beautifying in the Torah itself, in the Song of the Sea's "This is my God and I will glorify Him."[3] Later in Exodus, we find the Torah's chief *hiddur mitzvah* enactor: Bezalel, the chief artisan of the Tabernacle, who formed its implements. Even "mere" decoration enhances objects that facilitate and foster a Torah-shaped life.

In this view, the ketubah's center—the text—is the most important part. The margins' colors, patterns, symbols, and energy are peripheral, merely an aesthetic impulse to celebrate marriage and family in the context of Jewish community. Halakhically, this may be true. But just as an individual Jewish marriage cannot be reduced to a legal document, nor can the imagery and colors in the borders of these ketubot be dismissed as tangential. Rather, between the margins and the center of these legal artworks, I perceive creative tensions between tradition and innovation in Jewish life today.

Many of these ketubot evidence frictions between traditional gender roles and their contemporary critiques, tensions captured between marginal imagery and central text. Jewish couples influenced by the movements of feminist Jewish theology and halakhah may be reluctant to display a ketubah that reflects values they perceive as antiquated. On historic ketubot, artists often depicted portraits of biblical unions—Adam and Eve, Isaac and Rebekah, Jacob and Rachel or Leah—as ideals. But today's marital art is much more likely to contain calligraphed verses from the *Song of Songs*, which Jewish feminists such as Marcia Falk and Rachel Adler have upheld as the TANAKH's shining example of mutuality in romantic love. Open-ended symbols for love, such as Dafna Jalon's intertwined trees (p. 131), Judith Joseph's trees growing toward each other (p. 133), or Nava Shoham's heart and infinity sign (p. 155) avoid imposing stereotyped gender roles onto wife and husband. They also apply well to LGBTQ+ couples.

These contemporary marginal designs commonly coexist with the traditional halakhic ketubah text—despite the fact that couples today have a wide variety of text options. Couples who choose this pairing, I suspect, wish to honor this tension between honoring the ketubah text that grandma and grandpa used, and desiring to build a Jewish marriage that fits their values for the present and future. The ketubah does not solve this tension. Rather, it displays that tension on the bedroom wall.

Ketubot also reveal the creative tension between the Diaspora and Israel running through Jewish life past and present. Both historical and contemporary artists adorn this art form with symbols of Israel, such as flora, fauna, and Jerusalem cityscapes real or imagined (see "Appendix: Common Ketubah Symbols"). Whether couples live in Israel, intend to someday, or choose to visit, Israel imagery reminds them of the historic land that plays such a large role in Jewish life and consciousness. Ketubot such as David Moss's Jerusalem cityscape (p. 63) or Mickie Caspi's portal into the Israeli landscape (p. 79) provide passageways to the Holy Land.

Yet many couples wish to celebrate their homeland in the Diaspora alongside their connection to the City of Light. In his Alaska-themed ketubah (p. 73), Howard Fox paints two very contrasting climes: Alaska's outline, placed within its snow-capped landscape, lies in a frame of vistas of the Jordan River and Jerusalem's skyline. For the niche market of Alaskan Jews choosing a ketubah, this design celebrates their multiple homelands. While the ketubah text (and their marriage) literally lives in Alaska, their eyes remain on the distant City of Gold.

In short, the more closely we gaze at these ketubot, the more it becomes unclear what is central and what is marginal—and for whom, and in what context. For a *beit din* (Jewish religious court), the text is central and the image marginal. For the relatively secular Jewish couple who may only attend High Holidays at the local Reform temple, the text may be a nice nod to tradition, but the main interest likely lies in the margins. As scholar of Jewish ritual Vanessa Ochs puts it, such Judaic objects are "repositories and producers of cultural memory," material witnesses to parallel social changes and ritual changes.[4] These ketubot don't just depict Jewish marriage as some static, frozen form. They chronicle change and attempt to envision the past, present, and future, with all the complications of living in a tradition spanning thousands of years. And just as contemporary artists are challenged to innovate new ketubah designs in an increasingly crowded market, so the visual interplay in these ketubot—between center and margin, between text and image—challenge new couples to creatively shape the next generation of Jewish life.

Acknowledgments

Over six decades of life, I have learned that some of the most meaningful creations are the result of many people's efforts. This book is no exception.

After conducting dozens of interviews with key figures who witnessed the early days of the artistic and cultural movement that is the ketubah renaissance, the first turning point came in 2019 when it occurred to me to ask writer and editor Jessica Carew Kraft, one of Ketubah.com's top-selling artists, to assist with this book.

What started as one hopeful conversation grew into a rich collaboration. She assisted me in researching and writing this volume, and in seeking out the most notable contemporary ketubot from galleries, online portfolios, hundreds of recommendations, Ketubah.com's archives, and museums and institutions across the world. Jessica provided the structure and discerning judgment for managing such a sprawling endeavor, brought her skills and dedication to every aspect of this project, and even suggested the very apt cover image. Without her, my vision for this book would never have been brought to life.

The next decisive turning point began in 2022 under the capable stewardship of Joy Weinberg, managing editor of The Jewish Publication Society (JPS) and this book's editor. She recognized that my original ten-thousand-word essay submission needed to be expanded into chapters that delved deeply into the rich history of multiple facets of the ketubah through time, up to our modern day and beyond. Joy guided this process, asking tough questions, making valuable suggestions, and strengthening the writing. She also helped curate and enhance the imagery to showcase the finest of visuals for this coffee-table book. I feel truly blessed; without Joy, you would not be holding this volume in your hands today.

I am deeply grateful to so many others who generously contributed their time, knowledge, and skill in ways both large and small over the many years. While it is impossible to thank everyone here by name, I will attempt to call out a few individuals. Any inadvertent omissions are entirely my own.

David Moss: For unwittingly planting the seed for my career and for this book when you presented a slideshow about the inimitable *Moss Haggadah* to my fellow students at the Pardes Institute in Jerusalem one evening in the spring of 1995.

Ardyn Halter: For being the first to open my eyes to the stunning tradition of illuminated ketubot when I visited your home and studio in Pardes Chana soon afterward.

Dorion Liebgott: For greeting me in your living room in the autumn of 1995 and introducing me to Ruth Stern Warzecha and the many accomplished ketubah artists of Toronto soon after my return from Israel.

Jay Greenspan: For welcoming me into your small artist-in-residence studio at the Heschel School on New York's Upper West Side in 1997 when I was first starting out.

Shalom Sabar: For taking this project seriously from the first moment, even though you didn't know me from Adam, and for coining the term "Ketubah Renaissance" to which this book owes its title. (Thank you, Izzy Pludwinski, for the introduction.)

Rabbi Barry Schwartz, The Jewish Publication Society (JPS) director during the early days of my working with a publisher: You boosted my confidence by seeing the potential and championing this book when still in its infancy.

Elias Sacks, JPS director during much of the time the manuscript was being edited by JPS: For your deep listening, can-do spirit, and tireless—and highly effective—resourcefulness and vision.

Sharon Mintz: For sharing your incredible depth of knowledge and for opening the door to the JTS Library collection.

Joanna Homrighausen: For bringing your academic passion and infectious enthusiasm from our very first contact. (Thank you, Naomi Teplow, for the introduction.)

Eva Gurevich: For your scholarly research to help flesh out the historical foundations on which this revival stands.

Patty Leve: For creating the calligraphic fonts used for typesetting the ketubah texts on various ketubot, published by Ketubah.com, in this book's "Ketubah Gallery."

Shell Rummel and Enya Keshet: For penning the meaningful words of the ketubah texts that were typeset in Patty Leve's fonts.

Aliza Zauderer, Romina Rodriguez, Nava Hoffman, Tani Gordon, and everyone at Ketubah.com: For capably and tirelessly contributing your skills from design to color correction to permissions and beyond. And for making my job the best one in the world because I get to work with all of you.

To the many people I interviewed for this book for sharing your lived experience, especially during the early days of this story, including: Michael Brooks, Mickie and Eran Caspi, Laya Crust, Marc Dollinger, Amy Fagin, Pamela Feldman-Hill, Joanne Fink, B. J. Greenspan, Sivia Katz, Patty Shaivitz Leve, Dena Levie, Danny Levine, Lori Loebelsohn, Stuart Matlins, Cindy Michael and Ray Michaels, Jeanette Kevin Oren, Izzy Pludwinski, Mordechai Rosenstein, Karen Shain Schloss, Zev Shanken, Nanette Stahl, Rabbi Michael Strassfeld, Sharon Strassfeld, Naomi Teplow, Betsy Teutsch, Stacey Zaleski.

Thank you to the Dorot Foundation, which generously supported the early editorial process of this book with a grant.

Thank you also to the staff at the University of Nebraska Press for copublishing this volume.

To Mum and Dad: For giving me both roots and wings. For sending me to Jewish day school after your trip to Israel in 1969. For having a copy of *The Jewish Catalog* on the shelf at our cottage in the Laurentians outside Montreal in the early 1970s. For enrolling me in a Hebrew calligraphy class at our shul when I was twelve years old. And especially for loving and encouraging me to be fully myself.

A quarter century ago—"one August day, about 3:00, at the Bloor JCC"—I met someone who would change my life forever. Three years later, Cheryl and I signed our ketubah and stepped under a chuppah that had been lovingly constructed from her grandmothers' tablecloths. Thank you, Cheryl Epstein, for being my person. And for putting up with my incessant and often incomprehensible passion for words, languages, and alphabets even though they are not really your thing. I love you to the moon and back.

Introduction

Two Journeys

It has been over a decade since my first inkling of the need to tell this remarkable story. At that time, in response to an invitation from the Jewish Community Center in London, Ontario, I delivered a color PowerPoint presentation, "Very Old and Extremely New: The Ketubah, the Internet, and Beyond." Inspired by its reception, a few months later I wrote to the pioneering modern ketubah artist David Moss, floating the idea of an exhibition to chronicle the modern rebirth of the art ketubah. For years after that I worked intermittently—when I could find a moment between running a small business and raising a young family—on my idea of a coffee-table book that would do justice to this artful Jewish revival.

MY JOURNEY

In my late twenties, I left my corporate job to study at the Pardes Institute, a remarkable center of text-based Jewish learning in Jerusalem. As I prepared to embark on this journey, I had the idea of opening a gallery of fine art Judaica when I returned to my home in Canada. One spring evening in 1995, David Moss brought a slideshow presentation to Pardes about his breathtaking *Moss Haggadah*. Not long afterward, a friend who knew of my growing interest in Judaica insisted I visit Pardes Chana, the artists' colony near Haifa, and meet with the fine artist Ardyn Halter.

I have a dreamlike memory of arriving at his home surrounded by a garden of fruit trees, the afternoon sunlight dappling their leaves. Halter welcomed me and showed me his studio. When he brought out his ketubah designs, I felt I had stumbled upon an artistic Garden of Eden. Despite a dozen years of Jewish day school and further Jewish education, I had never heard of the Jewish marriage contract, let alone a decorated one. Believing the beautification of this Jewish ritual item in our modern day would be a perfect addition to the fine art Judaica gallery that I planned to open on my return home, I immediately arranged to represent Halter as a ketubah artist in North America.

Back in Toronto, I sought out exceptional artists producing the highest quality work for Jewish weddings. Soon, this passion became my profession. In 1996, I launched Ketubah.com, what would become the world's largest and most comprehensive online market for ketubot.

From day one, I had the opportunity to work and share ideas with leading and emerging contemporary artists who were creating ketubot. Later, my acquired knowledge of the ketubah text facilitated my company's acceptance of ketubah art from a wider range of talented artists who were freed from the need to master the text themselves. Cultivating relationships with artists, rabbis, brides, grooms, and their families has been one of the biggest blessings of my life.

I also innovated. In 2005, my user-friendly online tool solved a decades-long ketubah-related challenge: enabling couples who do not know the Hebrew language to easily submit their Hebrew names online (see chapter 5). Two years later, we began offering archival quality on-demand printing and in 2019, inhouse laser cutting. In essence I have had the honor not only to witness and promote but to help shape the development and production of contemporary ketubah art over the past three decades.

I am now thrilled to share some of my passion with you for what the Judaic scholar Moses Gaster has called the "most fascinating and romantic chapter in the history of Jewish civilization."[1] This volume, featuring some of the most notable examples collected over the past twenty-eight years, illuminates the contemporary revival of a very old and ubiquitous Jewish tradition: the artistic ketubah.

THE KETUBAH'S JOURNEY

Originally created 2,500 years ago as a unilateral marriage contract stating what the groom would provide for his bride, the ketubah (or ketubot in the plural Hebrew form) has become a richly creative expression of love and commitment.

History of the Marriage Contract

As one of the most important mitzvot in Judaism, marriage encourages a harmonious and holy union traditionally between a woman and a man. At its outset the ketubah was designed to strengthen the institution of marriage, protect a woman's rights during the union, and ensure her financial security when she was no longer married. The groom's financial and marital obligations to his wife were hence spelled out in Aramaic, the vernacular language of the Jews at the time.

Before a Jewish wedding, a learned individual—often a rabbi—would traditionally officiate at the ketubah ceremony, directing two male witnesses unrelated to the bride and groom to sign the document, as was the custom for all legal documents produced under *beit din* (Jewish religious court) authority. True to this context, the ketubah's language is about as romantic as an insurance policy or an alimony agreement. This is not entirely surprising since, over the centuries, it could serve both functions. Yet the ketubah was quite progressive, because no other culture at the time protected wives in such a comprehensive way. This revolutionary contract protected the wife in the event of her husband's death and discouraged a hasty divorce from him that might disadvantage her economically.

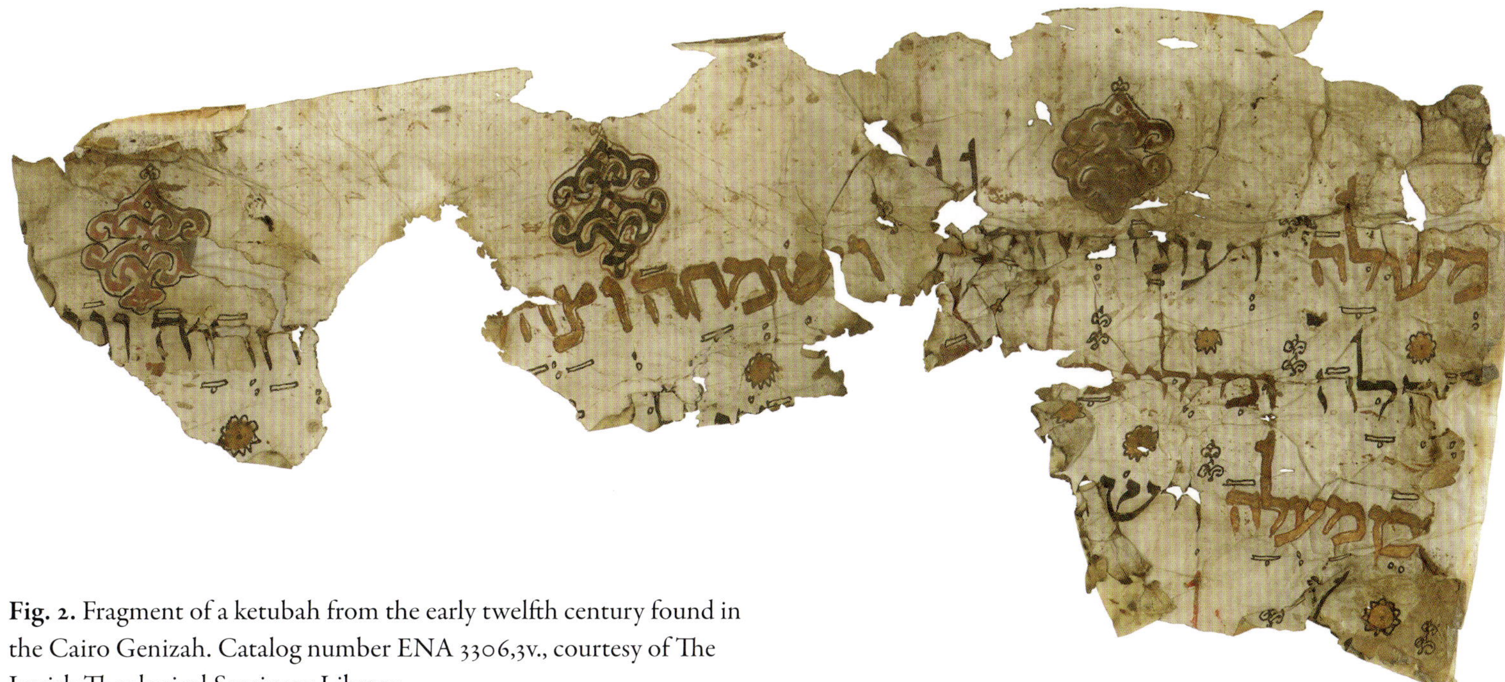

Fig. 2. Fragment of a ketubah from the early twelfth century found in the Cairo Genizah. Catalog number ENA 3306,3v., courtesy of The Jewish Theological Seminary Library.

This covenant, which echoes the Jews' original covenant with God, was taken so seriously that the Rabbis of the Talmud declared that a husband could not live with his wife even one hour without having a proper ketubah.[2] An entire Talmud tractate called "Ketubot" addresses the marriage contract's customs. The oldest extant ketubah, written on papyrus, dates from the fourth century BCE in Egypt. Another ancient example, from the second century CE, was discovered near the Dead Sea; thousands of years ago a woman known as Babatha likely fled the Bar Kokhba revolt and left her important papers, including a ketubah, stored in a cave for protection.

Starting around the tenth century CE, the ketubah began to be decorated and beautifully presented at public signing ceremonies as a celebration of the couple's love, initially in Eretz Yisra'el and Egypt.[3] We know this thanks to the discovery of the Cairo Genizah, a vast repository of worn Hebrew texts dating back over one thousand years, housed in the city's Ben Ezra Synagogue. When the genizah was opened and archived in the late nineteenth century, several artistic ketubot were found, some from the eleventh and twelfth centuries and one dating back to the tenth century.

The text of the ketubah was codified much earlier, however, in the first century BCE by the Sanhedrin (Jewish legislative body of rabbis), likely under the leadership of Rabbi Simeon ben Shetach. While many alternate versions of the text now exist, the ancient standardized version, now two thousand years old, is still used today at Orthodox weddings.

The full name of this document is *shetar ketubah* or "ketubah document." The word ketubah, meaning "written," is derived from the Hebrew root consisting of the letters *kaf, tav*, and *bet*—a root that also finds expression in similar Aramaic and Hebrew words relating to the action of writing and written documents. *Mikhtav*, for example, means letter. *Ketuvim*, which means writings, is the third section of the TANAKH, which includes the books of Esther, Psalms, and Song of Songs, excerpts of which have adorned ketubot for centuries.

Uses of Historical Ketubot

Historical ketubot serve multiple purposes today. They can aid in scholarly understanding of diaspora communities, such as when certain societies were formed and when they—along with their customs and institutions—may have dispersed. These personal documents can also provide information about the socioeconomic status of various communities. For instance, ketubot from the era of Russian pogroms—small, hastily and irregularly written, and made of lower-quality materials—reflect the poverty and fear then plaguing those communities. By contrast, the more stable and wealthy communities of Spain, Italy, and Iran produced ketubot on the highest quality parchment and decorated them in keeping with the most refined artistic work of the time.

Ketubot can help with the study of historical Hebrew scripts or trace an individual's lineage. Since the text pertains to the status of women, they can also shed light on the rarely documented lives of Jewish women throughout history. In our era, historical ketubot additionally provide visual inspiration for new designs that recall earlier aesthetic sensibilities.

History of Ketubah Artistry

Early ketubah artistry was influenced by the medieval tradition of illuminating (literally "adding light to") manuscripts, often with gold leaf. Following this decorative convention, scribal text was set inside an ornamental frame. This can be seen in stunning examples such as the Sarajevo Haggadah (1350) and the Rothschild Miscellany (1479).

When the Jews were expelled from Spain in 1492, they brought the artistic ketubah to new lands across the Mediterranean, North Africa, and the Middle East, but adapted to the aesthetic styles of their new regions. Thus, the style and decorations on historic ketubot tend to be reminiscent of the artistic and architectural styles of the broader non-Jewish milieu in which they were created. Motifs that were common on the title pages of holy books at the time—such as doorways, columns, and arches—were also used in ketubah decoration.

In 1853 a magnificent art ketubah was created for a marriage of a member of the Sassoon family, Baghdadi Jews in India who were known as "the Rothschilds of the East." (See the Sassoon Ketubbah [1853] shown here.) "Profusely ornamented with gold floral designs, opens with two panels containing decoratively penned blessings customarily found on marriage contracts from India," as Sotheby's catalog explains, it sold in 2020 for $63,000, the highest price ever paid for a ketubah.[4]

Muslim tradition similarly legislates a marriage contract, so Jews in Muslim lands were influenced by the style of their Muslim neighbors' contracts and other Islamic patterns found in books and carpets. Under Muslim rule, ketubot typically avoided the use of human figures and instead integrated plant, animal, and geometric motifs. Some were laid out like the design of an Oriental or prayer rug, with ornate decoration framing the contract text in a "carpet page" format often used in Muslim, Hebrew, and Christian illuminated manuscripts dating back to the tenth century. Lavishly decorated ketubot became common in Persia, with each Persian city developing its own ornamental tradition and adhering to a consistent layout, color, and design. For instance, ketubot from Isfahan, Persia, feature that city's symbol of a lion in front of the rising sun (see page xxx).

Beginning in the sixteenth century, artistic ketubot flourished in Italy, perhaps because Italians had their own rich tradition of decorated documents, but also because of the

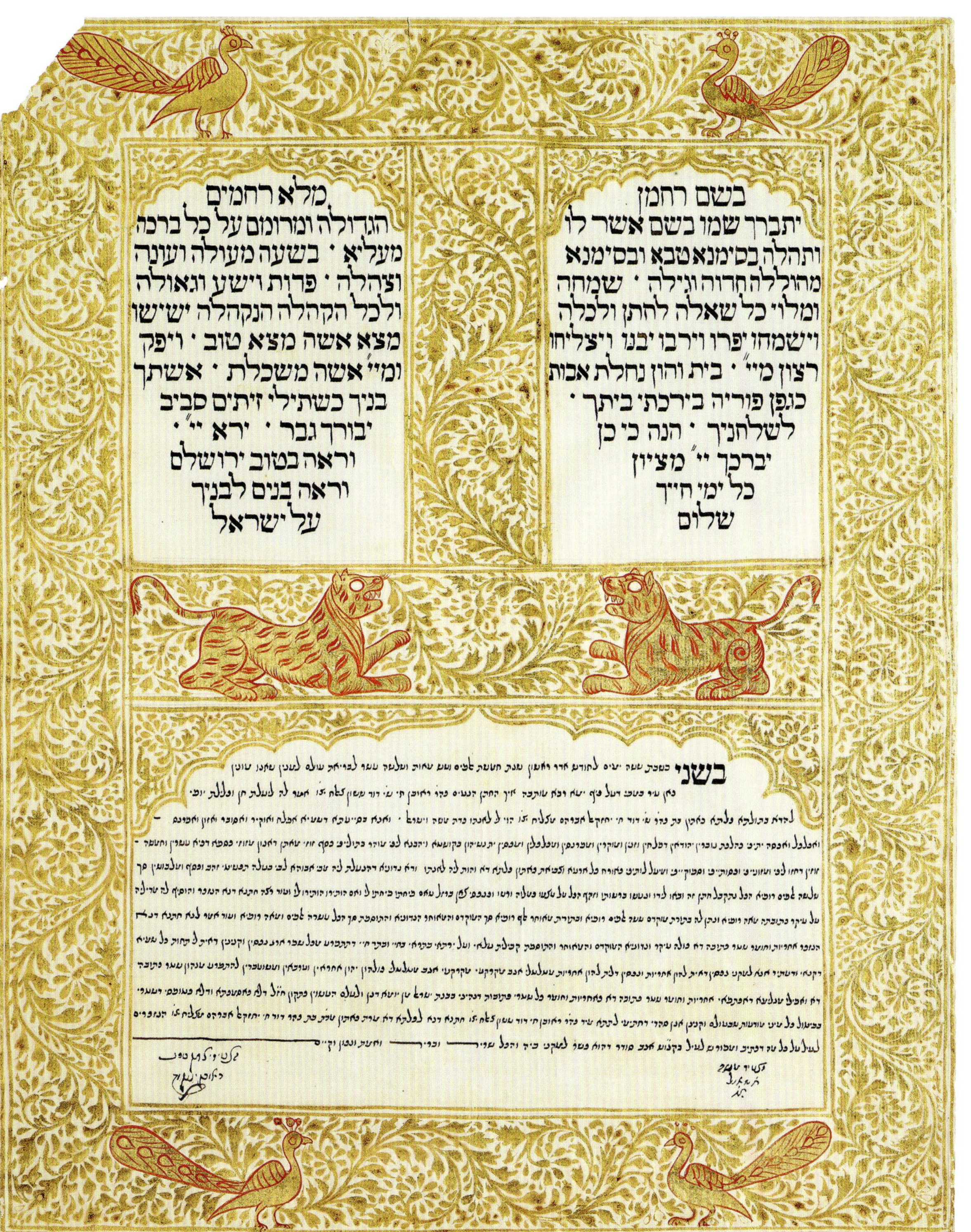

Fig. 3. The Sassoon Ketubbah, Bombay, 1853. Courtesy of a Private Collection.

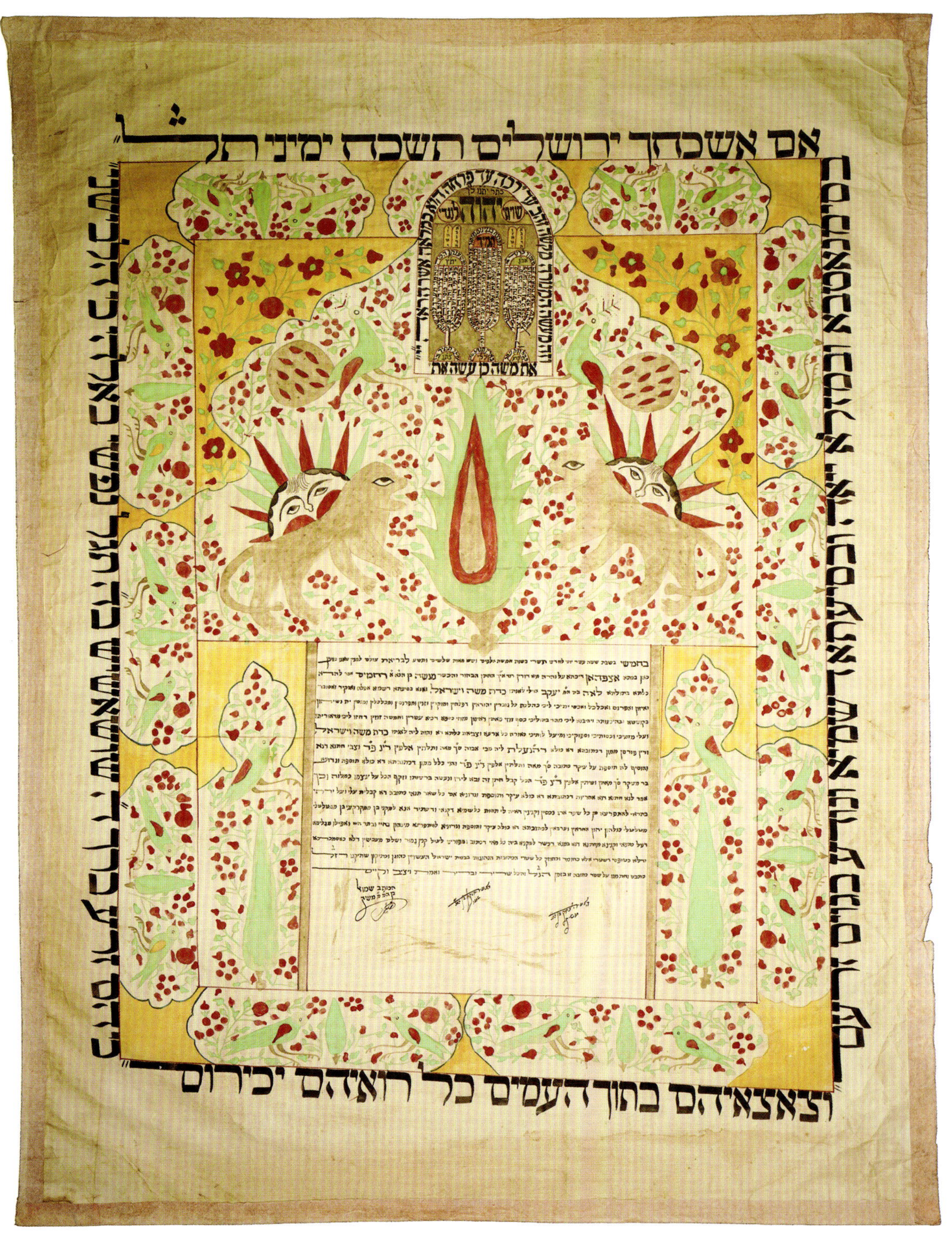

Fig. 4. Ketubah from Isfahan, Persia, 1878. Courtesy of the Beinecke Rare Book and Manuscript Library, Yale University.

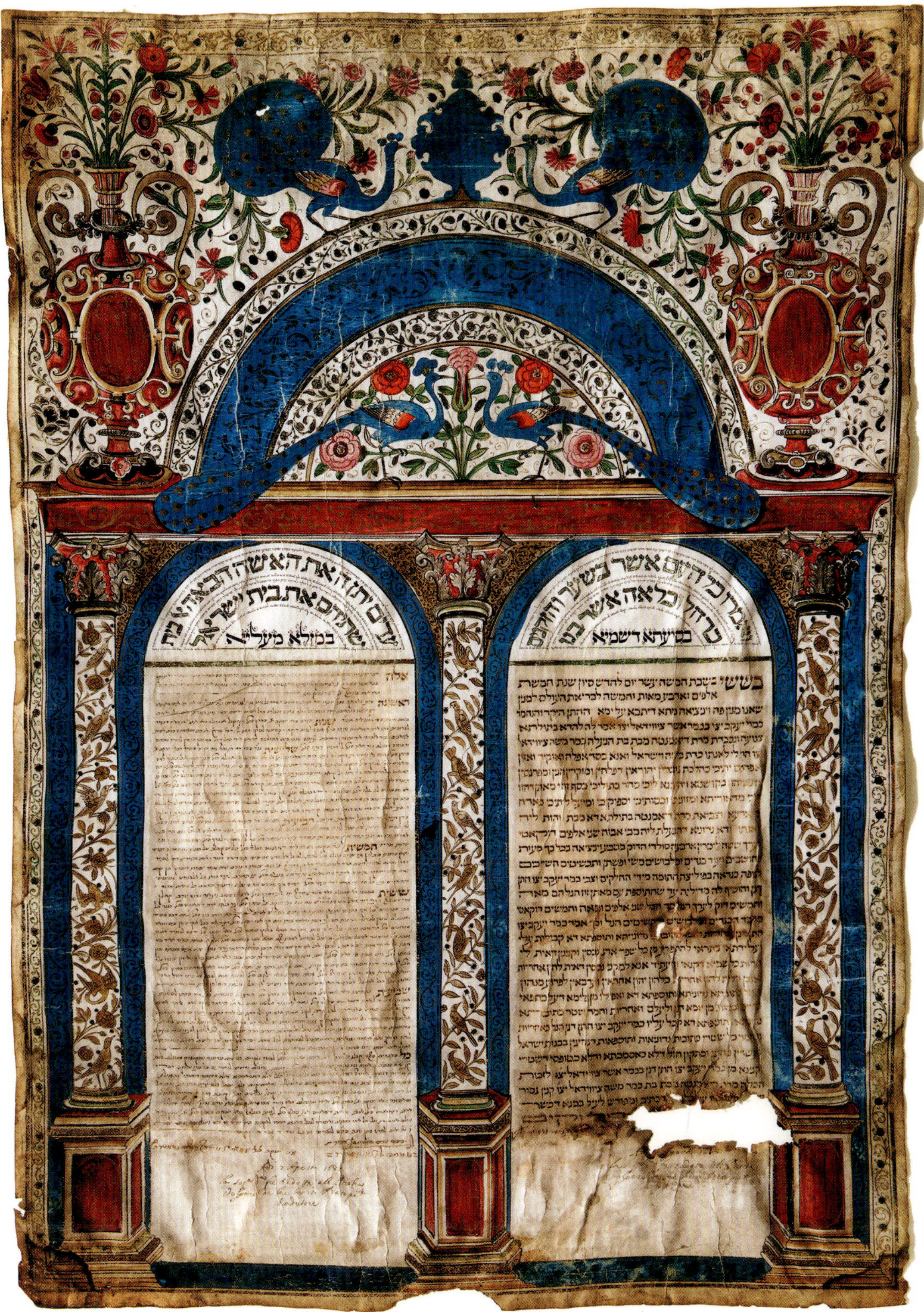

Fig. 5. Ketubbah, Venice, Italy, 1645. Courtesy of ROM (Royal Ontario Museum), Toronto, Canada. This acquisition was made possible with the generous support of the Louise Hawley Stone Charitable Trust.

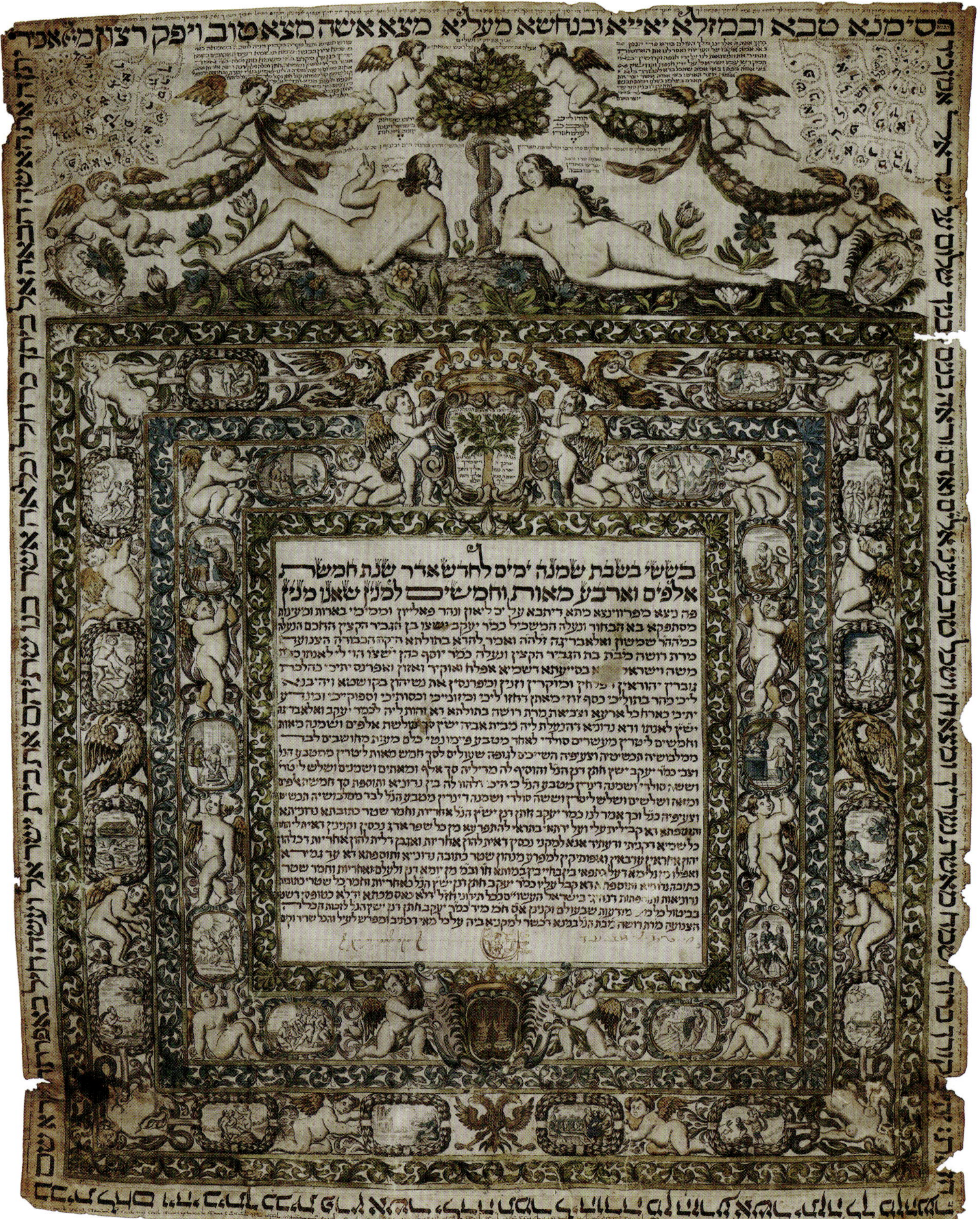

Fig. 6. Ketubah from Nice, 1690. Courtesy of the Beinecke Rare Book and Manuscript Library, Yale University.

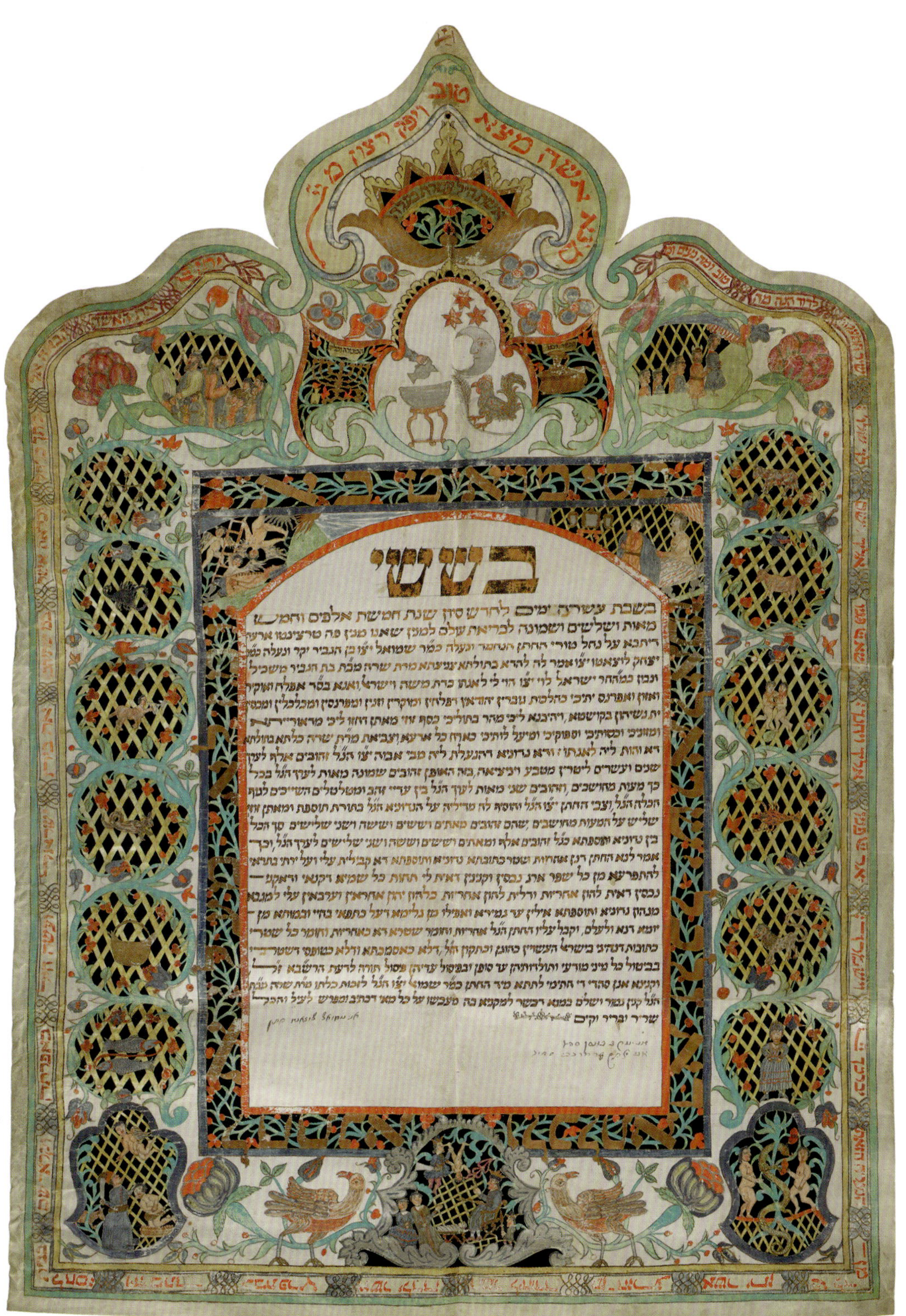

Fig. 7. Papercut ketubah from Tarcento, Italy, 1778. Copyright of the University of Manchester.

Jewish community's increasing affluence in this era, thanks to their success in the fields of commerce and moneylending, among others.

Italian ketubot became notable for their baroque decorative and architectural flourishes, zodiac symbols, and coats of arms from the uniting families that imitated the traditions of the gentile nobility. One magnificent, early example from Venice glows with gilded pillars and arches, ornate vases, and four stately red-winged blue peacocks (see page xxxi).

In spite of the second commandment's prohibition against graven images, some ketubot from this region included illustrated human figures from various biblical scenes. For example, practically every inch of an Italian ketubah from Nice is filled with nudes, from a large recumbent Adam and Eve to dozens of winged cherubs to biblical scenes with characters in various states of undress, reflecting the influence of the dominant Christian artistic culture of the time (see page xxxii).

Beginning in the eighteenth century, papercutting was sometimes used to dramatic effect on Italian ketubot. The border of this parchment papercut from Tarcento (1778) is resplendent with designs painstakingly cut to form gilded Hebrew letters, and with latticework ingeniously holding the Zodiac signs and biblical figures in place.

The embellishment of Italian ketubot became so elaborate in the port city of Ancona that families began competing to create the most opulent documents possible. By the eighteenth century, local rabbis in that city were sufficiently concerned about the resulting community discord that they enacted laws limiting the maximum amount families could spend on ketubah decoration.

In the Ashkenazic communities of Eastern and Central Europe, decorated ketubot were uncommon, since the ketubah was generally regarded as a matter-of-fact legal document with standardized financial terms and there was no tradition of displaying it to wedding guests. Yet the survival of an illustrated ketubah from fourteenth-century Krems, Austria, depicting the bride and groom in medieval wedding costumes and exhibiting distinctive, square Hebrew lettering (shown in two details here) indicates that Ashkenazic marriage contracts must have been occasionally glorified.

Artistic ketubot became less common from the eighteenth through nineteenth centuries, prompting one scholar to declare that the tradition was almost "entirely done away with" by 1925.[5] The prominent ketubah artist David Moss wrote of this period: "A rich, thousand-year-old tradition of imagination, color, and joy had withered."[6]

A Modern Renaissance

During the British Mandate (1920–48), there were glimmers of a ketubah resurgence in the Land of Israel, the birthplace of the decorated ketubah a millennium earlier, with some Jewish marriage contracts created as an expression of secular Zionism (see chapter 1, "The Ketubah in Israel"). Yet, this spark did not ignite then nor there.

Beginning in the late 1960s, a renewed interest in art ketubot in North America, this time among Ashkenazic Jews, ushered in what ketubah scholar Shalom Sabar has called "a veritable renaissance of the illuminated ketubah."[7] Free to explore a wide variety of materials, imagery, fonts, colors, and styles, hundreds of artists and calligraphers adopted the art form, imprinting their unique aesthetics onto each design (see chapter 2, "A Landmark Era for the Art Ketubah").

Notably, this rebirth blossomed at a time when most North American Jews married under state rather than halakhic authority. This untethering from traditional Jewish law also opened the door to reimagining the ketubah text: modifying the original Aramaic text and offering new

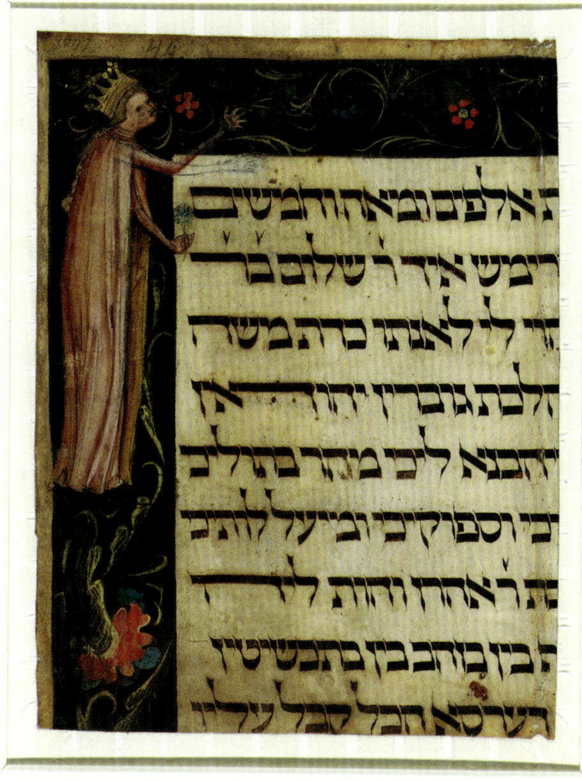

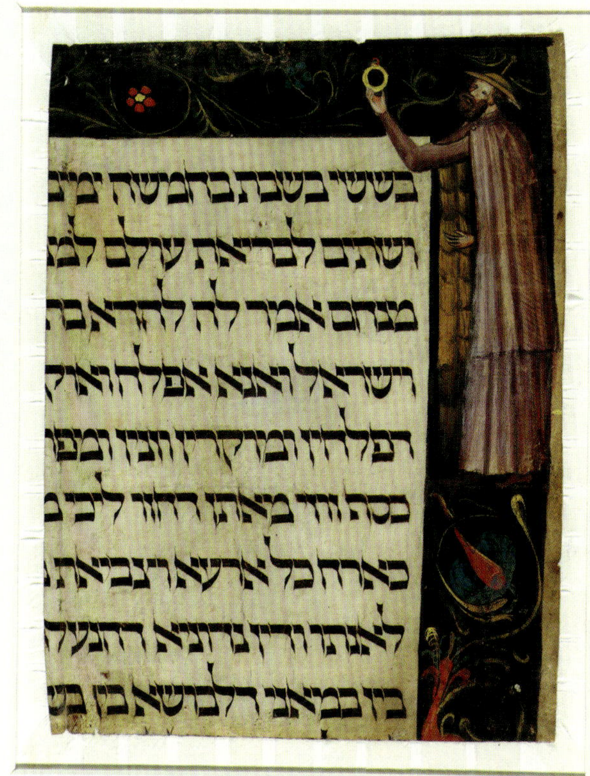

Figs. 8a & 8b. Top left and top right segments of a ketubah from Krems, Austria, 1392. Courtesy of the Austrian National Library.

poetic, egalitarian Hebrew and English texts reflecting the values of many modern Jews (see chapter 3, "Ketubah Text Transformations and Use at the Wedding Ceremony"). These, in turn, helped this fledgling reawakening grow into a widespread revival.

During this period of textual innovation, ketubah artists and calligraphers explored new ways of putting these texts to paper. From David Moss's "macrography" to the creation of calligraphic digital fonts, the letter forms themselves were stretched far beyond the handed-down realm of the Jewish scribe writing Torah scrolls (see chapter 4, "The Script of the Ketubah").

Since its beginnings in the tenth century, the creation of art ketubot has followed a fascinating ebb and flow between bespoke handwork, mechanical production, and hybrids thereof. Eleven centuries after the ketubah's origins as personally commissioned artwork, things have come full circle, with, for example, on-demand printing and lasercutting enabling the modern production of personalized ketubot showing each couple's selected design and text (see chapter 5, "The Art of Ketubah Production").

Arguably, it is quite Jewish for a tradition to be questioned, renovated, and adapted to current circumstances. Since Abraham, Jews have challenged what has come before and created innovative ways to navigate evolving ideologies and worldviews. Looking ahead, new questions emerge, among them how will the ketubah respond to AI (see chapter 6, "The Ketubah in the Twenty-First Century")?

From one ancient Aramaic contract has sprung a stunning variety of ketubot that speak to and inform contemporary Jewish conceptions of love and art. This volume's sixty full-page, color reproductions of many of the most influential and beautiful ketubot of the last half-century are testament to my heartfelt attempts to honor and document both the traditions and innovations of Jewish marriage contracts in our era (see chapter 7, "Gallery of Ketubah Plates").

Finally, to learn more about common ketubah iconography—a window into Jewish experience and identity past and present—please see the appendix, "Common Ketubah Symbols."

My hope is that the seven chapters ahead will inform and inspire, delight and deepen your connection to the Jewish marriage document. Welcome to a fascinating legacy and a future full of possibility—the world of the Ketubah Renaissance!

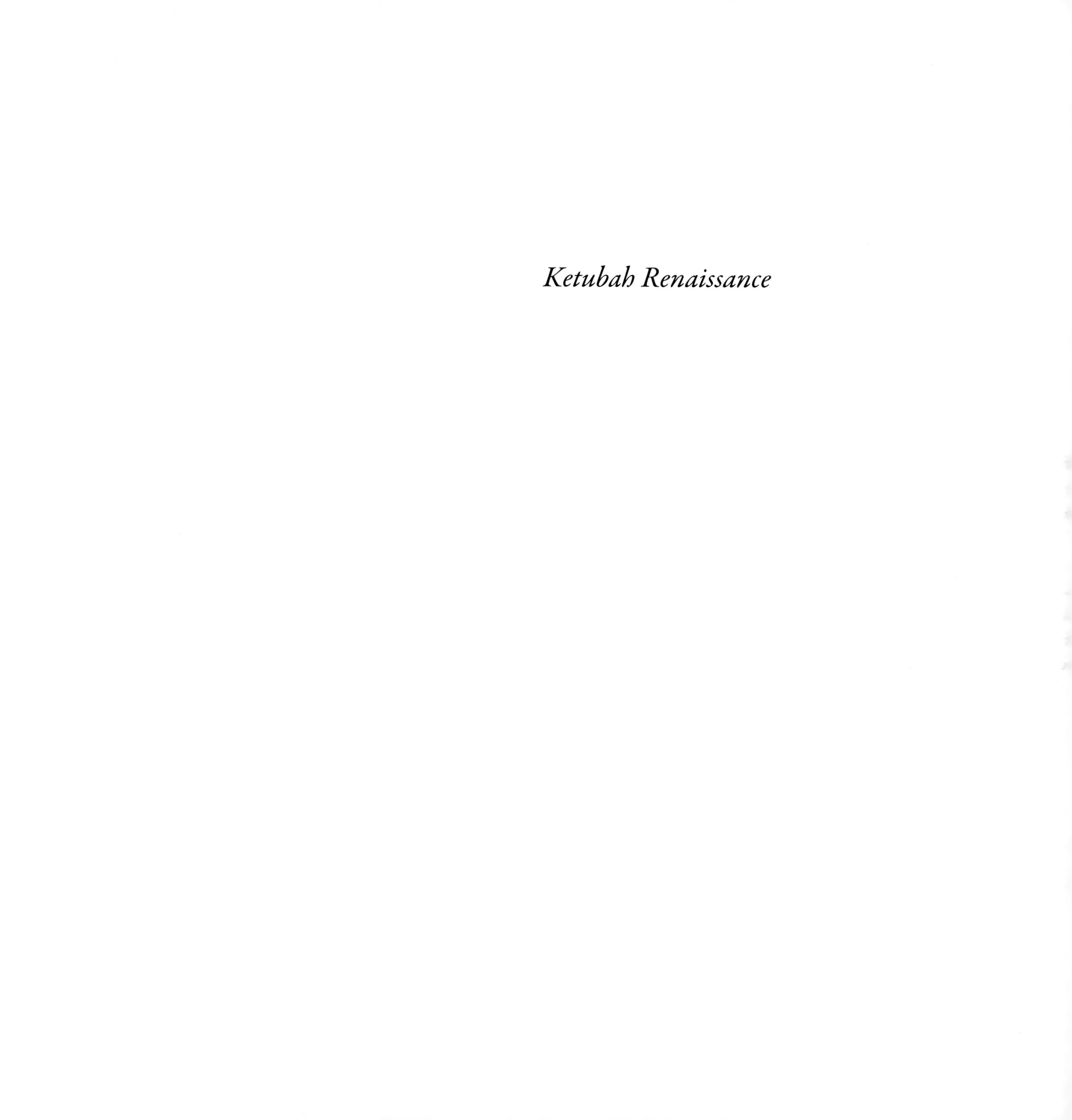

Ketubah Renaissance

1 The Ketubah in Israel

From the sixteenth to the nineteenth centuries, a tradition of decorating ketubot coevolved in many Jewish communities in different parts of the world, especially Europe and many Islamic countries—including in the Land of Israel, then in Muslim hands.

A common theme across all of these communities at the time was the use of Judaic symbols in distinct and ornamental forms. Important motifs from the Torah, such as the seven species of natural produce from the Land of Israel, the twelve tribes, and the Judean desert landscape, were combined with potent symbols of the Jewish nation, such as the Tower of David, the Star of David, the Western Wall, and the Temple Mount. During this period that preceded the emergence of modern Zionism, Jews were attracted to visual symbols that harkened back to the storied Jewish past, whether to images of ancient times depicted in the Torah or to those of the somewhat more recent antiquity, particularly to images of Jerusalem that expressed the age-old prayer for a return to the Holy Land.

PRINTING INNOVATIONS

In the nineteenth century, innovation centered around the easily reproducible Hebrew alphabet. As Hebrew typography flourished, the alphabet began to take on more artistic and decorative value. Printshops in Jerusalem, initiating the first printing of ketubot in the 1840s, produced individual broadsides that resembled the title pages of Hebrew books, with small decorative images made by carved blocks or stamps in the borders. Blessings and inscriptions adorned the tops of standardized designs that integrated architectural themes of gates—representing the entryway to the Kingdom of Heaven and the building of a new home in the House of Israel—and columns decorated with vegetation.[1]

Printed ketubot had the advantage of being inexpensive, costing only a fraction of their handmade counterparts, even when compared with an unadorned handwritten ketubah. They were also readily available, with ketubah texts preapproved by the rabbinate. In some cases they were printed with a partially "pre-populated" text worded appropriately for first marriages only, thus expediting the wedding officiant's completion of the majority of ketubot. Alternatively, for cases where the bride was a widow, a divorcee, or a convert, some ketubot were printed with a text that required the insertion of additional information. The demand for these simply decorated form ketubot proliferated, partly spurred on by increased rates of divorce and remarriage in the Land of Israel during the British Mandate period (1920–48).

For Ashkenazic communities, among whom the decoration of ketubot had not taken hold, the printing process introduced the integration of pictures and symbols around the ketubah text—literally taking a page out of the accepted norm for printed Jewish books. More broadly, interest in the Diaspora for printed ketubot from the Land of Israel would eventually dampen the demand for hand-decorated ketubot, even among Sephardic communities.

RISE OF SECULAR ZIONISM

The rise of secular Zionism in the late nineteenth and early twentieth centuries continued to broaden the motifs couples could select for their ketubot. As Jewish communities were becoming secularized worldwide, Zionist leaders encouraged Jews to observe traditions that were more inspired by a sense of Jewish history and nationhood than by religious belief. By the turn of the century, the Zionist dream dominated politics and social life in the Holy Land and began influencing artistic expression and the design of everyday items, including Judaica. The secular Zionist movement reached its peak in the kibbutz communities, which introduced many innovations to the creation of decorated Jewish marriage documents—often referred to as "marriage scrolls," and virtually never as ketubot. Secular Zionist culture was diminishing the status of the document that had accompanied the Jewish family through centuries of diaspora life.

Meanwhile, the ketubah's simplified design emphasized the new ideal of "making the desert bloom" in these collective agricultural communities. Men and women were depicted in egalitarian fashion, working the land—a glorified Israeli landscape—and joining together as partners in love, friendship, and communal life in a new nation-state.

BEZALEL AND BEYOND

By the 1920s, some artists began to infuse old cultural symbols with new importance in light of the aspiration toward a modern Jewish state. They emphasized the country's history and landscape, as well as stories from the Torah that displayed the heroism and independence that members of the new nation wished to embody. The Bezalel art school in Jerusalem became a hotbed for this revival, which included the beginning of a new illustrated tradition of ketubot, led by academy teachers Shmuel Ben-David and Ze'ev Raban. An iconic Ben-David ketubah from this era, created for the prominent Jerusalem family Zonnschein (groom) and Zuta (bride) in 1926, features the Jerusalem landscape with an embracing Zionist pioneer couple at the entrance to a white tent in the foreground. A quintessential Raban ketubah from this period (shown here) depicts Adam and Eve in the Garden of Eden, flanked by heraldic lions and stylized foliage.

Notwithstanding these developments—and in spite of the fact that some of the very earliest decorated ketubot first appeared in Eretz Yisra'el a millennium before—a widespread rebirth of the decorated ketubah was not to take hold in Israel. It wasn't until the late 1960s and early 1970s in America that a broad-based revival of modern ketubah art would truly begin, and only in the 1990s did a significant number of Israeli artists start to produce artistic ketubot primarily for the tourist and diaspora markets.

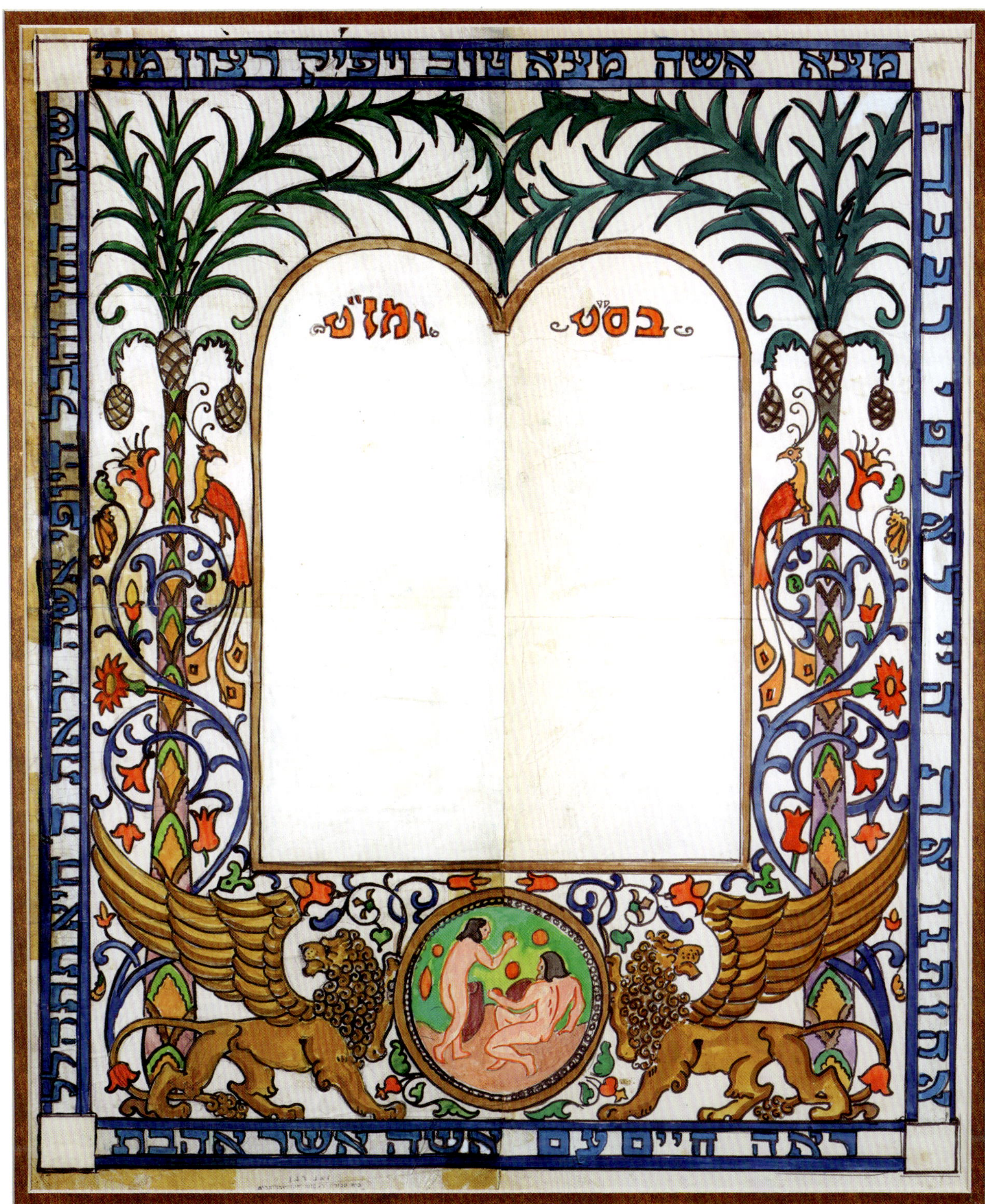

Fig. 9. Ketubah template created by Ze'ev Raban, 1950. Courtesy of the Braginsky Collection, Zurich. Photography by Ardon Bar-Hama, Ra'anana, Israel.

2 A Landmark Era for the Art Ketubah

Before the mid-twentieth century, the art that decorated ketubot was greatly shaped by the ketubah's time and place of creation. For example, ketubot from nineteenth-century Isfahan, a city in modern-day Iran, were typically painted on paper and featured red floral motifs surrounding two lions with rising suns, a popular symbol of Persia (see page xxx). In contrast, ketubot from eighteenth-century Venice were generally executed on parchment and tended to be more architectural in nature, often featuring figurative elements such as biblical scenes and zodiac signs in a more restrained color palette (see page xxxi).

Additionally, up through the first half of twentieth century in North America, Jewish fine artists were largely not interested in ketubot. Especially before the 1960s, Jewish artists in the United States sought to release themselves from the limitations of Jewish tradition, "concerned that their work would not appeal to a broad public if it seemed 'too Jewish.'"[1] Instead, they incorporated the popular trends of modernism and abstraction into their decidedly "non-Jewish" creations.

All this would change between 1961 and 1975, a period that would come to be recognized as a landmark era for the art ketubah. Especially in North America, Jewish artists would now seek out the freedom to express their Judaism in fresh, authentic ways.

Several factors influenced this sudden and notable diversion from any previous tradition of artistic ketubot.

EARLY STIRRINGS

One major influence was the post–World War II cultural zeitgeist. The Allies had won the war, America was experiencing a period of unprecedented prosperity, and the baby boom was in full swing. The devastation of the Holocaust, the resolve of survivors to build new lives, and the creation of the State of Israel simultaneously challenged what it meant to be Jewish and opened up entirely new possibilities of expressing that identity.

Notably, even in the midst of the Holocaust, there were marriages and at least one ketubah we know of: that of Berta Grossova and Otto Wolf from the Theresienstadt concentration camp in 1942 (see page 6).

After the war, artists from all over the world began experimenting with form and style. Modernist, abstract expressionist, and pop art movements took hold. Jewish fine artists who worked with Jewish symbols and themes—for example, Marc Chagall, Barnett Newman, Chaim Soutine—also created new modes of representation for them.

In 1955, the prominent South African Jewish educator Harry Abt pointed to the absence of the artistic ketubah in mainstream Ashkenazic Jewish marriages as a gap in Jewish ritual practice, writing in the South African monthly magazine *Jewish Affairs* that the ketubah was being neglected as an opportunity to "enhance the ceremony."[2] Having seen many elaborately decorated ketubot of historic Jewish communities, he lamented that the ketubah had now become a

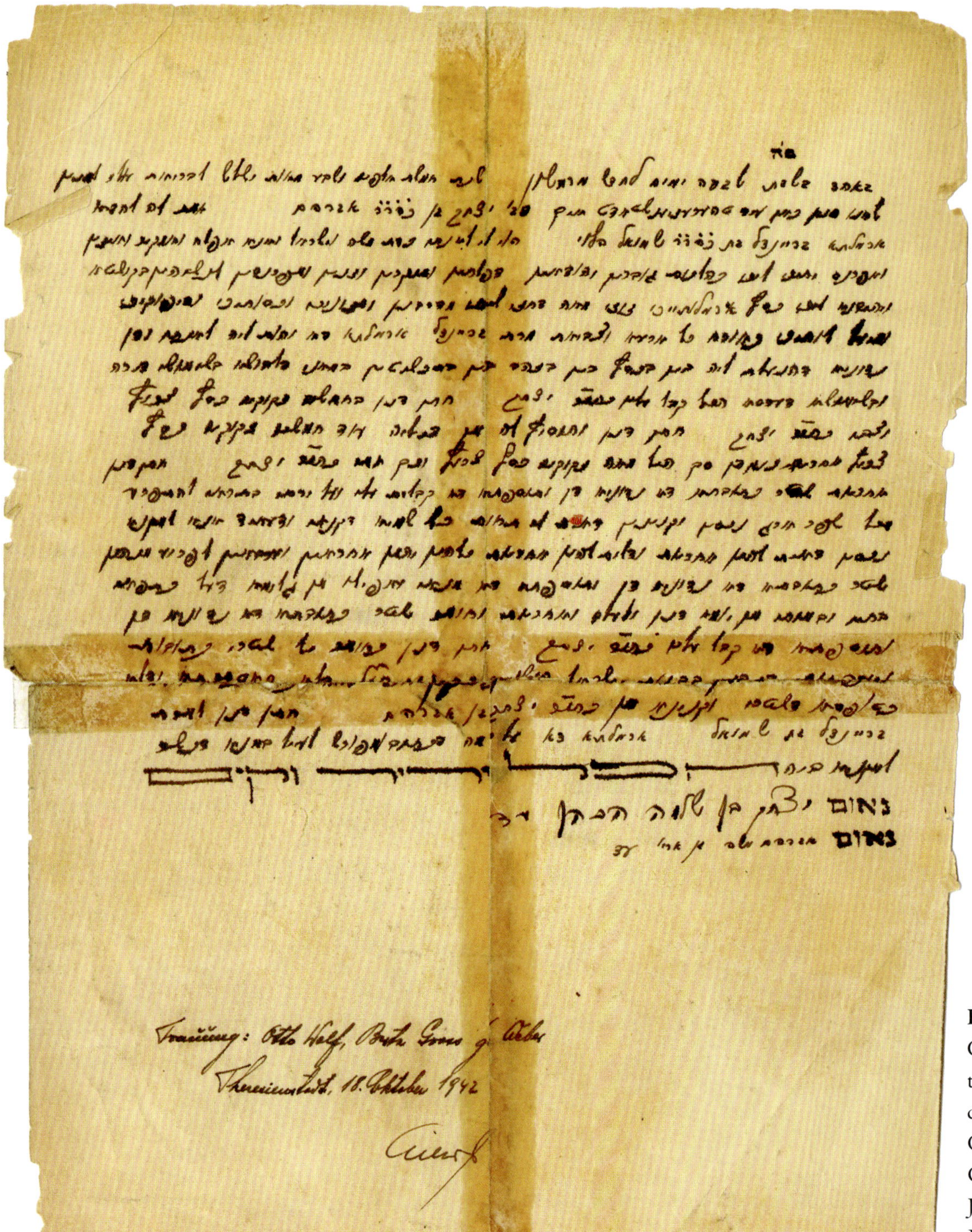

Fig. 10. Ketubah of Berta Grossova and Otto Wolf from the Theresienstadt concentration camp, 1942. Ketubah of Berta Grossova and Otto Wolf, 2022.13.1, Collection of the Museum of Jewish Heritage—A Living Memorial to the Holocaust, Gift of Jeffery W. Dunn.

formulaic document printed on an ordinary piece of paper. "Revive the artistic ketubah," he urged his audience, so it will "once again become a thing of beauty in addition to being a legal document."[3]

Perhaps heeding this call just a few years later, in 1961, the Albert A. List family of Connecticut commissioned the Lithuanian-born American Jewish fine artist Ben Shahn to create a ketubah—not for a wedding, but as a work of art. After World War II, Shahn had transitioned from his prewar social realism to a new style that included Jewish religious symbolism. He became "fascinated with letters, both Hebrew and English, which became essential elements in his work," writes Norman L. Kleeblatt, a longtime curator at The Jewish Museum in New York.[4] A striking example is "Today Is the Birthday of the World," a work of non-ketubah art in the Jewish Museum's holdings that features the Hebrew words of a well-known prayer from the Rosh Hashanah prayer book (or *maḥzor* in Hebrew).[5] In 1954 Shahn published *The Alphabet of Creation*, an art book that contained his unique combination of the letters of the Hebrew alphabet; this image became his seal (reminiscent of the red artist's stamp or "chops" seen on traditional Chinese paintings), appearing on his landmark 1961 ketubah and on many of his prints and drawings after 1960.

Ben Shahn's ketubah (see page 57) integrated floral and foliage decorations around and within the artist's distinctive Hebrew calligraphy. "All letters, of course, were once pictures," Shahn explained. "One works painstakingly, almost painfully, the lip fixed between the teeth, contemplating, wondering about the mysteries, the mystic relationship of the letters growing under one's hands."[6]

In the late 1960s, the sculptor and printmaker Chaim Gross began experimenting with two dimensional pieces that featured whimsical, multicolored, interwoven words in Hebrew and English as the primary design element. These striking prints ("Eternal Peace" is a lovely example) as well as his Aubusson tapestries and sculpted wool area rugs (produced by Eric Fields Carpet Makers) displayed a whimsical, colorful style of Hebrew (and English) words as art and emblematized this period of Jewish visual reinvention in America.[7] The influence of this work is clear in the limited edition ketubah print Gross produced in the 1970s, inscribed and gifted to a friend for use at her wedding in 1978 (see page 59).

By 1969, less than fifteen years after his initial article, Harry Abt noted in *Jewish Affairs* that many local artists across the Diaspora had started creating ketubot for Jewish weddings.[8] The renaissance was slowly stirring to life, awaiting a spark to fully ignite its potential in the decade to follow.

RENEWAL OF JUDAISM ON ONE'S OWN TERMS

A generation after the Holocaust, Jews in North America were—finally—readily assimilated. Especially after Israel's triumph in the Six-Day War in 1967, they felt comfortable enough to openly express their Judaism and renew their connection with Jewish tradition in novel ways on their own terms.

Beginning in the 1960s, artisans of all backgrounds brought a renewed emphasis on mastery, craftsmanship, and traditional ways of making things beautiful. At first, Jewish artisans applied their skills to secular items, both practical and decorative, in fiber, ceramics, glass, metals, and other media, striving to infuse joy, movement, and color into their creations. Soon they began to apply this approach to the design and creation of Judaica, manifesting a contemporary expression of *hiddur mitzvah*—beautifying items used to fulfill the commandments. Items for home-based rituals, such as menorot, kiddush cups, candlesticks, mezuzot, seder plates, and mizrach placards (positioned on the eastern wall of the home to remind the family of the direction of prayer) were reimagined in more visually innovative ways than ever before.

By the late 1970s, demand grew for Judaic objects that were decidedly "not your bubbe's style," both for private and public Jewish realms. In place of traditional Judaica items that often had either an ornate European style or, alternatively, an inexpensive "made in Israel" aesthetic, there emerged home ritual items with cleaner lines and a contemporary design feel. Gary Rosenthal sculpted welded metals combining copper, brass, steel, and fused glass to create "Judaica that was beautiful enough to leave out on display even when it was not being used."[9] Potters such as Irene Helitzer and Renee and Howard Vichinsky pushed the boundaries of ceramics, creating modern shabbat candlesticks and ritual objects for holidays that resembled home decor items from high-end shops. Textile artists joined together in the Pomegranate Guild of Judaic needlework, with creators such as Reeva Shaffer and Temma Gentles reimagining items like *tallitot, kippot,* challah covers, and chuppot (wedding canopies).

In 1978, Billy Mencow opened Kolbo Fine Judaica, a small gallery in Harvard Square carrying "new American artists who were passionate about crafting beautiful and masterfully made [Judaica] pieces."[10] While at first the gallery focused on ceramics, over time it "introduced an expanded view of Judaica [items] . . . that were artistic and cutting edge in design."[11] Over time, other fine art Judaica galleries opened, from Bob and Bob Fine Jewish Gifts in Palo Alto to Dorion Fine Judaica in Toronto.

In 1980, Temple Ansche Chesed on New York's Upper West Side launched its first of what would become an annual Hanukkah Arts Festival and Judaica Crafts Fair.[12] This event, along with the Judaica and Crafts Fair at the biennial conventions of the Women's League for Conservative Judaism, helped to build—and satisfy—the burgeoning demand for this new style of Judaica. Synagogues were also a driving force for this surge in Jewish creativity, both through their Sisterhood Judaica shops and also as purchasers of ceremonial objects such as Torah mantle covers and Torah ark curtains (*parochet* in Hebrew) by fabric artists like Jeanette Kuvin Oren (see her fabric ketubah on page 137).

THE JEWISH CATALOG AND DO-IT-YOURSELF JUDAISM

The late 1970s saw a growing trend of Jewish couples commissioning artistic ketubot for their weddings. One of the early tipping points for these ketubot came in 1973, when The Jewish Publication Society published *The Jewish Catalog: A Do-It-Yourself Kit* by Richard Siegel, Michael Strassfeld, and Sharon Strassfeld.[13] Siegel had previously conceived of this manual while writing his master's dissertation entitled "A Theoretical Construct for a Jewish Whole Earth Catalog" in Contemporary Jewish Studies at Brandeis University.

Directly modeled on *The Whole Earth Catalog*, a counterculture bible first published in 1968 to provide "access to tools" that would help the reader "find his own inspiration, shape his own environment, and share his adventure," *The Jewish Catalog* was a DIY guide to the modernization of ancient traditions, driven by a desire to express Jewish identity individually.[14] All over America, Jewish communities were looking for ways to democratize Jewish ritual and open it up to those previously excluded from it, including women and children. *The Jewish Catalog* had the effect of empowering many Jews seeking a way to "do Jewish" that felt relevant to their lives during an era deeply affected by social change. Serving as a basic reference on Judaism and

American Jewish life, it also playfully compiled Jewish crafts, recipes, meditational practices, and political action ideas, all targeted to Jews who felt excepted from mainstream Judaism. It would go on to become one of the best-selling books in American Jewish history, and spawn two sequels within seven years.

The Jewish Catalog's chapter on scribal arts included two DIY articles that helped ignite the ketubah renaissance. The first article, "A Practical Guide to Hebrew Calligraphy" by Jay Greenspan, was not only "intended to be a short, basic guide to the fundamentals and techniques," but also "a springboard . . . in whatever good paths your . . . creative expressions lead you."[15] In the second article, "The Lovely Art of Ketubbah-Making," David Moss lamented the "horrible mass-produced 'dimestore' ketubbot with which most people are now getting married."[16] He urged aspiring calligraphers to apply their creativity directly to this old tradition, and guided them on how to fashion their own ketubot, with examples from his own initial experimentations. According to Moss, "The hours really fly by when you are working on something you know will be used, appreciated and cherished."[17]

Within a short time the tradition was being renewed, with artistically inclined family members creating ketubot for their loved ones' weddings alongside a growing professionalization of ketubah artistry. By the time the *Second Jewish Catalog* was printed three years later in 1976, it listed three dozen calligraphers and four ketubah distributors actively selling to modern Jewish couples.

Nearly fifteen years later, in 1990, The Jewish Publication Society would further the ketubah renaissance by publishing *Ketubbah: Jewish Marriage Contracts of the Hebrew Union College Skirball Museum and Klau Library*, Judaica scholar Shalom Sabar's first coffee-table book that cataloged the remarkable historical ketubah collection at the Skirball Center in Los Angeles. Sabar's authoritative volume, the first major art ketubah book since David Davidovitch's landmark *The Ketuba: Jewish Marriage Contracts Through the Ages* (1968), would also mark the increasing importance twentieth-century Jews placed on ornamented marriage contracts.

THE CHAVURAH MOVEMENT

Among many other innovations, *The Jewish Catalog* also helped to spread the nascent "chavurah" or lay-led religious movement across the United States. In turn, this initiative of Conservative Judaism, which began launching congregations without a central ordained leader in 1968, also contributed to popularizing American artistic ketubot.

Young Jews were becoming disenchanted with what felt like a heavy, formalized, and not very personal synagogue environment. They sought an alternative to what they saw as an over-institutionalized and spiritually lacking North American Jewish establishment.

This drive for a more intimate and individualized Jewish worship experience animated the members of the first chavurah: Chavurat Shalom in the Boston area, which included *The Jewish Catalog* coeditor Richard Siegel. The young rabbis, academics, and political activists who joined together with Siegel at Chavurat Shalom to experiment with prayer and study would go on to become leading figures in Jewish life in the second half of the twentieth century. Several members of the broader chavurah movement, including David Moss, Jay Greenspan, and even Rabbi Zalman Schachter (Reb Zalman)—a co-founder of Chavurat Shalom who wrote ketubot by hand for chavurah members such as Michael Brooks—were prominent in repopularizing ketubah traditions within and beyond the movement.

DAVID MOSS AND JAY GREENSPAN

The artists David Moss and Jay Greenspan were members of the New York Chavurah and roommates at the Jewish

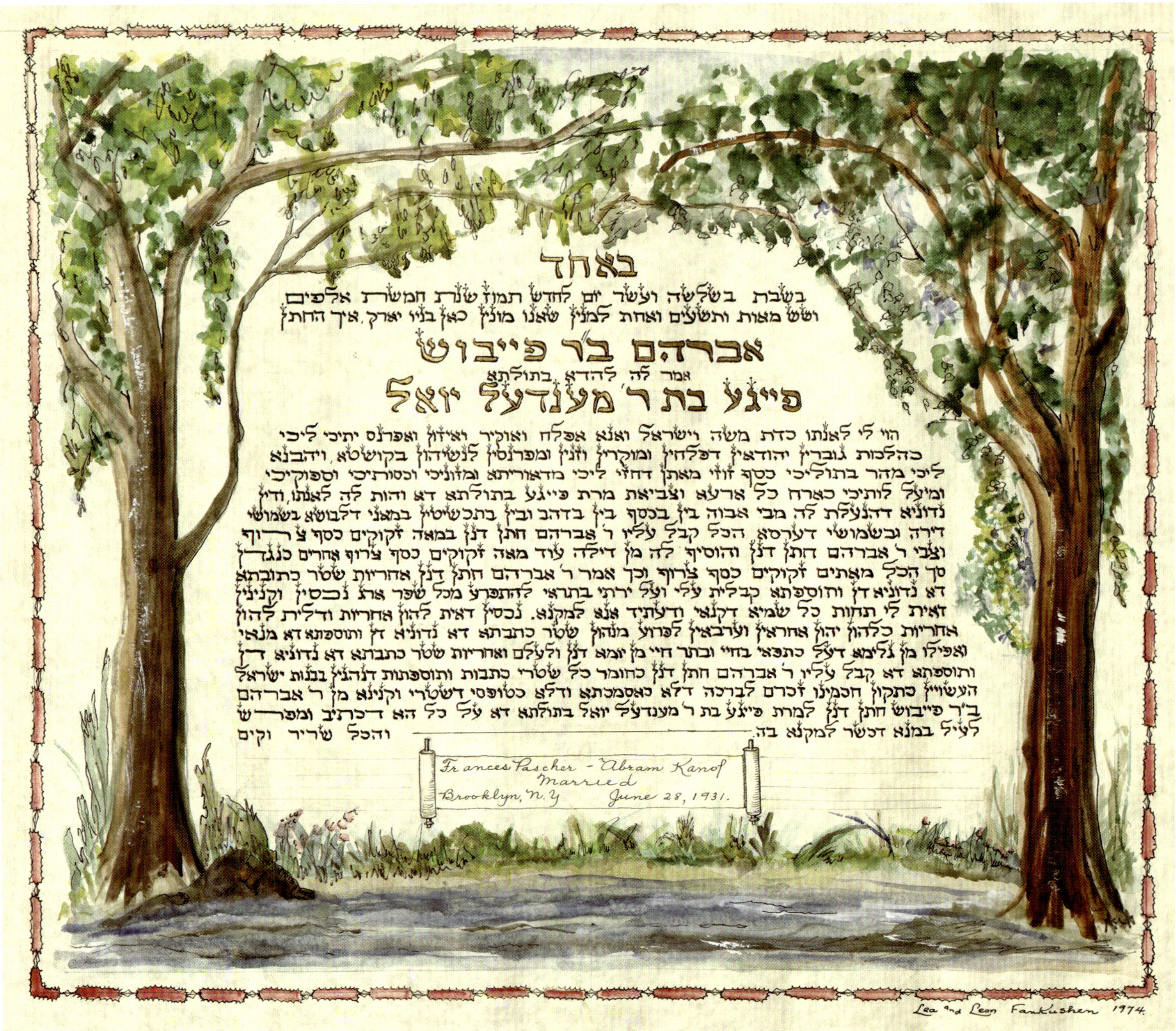

Fig. 11. Ketubah by Leon and Elenora Fankushen, 1974. Courtesy of David Fankushen.

Theological Seminary in 1969–71 when they both became enamored with the artistic possibilities of the ketubah. Moss, in particular, was impressed by the 1968 publication of David Davidovitch's coffee-table volume. Deeply moved by its collection of illuminated contracts from history, he was saddened that the tradition was no longer practiced and vowed to try to revive it. A powerful encounter with a Hebrew calligrapher while he studied at the Hebrew University in Jerusalem in 1968 inspired him to learn to scribe.

When Moss returned to the United States, he volunteered to create a ketubah for friends. It was a big success. For centuries, Hebrew quotes, such as from the *Song of Songs*, had been included as a component of the decorative border surrounding a ketubah's text. In a bold break with one of the "handed down" conventions of the art form, Moss crafted a visually stunning ketubah design that was entirely constructed from the actual text of a ketubah, complete with the couple's names, furthering Ben Shahn's earlier innovation.

Moss and Greenspan discussed the great potential for a ketubah revival. Moss started making more ketubot for people he knew, blazing the path for a broad-based renaissance. Much later, he would famously recollect how surprised and delighted he had been to receive $50 for a commissioned ketubah—at the time it felt like more than enough compensation.

Moss and Greenspan's commissions for friends led to their professionalization as Judaic artisans. Soon, the two were offering ketubot for sale to a wider market of Jews who saw their ketubot on display at a couple's wedding or when visiting the newlyweds' home afterward. This nascent ketubah market inspired other Jewish artists to adopt the art form.

Over the years, Moss held much anticipated creativity master classes at Camp Ramah sites in Canada and the United States that attracted and motivated a generation of ketubah artists. In 2004, he published *Love Letters*, a sumptuous art volume chronicling his creative journey and featuring dozens of the ketubot that couples had commissioned him to produce over the decades. In 2009, Moss co-founded Kol HaOt in Jerusalem's Hutzot HaYotzer artists' colony, with the mission of "sharing the foundations of Jewish identity freshly clothed in attractive, stimulating and irresistible forms."[18]

In 1981, Greenspan published *Hebrew Calligraphy: A Step-by-Step Guide*, an authoritative book on the topic. For many years he taught calligraphy at New York's 92nd Street Y; many ketubah artists, such as Miriam Karp, would later credit their craft to his skill and patient teaching. Greenspan was also artist-in-residence at The Heschel School on the Upper West Side, where the author had the pleasure of meeting him in the late 1990s.

MOSS AS INNOVATOR, HISTORIAN, AND PERSONALIZER

David Moss not only published the first article about how to create an artistic ketubah. His work was also featured on the cover of B'nai B'rith's *National Jewish Monthly* magazine several times in the early 1970s, including the ketubah he made for his wife, Rosalyn (see page 12).

Then in 1974 he spearheaded the first contemporary art exhibition of ketubot—"A Tradition Reborn"—at Berkeley's Judah L. Magnes Museum while serving as artist-in-residence there. As he would later reflect in *Love Letters*, he opened up a "little ketuborium" in the carriage house behind the museum to sell his work.

During this time, Moss delved into the museum's rich collection of historic ketubot. As he put it, "The artistic variety and regional diversity of the ketubot from the past inspired me to improvise and experiment."[19] His early ring-shaped ketubah (see page 61) is a beautiful example of his innovation. When faced with a hole in the piece of parchment the couple had provided, he devised a novel ketubah design in

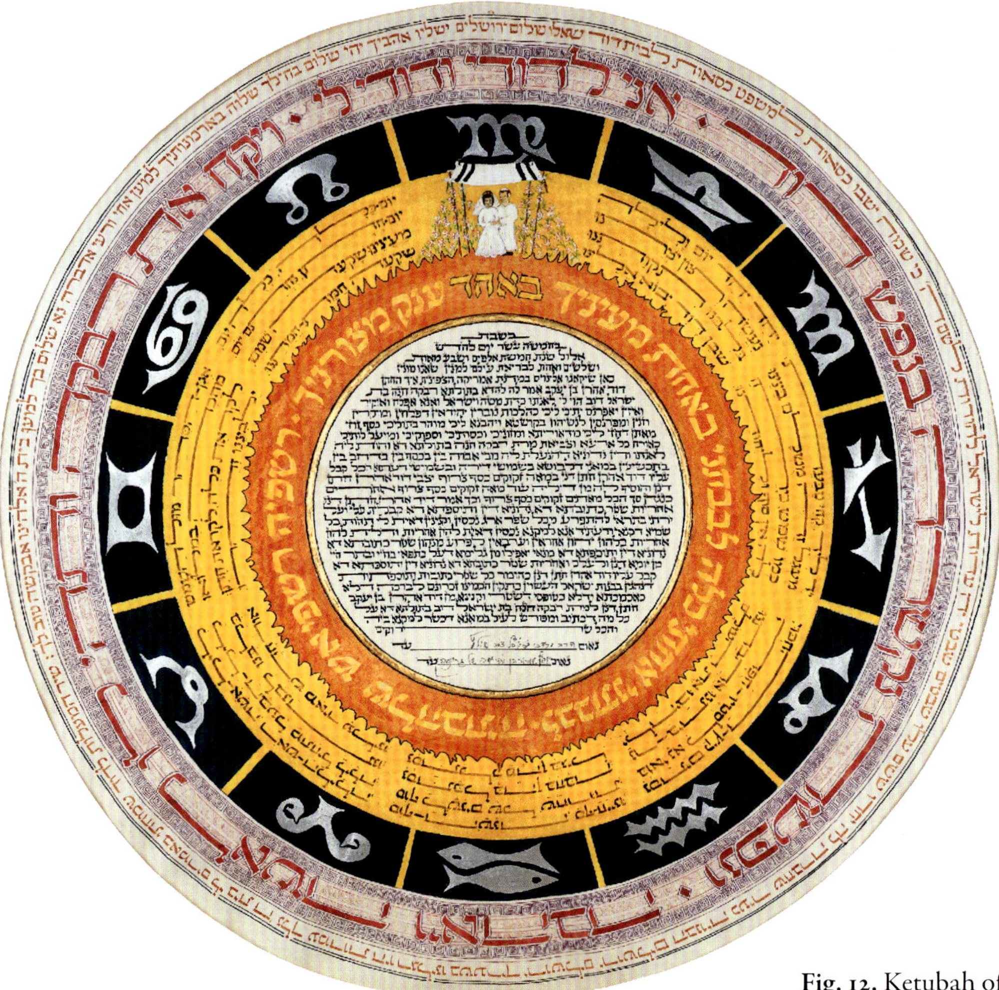

Fig. 12. Ketubah of Rosalyn and David Moss, 1971. Courtesy of David Moss.

the shape of a communal Central European wedding ring. Moss became one of the most successful ketubah artists both for his inventive designs and his scholarship on how the ketubah document had evolved.

He was also known for his attentive personalization of each ketubah commission. He developed a new way of incorporating the personal symbols meaningful for the couple that went beyond putting a new spin on the classic Judaic motifs. As Moss described in *Love Letters*:

> I developed a method that . . . begins with my attempt to learn as much as possible about each person's tastes, values, families, names, sensitivities, interests, and world views. I become attuned not only to their direct answers to my questions, but also to the subtle hints in their conversation or in a letter they have written that might lead me in unexpected directions. . . . Amazingly when I sit down to translate a couple's lives into a unique work, a phrase always jumps out, an image moves to the foreground. Some glance between them, an underlining in a letter, or

> a comment uttered with passion . . . provides me with an artistic opening into their world. From this entryway, I turn to Jewish literature to find the verse, midrash, image, quote, symbol . . . that embodies the couple's uniqueness.[20]

For example, his 1975 "Ketubah of Leslie Kane and Manuel Fishman" (see cover and page 65) portrays seven concentric forms, together reminiscent of a TV screen—a marriage of the layered meanings of this number in relation to Jewish weddings (see appendix) with the couple's interest in media. Additionally, the signs of the zodiac are crowned by a lion representing the month of Av in which the couple married.

WOMEN'S CONTRIBUTIONS

While male artists initially catalyzed the ketubah renaissance, today most ketubot are made by women. How did this come to be?

Historically, women were excluded from important realms of Jewish learning and leadership. For example, up until very recently, only men could be rabbis. In 1972, Sally Priesand became the first woman to be ordained as a rabbi by a Jewish seminary.[21] Even though she was trained and ordained in the progressive Reform movement, it was an uphill battle in ways both large and small; while her classmates lived conveniently near classes in the male-only dorms, she had to live off campus. Priesand persisted, eventually finding a pulpit and marking an important, hard-won departure from the handed-down patriarchal tradition. Rabbi Priesand's approach to her congregants was reminiscent of the contemporaneous spirit of *The Jewish Catalog*: "When I came to this congregation, I was very open with them: 'Look, I'm not here to be Jewish for you. I'm here to suggest ways that we can all be Jewish together.'"[22]

Similarly, throughout Jewish history women were blocked from the scribal arts. In fact, the first *soferet* (female scribe) was only certified in 2003.[23] According to Jen Taylor Friedman, the first *soferet* known to have completed a Torah scroll, there was great resistance to her and her journey. "Even buying the necessary materials . . . can be tricky. If it's me buying, they won't sell it to me. . . . I have a faithful spy network, and send people to buy it for me."[24]

By contrast, there was nothing to stop women throughout the ages from writing or decorating ketubot. Although there was a talmudic prohibition on women—and other "outsiders" such as star worshippers—writing a Torah, it was permissible for a woman to write a megillah (scroll, such as the Scroll of Esther). Halakhah did not require that a ketubah be written by a *sofer*—or, for that matter, that a Jewish wedding be performed by a rabbi. Unlike the processes for being recognized as a *sofer/et* or ordained as a rabbi, a ketubah writer did not need to be trained or certified by any established body or authority.

Nonetheless, as far as we know, women did not embark on writing ketubot until later in the twentieth century. In the early 1970s, the idea of a woman writing a ketubah was still novel. Yet, as ketubah commissions multiplied, women started playing a central role, making significant contributions to a traditionally male domain in both artistry and text, and invigorating the full-blown revolution of writing and decorating ketubot.

As ketubah artist Laya Crust characterizes her creative experience:

> When I was a child, I experienced music as color. . . . When I went to shul, I stepped inside a kaleidoscope. The lilting rhythm of the Hebrew prayers swirled themselves into endless combinations of hue and tone. . . . [Now, as an adult] designing ketubot is as close as I have come to that transcendent synthesis of liturgy and color.[25]

A number of contemporary factors empowered women calligraphers and artists to take their rightful place as ketubah designers, creators, and innovators. The women's liberation and feminist movements in broader North American society included significant participation and leadership by Jewish women, and in turn influenced women to pursue roles in Jewish living that had been traditionally reserved for or occupied by men. The aforementioned zeitgeist of the late 1960s and early 1970s in North America inspired Jewish women to try their hand at Jewish artistic expressions, including mastering Hebrew calligraphy.

The opportunity to contribute to and reinvent a Jewish ritual item related to marriage, family, and home—that is, traditional "women's realms"—may have provided an added attraction. The process of meeting with individual couples (often in a home setting), listening deeply for what was important to them, translating that into a unique piece of commissioned ritual art, and participating in their journey toward creating a life together, may have been particularly meaningful, tapping into an array of skills, from the technical and artistic to the interpretive and interpersonal. Lastly, since ketubot could be produced in a modest home studio, this pursuit lent itself to balancing professional and family responsibilities.

Some of these early ketubah makers were calligraphers first; they either collaborated with an artist (as Robin Hall did with her then-husband Richard Sigberman; see their ketubah on page 91) or developed their own artistic abilities. Others were artists first, with backgrounds ranging from a bachelor of fine arts to formally trained graphic designers to self-taught artisans. They either learned Hebrew calligraphy, developed their own style of drawing each letter, or collaborated with a calligrapher (as Carol Fisher Moch did with her husband Stephen Fisher Moch). These and other early pioneers in this field—Betsy Platkin Teutsch, Claire Mendelson, Sivia Katz, Karen Shain Schloss, and Judith Joseph, to name just a few—were at the forefront of a new generation of women who embraced the opportunity to bring creativity to Jewish art forms, expressing and reinforcing Jewish identity in the home.

A FOUNDATIONAL PERIOD

In retrospect, the various sociocultural influences that converged in the North American environment to support the revival and proliferation of artistic ketubot from 1961 to 1975 would lay the foundation for making the art ketubah a fixture of an increasing number of Jewish—and interfaith—weddings; and also lead to various revisions of the ketubah text, diversifying across Jewish denominations—and different types of couples—in the decades to come. David Moss aptly framed the imaginative renewal of the illuminated ketubah as an essentially Jewish endeavor: "Just as we have expanded the Torah—a book of laws and covenant—into an enormous literature of discourse, imagination, embellishment, legend, and lore, so too have we transformed the ketubah into an exuberant form of visual art."[26]

3 Ketubah Text Transformations and Use at the Wedding Ceremony

Over two millennia, the text of the ketubah has followed a storied path through Jewish history. Buffeted by the twists and turns from the Holy Land to the Diaspora, it has been shaped by debates among the Rabbis of the Talmud and modified in response to upheavals such as the expulsion of the Jews of Spain. Yet, it was not until the late 1960s—very recently in the overall Jewish passage of time—that the ketubah text was transformed to serve a different function than the one delineated in the Jewish legal tradition.

ORIGINS OF THE KETUBAH TEXT

The ancient Rabbis instituted the ketubah to protect a woman from being divorced too hastily—as the Talmud (third- to eighth-century compilation of extensive rabbinical discourse) explains, "so that she will not be demeaned in his eyes such that he will easily divorce her."[1]

The Torah allowed a husband to divorce his wife at his discretion, without any obligation to her. Deuteronomy 24:1 states: "A man takes a woman [into his household as his wife] and becomes her husband. She fails to please him because he finds something obnoxious about her, and he writes her a bill of divorcement, hands it to her, and sends her away from his house." Under the biblical directions, if a husband were to evict his wife for any reason, she had no property or security to fall back upon. She and often their children would be in a tremendously vulnerable situation.

The ketubah, literally "that which is written" (and short for *shetar ketubah*, referring to the marriage deed), made it difficult for the husband to divorce his wife by obliging him to pay her as a divorcee the sum mentioned in the contract. The Mishnah (collection of rabbinic traditions redacted by Rabbi Judah Hanasi at the beginning of the third century CE) became the first legal corpus to address the ketubah, devoting the *Ketubot* tractate (book) to it,[2] and subsequent discussion of the marriage contract appeared in the Talmud and other rabbinical commentaries. In both the Mishnah and Talmud the word *ketubah* could also refer to the wife's claim to payment specified in the marriage deed. The bridegroom could not cohabit with his bride until he gave her a ketubah; if it was lost, he had to issue her another one.

The earliest surviving Jewish marriage contracts date back to 449 BCE, from the Jewish community at the Egyptian border fortress Elephantine.[3]

EARLY KETUBAH TEXT VARIATIONS

Ketubah texts came to vary greatly over the centuries. The Talmud had provided a detailed legal discussion on the ketubah, but not its exact language. Starting in the ninth century, several rabbinical figures such as Rav Hai Gaon and Rav Saadia Gaon offered standardized formulae. Later, medieval rabbinical authorities such as Maimonides (Moses ben Maimon, 1138–1204) did so as well.

Maimonides's text not only enumerated the husband's payment to the wife upon divorce; it specified the husband's obligations toward her during their marriage, including providing her with food, clothing, and conjugal rights:

"And I [the bridegroom], with the help of God, will work to honor you [the bride], sustain you, nourish you, provide for you and clothe you according to the custom of Jewish men who faithfully honor, sustain, nurture, provide for and clothe their wives . . . and I will give you conjugal rights."[4]

Over the centuries and across the globe, Jewish communities modified the ketubah to fit their particular needs. The ketubah might stipulate the husband's obligation to free his wife from captivity and to bury her, as written in the Mishnah. The ketubah might also include the inheritance rights between the husband, the wife, and their children in regard to her dowry, the monies specified in the ketubah, and his estate. Additionally, the ketubah might delineate how divorce could be initialized by the husband or the wife.

THE FIRST FORK: BABYLONIAN VS. JERUSALEM KETUBAH TRADITIONS

As it developed, the ketubah went through several important "forks in the road."

The first authoritative fork in the ketubah tradition occurred during the talmudic period. The two major rabbinical centers of the time were in the Land of Israel and in Babylonia (Bavel in Hebrew, modern-day Iraq). Both centers produced edited volumes of their rabbinic traditions: the Jerusalem Talmud (Talmud Yerushalmi) and the Babylonian Talmud (Talmud Bavli), respectively.

Contemporary examination of second- to twelfth-century CE "Palestinian-style ketubot" (as termed by scholar of ancient ketubot Mordechai Friedman), written in Hebrew, Palestinian Aramaic, and Greek and found in the Judean Desert, show the "Palestinian tradition" to have had several unique formulations, including differences in language and legal ramifications.[5] Stipulations on matters of inheritance if either of the spouses died appeared in second-century CE Aramaic and Greek documents from the Judean desert but not in the Babylonian tradition. The Jerusalem Talmud also uniquely included stipulations for mutual divorce, or a divorce that could be initialized by either party.

In time, the Babylonian Talmud was deemed the more authoritative of the two. Accordingly, from the time when the great rabbis of Babylon began to codify the predominant ketubah texts, until the second half of the twentieth century—when major revisions to the standard ketubah texts were first introduced—the text followed this tradition.

THE SECOND FORK: SEPHARDIC VS. ASHKENAZIC TEXTS

By the Middle Ages, most Jewish communities accepted the core formulae for ketubah texts provided by rabbinical authorities, with additional modifications according to local rabbinical authorities, customs, and historical circumstances.

The eleventh century, however, saw the development of two major Jewish traditions—Ashkenazic and Sephardic versions of the ketubah texts—that would continue in use through today. Many variations were common even within each of these two traditions, but several major differences between the two traditions remained consistent over time.

The first difference concerned the prohibition of polygamy in Sephardic but not in Ashkenazic ketubot. Ashkenazic Rabbi Gershom ben Judah (c. 960–1040) had prohibited both polygamy and forced divorces; his authority extended to the Franco-German Jewish communities; and many of their descendants, moving to Poland and Eastern Europe, followed the Ashkenazic rabbinical tradition. Since Ashkenazic Jewry took Rabbenu Gershom's ruling forbidding polygamy for granted, it was understood that the ketubah text did not need to specify the prohibition. By contrast, Sephardic Jews (or Iberian Jews dispersed after the 1492 expulsion from Spain and 1496 expulsion from Portugal who subsequently moved to North Africa, the Ottoman Empire, and the Americas) followed their own—and not Ashkenazic—rabbinical authorities. So it is that to this day, Sephardic ketubot explicitly prohibit polygamy, while Ashkenazic ketubot do not mention the matter.

There are other differences between the traditions. An addition in Sephardic texts prohibits a husband from leaving the couple's country of residence and from selling or mortgaging his wife's belongings without her consent. In the Ashkenazic tradition the monetary contributions are specified in zuzim (silver coins mentioned in the Mishnah), whereas Sephardic ketubot call for a large sum in local currency (for example, dollars) and mention the bride's dowry. The final phrase of the Sephardic text also includes two additional words. Instead of "Hakol Sharir v'Kayam," usually translated as "All of this is valid and binding," it says "Hakol Sharir v'Barir v'Nachon v'Kayam," "All of this is valid *and clear and correct* and binding."[6]

HALAKHIC KETUBAH TEXTS AND THEIR MODERN STANDARDIZATIONS

To this day, the halakhic ketubah text is written in Aramaic, the lingua franca of most Jews at the time the text was composed, as it has been for two millennia. To make it more accessible today, the Aramaic text is sometimes supplemented with a shorter poetic English text, though this is not a translation but rather a sort of embellishment that does not affect the religious legal standing of the halakhic Aramaic text.

Notably, the standard halakhic text is written from the perspective of the witnesses who sign it. The proceedings are documented in third person, such as "And thus he said to her: be thou my wife according to the law of Moses and Israel . . . and she was satisfied and became his wife." . . . "And we saw that the dowry came into his possession."[7]

Great care is taken to protect against either party making additions without the knowledge of the other or the witnesses. The text must be both right- and left-justified, snugly forming a perfect rectangular shape. Moreover, the decorations on the page must be entirely separated from the text, specifically surrounding it on all four sides. Additionally, the conclusion must summarize the contract's contents, and the two witnesses are instructed to sign the document very close to the last line, so that nothing else can be added.

After the State of Israel's establishment, the Israeli Knesset (parliament) passed a law granting the Ministry of Religions jurisdiction over marriages and divorces, and the Chief Rabbinate of Israel began issuing ketubot to marrying couples according to the groom's family background—Sephardi, Ashkenazi, or Yemenite. Per the Chief Rabbinate, an additional sum, specified in shekels, must be granted to the wife in case of divorce or the husband's death. The Rabbinate also maintains a copy of every ketubah in its archives. If the bride and groom wish to use their own ketubah, say one written in calligraphy, their marrying rabbi must give permission.[8]

After the modern centralizations of rabbinical organizations in America, these institutions issued their own standardized versions of the ketubah text, leaving it to the officiating rabbi to choose the desired version and complete the ketubah details. In addition to producing its standardized versions,[9] the Rabbinical Council of America (Orthodox) also instituted—and suggested couples sign—a halachic prenuptial, to avoid the possibility of the bride becoming a chained woman (*agunah*).[10]

ELEMENTS OF THE HALAKHIC KETUBAH TEXT

Whether Ashkenazi or Sephardi, whether issued in Israel or the Diaspora, the halakhic ketubah text generally begins by stating the day of the week and the wedding date according to the Hebrew calendar. Consistent with the Jewish concept of each day running from sunset to sunset—just as Shabbat is considered to begin on Friday at sunset rather than on Saturday—a wedding ceremony that takes place after sunset is recorded in the Hebrew calendar as the new day that began after sunset.

The formula used to express the day of the week is different from the wording used in modern Hebrew. For example, if a wedding takes place on a Sunday, one might expect the ketubah to read "*b'yom rishon*," or "on the first day," but instead it says "*B'echad b'shabbat*," meaning "on the first day after (or in relation to) the Sabbath." After the date comes the location (city/town and state/province) of the wedding. Historically, during times when place names changed frequently due to war, the name of a nearby river would also often be included to help pinpoint the site.

Next to be delineated are the Hebrew names of the couple with reference to their parents, for example, Malkah Golda bat [daughter of] Moshe Aharon v'Esther Frima. If the groom or either of the fathers is a Cohen or a Levi, the words "Ha-Cohen" or "Ha-Levi" will follow their Hebrew name(s). If either the bride or the groom is a convert, the parents' names are listed in Hebrew as "Avraham and Sarah," welcoming them into the people descended from the first Jewish couple.

Following the introductory section, the ketubah lists the husband's (or his heir's) financial obligations to his wife in case of divorce or the husband's death. The Mishnah specified this remuneration as a minimum of 200 zuzim for a virgin and 100 for a divorcée or widow.[11] Traditionally the ketubah text used different Aramaic words to refer to the bride based on her marital history—previously unmarried or virgin (*betulta*), divorcée (*matrachta*), or widow (*armalta*)—and whether she was a convert (*giorta*).[12] Some rabbis prefer to omit the focus on the woman's personal status and instead use the general term for a woman (*itettah*).

Over the ages an equivalent remuneration in the local currency was sometimes noted within the text. In Israel today, the Chief Rabbinate requires a large monetary amount ranging from tens of thousands to a million shekels.

THE THIRD FORK: CONSERVATIVE MOVEMENT INNOVATIONS

The third fork in the road of the development of the ketubah text, the Conservative movement's addition of wording to the handed-down halakhic ketubah text, was a bold step to address an age-old problem. Many Jewish women were (and remain) relegated to the position of *agunah* (one who is "anchored" or "chained") if their husbands refused to grant them a *get* (Jewish divorce) to release them from an unhappy marriage. Still bound to their husbands, these women could not remarry unless their husbands provided them with the *get*.

The "Lieberman Clause"

In 1953, to protect a woman from becoming an *agunah*, Conservative Rabbi Saul Lieberman created what became known as the "Lieberman clause," an insertion into the traditional halakhic text that allowed either the wife or the husband to initiate a religious divorce on equal grounds. Per the Lieberman clause, the groom and the bride:

> further agreed that should either contemplate dissolution of the marriage, or following the dissolution of

their marriage in the civil courts, each may summon the other to the Beit Din of the Rabbinical Assembly and the Jewish Theological Seminary of America, or its representative, and that each will abide by its instructions so that throughout life each will be able to live according to the laws of the Torah.[13]

In some circles, amending the longstanding halakhic ketubah text with additions was viewed as radical. At one time it looked like the Rabbinical Council of America (Orthodox) might also adopt the Lieberman clause, but in the end the RCA did not, and most Orthodox rabbis today do not accept it.

Today a growing number of modern Orthodox couples sign a separate prenuptial agreement in order to avert the *agunah* issue, while keeping the halakhic ketubah text intact. Still, despite ongoing advocacy, the plight of anchored wives remains a problem, especially in Israel and in some observant Jewish communities in North America.

Rabbi Gordon Tucker's Egalitarian and Traditional Approach

Going beyond the Lieberman clause, Conservative Rabbi Gordon Tucker authored an egalitarian ketubah text for couples who objected to the one-sided nature of the conventional contract, but still preferred a more traditional ketubah text. Some aspects of the halakhic ketubah, such as varying financial amounts based on the bride's former marital status, were eliminated to make the document a mutual agreement between equals. Other terms were expanded to become mutual obligations of the groom and bride, such as a two-way ring exchange and a reciprocal *kinyan* (formal exchange of an item, such as a handkerchief, that renders a contract binding according to halakhah). The *kinyan* text partially reads: "The bride accepted a ring from the groom, and the groom accepted a ring from the bride, for the purposes of creating this marriage and to symbolize their love."[14]

Unlike the Lieberman text, the Tucker text is written in Hebrew rather than Aramaic, making it contemporary and accessible. It usually also includes a complete English translation. Additionally, unlike the Orthodox text—or the very similar Lieberman text—the direct translation of this text sounds more like a contemporary commitment of love than an ancient legal contract. Still the Tucker text reads somewhat like a halakhic document, following the cadence and some of the content of the halakhic text, so that most Conservative rabbis accept it. It is a popular choice for egalitarian-minded couples being married by a Conservative rabbi.

THE FOURTH FORK: NON-HALAKHIC KETUBOT

The fourth and most recent fork in the road began in the late 1960s and early 1970s, during—and helping to fuel—the contemporary art ketubah revival. Unlike the aforementioned halakhically rooted texts, most of these new texts were deliberately conceived outside the framework of the Jewish legal tradition. Couples and calligraphers, ketubah artists and clergy fashioned their own interpretations of what a ketubah text ought to stipulate or describe. Often speaking of Jewish values and aspirations, these texts no longer functioned as legal contracts, and instead were typically more akin to poetic documents of love.

First and foremost, the verbiage made clear that the marriage was a union of two equals. All declarations and commitments had to apply reciprocally to both parties.

The Aramaic language used in traditional ketubot was replaced with modern Hebrew, English, or another vernacular language for accessibility. Over time, the English section of the text came to take precedence in the eyes of English-speaking couples, with the Hebrew validating the Judaic origins of the document and satisfying the officiating rabbi's requirements.

Visually as well, the design, shape, and placement of the text also underwent transformation. Whereas traditionally the text was centered on the page and occupied most of the space, with any ornamentation or illustration essentially serving as a full framing device, on modern and contemporary ketubot, the possibilities for integrating artwork became as numerous as ketubah artists' imaginations. Halakhic stipulations were relaxed. Color and imagery might be featured on the center or top or bottom or side or corner of the page or even form the entire background over which the entire text was printed. Some contemporary couples chose to give the artwork more prominence, and this, in turn, reflected a shift in how the ketubah itself was perceived. Rather than a legal or protective document, it was increasingly viewed as a ritual object meant more for commemorative display as a cherished memento of the wedding day.

Unlike a birth certificate or will that was filed away, it was more akin to a professional diploma—occupying an important place as a qualification or certification for operating a Jewish family home. It could also serve as moral affirmation for the couple to continue their commitment to marital harmony. Harry Abt wrote of the possible use of looking at the ketubah during an argument to help resolve conflict: "They will clasp their hands, and the harmony of married life will be restored through the impact of a work of art."[15] Or as the ketubah artist Gad Almaliah put it simply: "It will always be there on the wall, you promising to be nice."[16]

Reform Ketubot

Egalitarianism influenced and supported the development of new standardized ketubah texts within the Reform movement and beyond—essentially poetic expression of an egalitarian relationship between the bride and groom, who enter into marriage as political, economic, and legal equals.

In 1984 the Reform movement, the largest Jewish denomination in North America, issued a poetic, bilingual Hebrew and English ketubah text for American Jews that excluded all of the financial obligations and legal aspects of the Orthodox versions.

One Reform ketubah text reads in part:

> The groom and bride declared: "As we begin our life together, we promise to love, respect, encourage, and inspire one another. We will always endeavor to be open and honest, understanding and accepting, loving and forgiving, trusting of and loyal to one another. We promise to do the most that we can to bring out the best in the other. . . . Let us build a home that emanates warmth, generosity, and love, in accordance with Jewish traditions. . . ."[17]

In 1994 the American Conference of Cantors (organization of Reform cantors) issued a ketubah text with some small but important innovations in the signature lines at the bottom. The use of the word "officiant" instead of "rabbi" opened up this text for use by the many cantors who perform wedding ceremonies. The inclusion of both the male and female Hebrew words for "witness" explicitly acknowledged the departure from the halakhic requirement that ketubot only be signed by men.

In Canada, where the practice of Reform Judaism tends to be more traditional, the Reform rabbinate issued a standard ketubah text that prevented a woman from becoming an *agunah*. Canadian clergy inserted the phrase "by the consent of the *beit din [religious court]* of [city name]" into the handed-down formulation "be my wife according to the law of Moses and Israel," and, since this was an egalitarian text, then repeated this phrase, beginning with "be my husband. . . ."[18] Similar in thrust to the Conservative movement's Lieberman clause, this text effectively stipulated that, in the event of divorce, the couple had to go before the Reform *beit din* to release each other.

Humanistic Judaism

In 1999, the Association of Humanistic Rabbis introduced two humanistic ketubah texts that "speak of love and commitment without references to property or divine creation of the world."[19] One text celebrates Jewish culture and heritage in the new marital partnership, saying, "Let us weave our commitment to the Jewish people and culture into the fabric of our lives. Together, let us build a Jewish home filled with loving affection, laughter, wisdom and a dedication to peace and harmony for all humanity."[20] Another text, designed for interfaith or intercultural couples, reads in part: "Together, we shall create a home filled with learning, laughter and compassion, a home wherein we will honor each other's cherished family traditions and values. Let us join hands to help build a world filled with peace and love."[21] The two texts are available in both Hebrew and English, and some couples choose other languages meaningful to them. A Humanistic rabbi may also sign other ketubot (see below).

Interfaith Couples

From the 1980s onward, numerous new texts were also created to sanctify interfaith, LGBTQ+, and multilingual unions, along with wedding vow renewals and anniversaries. Thus the ketubah was adapting to new social realities.

Interfaith couples became a particularly robust audience for ketubot. In fact, the non-Jewish member of the couple was often the one motivating the Jewish beloved to honor Jewish tradition by displaying a meaningful, beautiful document at their wedding and hanging it in their home. Many interfaith couples—and some secular-minded Jewish couples too—viewed the ketubah, the chuppah, and the breaking of the glass as the core ritual symbols of their Jewish wedding.

One interfaith ketubah reads in part:

> We pledge to each other to be loving friends and equal partners in marriage, to talk and listen, to trust and appreciate one another, and to respect and cherish each other's uniqueness. May our love provide us with the freedom to be ourselves, and the courage to follow our mutual and individual paths. As we share life's experiences, we vow to create an intimacy that will enable us to express our innermost thoughts and feelings; to be sensitive to each other's needs; to comfort and strengthen each other through life's sorrows and joys. We promise to embrace our differences and overcome challenges together with compassion and compromise.[22]

LGBTQ+ Couples

Notably, the use of ketubot at LGBTQ+ weddings predated state and federally sanctioned lesbian and gay marriage. The ketubah artist Mickie Caspi was pivotal in this movement; she and her husband Eran Caspi developed some of the first standardized texts for non-heterosexual unions in 1993. Ingeniously, they left out the last letters of the words in the Hebrew text that required different plural forms and verb conjugations depending on whether the ketubah was for two women or for two men. Emphasizing the creation of an all-inclusive society and the couple's desire to provide each other with the protections and privileges of all loving couples, the text reads in part:

> We also promise to establish a home amid the community of Israel, committed to the creation of an all-inclusive society; a loving environment dedicated to peace, hope, and respect for all people.[23]

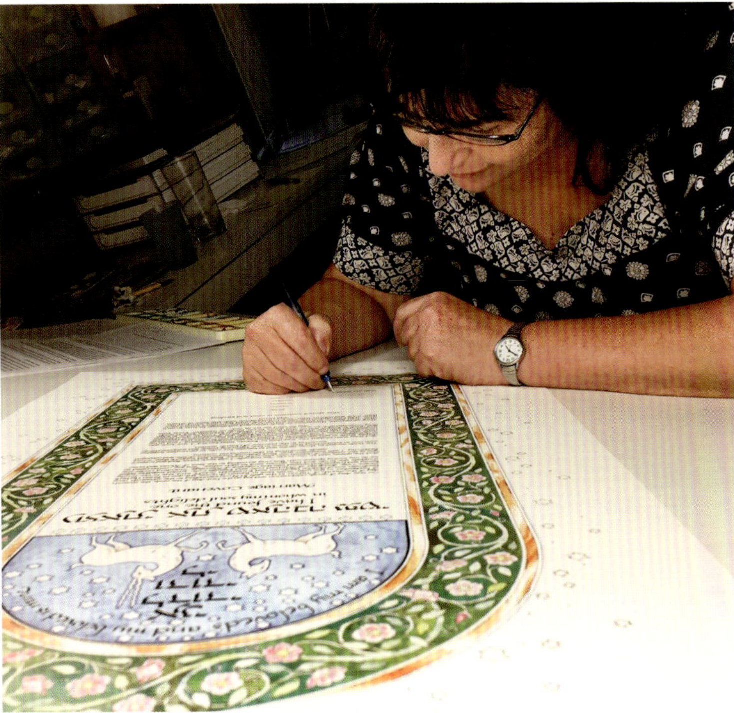

Fig. 13. Ketubah artist and calligrapher Mickie Caspi in her studio. Courtesy of Mickie Caspi.

This ketubah text for LGBTQ+ couples was quite radical and ahead of its time. According to Caspi, it was originally launched under the title of "Gender Neutral Ketubah Text" to help mitigate resistance from some Rabbis and Judaica store owners.[24]

Lovers' Covenant

Another notable innovation was the 1998 creation of the *brit ahuvim* (or lovers' covenant) text by feminist theologian Rachel Adler (b. 1943), printed in her book *Engendering Judaism*.[25] Adler turned away from the language of acquisition to the metaphor of a covenant (*brit*) to define the marital relationship as a mutual responsibility, grounded in love and the promises the two members of the couple make to one another.

The text brings forward several examples of biblical covenants, such as the covenants between God and Noah, God and Israel, David and Jonathan. The covenant between God and Zion from Hosea 2:21–22 reads in part:

> And I will espouse you forever: I will espouse you with righteousness and justice,
>
> And with goodness and mercy, And I will espouse you with faithfulness; Then you shall be devoted to GOD.[26]

Nonbinary Couples

The most recent innovation has been the introduction of texts for nonbinary couples, where at least one of the beloveds identifies as gender nonbinary. These texts are virtually identical to other egalitarian texts but incorporate some innovative Hebrew grammatical forms that have sprung up as a grassroots modification of the heavily gendered Hebrew language. The most striking is a new ending for plural nouns and present tense plural verbs that comprises both the usual female "*-ot*" and male "*-im*" endings. For example, "the beloveds" are "*ha-neh-ehav-im-ot*."

One nonbinary ketubah text reads in part:

> Our hearts fuse together, creating a unique bond with friendship and compassion at its core. . . . We shall nurture one another emotionally, spiritually, and intellectually, always mindful of our respective qualities and strengths.[27]

ANCIENT ROOTS OF MODERN TRADITIONS

Today, the majority of art ketubot chosen by Jewish couples in North America do not adhere to ancient guidelines. Notably, the reciprocity inherent in these texts may reflect the influence of Christian wedding customs, which include vows the couple make to one another during the wedding ceremony, as well as the exchange of rings. These two borrowed innovations brought into contemporary Jewish weddings contrast with the former unilateral practice of the Jewish groom's declaration to the bride and the accompanying presentation of a single ring from him to her.

Today's romantic and inspirational ketubah language may also be rooted in the introductory decorative blessing statements, or rhyming poems in honor of the bride and groom, that appeared on many ketubot across the centuries to express good wishes for the happiness of the newly married couple. The tradition continues in our day, even though the texts of many modern ketubot are more romantic and inspiring in and of themselves. Some of the old scriptural quotes continue to be used—for example, "I am my beloved's and my beloved is mine (*Ani le dodi ve dodi li*)" and "I have found the one I love (*Matzati et she'ahava nafshi*)," both from "Song of Songs" (6:3 and 3:4 respectively), a series of love poems attributed to King Solomon in Jewish tradition.

Likewise, many ketubah artists create their own texts that integrate poetry, romantic Hebrew quotations, and sometimes personal statements from the couple. Some artists offer this type of text in the couple's language paired with the traditional Aramaic text. Such a hybrid text binds contemporary couples to the ancient tradition while also empowering them to craft agreements reflecting their values and contemporary cultural norms.

THE KETUBAH IN THE WEDDING CEREMONY

The ketubah is an integral part of the wedding ritual, appearing at least two times during the wedding day.

Signing of the Ketubah

The ketubah signing usually happens in a special ceremony right before the wedding starts. At Orthodox weddings, this usually occurs at a gathering of the groom and male guests at the groom's table (*chassan's tisch*), where two male witnesses sign the ketubah. At egalitarian weddings, the marrying couple, two (or more) witnesses, and the officiating rabbi or cantor usually sign the ketubah in the presence of immediate family and closest friends (such as the best man and maid of honor) prior to standing under the chuppah. Some modern ketubot even include a signing line for every wedding guest, in a nod to the Quaker wedding certificate tradition that incorporates the signature of everyone in attendance.

One signature that often remains missing is that of the ketubah artist. With the exception of ketubot created by well-known artists like Chaim Gross and Ben Shahn, the artist generally does not receive recognition. Ketubah creation is, therefore, the reverse of most notable works of art held in esteem by the public, in which the artist's name is prominently displayed and the owner or commissioning party is typically unseen.

Reading of the Ketubah

At Orthodox and Conservative wedding ceremonies, the entire ketubah is read aloud between the giving of the ring and the *Sheva Brachot* (seven wedding blessings), thereby serving to divide the two parts of the traditional ceremony. At egalitarian ceremonies, either the full Hebrew text or sometimes just an excerpt will be read, particularly the beginning that contains the date, the location, and the couple's names, often followed by the full English text.

CONSIDERATIONS FOR COUPLES

Today, couples are advised to consult with their chosen officiant about the type of text they may be required or encouraged to use. Most rabbis either insist on or express preferences for particular texts.

Wedding officiants who require a ketubah text rooted in halakhah—such as the Orthodox text or the Lieberman (Conservative) text—will typically want to review and approve the chosen ketubah text before the couple's particulars are filled in. Most officiants who are proficient in Hebrew and Aramaic will also proofread the completed text to ensure that the names, location, and wedding date are accurate and spelled correctly. Doing so in advance of the wedding day is preferable, to ensure that any textual corrections are made before the contractual signing on the day of celebration.

On its storied path through Jewish history, the text of the ketubah has worked hand-in-hand with a flowering of unprecedented visual innovation in ketubah decoration, enabling today's spectrum of couples to express Jewish tradition on their own terms at the intimate moment when they publicly declare the new life they are creating together.

4 The Script of the Ketubah

Alongside innovations in the content of ketubah texts, the ketubah revival period would usher in novel ways of executing the script of—and around—the ketubah document. In other words, the renewal during this period extended beyond the realm of *what* was written and into the dimension of *how* it was written.

HISTORY OF HEBREW SCRIPTS

Initially, of course, all Hebrew scripts were handwritten. The familiar square style of its letter forms, known as *Ktav Ashuri* (Assyrian script), was developed from the Aramaic alphabet used in the Persian Empire, which conquered the Babylonian Empire in 539 BCE and allowed Jews to return to ancient Israel.[1] According to the talmudic sages, Ezra the Scribe (d. 440 BCE) adopted *Ktav Ashuri* for use as scriptural Hebrew to spread the teaching of the Torah to the Jewish people who returned from the Babylonian exile.[2]

In so doing, *Ktav Ashuri* replaced the more angular, linear letter forms of *Ktav Ivri* (Paleo-Hebrew script) that descended from the ancient Phoenician script and was in use until the second century CE.[3] As the Talmud recounts: "Initially, the Torah was given to the Jewish people in *Ktav Ivri*, the original form of the written language, and the sacred tongue, Hebrew. It was given to them again in the days of Ezra in *Ktav Ashuri* and the Aramaic tongue. The Jewish people selected *Ktav Ashuri* and the sacred tongue [Hebrew] for the Torah scroll. . . ."[4]

As the Jews dispersed after the destruction of the Second Temple in 70 CE, different Hebrew scripts developed among the Jews around the world.[5] However, the script of the Torah scroll remained virtually unchanged.[6] The Talmud recounts that the Torah was revealed to Moses in the "crowned style," where decorative "crowns" are placed on specified letters, and discusses the rules of placing "crowns" on those specified letters.[7] A professional scribe known as a *sofer stam* faithfully reproduces the traditional forms of the letters in three primary sacred scrolls used in religious practice: *sefer Torah*—a Torah scroll read and used in the synagogue service; *tefillin*—a set of small black boxes, worn on the head and forearm during morning prayers, containing scrolls of parchment inscribed with Torah text; and *mezuzah*—a parchment inscribed with biblical text affixed to the doorposts of a Jewish dwelling. In so doing the *sofer* follows the "crowned" scroll style directions from the ancient manual "*Sefer HaTagin*" (*tag* means crown in Aramaic).

HISTORY OF KETUBAH SCRIPTS

For most of Jewish history, ketubot were also handwritten. However, unlike a Torah scroll, this was done in a variety of scripts. Since ketubot did not need to be written by a *sofer*, and as such were not governed by the strictures of the highly standardized script required when writing a Torah, tefillin, or mezuzah, they could be written in a variety of nonscribal script variations that existed in various geographies over time. In further contrast to a *sefer Torah*—and unlike the majority of Hebrew manuscripts—a ketubah contains two important pieces of information: a date and a location. Thanks to being anchored in time and geography, the script of the ketubah has contributed to the study of historical Hebrew scripts.[8]

As Moses Gaster (1856–1939), the celebrated Romanian-British linguist and Jewish manuscript collector, wrote, from ketubot "we learn to appreciate Jewish penmanship, and we find a new basis for the study of reliable Palæography" (the study of ancient writing systems).[9] Moreover, according to Gaster, ketubot are "the richest mine of Jewish History in all its aspects. . . . And as for Jewish Art, a new treasure house is found in the Ketubah."[10]

(R)EVOLUTIONS IN PRINTED HEBREW TEXTS

When Hebrew texts began to be mechanically printed in the fifteenth century, the first prints resembled manuscripts and handwritten scripts.[11] Interestingly, compared to several other written languages prevalent at the time, Hebrew was uniquely suited to the printing press. Since its letter forms derived from the shape of a square, these were easily transformed into letter blocks. Additionally, in contrast to letters in other Near Eastern languages (such as Arabic and even Hindi), Hebrew letters seldom change form based on their placement in a word and never need to connect with the letters that precede or follow them.[12]

The revolutionary advent of the printing press led to preprinted, typeset ketubot with blank spaces where details about the bride and groom would be filled in by hand.

Fast-forward to the 1980s. In place of a typeset text, many preprinted ketubot now included a high-resolution reproduction of a text that had been hand-calligraphed, with the appropriate blank spaces, by a ketubah artist. Sometimes the officiating rabbi or cantor would handwrite the wedding particulars into the spaces, but increasingly the artist who created the document or a local calligrapher would render these in a matching hand.

By definition the "one size fits all" spaces in the texts of these preprinted ketubot could cause calligraphic challenges when filling in the couple's names. In some texts the spaces were too small for even the briefest of names, requiring the calligrapher to write the names in a nearly micrographic font. Other preprinted texts, perhaps demonstrating greater foresight, contained extremely large spaces to accommodate even the lengthiest of names, and therefore called on the calligrapher to insert extra calligraphic flourishes around the names to fill any remaining space.

Since the turn of the (twenty-first) century, the realm of printed ketubot has yielded to another revolution. With the help of specialized font foundries—organizations that publish typefaces and release fonts—calligraphers can convert their hand lettering into a digital font. Once this is done, a variety of ketubah texts can be prepared in advance and then, using commercially available design software, be filled in digitally with that same font—yielding a result for a particular couple that is hard to distinguish from handwritten calligraphy! For example, calligrapher Patty Leve converted her handwritten lettering, itself based on old Sephardic scripts that integrated more rounded letter forms, into a timeless digital font.

With current design and printing technology, it could be said that a tradition has now come full circle. In place of a handwritten text, a digitally produced ketubah can approximate a complete, visually cohesive calligraphic text. As a result, fill-in texts have nearly disappeared. Twenty-first-century couples, many of whom grew up in the digital age, have come to expect seamless text.

RENEWED INTEREST IN HEBREW LETTERING

Toward the middle of the twentieth century, inspired by a rich tradition of Hebrew scribal arts, some artists and graphic designers began engaging with Hebrew letter forms with fresh interest. In 1950, Reuben Leaf (b. Lifshitz) published *Hebrew Alphabets: 400 BCE to Our Days*, the first comprehensive guide to over two millennia of Hebrew lettering for artistic purposes. A Ukrainian-born graphic artist who took part in the Jewish artistic revival of the twentieth century, teaching at the Bezalel Academy of Art in Jerusalem in its early years before moving to New York City during the First World War, Leaf advised Jewish artists to "realize that the Hebrew alphabet, in its manifold shapes and renderings, is an integral part of the cultural legacy of the Jew; the accepted and sanctified shapes of the Hebrew alphabet are not only time-honored, but an inseparable part of his consciousness." He went on to caution: "No responsible artist will, therefore, take liberties and trifle with basic forms, lest he destroy or impair its legibility."[13]

In the late 1960s and early 1970s, Jay Greenspan and David Moss (see chapter 2) embarked on early experiments in Hebrew script for ketubot. A trained *sofer stam*, Greenspan proceeding to specialize in Hebrew calligraphy. He authored *Hebrew Calligraphy: A Step-by-Step Guide*, a well-regarded manual instructing artists on how to form the letters, in 1981. Practicing Hebrew calligraphy connects Jews to their history, he explained. "At any moment, as you practice a page of letters or work on an illuminated project, you can join in this unbroken line of tradition that extends from the first tablets carried in the ark of the Tabernacle down through all the past and present generations that have taken, and still take, those words to heart."[14]

LETTERING INNOVATIONS IN THE KETUBAH TEXT

David Moss was influential in transforming how Hebrew script was used in the artistry of ketubah design. While many of his earlier works employed Hebrew lettering as a decorative element, he soon began using the letters of the ketubah text itself to construct his designs. In one such early work from 1972, the words of the ketubah formed the shape of Solomon's Temple atop a traditional Jewish engagement ring (see "Ketubah of Susan and Ze'ev Shainhouse," page 61).

Whereas the old practice of micrography had employed very small Hebrew letters to design visual elements, Moss's revolutionary approach could be called "macrography," making use of very large letter forms instead, to powerful visual effect. In 1989 the American artist Gregg Handorff also pressed the entire ketubah text into service, with multicolored, handstamped, playful Hebrew lettering bursting out of the constraints of the genre. Once again, the font had become art (see "Untitled," page 81).[15]

Creating a new script style could be a painstaking practice. Scripts inherently conveyed emotional attitudes—they could be conservative, dynamic, calm, lyrical, luxurious, minimalist, among others. Tone-wise, a given script style needed to match the ketubah's intended message—traditional, romantic, expansive, modest, or the like. To achieve a pleasing, harmonious, and legible read, artists also weighed the color and sizing of the letters, along with the regularity and rhythm of the strokes—all in all, transmitting something of their own character as artists in the process.

As the modern renaissance of the art ketubah gradually began to take hold, artists furthered the development of Hebrew calligraphy in new creative ways. For example, while historically most Hebrew lettering had been written in black ink, ketubah artists began treating the letters more playfully, even "colorizing" the Hebrew script. Some ketubah artisans even broke away from Leaf's strict ideal and "took liberties" with the letter forms in the service of innovative lettering that complemented their artistic border style and appealed to contemporary couples. The eye-catching fonts and script styles they developed specifically for ketubot sometimes significantly diverged from traditional scribal styles. One striking example is the ketubah script developed by Stephanie Caplan (see "Pomegranate," page 107), inspired by the contemporary English lettering style of Brody Neuenschwander.

Some ketubah artists experimented with "interlinear" layouts of bilingual ketubah texts, in which lines of text alternated between the original Hebrew and its English translation. Best suited to non-halakhic texts in which the Hebrew and English texts were of similar length, this approach appealed to couples seeking the visual connection to tradition provided by the Hebrew text coupled with the more accessible English text that expressed their values and commitment to each other. Jonathan Kremer, for one, produced ketubot notable not only for their interlinearity, but also for the use of calligraphic strokes as the main visual element (see "Untitled," page 93).

LETTERING INNOVATIONS BEYOND BORDERS

In the 1970s, Chaim Gross (see chapter 2), one of America's foremost modernist sculptors and printmakers, created a ketubah bordered by large, riotous Hebrew letter forms—the results of a decade of experimentation with multicolored prints and tapestries (see "Marriage Contract," page 59).

In 2002, the Israeli ketubah artist Izzy Pludwinski crafted the decorative border of his "Wildscript Roundel" ketubah out of a cursive Hebrew script that generally had not been seen on ketubot. Originating in Central Europe in the thirteenth century, this script was widely adopted after the creation of the State of Israel, when Hebrew officially became the national tongue. Pludwinski adapted this traditional script in boisterous and colorful form (see page 115), deploying large lettering with biblical quotations, "the sound of mirth and gladness, the voice of bridegroom and bride" (Jer. 33:11), and "I am my beloved's / And my beloved is mine" (Song of Songs 6:3).

Perhaps Pludwinski, like Moss, could be said to be producing "macrography." Unlike micrography, which requires the viewer's close scrutiny to recognize the letters, here the viewer needs to take a step back to fully comprehend the script.

In 2007, Oded Ezer, the bleeding-edge Israeli designer of digital fonts, uniquely rendered a ketubah text in five different languages—Hebrew, English, French, Spanish, and Yiddish—and also expanded the ketubah's first Hebrew word (the day of the week of the wedding) into giant letters, parts of which escape the two-dimensional confines of the page (see "Untitled," page 123). This augmentation is an energetic twist on a pattern found on many historical ketubot, which itself was influenced by the practice of enlarging, and even gilding, the first letter on Christian illuminated manuscripts in medieval times. Although strictly speaking this innovation occurs within the ketubah text, since the metamorphosis of this first word becomes the focal design element of this "borderless" ketubah, it seems more fitting to group it among breakout innovations in ketubah borders.

HISTORICAL JOURNEY OF REINVENTION

Such is the historical journey of the ketubah script, from its earliest roots in handwritten scribal arts to mechanically typeset texts and finally to digitally printed calligraphy. From the late 1960s onward, a new generation of calligraphers pushed expressive boundaries, taking liberties with letter strokes, letter spacing, and letter connectivity. While scribes had long prized the standard, uniform treatments of Hebrew letter forms, ketubah artists increasingly unbounded themselves from these constraints. As the ketubah artist Judith Joseph once wrote, "As a calligrapher, I see the Hebrew letters as little dancers."[16] Akin to jazz improvisation, Hebrew letter forms became like musical notes that could be playfully shaped into never-before-seen arrangements, inviting new, personally meaningful connections with the handed-down "standards."

5 The Art of Ketubah Production

For centuries, each ketubah was handmade individually. The text was written with ink made from time-tested, naturally occurring materials, using a quill made from the feather of a kosher bird, either on parchment produced from the skin of a kosher animal or on high quality paper. Artisans inked or painted the decorative border, and sometimes added handmade flourishes such as papercuts or illumination (a literal "lighting up") with genuine gold leaf. As was the case with other illuminated manuscripts, a multiplicity of master artisans with diverse skills from calligraphy to gilding collaborated (sometimes in an atelier or workshop) to produce each unique piece.

PRINTING

The 1440 invention of Gutenberg's printing press lay the groundwork for new possibilities in ketubah production. The first printing of Hebrew volumes (Rashi's commentary on the Pentateuch and Jacob b. Asher's *Arba'ah Turim*) took place relatively soon afterward, in 1475, but it would be several centuries, until in the first half of the 1800s, that the use of printed text in the ketubah become popular among Ashkenazic communities in Amsterdam, London, Lemberg (Lvov, known today as Lviv), and Eastern Europe.

One early example of a ketubah using printed text, from 1830 in Swansea, features a printed text and engraving from the Amsterdam Ashkenazic community, which issued the same ketubah for use by its couples. There, too, a popular printed ketubah with an engraved border was produced for export to the British Isles and as far as India. Various printers would use a similar design throughout the nineteenth century.

In 1782 a Hebrew printing press was established in Lemberg, which would grow to become one of the centers of Hebrew printing. Many printers there became renowned for Hebrew book printing, and the printer's name would often be printed on the ketubah. In the Russian Empire, the printed ketubah commonly included a Russian inscription noting the document's purpose and the censor's permission.

As a variety of printmaking techniques became available over time—among them engraving, lithography, silkscreen, offset, and eventually giclée printing—these methods were applied to ketubot production. The printing method employed was generally a function of the available skills, facilities, and communal preferences at the time and place, rather than the needs of particular couples.

ENGRAVING

One of the most ancient techniques in printmaking, engraving involves cutting a series of lines or grooves into a hard surface, such as copper, to produce a design that can then be printed on paper. First used to produce art on paper in Germany in the 1430s, the decorative art form was famously embraced by Rembrandt in the mid-1600s. In fact, both engraving and printed images became popular in mid-seventeenth-century Amsterdam. Ashkenazic Jewish communities in Amsterdam, London, and elsewhere appear to have issued ketubot for their congregations, with identical texts but differing engraved borders. The master engraver Shalom Italia (1619–c. 1655) inspired several copper engraved ketubot, including the elaborate border of "Wedding of a Brazilian Bride in Amsterdam in 1663."[1] Various extant copies of this elaborate ketubah border containing a handwritten ketubah text as well as a *tenaim* (wedding "conditions" document) were printed on parchment from 1663 to 1771 for particular wedding couples.[2]

Engraving was a popular medium early on in ketubah production. The engravings could contain intricate details, the same image could be used multiple times, and that image could be enhanced with some coloring. A major disadvantage was the risk that a careless scribe, writing on the piece after the engraving, could go over the engraving.[3] Beyond this, an engraved work was pricey to produce. In nineteenth-century Europe and North America, other printing techniques, such as lithography, would largely take its place.

Today, engraving is rarely if ever used in ketubah production. Modernity offers high quality options that are less expensive and time-consuming.

SCREEN PRINTING

Modern screen printing is a descendent of a method whereby a design is printed by passing ink through the permeable part of a fabric mesh, traditionally silk (hence the alternate term silkscreen). Wherever ink is not wanted, a stencil blocks the ink from reaching the paper.

Developed in the Far East over a thousand years ago, screen printing first entered Western Europe in the late 1700s. Two centuries later, in the 1950s, it took off in popularity, and it came to distinguish the postmodern pop art of the 1960s and 1970s. Silkscreening helped animate a modern, colorful aesthetic, especially in blocks of color (as opposed to lines or details). Also, it could be applied to diverse materials, from fabrics to paper to glass.

Yet, this printing process is slow, and details and tone gradations are challenging to achieve. In the era of digital printing, silkscreen printing has diminished in popularity.

Chaim Gross's 1970s marriage contract, page 59, is an early example of a silkscreened ketubah, and Ardyn Halter's 1991 "Seven Species" ketubah, page 97, is testament to the medium's continued use in our day.

LITHOGRAPHY

Lithography, from the Greek words for "stone" and "to write," was invented in 1796. The image to be printed is placed on a flat plate of zinc or aluminum; portions of the surface are chemically treated to repel or retain ink; paper is then run over the plate several times to print different colors, and a very richly colored and accurately reproduced image emerges.

Lithography made it both cheaper and easier to produce prints. A lithographer could produce an extremely large number of prints from a single drawing. Once technological advancements allowed for adding color and increasing the printing base size, its commercialization followed.

Lithography reached its heyday as a ketubah medium in the late nineteenth and early twentieth centuries, though beautiful examples appear earlier, among them the 1852 marriage contract produced and signed by the German-born American lithographer Julius Bien, who also served as president of B'nai B'rith for more than three decades.[4] By the end of the nineteenth century, colored lithographic ketubot became popular in some Ottoman Empire Sephardic communities as well as Rhodes.

Lithography's general appeal would diminish with the rise of photogravure for printing newspapers and other publications, but it is still used today in ketubah production, as, for example, Moroccan-born artist Amram Ebgi's ketubah created in 2000, page 111.

OFFSET PRINTING

Descended from lithography, commercial offset printing is used to produce full-color items, from newspapers and posters to promotional brochures and packaging. Instead of being printed directly from a metal plate, the image is printed from a rubber blanket cylinder, to which the image has been transferred or "offset."

The printer Ira W. Rubel of Nutley, New Jersey, accidentally discovered the offset process in 1904, and built a press shortly thereafter. By the 1980s, offset printing had become the ketubah-printing standard, thanks to its widespread availability and overall cost effectiveness.

Still, offset printing presented both pros and cons. On the downside, the time and skill required to prepare the film, plates, and gigantic printing machinery for each run necessitated expensive setup fees—even before the first print was produced. Consequently, ketubot were printed in extensive runs consisting of a single design applied to a variety of ketubah texts, and a different black plate substituted for each text version. But this was far from a failsafe process. In addition to the large upfront investment, a ketubah artist ran the risk of miscalculating the right number of each kind of ketubah text to produce—or worse, of discovering after the fact that very few ketubot with a particular design would ever sell.

On the plus side, offset printing allowed artists to produce multiple copies of their work, often in limited editions, with each ketubah signed and numbered. Thanks to the relatively low production cost per print, they could offer high quality printed ketubot at a fraction of the cost of time-consuming original, commissioned works, sometimes directly to couples and even at a wholesale discount to Judaica shops. Additionally, since the production cost per ketubah was quite low, offset designs that sold even moderately well could be profitable.

Offset printing of ketubot remains popular today. See Betsy Platkin Teutsch's 1997 "Trees of Life" ketubah, offset printed with additional reflective gold foil mechanically applied, on page 105.

GICLÉE PRINTING

Toward the end of the twentieth century, the development of giclée printing helped alleviate some of the problematic aspects of printing ketubot using previous methods.

The term "giclée," derived by printmaker Jack Duganne in 1991 from the French word for "spray," denotes heirloom quality ink-jet printing, with the archival quality inks and papers yielding superior image fidelity.

At first most giclée prints were digital reproductions of conventionally made paintings or drawings. However, with the rise of digital image software like Adobe Creative Suite, a ketubah design could be entirely created on a screen, all the while the finished print resembled artwork created with traditional media. Today, some contemporary ketubah artists work with fully digital processes, from initial design to printing. Others use a hybrid process, creating original artworks by hand that are then scanned and digitally combined with a ketubah text before being giclée printed. See, for example, Jessica Carew Kraft's 2009 "Four Seasons" ketubah, an extremely popular, digitally designed giclée print, on page 135.

Micah Parker was the first ketubah artist to harness the power of giclée printing. In the late 1990s, he pioneered the design and production of giclée-printed ketubot. Even more presciently, in 1999, he launched an online collection of ketubah designs by a variety of artists, all of which were available with a wide array of interchangeable, seamlessly filled in texts. Couples were thrilled to find that now their desired ketubah text was always available on the design they set their hearts on.

Giclée offered artists important advantages, such as printing "on demand" instead of committing to, investing in, and storing, a large print run; as well as printing in their own studio, rather than relying on an external third-party printer. It also opened up the field to more artists, since it eliminated the need to master calligraphy. Over time, with the advent of ketubah publishers with expertise in handling ketubah texts, a command of Hebrew was no longer necessary either.

Interestingly, giclée printing also contributed to a small but notable surge in DIY (Do It Yourself) ketubot, driven by a broader DIY wedding trend. Someone who is not a ketubah artist—the wedding couple, a friend, relative, or designer—can add a decorative border (either digitally or by hand) to a complete, filled-in ketubah text that is printed on fine art paper or provided in a suitable digital format. Overall, by 2020, giclée printing had substantially replaced offset printing in ketubah production.

PAPERCUTTING AND LASER CUTTING

The historical artistic technique of papercutting is enjoying a recent resurgence, as it adds elegant texture and dimension to ketubah designs.

Yet Jews were creating cut paper work by 1345, when Rabbi Shem-Tov ben Yitzhak ben Ardutiel of Spain authored the comical Hebrew treatise *The War of the Pen Against the Scissors*. He explains that he chose to cut the letters out of the paper (apparently in concert with a trend of the time) when the ink in his inkwell froze on a cold winter's night.[5] Ketubot were cut out of parchment (*klaf*) at least as early as 1756 in Modena.

Beautifying ritual items such as *mizrach* placards (indicating the direction of prayer) and Jewish holiday decorations, papercutting became popular in part because it was so accessible, even to Jews with modest means. One simply needed paper, pencil and a penknife; colored crayons or watercolors could be used to add an economical and vivid flourish. Paper was also inexpensive and replaceable, allowing the papercut artist to take creative risks without overconcern about the potential consequences of failure.[6] Sharp shears or a shoemaker's knife were the cutting tools of choice and inscriptions with Hebrew phrases were common decorative elements. Papercuts could even be placed against a windowpane, to give the effect of a "poor man's" stained glass. Jews from Galicia and the adjacent Carpathian Mountains regions, Poland, the Pale of Settlement (in Czarist Russia), Alsace, Bohemia-Moravia, Austria-Hungary, Italy, Ottoman Turkey, North Africa, Eretz Israel, Syria, Iraq, and the United States, among others, would embrace this inviting medium.

Papercutting by Eastern European Jews flourished in the nineteenth century, began to lose popularity as an art form in the 1920s, and subsequently diminished during the Holocaust. Much Jewish ceremonial and folk artwork was lost, and such frail items as papercuts were especially difficult to preserve.

In the 1970s and 1980s, ketubah artists revisited and newly applied this exacting, manual technique in innovative ways. Papercutting helped actualize some of the earliest ketubot of the contemporary Ketubah Renaissance. See, for example, David Moss's 1972 "Ketubah of Susan and Ze'ev Shainhouse," page 61.

Then the late 1990s saw the development of an industrial process involving laser cutting to imitate papercuts. In a nutshell, a laser beam follows a digital "cutting file" and excises the negative spaces from a sheet of paper instead of having those spaces cut out by hand. As laser equipment prices decreased and more reliable laser technology came on the market, this production method became sufficiently dependable and cost-effective for artistic use, including for ketubah production. One could prepare papercut-styled designs using digital design tools without first cutting an original by hand. Additionally, laser cutting allowed for a high level of precision, which led in turn to eye-catching, intricate ketubah designs.

This development did for papercut ketubot what giclée printing did for painted ketubah designs: it opened the door for the mechanical replication of a single design, in this case on a "cut-on-demand" basis. With laser cutting, Ruth Stern Warzecha's 2008 hand-cut original papercut, "Gefen Papercut—Charcoal" on page 129 became affordable to couples as a "cut on demand" limited edition. As with giclée printing, lasercut reproductions could be produced from both hand-rendered originals and digitally produced designs. For instance, Enya Keshet's 2019 "Sasson Papercut Luxe," page 165, is an entirely digital papercut design (it never began with a hand-cut original) produced via laser cutting.

In addition to making papercut designs financially accessible to more couples, lasercutting opened the door to further design innovations both by artists and ketubah publishers. Designs could now easily be offered in a variety of colorways. Personalized papercuts could include a cut-out of the couple's names integrated within the decorative border.[7] Multilayer designs employing both paper and new materials, including wood, became practical as well.[8] For example, "Growing Together" by Dafna Jalon, page 131, is a "3D" ketubah constructed with precision-cut spacers. Ruth Becker's 2010 work, "Revelry 18-Layer," page 139, is a breakthrough eighteen-layer design pushing lasercutting technology to achieve a sculptural effect.

HAND FINISHING

There is a long history of adorning ketubot with artisanal handwork. The process of hand finishing is rooted in illuminated manuscripts, so named because they reflected light thanks to painstaking additions of gold leaf. Furthermore, embellishments by hand were consistent with the then entirely manual process of creating ketubot, from handwritten texts to hand-painted borders and beyond. Surprisingly, the advent of digital production methods has ushered in a resurgence of hand finishes, though this time paired with giclée printing, laser cutting, or both.

Certainly, before digital printing emerged, some ketubot printed via the offset method included gold- (or silver-) colored foil that was mechanically applied to highlight key design elements. See, for example, Betsy Platkin Teutsch's 1997 "Trees of Life" ketubah, page 105. And there were occasional innovations, such as Gad Almaliah's c. 1990 "Pesukim" ketubah, page 89, in which thin pieces of metal containing hammered-in designs have been affixed onto paper printed with the ketubah text. However, today there is a veritable explosion of manual decoration, including the addition of 23K gold leaf, Swarovski crystals, faux pearls, and even embroidery. See, for example, Britt Yudell's 2020 "White & Gold Garden Embroidery" ketubah, page 167.

MASS-MARKET KETUBOT

Starting in the 1980s and 1990s, couples with modest budgets or shorter timelines increasingly shopped for their ketubah at their local Judaica shop. Modern Judaica galleries like Kolbo in the Boston area, Afikomen in Berkeley, West Side Judaica in Manhattan, and Gallery Judaica in Los Angeles played central roles in broadening the appeal and distribution of artistic ketubot by offering ketubah prints by different artists with multiple text variations. These ketubot often acted as magnets for a new generation of engaged couples who were in the market for wedding items such as kippot and could become valuable lifelong customers. During this pre-internet period, a modest selection of ketubot was also available for sale via major full-color Judaica mail-order catalogs such as "The Source for Everything Jewish" and the "J. Levine Judaica catalog," which aimed to reach geographically dispersed consumers interested in modern Judaica. In short, by 1995, when this author met his first ketubah artist, the widespread availability of high-quality prints in the $150 to $300 range had firmly established the art ketubah as a beautiful fixture at the majority of Jewish and interfaith weddings in North America.

ESTABLISHMENT AND BENEFITS OF DIGITAL PRODUCTION

Digital production methods became cost-effective and widely available roughly in parallel with the mainstreaming of the internet around the turn of the twenty-first century. Together with the information superhighway, these techniques opened up unprecedented avenues for ketubah artists, couples, and wedding officiants, solving longstanding challenges for all three groups.

Surmounting Language Barriers to Creating Art Ketubot

Previously, ketubah artists—even native Hebrew speakers—often faced steep learning curves when working with ketubah texts. This was especially true with Orthodox and most Conservative ketubah texts, because they are written in Aramaic (not Hebrew) and include a number of "spaces" to be filled in differently depending on the couple (primarily related to the bride's previous marital status). Artists found it far from easy to master Aramaic.

Fortunately, recent digital advances in "on-demand printing" have opened up the creation of art ketubot to virtually all artists and designers, regardless of their knowledge of Aramaic or the Hebrew Alef Bet. Artists can now submit their handmade or digital ketubah designs to a specialized, fine art ketubah publishing house, which takes care of filling in the individual elements of the ketubah text needed by each couple. Ketubah artists who choose this process then have the opportunity to focus completely on their art.

Avoiding Errors and Aesthetic Flaws in Printed Ketubah Texts

Before the advent of digital printing, some ketubah texts were printed with errors that had to be addressed by the artist or officiating rabbi, sometimes at the very last minute. For example, a Hebrew word or phrase might be printed in the wrong place in the text, or not appear at all. Also, the spaces within the preprinted text were often so small that it was barely possible even for a skilled calligrapher to fit in a longer name without resorting to micrography that verged on being illegible.

Digital printing eliminates these issues by replacing static preprinted texts with digital texts that have flexible spaces of theoretically infinite size. Ketubah texts filled in digitally on a computer monitor can be fixed at any time and can beautifully and seamlessly accommodate even the longest (or shortest) names before being set to print.

Overcoming Frustrations in Finding the Perfect Ketubah

Before digital production, couples often experienced limitations and frustrations when shopping for their perfect ketubah. Some fell in love with a particular design, only to discover it wasn't available in the text they wanted or needed to satisfy their wedding officiant's requirements. If, say, they needed a halakhic text or a non-halakhic egalitarian text, sometimes the artist who created the design they loved did not print any ketubot with that text. Artists then tended to offer a limited number of text options, either to mitigate printing costs or to provide ketubah options in keeping with their personal beliefs. In other instances, the stock of a couple's chosen design printed with their selected text actually existed but would run out. This could be even more disappointing: couples would think their desired ketubah was available, and later discover that, in fact, it was unobtainable.

Ketubah shoppers could find themselves riding a similar emotional rollercoaster for yet another reason. For non-halakhic texts—including Reform, interfaith, LGBTQ+, and others, which together represented a substantial majority of the market—different artists would often write their own texts, usually in English with a Hebrew translation. As a result, couples shopping either at a brick-and-mortar Judaica shop or an online store were often frustrated that they could not "mix and match" ketubah designs and texts. In short, they would need to settle for either their preferred design or text, but not both.

With the advent of on-demand printing, these problems largely vanished. Various ketubah publisher sites—and also the websites of individual ketubah artists—began to offer ketubah designs, all of which were available with a wide array of texts. Even if a design was produced in a limited edition (meaning an upfront commitment that only a defined number of ketubot with a particular design would be printed, with any of the range of available texts), no text itself would ever run out. As a side benefit, artists were never left with "stranded" ketubah prints. By definition, the supply of ketubot printed—both overall and in each text version—exactly matched the demand. And online ketubah shopping at a ketubah publisher's site could be even more rewarding. Couples could mix and match any of hundreds of designs by scores of artists with any of the dozens of available texts.

Dramatically Decreasing the Cost of Custom Texts

Occasionally in the "before digital" (BD) era, couples could in fact arrange their chosen text on their chosen ketubah design, but doing so came at hefty price. When producing a ketubah using the offset (or similar) printing method, some artists included a small number of textless ketubot in their print runs. These blank—or "decoration only"—ketubah borders could be filled in with an entire handwritten text of the couple's choosing, resulting in a beautiful, hand-calligraphed ketubah that also tapped into the practice of times gone by. However, the time-consuming nature of adding the text by hand wasn't for everyone. The hand-calligraphed text usually costs more than the price of the ketubah itself.

Digital production eliminated the time-consuming expense of calligraphing a complete text by hand. As a result, the additional cost of a custom text became affordable for most ketubah shoppers. Today, a growing number of couples opt to write their own English text. Some pair it with a halakhic Aramaic text, while others place a literal Hebrew translation above it on their preferred ketubah design. Some even take advantage of an added bonus of digital text preparation and add a text in a third language to honor the cultural roots of one of the beloveds, running the gamut from Spanish to Mandarin and beyond.

Offering Halakhic Ketubot for Divorced, Widowed, and Converted Brides

Before the invention of giclée printing, most preprinted Orthodox ketubot were only usable for previously unmarried brides who were born Jewish. This "first marriage" text, used by Orthodox couples as well as non-Orthodox couples being married by an Orthodox rabbi, had the advantage of being substantially easier to work with; other than the date, location, and names of the bride and groom, everything else was already filled in. (This preprinted text did not accommodate the modifications related to the bride's status and the resulting financial terms in the contract.) Yet it left divorced, widowed, or converted brides with very few choices in ketubah designs. Today, however, since most ketubot are printed "on demand," these couples can select the ketubah design of their choice as well.

Simplifying the Hebrew Names Submission Process

For forty years the Israelites wandered in the desert en route to the Promised Land. And for four decades, ordering a printed ketubah or an original commission involved a cumbersome process of completing a form that required one to specify the Hebrew names of the wedding couple and their parents—often a stressful exercise for the couple who needed to gather this infrequently used information. This process could also be inefficient and time-consuming for the officiating rabbi or cantor, who was generally the one to handwrite the names in Hebrew letters.

It could also throw a wrench in things on—or soon before—the wedding day, when the filled-in ketubah was available for inspection and an error was detected. There are happy stories of heroic efforts by local calligraphers who made corrections in a matching hand on short notice. Sadly, there were also instances when this could not be accomplished. The couple's lovingly selected art ketubah needed to be set aside or supplemented by another simple, unadorned ketubah, signed by the witnesses, which became the official marriage document.

Giclée printing helped reduce one stressful aspect of this challenge. A filled-in text proof was sent to the officiating rabbi or cantor to approve *before* the final text was printed.

The next step forward occurred in 2005 with a groundbreaking online innovation. The Ketubah Text Tool (originally the Ketubah Personalization Wizard)—this author's invention—allows couples to use an intuitive step-by-step interface to enter the required Hebrew information without any knowledge of the *Alef Bet*. Working from a curated database of Hebrew names, this tool automatically populates the selected names in Hebrew letters. Once the couple completes the process to the best of their ability, they click to share the information with their rabbi, cantor, or other wedding officiant. The officiant then completes or revises the names as needed, including important details such as the indication of "Cohen" or "Levi" and, if desired, the addition of two Hebrew letters, *zayin* and *lamed* (the initial letters of the words *zichrono/a livracha*, or "may his/her memory be a blessing") after the name of a deceased parent.

In addition to Hebrew names, the Ketubah Text Tool includes Yiddish names—which are sometimes difficult to spell correctly, since Yiddish indicates vowel sounds with a system of consonants instead of the *nikud* ("the dots") used in Hebrew for this purpose. It also calculates the Hebrew date—based on the wedding date and whether the ceremony takes place before or after sunset—and, for halakhic ketubah texts, suggests modifications to the ketubah wording based on the bride's status. In keeping with the times, a more recent enhancement allows couples to indicate their preferred pronouns.

Overall, on-demand printing using digital calligraphy coupled with the online gathering of Hebrew names could reasonably be called a disruptive technology. Among other benefits, it has radically reduced the turnaround time for an heirloom quality, ready-to-sign ketubah. While it is still generally recommended to order a ketubah a couple of months in advance, for couples and officiants who are able to move quickly to finalize the requisite Hebrew names and sign off on completed text proofs, seasoned ketubah publishers can generally accommodate even the very shortest of timelines, within days if necessary!

RESURGENCE OF HISTORICAL DESIGNS AND PAPERCUTS

Interestingly, the newest technologies have recently paved the way for a fresh interest in some of the oldest ketubot. Thanks to high-resolution photography, graphic design software, giclée printing, and lasercutting, a growing number of couples are selecting heirloom quality, authorized reproductions of historical ketubah designs. Once a precious ketubah has been carefully scanned at high resolution, often by The Jewish Museum (New York) or The National Library of Israel (Jerusalem), both of which hold vast permanent collections of historical ketubot dating back to the fifteenth century, the original text can be removed and replaced with a contemporary, personalized text selected by the couple. Couples choosing an ancient ketubah design may have a particular connection to the country or culture in which the ketubah was originally created, may wish to feel connected to the generations who have come before them, or may treasure the old-world feel of historic documents, such as this breathtaking ketubah from 1614 Venice.

The couple can simply order it online just as they would any other ketubah, selecting their preferred design and text and uploading their names and wedding particulars. The result is a museum-quality print or lasercut of a historical treasure alongside a text personalized for their contemporary simcha.

In essence, over the last few decades, despite—and also thanks to—revolutionary technology and production methods, acquiring a ketubah has come full circle. Unlike in the recent past, when large print runs had to be arranged in advance for many (yet to be determined) couples, the process bears a surprising resemblance to how it was centuries ago. Today, as in yesteryear, a ketubah artist—or ketubah atelier—produces a single archival quality ketubah for one couple, with their selected design and text, in the size and on the print stock of their choice.

As Shalom Sabar noted (see Introduction), in the century before the start of the modern ketubah revival, the availability of inexpensive printing contributed to the demise of the illuminated ketubah. Yet, in a marvelous reversal, over the last half century, it could reasonably be said that without affordable, high quality printed reproductions in a variety of texts, the widespread ketubah renaissance would never have come to fruition.

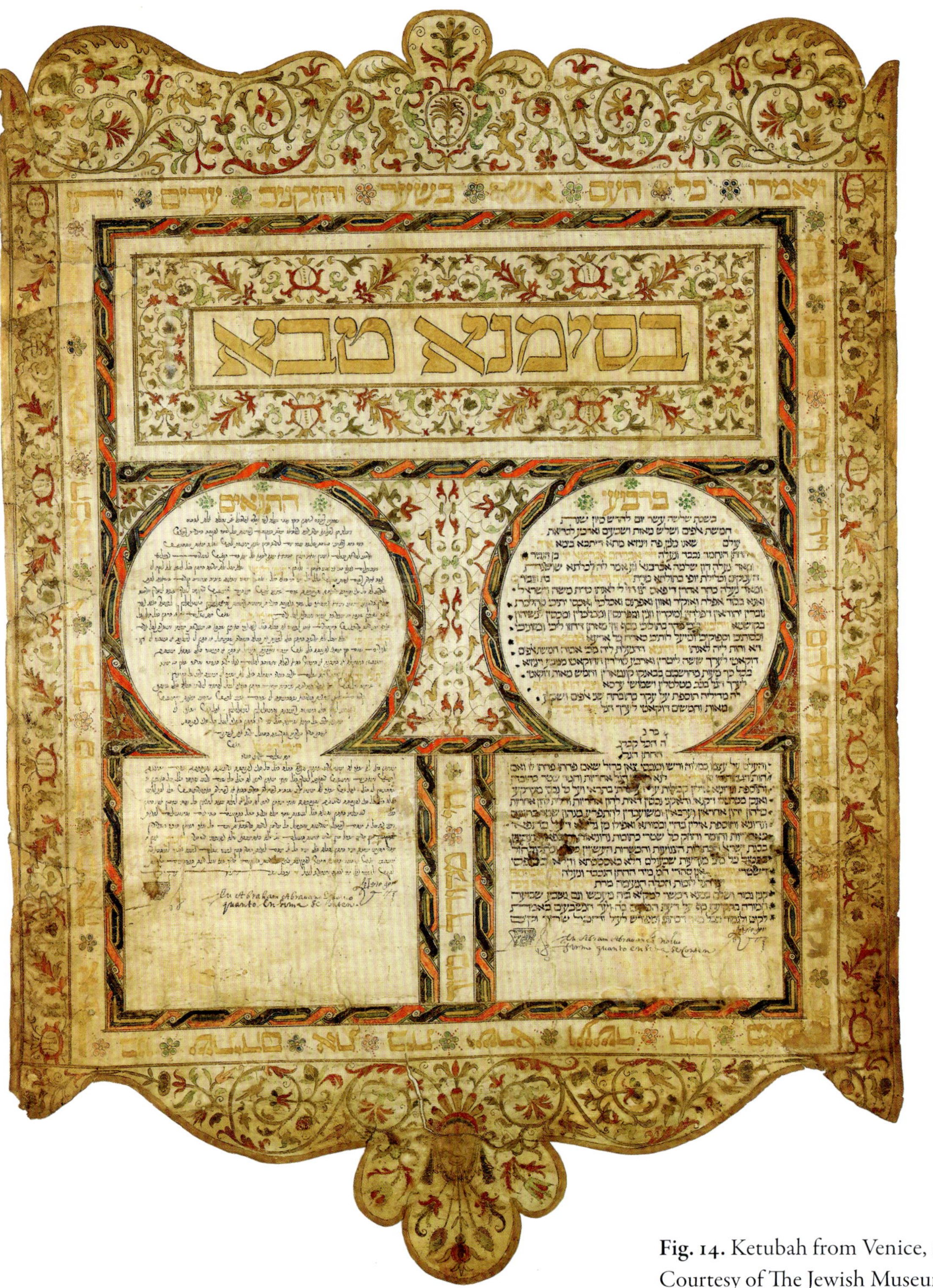

Fig. 14. Ketubah from Venice, 1614.
Courtesy of The Jewish Museum, New York.

6 The Ketubah in the Twenty-First Century

The social, economic, and technological changes of the last half century have altered mainstream Jewish life in ways the talmudic Rabbis could never have imagined when they codified the ketubah.

During this period, gender roles became more egalitarian and, more recently, gender fluidity entered the mainstream. Interfaith marriage among Jews went from being a rarity to becoming the norm.[1] Same-sex marriage was legalized first in Canada and then in the United States, and LGBTQ+ couples increasingly wed. Online shopping gained prominence.

The ketubah is a touchpoint for these and many other transformations. It continues to operate and evolve in new contexts and configurations.

MULTITUDE OF DESIGN OPTIONS

Today's couples have a multitude of ketubah design options. Thousands are displayed on artists' websites, Etsy shops, and social media, as well as on sites like Ketubah.com, the first online gallery dedicated to ketubot, launched by this author in 1996.

The range of ketubah designs is broader than ever. Some couples are drawn to perennial Jewish motifs, such as flowers, grapevines, wedding bands, scenes from Jerusalem, the Tree of Life, hamsas, and menorahs, in a modern rendering or in imitation of historic styles. (See the appendix, "Common Ketubah Symbols.") Since the turn of the twenty-first century, however, more couples are choosing ketubah designs that have subtle Jewish symbolism or none at all. Some prefer a ketubah that incorporates space-age materials or the aesthetic of famous artists like Gustav Klimt or Mark Rothko. Others gravitate to starkly modernist, whimsical, or minimalist designs, or a more experimental medium. Some ketubot incorporate digital photography, sculptural objects, or fabric scraps, while others are masterfully etched in glass.

PERSONALIZATION

Even with the vast array of ketubah prints, laser cuts, and unique designs currently available, some couples still opt for custom artwork that incorporates their birthplaces, the locale of their first meeting, their professions, alma maters, favorite colors, even their pets.

As discussed in chapter 2, one of David Moss's most significant contributions to the revival of the artistic ketubah was his loving attention to the bride and groom, culminating with a handwritten letter explaining what inspired him to create their commission. As the artist Judith Joseph has said: "It is my goal as a ketubah artist to tell the story of the couple who are getting married."[2]

Today, most couples look to fall in love with the art of their ketubah first. They may also take into account their wedding theme or home decor. There are generally a variety of available options to personalize the final look, such as choices of size, colorway, print stock (paper, canvas) and hand finishes (gold leaf, Swarovski crystals). Next, they select a text that is meaningful to them and acceptable to their rabbi or wedding officiant. After the wedding, they have the ketubah framed and hung in a place of honor, either in a private space such as a bedroom or in a more public locale, such as a living or dining room, where it can be shared with and admired by guests.

THE KETUBAH IN THE FUTURE

A number of recent developments and emerging trends may influence the ongoing evolution of art ketubot in the next decade and beyond. As with any attempt to glimpse the future, predictions are fascinating to consider, but of course fall into the realm of educated guesses. Here are some of mine.

Gender, Pronouns, and Ketubah Texts

As we've seen, significant innovations in the realm of the ketubah text include verbiage designed to ensure that Jewish divorce is available to women in the case of marital breakdown, and, more broadly, a wealth of texts imagined outside of halakhah. The most recent textual innovation, addressing contemporary concepts of nonbinary gender identity, calls for the use of new gender-inclusive pronouns, plural forms, and verb conjugations in the Hebrew. Looking ahead, if the current trajectory persists, other wordings—or entirely new texts—may be invented to acknowledge and honor the ever-evolving identities of the beloved parties under the chuppah.

Interfaith Ketubot

When interfaith texts first appeared on the scene, there was a sense that higher rates of intermarriage would lead to a reduction in the overall interest in—and sales of—art ketubot, but so far, this has not turned out to be the case. Many interfaith couples choose to incorporate a ketubah into their wedding ceremony. As discussed, they, like many secular Jewish couples, see the ketubah as one of the new "big three"—together with a chuppah and the breaking of the glass—that make a wedding feel Jewish.

Note that nearly 60 percent of the children of interfaith couples are being raised as Jews.[3] With supportive organizations and programs such as PJ Library, there is evidence that these families continue to value Jewish identity on their own terms. With the ongoing trend of intermarriage, it is likely that in the near future, the proportion of ketubot with interfaith texts will continue to increase.

Looking further ahead, there remains a question about whether the next generation—the grandchildren of the interfaith couples—will connect with Jewish identity or tradition, and if so, to what extent are they likely to include a ketubah in their own wedding ceremonies.

Anniversary Ketubot

Some of David Moss's early ketubot were in fact commemorative anniversary documents rather than wedding contracts. Since then, there has been a small but steady demand for these beautiful items, both as commissioned originals and as fine art prints. An anniversary ketubah is a meaningful present from one spouse to another, or the perfect group gift for parents, or grandparents, "who have everything." It is suitable for couples who never had an art ketubah—and wish they did—as well as for those who already have one and are drawn to the idea of renewing and celebrating their commitment with new art or text. With increasing life expectancy and a growing number of anniversary ketubot specially designed for big anniversaries—silver (25th), gold (50th), and even diamond (60th)—it seems likely that demand for anniversary ketubot will grow in the next few years.

Israeli Market for Art Ketubot

While Israeli artists have made substantial contributions to the art ketubah renaissance (see especially chapters 1 and

7), their output has almost exclusively served the North American market, either via online sales or by selling directly to visiting tourists. Native Israeli adoption of the art ketubah has been minuscule at best, and almost entirely contained within the "Anglo Israeli" communities originating from the United States, Canada, the UK, South Africa, and Australia. Why is there virtually no market for art ketubot in Israel?

Most Orthodox Israelis relate to the ketubah solely as a legal document and, consistent with longstanding practices such as putting the ketubah away for safekeeping or storing it at the bride's parents' home, the couple would not hang their ketubah on the wall. And, as noted earlier, among the Ashkenazic half of the Israeli population there is no tradition of decorated ketubot. Moreover, many secular Israelis (in Hebrew, *chilonim*) resent the Orthodox rabbinate's authority over lifecycle events including marriage. In response, quite a number of these couples leave the country to be married in a civil ceremony abroad; although the Israeli government only recognizes weddings officiated by Orthodox rabbis within Israel, it does sanction the marital status of all weddings of Israeli citizens performed outside of Israel, regardless of the officiant's affiliations there. *Chilonim* who view the ketubah as a document imposed on them by the Israeli rabbinate have little appetite to decorate, invest in, or display one in the home.

Looking ahead, it would seem unlikely that widespread interest in art ketubot could develop among Israelis. Yet, as author Yossi Klein Halevi observes, while secular Israelis are seeking less religion, they are simultaneously drawn to more tradition. In that light, could an art ketubah with a non-halakhic text become a meaningful part of secular Israeli wedding ceremonies?

On the one hand, this is exactly what happened in the North American Jewish community over the last half century. Before the ketubah renaissance, virtually no one had an art ketubah. Yet today, the majority of Jewish and interfaith weddings include one. During the decades of the ketubah revival, North American Jews strove to connect with their traditions on their own terms—and one important aspect of their reimagined Judaism was the modernization of the ketubah text to align with post-halakhic, egalitarian values.

As Jews drove to integrate more fully into North American society—and were increasingly accepted—there was tension between the desire to be less religious (or at least less observant of the handed-down commandments and interpretations) and the yearning to deepen their connection with Jewish traditions, especially in "old-new" ways that felt more creative and less onerous.[4] The art ketubah fit the bill perfectly. It was a beautiful example of *hiddur mitzvah* that already existed in geographically diverse communities across the ages. It did not need to be invented but was ripe for revival and reinterpretation—that is, it was just the thing.

Ultimately, however, the reasons underlying this substantial change in the North American Jewish community are not present in Israel; nor is there evidence of other local impulses likely to lead to the same end. If, however, the Israeli rabbinate does come to recognize non-halakhic (or even civil) weddings performed in Israel, there may yet be a chance for broad-based adoption of art ketubot in Israel.

Technological Cross-Pollination

The widespread popularity of art ketubot has triggered user-friendly technological innovations to help put brides and grooms at ease regarding their Hebrew names (see chapter 5). While the majority of North American Jews have a Hebrew name, many have limited facility with the Hebrew language. Furthermore, following the age-old formula, a person's "complete Hebrew name" also includes their parents' Hebrew names as well as the designation of "Cohen" or "Levi" if applicable—so, for example, Chaya Sarah bat Tzvi

Hersh ha-Cohen ve-Yocheved Avigayil. To make matters even more challenging, many Hebrew names (like "Hersh" above) are actually Yiddish names. Even though these names are spelled using the Hebrew alphabet, the Yiddish vowel system is entirely different—using letters instead of dots—and unfamiliar even to many rabbis.[5] The entire exercise can be stressful or even embarrassing on one of those infrequent occasions—bris/baby naming, bar/bat mitzvah, wedding, death/tombstone—when adult children need to scramble to find their / their parents' / their kids' Hebrew names.

Having experienced this relief at wedding time, Jews are now seeking similar help at these and other times of life. Jews by choice joining the Jewish people, Jews who were never given a Hebrew name, and Jewish couples starting a family often find themselves seeking out just the right Hebrew name for the given occasion. Today, there are websites with lists of dozens—or hundreds—of Hebrew names, from Chabad.org to theBump.com, and useful baby-naming articles on sites like Kveller.com. To take things to the next level, this author recently launched HebrewNamer.com, where queries such as "Suggest some Hebrew girls names after my late grandfather Irving" receive intelligent responses; a favorites list helps narrow down the final name selection; "complete Hebrew names" are easily created and shared with a synagogue, rabbi, or mohel/et; and cloud-based name storage for an entire family makes all family members' complete Hebrew names accessible whenever lifecycle events call for them. With the accelerating pace of AI, it can be expected that offerings in this realm will improve exponentially in the future.

Artificial Intelligence

In 2024, at the time of this writing, Artificial Intelligence (AI) has gone from being something for the future to a driving force in our day. Already we have witnessed the first haggadah (haggad.ai) whose commentary and images were created with AI tools. In the realm of ketubot, couples have used ChatGPT to write personalized texts and Etsy includes AI-generated, downloadable, print-it-yourself ketubah designs, with many more expected.[6] AI is likely to play an increasing—and possibly substantial—role in the design of ketubot, and in the composition of ketubah texts as well.

Will this disruptive technology drive a seismic shift in how ketubot are designed, ordered, or produced—or will it be harnessed to augment and make improvements in these areas while continuing to draw heavily on human creativity? At present, it is too early to tell.

Broadened Use

Yet another current trend is adapting the ketubah to mark other important occasions. For example, the union of two California congregations was solemnized with a thoughtfully written and elegantly typeset Spiritual Covenant set within a ketubah border. Camp Harlam in Kunkletown, Pennsylvania, commissioned alumna Hadass Gerson to design a ketubah for its sixtieth anniversary celebrations, with signature lines for the couples who had met at the Reform camp over the years (see page 175). The Jewish Museum in New York commissioned a marriage contract by Nigerian American artist ruby onyinyechi amanze for its permanent collection. Non-Jewish artist Brooke Borg has collaborated with Jewish ketubah artist Judith Joseph to create "ketubot" signed by family members to promote the healing of traumatic relationships. And on the back wall of Russ & Daughters restaurant in Manhattan hangs an original piece of art in the unmistakable shape of a contemporary ketubah—with a decorative border surrounding a heartfelt text to acknowledge the many years of service of a cherished employee.[7]

Looking ahead, the ketubah as an art form is likely to be inventively adapted to meet new needs and circumstances.

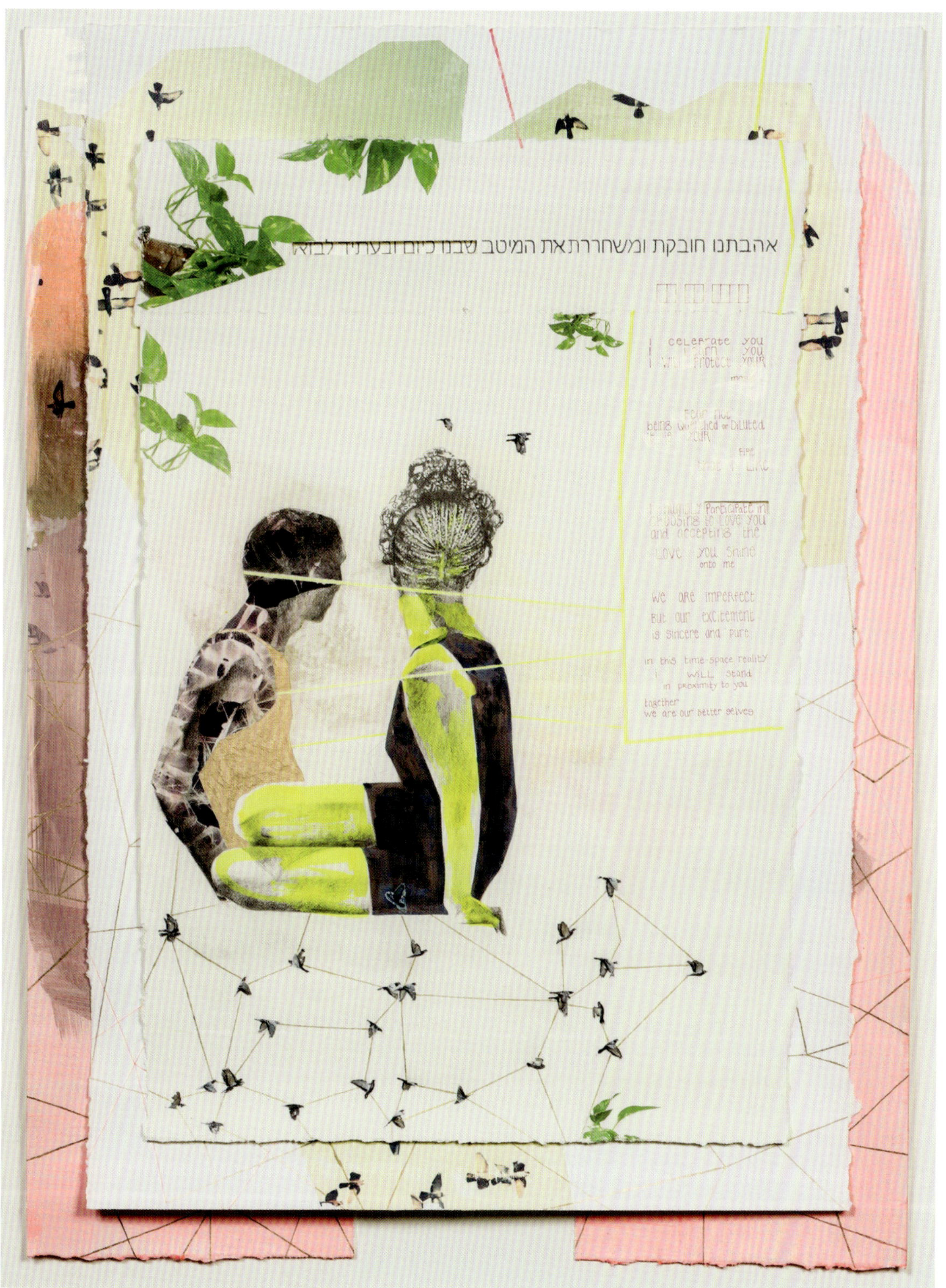

Fig. 15. ruby onyinyechi amanze, "Marriage Contract," 2017. Courtesy of ruby onyinyechi amanze.

IN CONCLUSION: AN EVOLVING TESTAMENT OF LOVE

The art ketubah, a remarkable artistic artifact and ritual item, has endured the trials of a millennium of Jewish history. Looking ahead, it will undoubtedly continue to evolve and transform to fit its time and context.

Yet, as its aesthetics and even its purpose keeps expanding, it remains rooted in a central aspect of the human experience that Jews continue to beautify and sanctify.

David Moss expresses that essence in his evocative 1973 poem "Lines Pulled Black on White." Inviting the reader to the wedding chuppah, it skillfully interweaves *Ketubta da, Nedunya dane*, and *Vetosefta da*, the Aramaic words traditionally read or sung aloud, forming the ancient cadence of the ketubah text:

Lines pulled black on white
Intend a dual unity,
Drawing separate lives together.
A golden rainbow garland,
Surrounding the ancient amulet,
Surrounding the aramagic letters,[8]
Makes a beaming brideheart beauty-beat;
Makes a pridegroom glow
Hot and happy.

Ketubta da—he reaches out to her;
Nedunya dane—and she to him;
Vetosefta da—adding mutual joys and sorrows.

Kehilchot guvrin yehudain
And he lifts up a handkerchief
Denahagin bevanot Israel
To wipe a love-tear from her eye.[9]

7 Gallery of Ketubah Plates

The pages that follow showcase sixty examples of the thousands of outstanding artistic ketubot produced from 1961 to the present. Given this embarrassment of riches, for every ketubah selected, there are scores of others that, space permitting, could have equally merited inclusion. In painstakingly selecting these ketubot, priority was given to those that represented visual breakthroughs—examples that were new and different for their time—with some of these further validated by their popularity among couples.

These stunning designs, displayed here in chronological order, were created using a remarkable range of techniques, from Gregg Handorff's potato-block prints to Jeanette Kuvin Oren's fabric artistry to Gad Almaliah's hammered copper illuminations. The represented artists created their ketubot in the United States, Canada, and Israel, with an interestingly high incidence of geographic cross-pollination—that is, of "Anglos" (both North Americans and Brits) living in Israel and Israeli artists living in North America. In general, a single—and singular—example of each artist's ketubah designs follows, in order to represent the widest variety of artists; however, to emphasize his central role in sparking the ketubah renaissance (see chapter 2), four David Moss ketubot are featured.

Many designs depicted here were created with titles, as they were mass produced. Others do not have titles, since they are either custom works or are simply untitled. While some ketubot in this collection include names, locations, and wedding dates, others are blank, and still others blur personal details to protect the privacy of the marrying couple. Whenever the ketubah materials significantly vary from the traditional media of paint and ink, the accompanying caption sheds additional light on their form and function.

It is my hope that the reader will experience the visual journey in the pages ahead as a sacred experience in and of itself.

Ben Shahn

“Marriage Contract”

1961

Immigrating to New York City in 1906, Benjamin Shahn (1898–1969, Kaunas, Russian Empire) developed interest in lettering and calligraphy early in life. Words, names, and quotations became visual elements in many of his compositions, and his art was shown in both solo and group exhibitions in major art museums worldwide. He became known as “the people’s painter” because of his social realist focus and themes of justice in his work.

In this decorated ketubah, the earliest ketubah from the ketubah renaissance period, Shahn makes several deviations from the traditional constraints of the ketubah—incorporating a playful Hebrew letter form, filling up spaces between the lines of text with flowers and leaves, and also placing his signature at the bottom of the page next to his red artist’s stamp containing every Hebrew letter.

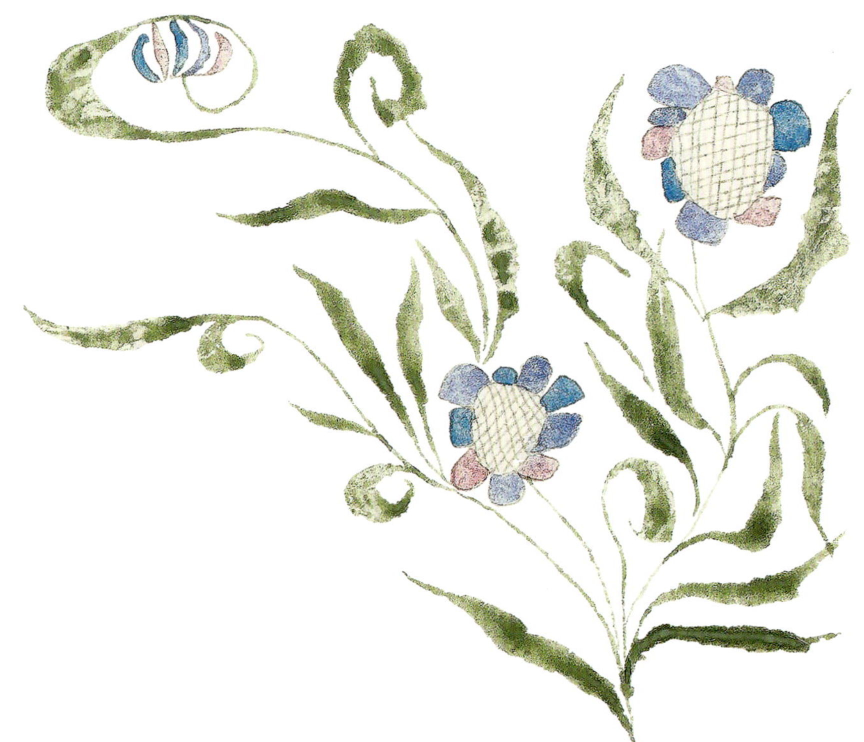

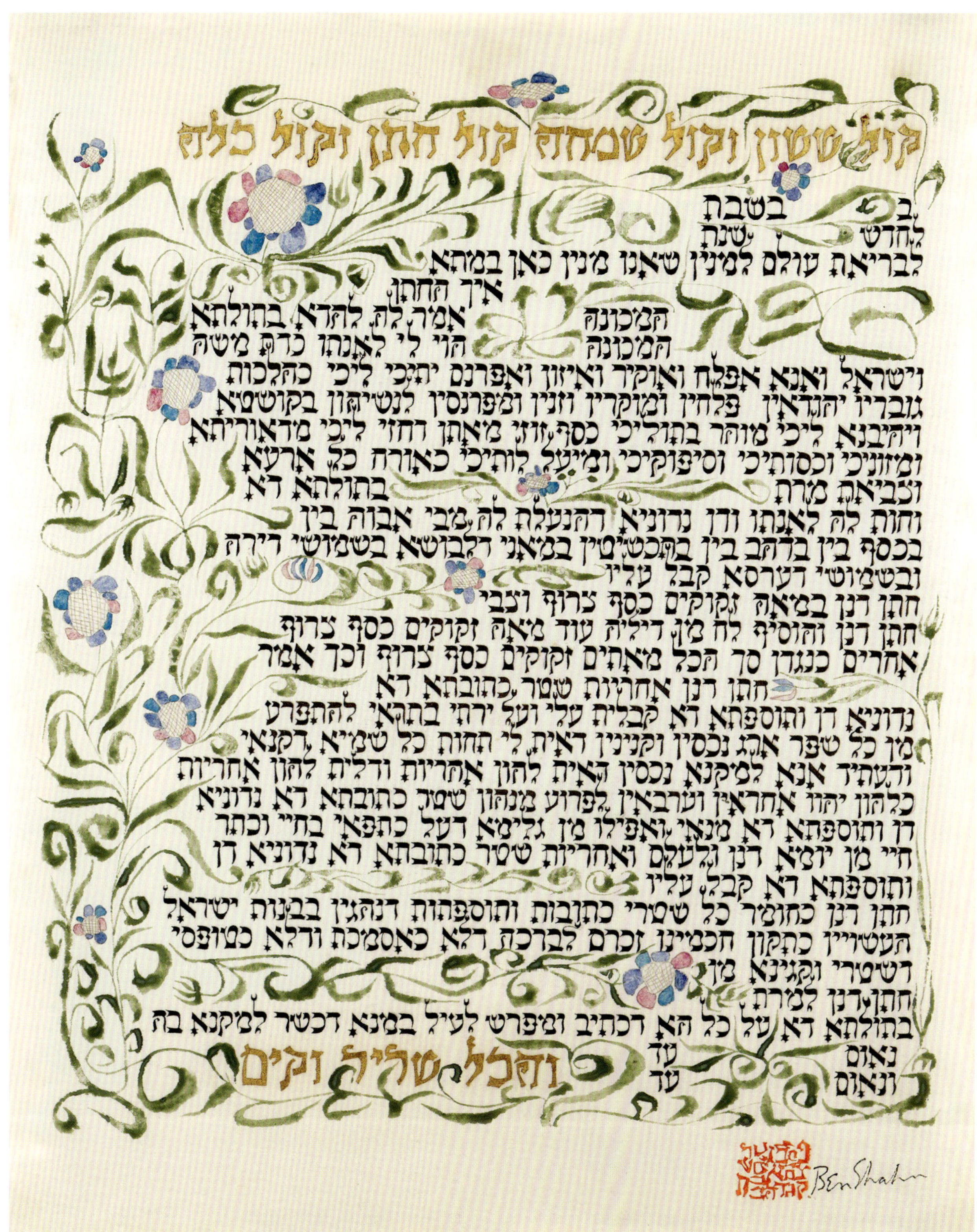
קול ששון וקול שמחה קול חתן וקול כלה
ב בשבת
לחדש שנת
לבריאת עולם למנין שאנו מנין כאן במתא
איך החתן
המכונה אמר לה להדא בתולתא
המכונה הוי לי לאנתו כדת משה
וישראל ואנא אפלח ואוקיר ואיזון ואפרנס יתיכי ליכי כהלכות
גוברין יהודאין פלחין ומוקרין וזנין ומפרנסין לנשיהון בקושטא
ויהיבנא ליכי מוהר בתוליכי כסף זוזי מאתן דחזי ליכי מדאוריתא
ומזוניכי וכסותיכי וסיפוקיכי ומיעל לותיכי כאורח כל ארעא
וצביאת מרת בתולתא דא
והות לה לאנתו ודן נדוניא דהנעלת לה מבי אבוה בין
בכסף בין בדהב בין בתכשיטין במאני דלבושא בשמושי דירה
ובשמושי דערסא קבל עליו
חתן דנן במאה זקוקים כסף צרוף וצבי
חתן דנן והוסיף לה מן דיליה עוד מאה זקוקים כסף צרוף
אחרים כנגדן סך הכל מאתים זקוקים כסף צרוף וכך אמר
חתן דנן אחריות שטר כתובתא דא
נדוניא דן ותוספתא דא קבלית עלי ועל ירתי בתראי להתפרע
מן כל שפר ארג נכסין וקנינין דאית לי תחות כל שמיא דקנאי
ודעתיד אנא למקנא נכסין דאית להון אחריות ודלית להון אחריות
כלהון יהון אחראין וערבאין לפרוע מנהון שטר כתובתא דא נדוניא
דן ותוספתא דא מנאי ואפילו מן גלימא דעל כתפאי בחיי ובתר
חיי מן יומא דנן ולעלם ואחריות שטר כתובתא דא נדוניא דן
ותוספתא דא קבל עליו
חתן דנן כחומר כל שטרי כתובות ותוספתות דנהגין בבנות ישראל
העשויין כתקון חכמינו זכרם לברכה דלא כאסמכתא ודלא כטופסי
דשטרי וקנינא מן
חתן דנן למרת
בתולתא דא על כל הא דכתיב ומפרש לעיל במנא דכשר למקנא בה
נאום עד
ונאום עד
והכל שריר וקים
Ben Shahn

Chaim Gross

“Marriage Contract”

c. 1970

The American sculptor Chaim Gross (1902–91, Galicia) was born into a Hasidic family and immigrated to New York in 1921. He became well known for creating sculptures of figures flung into space, such as performers or mothers playing with their children. His joyful, exuberant work expressed optimistic themes—fitting for a ketubah.

In this example, abstractions of organic forms are interwoven with images of birds, candles, hands, interlocked rings, flowers, goats, and deer. The largely pastel color palette was an innovative choice for the time period.

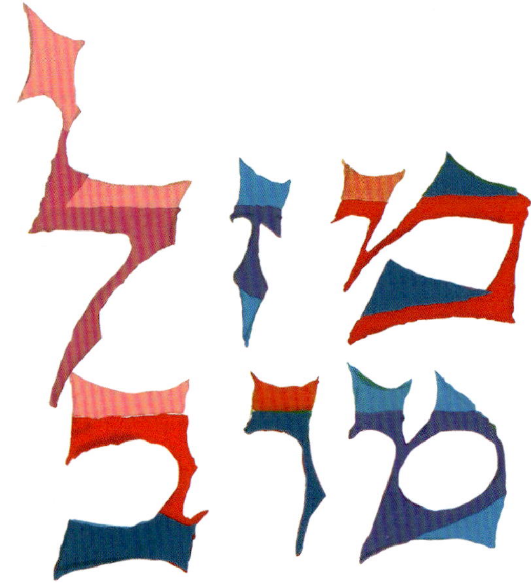

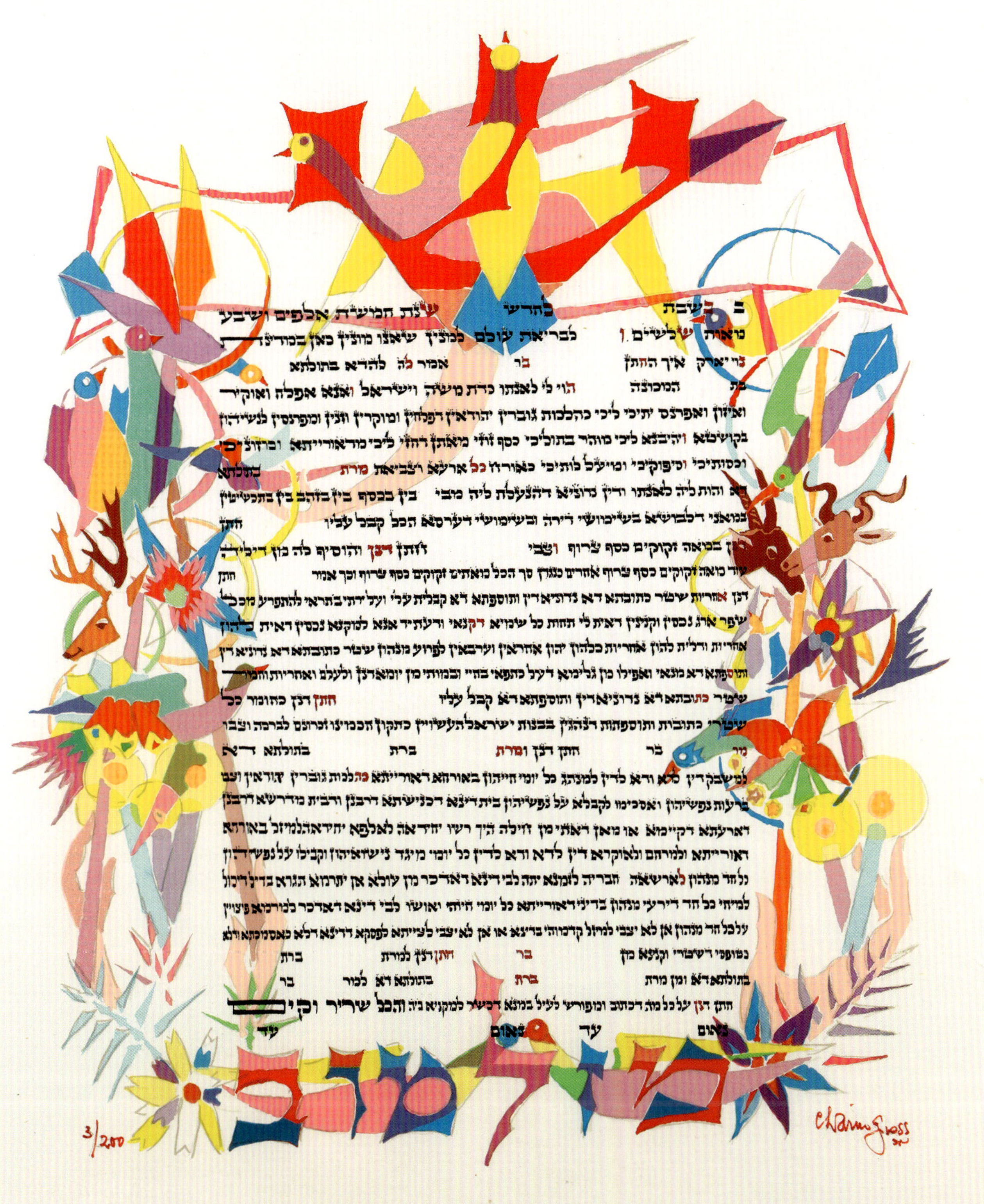

David Moss

"Ketubah of Susan and Ze'ev Shainhouse"

1972

Jerusalem artist David Moss (b. 1946, Ohio) is a self-proclaimed "mitzvah beautifier," illuminating, animating, and transforming Jewish texts, objects, spaces, and experiences. His work has been exhibited and acquired by museums and universities worldwide.

This design takes inspiration from the imperfections in the parchment he received from the couple. A round hole in it reminded him of a wedding ring. Perhaps the most exquisite Jewish rings ever made were the communal wedding bands created in Central Europe in the Middle Ages. Intricately fabricated in silver and gold with inset gems and owned by the community, they were given to the groom to present to his bride during the wedding ceremony. A customary building on the top symbolized the new home the couple was about to create.

Here, Moss's building resembles the Temple Mount. His use of enlarged words from the ketubah text as visual building blocks is completely innovative and would become a signature style of many of his more modernist designs.

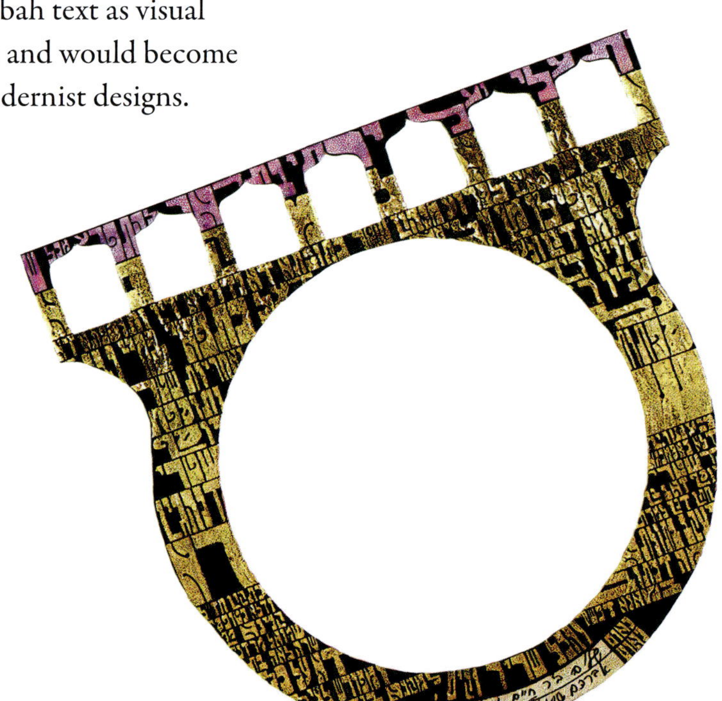

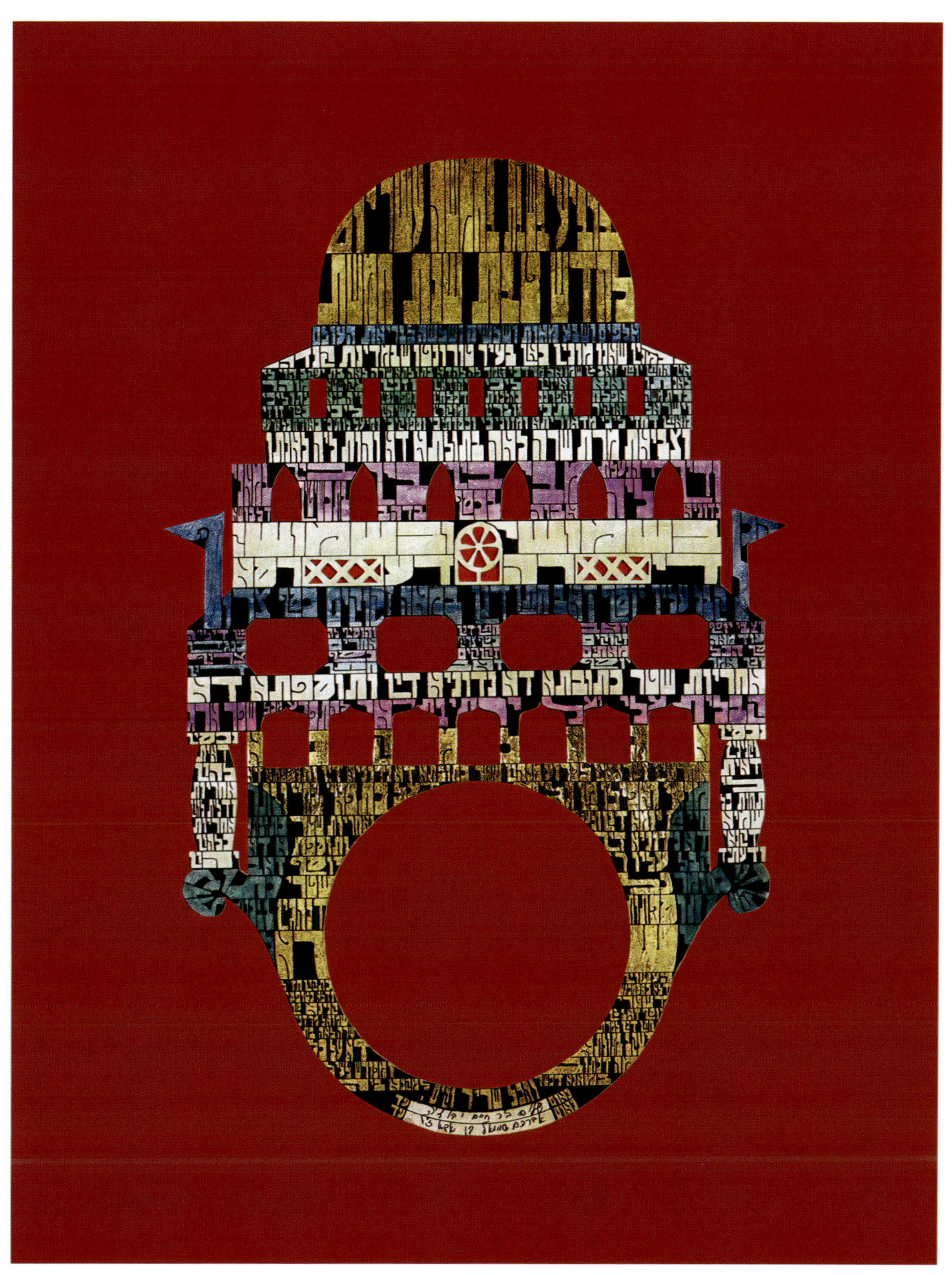

Courtesy of David Moss. From *Love Letters: The Ketubot of David Moss*. With permission of Bet Alpha Editions, California. © 2023 by David Moss.

David Moss

“Ketubah of Eisenberg Family”

1974

For this ketubah, Moss devised a new style of lettering that employs light on black for the ketubah text, and black on white for the surrounding verses. Psalms 128:5–6 reads: “May the Lord bless you from Zion; may you share the prosperity of Jerusalem all the days of your life, and live to see your children’s children. May all be well with Israel!” The verses speak to the welfare and peace of Israel and the continuity of the generations.

This ketubah is very geometric and playful. It seems to reference a child’s building blocks, bringing love and the home back down to the most basic elements.

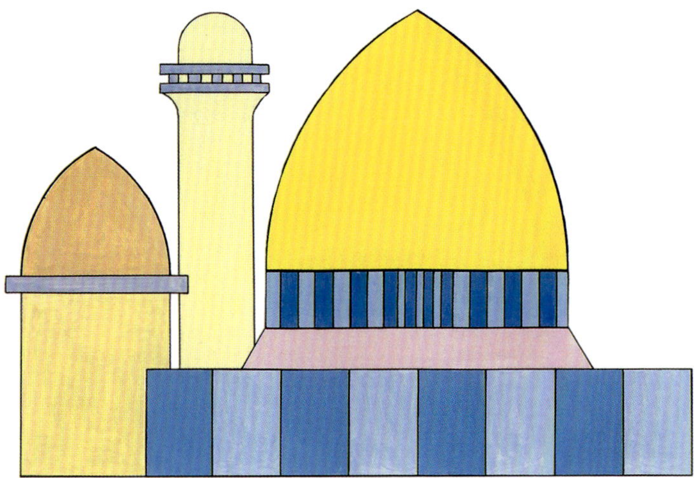

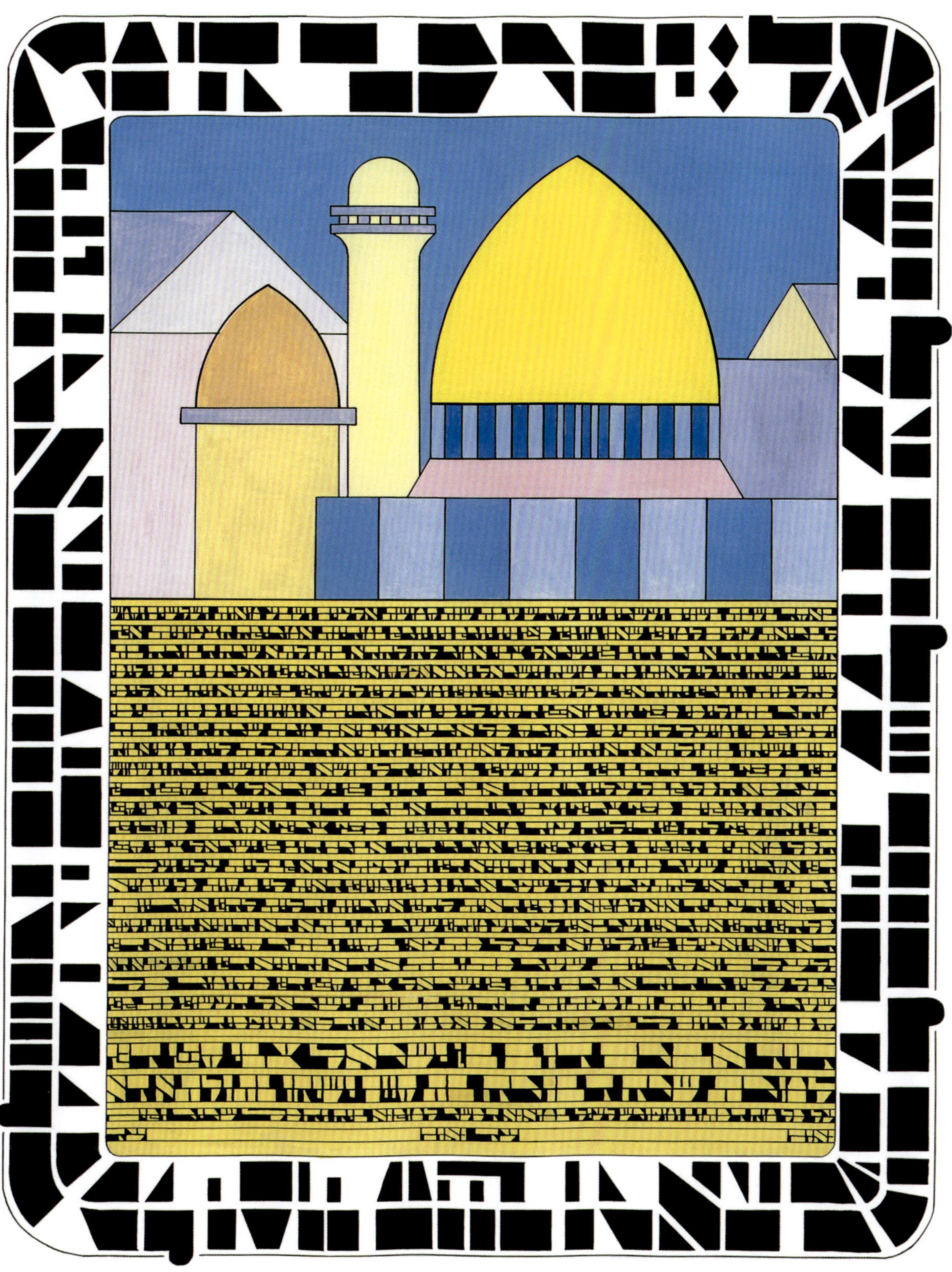

Courtesy of David Moss. From *Love Letters: The Ketubot of David Moss*.

David Moss

“Ketubah of Leslie Kane and Manuel Fishman”

1975

In the late 1960s David Moss imagined a new function for the traditional ketubah: as a source of Jewish introspection and personal growth for the betrothed couple.

Here, seven concentric forms of an evocative shape contain the ketubah text as well as other verses. The seven forms also reference the seven wedding blessings recited during the marriage ceremony (*Sheva Brachot*), as well as the Ashkenazic custom of the bride circling the groom seven times under the wedding canopy.

Personalizing the ketubah to the couple’s interest in media, Moss intended for the shapes to mimic the rounded-off rectangle of a television screen. These shapes might equally be seen as sacred tablets, ancient stones, or charmed amulets. He likened the winding of the text inward and outward through the forms to marriage itself: how it contains both inner- and outer-directed energy.

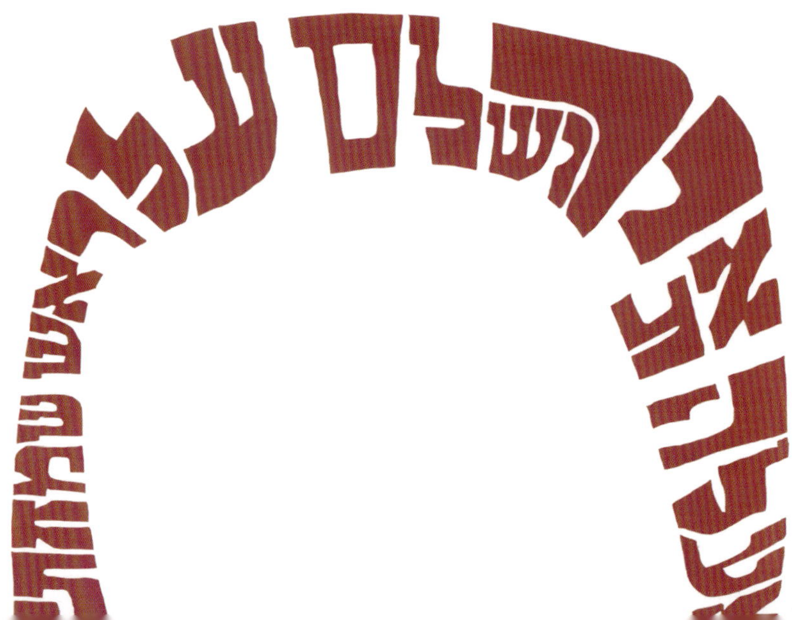

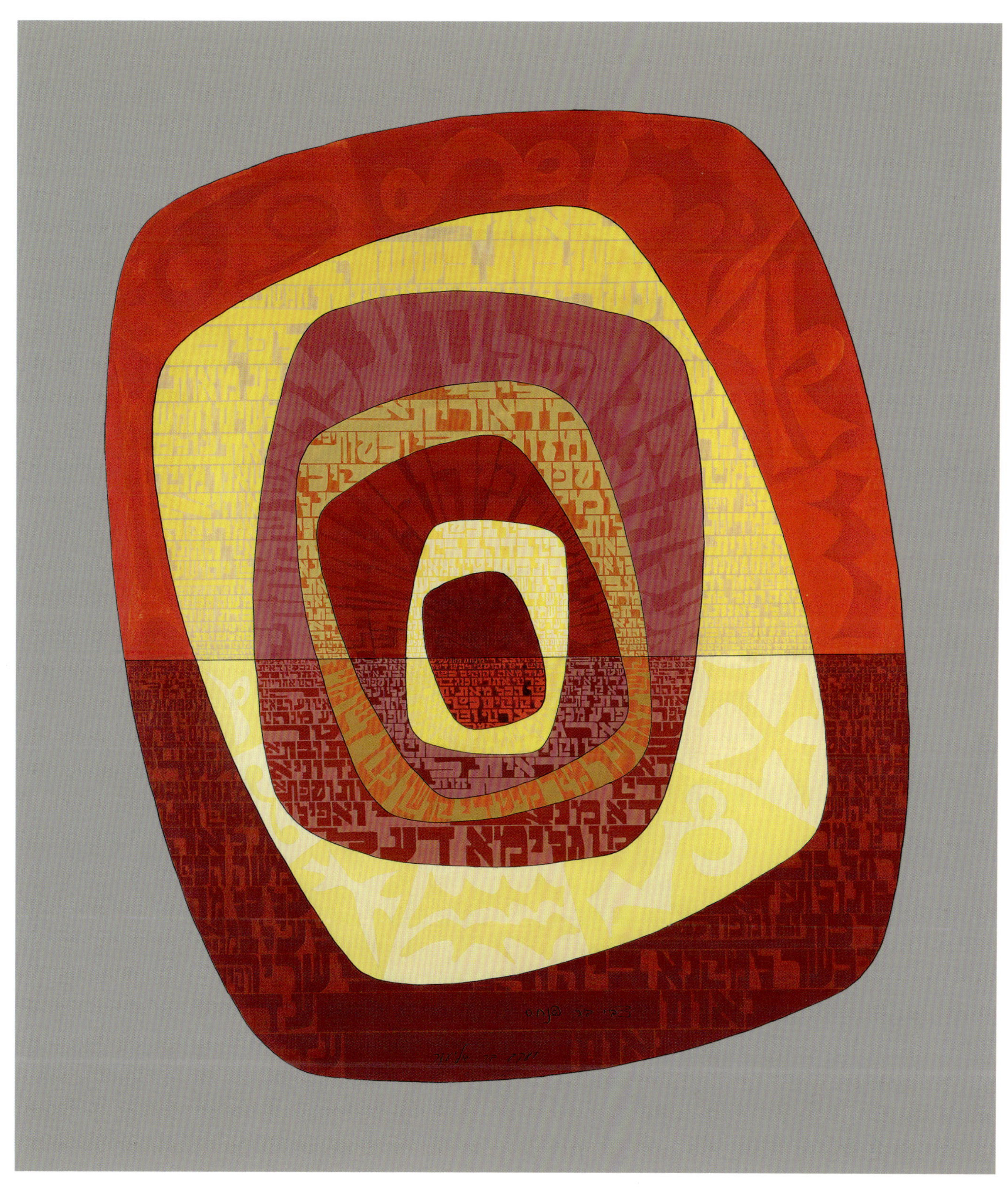

Courtesy of David Moss. From *Love Letters: The Ketubot of David Moss*. With permission of Bet Alpha Editions, California. © 2023 by David Moss.

Kopel Gurwin

Untitled

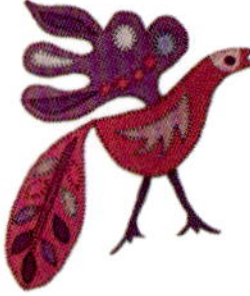

1979

Kopel Gurwin (1923–90, Vilnius, Lithuania) immigrated to Israel in 1950 after surviving the Holocaust. He became known for wall hangings and tapestries that integrated felt applique and intricate embroidery. The wall hangings incorporated a main motif and Hebrew text as well as these decorative elements. Today, Gurwin's works are displayed in the Knesset, synagogues, museums, galleries, and theaters in Israel and North America.

Gurwin created this mass-printed design for the Rabbinical Assembly (organization of Conservative rabbis) to use at weddings. Its hand-quilted fabric design makes unusual use of the traditional imagery of decorated arches to frame three texts in three languages. The center arch, containing the Conservative movement's Lieberman text (allowing either the wife or the husband to initiate a religious divorce on equal grounds) in Aramaic (see chapter 3), is flanked on the right by reciprocal Hebrew vows and on the left by a poetic English translation of the Hebrew.

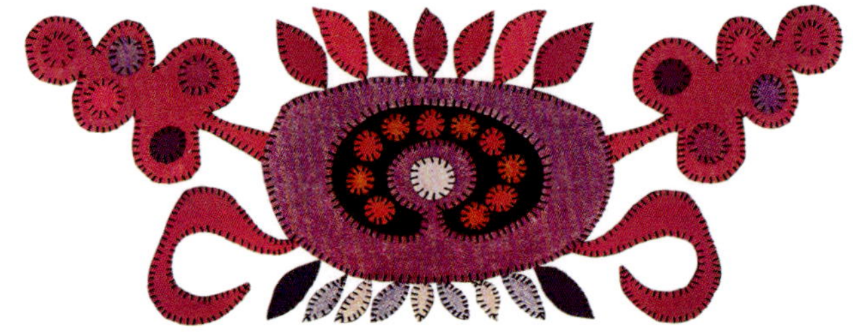

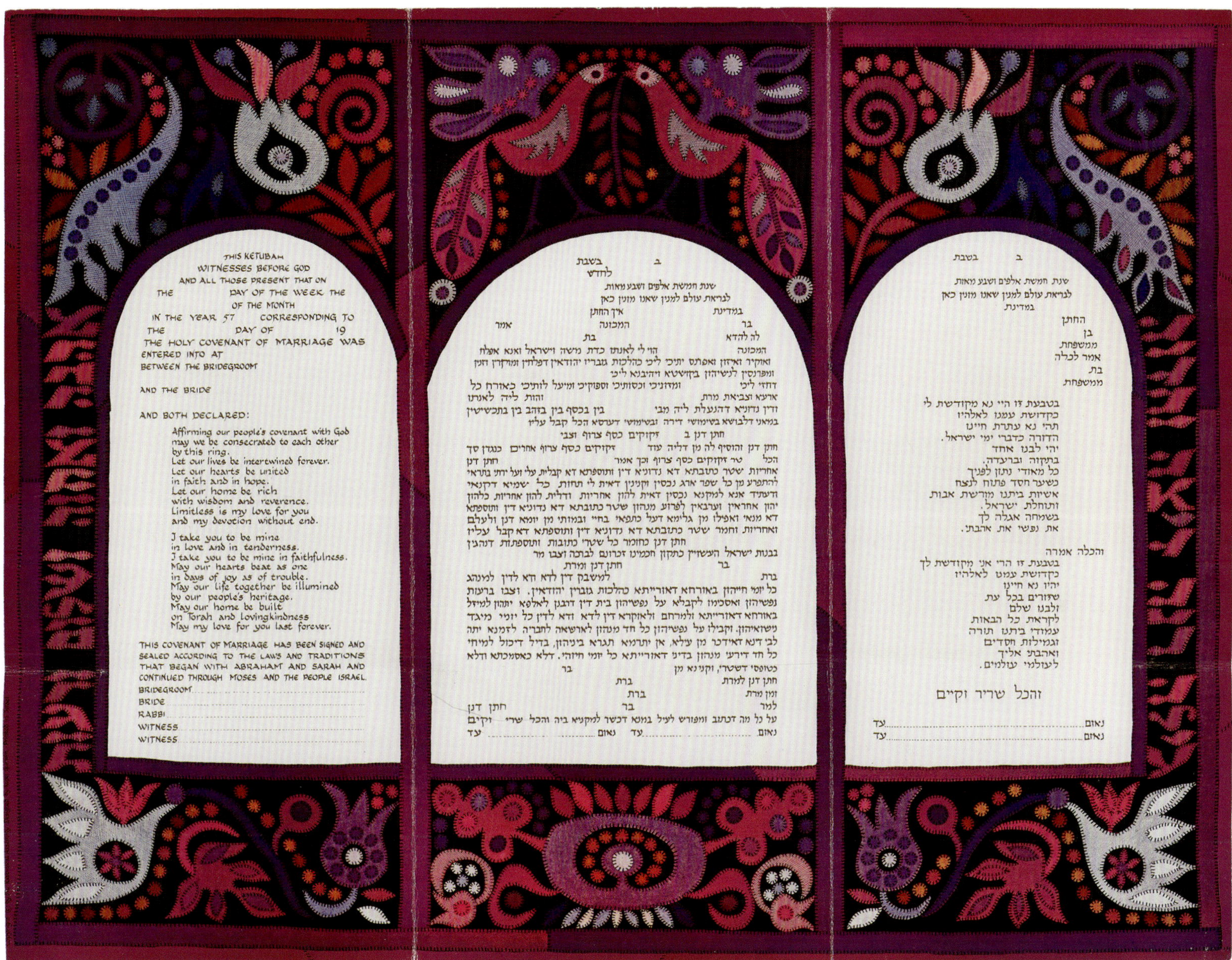

THIS KETUBAH
WITNESSES BEFORE GOD
AND ALL THOSE PRESENT THAT ON
THE DAY OF THE WEEK THE
OF THE MONTH
IN THE YEAR 57 CORRESPONDING TO
THE DAY OF 19
THE HOLY COVENANT OF MARRIAGE WAS
ENTERED INTO AT
BETWEEN THE BRIDEGROOM

AND THE BRIDE

AND BOTH DECLARED:

Affirming our people's covenant with God
may we be consecrated to each other
by this ring.
Let our lives be intertwined forever.
Let our hearts be united
in faith and in hope.
Let our home be rich
with wisdom and reverence.
Limitless is my love for you
and my devotion without end.

I take you to be mine
in love and in tenderness.
I take you to be mine in faithfulness.
May our hearts beat as one
in days of joy as of trouble.
May our life together be illumined
by our people's heritage.
May our home be built
on Torah and lovingkindness
May my love for you last forever.

THIS COVENANT OF MARRIAGE HAS BEEN SIGNED AND
SEALED ACCORDING TO THE LAWS AND TRADITIONS
THAT BEGAN WITH ABRAHAM AND SARAH AND
CONTINUED THROUGH MOSES AND THE PEOPLE ISRAEL.
BRIDEGROOM ....
BRIDE ....
RABBI ....
WITNESS ....
WITNESS ....

ב בשבת
לחדש
שנת חמשת אלפים ושבע מאות
לבריאת עולם למנין שאנו מונין כאן
במדינת איך החתן
בר המכונה אמר
לה להדא בת
המכונה הוי לי לאנתו כדת משה וישראל ואנא אפלח
ואוקיר ואיזון ואפרנס יתיכי ליכי כהלכות גוברין יהודאין דפלחין ומוקרין וזנין
ומפרנסין לנשיהון בקושטא ויהיבנא ליכי
דחזי ליכי ומזוניכי וכסותיכי וספוקיכי ומיעל לותיכי כאורח כל
ארעא וצביאת מרת והות ליה לאנתו
ודין נדוניא דהנעלת ליה מבי בין בכסף בין בזהב בין בתכשיטין
במאני דלבושא בשימושי דירה ובשימושי דערסא הכל קבל עליו
חתן דנן ב זקוקים כסף צרוף וצבי
חתן דנן והוסיף לה מן דליה עוד זקוקים כסף צרוף אחרים כנגדן סך
הכל טר זקוקים כסף צרוף וכך אמר חתן דנן
אחריות שטר כתובתא דא נדוניא דין ותוספתא דא קבלית עלי ועל ירתי בתראי
להתפרע מן כל שפר ארג נכסין וקנינין דאית לי תחות כל שמיא דקנאי
ודעתיד אנא למקנא נכסין דאית להון אחריות ודלית להון אחריות כלהון
יהון אחראין וערבאין לפרוע מנהון שטר כתובתא דא נדוניא דין ותוספתא
דא מנאי ואפילו מן גלימא דעל כתפאי בחיי ובמותי מן יומא דנן ולעלם
ואחריות וחומר שטר כתובתא דא נדוניא דין ותוספתא דא קבל עליו
חתן דנן כחומר כל שטרי כתובות ותוספתות דנהגין
בבנות ישראל העשויין כתקון חכמינו זכרונם לברכה וצבו מר
בר חתן דנן ומרת
ברת למשבק דין לדא ודא לדין למנהג
כל יומי חייהון באורחא דאורייתא כהלכות גוברין יהודאין. וצבו ברעות
נפשיהון ואסכימו לקבלא על נפשיהון בית דין דהבנן לאלפא יתהון למיזל
באורחא דאורייתא ולמרחם ולאוקרא דין לדא ודא לדין כל יומי מיגד
משואיהון. וקבילו על נפשיהון כל חד מנהון לארשאה לחבריה לזמנא יתה
לבי דינא דאידכר מן עילא, אן יתרמא תגרא ביניהון, בדיל דיכול למיחי
כל חד דירעי מנהון בדיני דאורייתא כל יומי חיוהי. דלא כאסמכתא ודלא
כטופסי דשטרי, וקנינא מן בר
חתן דנן למרת ברת
זמן מרת ברת
למר בר חתן דנן
על כל מה דכתוב ומפורש לעיל במנא דכשר למקניא ביה והכל שרי וקים
נאום .... עד נאום .... עד

ב בשבת
שנת חמשת אלפים ושבע מאות
לבריאת עולם למנין שאנו מונין כאן
במדינת
החתן
בן
ממשפחת
אמר לכלה
בת
ממשפחת

בטבעת זו הרי את מקודשת לי
כקדושת עמנו לאלהיו
תהי נא עטרת חיינו
הדורה כדברי ימי ישראל.
יהי לבנו אחד
בתקוה וברעדה.
כל מאודי נתון לפניך
כשער חסד פתוח לנצח
אשיות ביתנו מורשת אבות
ונחלת ישראל.
בשמחה אגלה לך
את נפשי את אהבתי.

והכלה אמרה
בטבעת זו הרי אני מקודשת לך
כקדושת עמנו לאלהיו
יהיו נא חיינו
שזורים בכל עת
ולבנו שלם
לקראת כל הבאות
עמודי ביתנו תורה
וגמילות חסדים
ואהבתי אליך
לעולמי עולמים.

והכל שריר וקיים

נאום .... עד
נאום .... עד

Catalog number Ket 511, courtesy of The Jewish Theological Seminary Library.

David Moss

“Anniversary Ketubah of Richard Marchick and Gloria Becker Marchick”

1980

David Moss’s personal, meaningful conversations with couples have informed his custom ketubah designs.

This ketubah celebrating the Marchicks’ twentieth wedding anniversary (the couple married in December 1960) showcases their favorite colors, symbols, and words from the family history—the time they spent in Jerusalem; their love of Shabbat; their chosen hometown, Orinda, California; and many happy memories with their children, who also provided design ideas. Decorated with scrolls and flowers, this is a more traditionally styled work than Moss’s typically innovative ketubah design, but his distinctive imprint is evident in the unique framing shapes and harmonious symmetry.

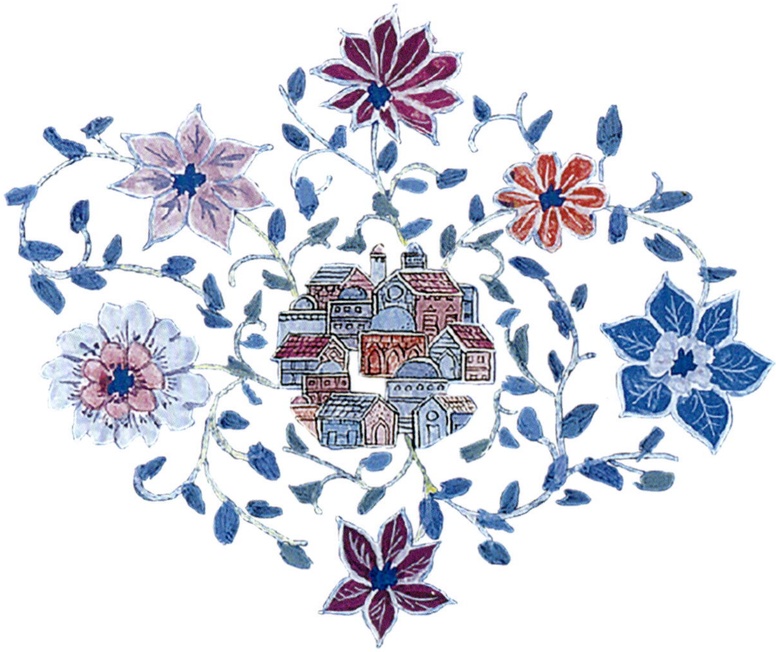

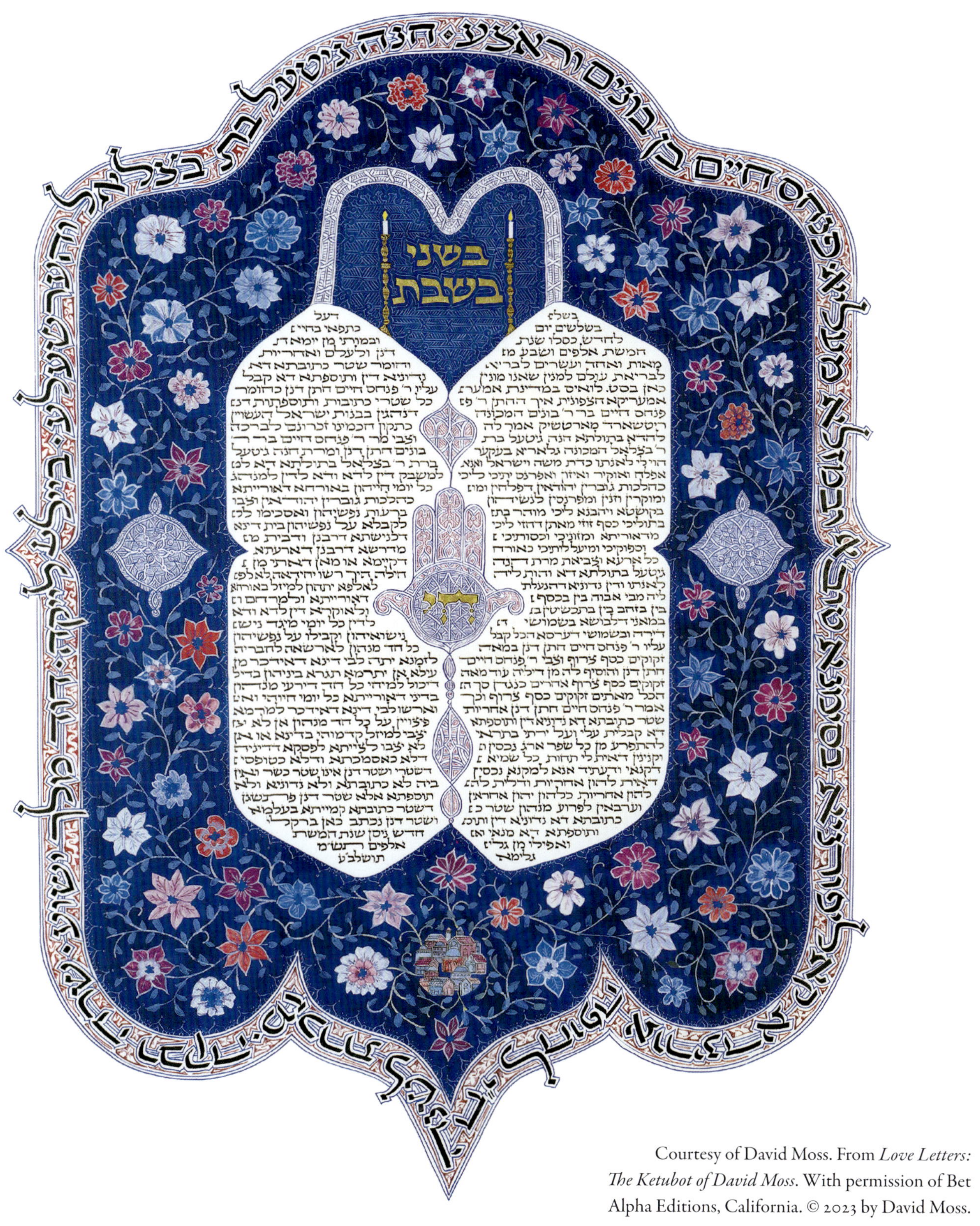

Courtesy of David Moss. From *Love Letters: The Ketubot of David Moss*. With permission of Bet Alpha Editions, California. © 2023 by David Moss.

Laya Crust

“Medieval Arch”

1982

A native of Winnipeg, Canada, the Toronto-based artist Laya Crust delves into Jewish history and reflects it in her art. Her art book *Illuminations: An Explorations of Haftarah through Art and History* (2022) offers artistic interpretations of the weekly supplemental Torah reading. Here, Crust presents a romantic scene integrating many common motifs of historical and contemporary ketubot—landscape, ornament, and architectural elements—with a distinctly medieval flavor. Inspired by a thirteenth-century illumination from Worms, Germany, she illustrates a medieval fantasy of Jerusalem, a Tree of Life depicting all four seasons, decorated columns and archway, and a sun and moon representing the passage of time. The vast terrain is drawn from the Israeli landscape, and the leafy border from thirteenth-century Flemish tapestries.

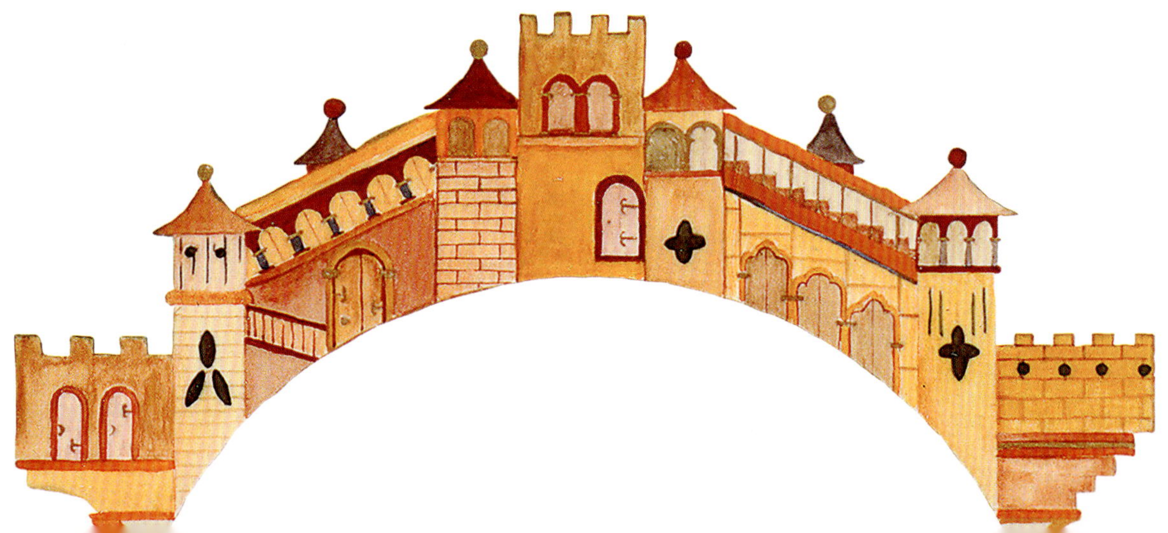

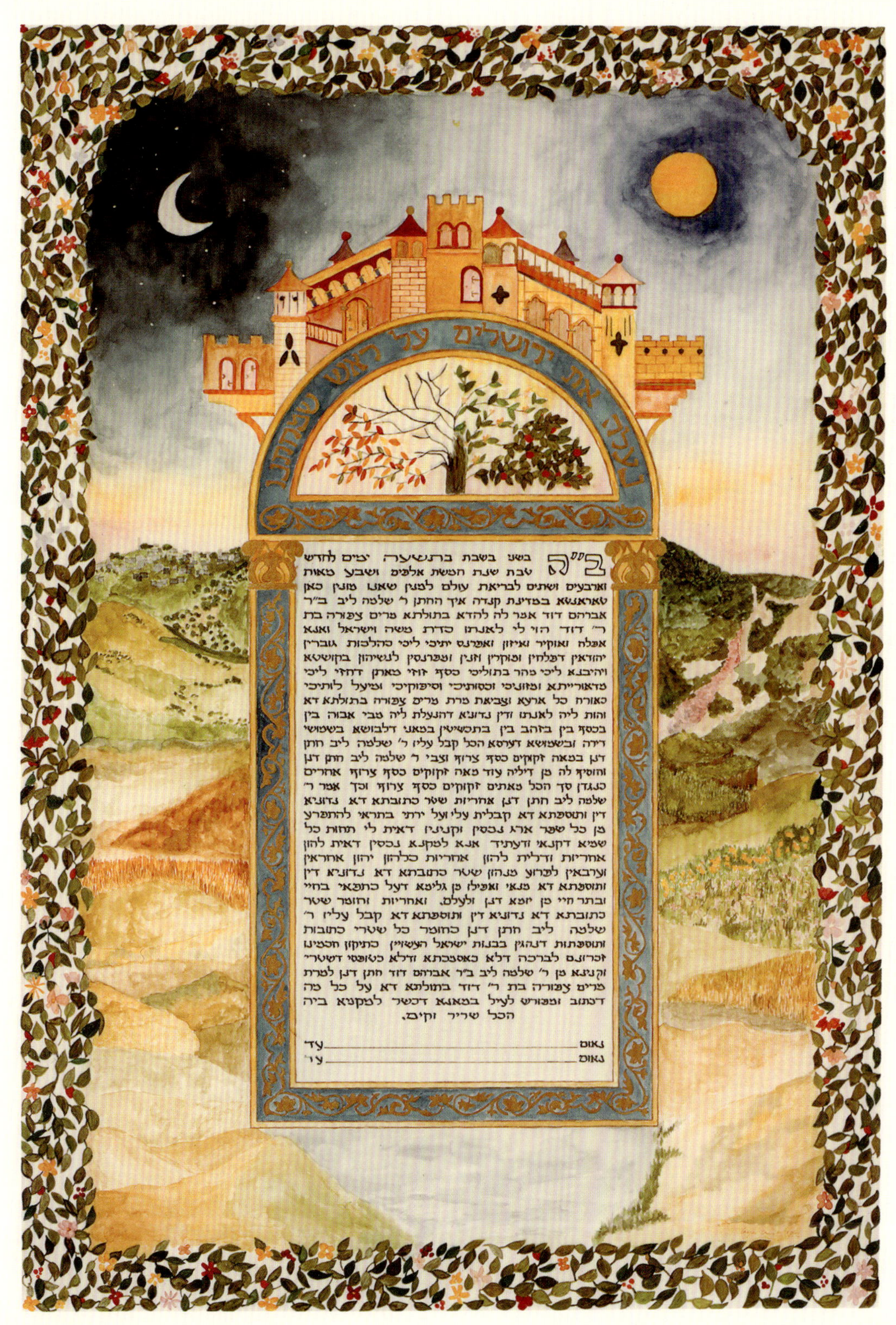

Courtesy of Laya Crust.

Howard Fox

"Alaska Ketubah"

1986

Born in Canada, the now Israel-based artist Howard Fox is known for his imaginative realism, a thoughtful crafting of environments. His work has been exhibited and collected internationally.

A couple from Anchorage commissioned this literally "out of the box" design. Fox juxtaposes two settings around a central map of Alaska: a scene from the far north—magnificent fauna gazing out at the viewer; and images from Israel—a Jordan River landscape and Jerusalem's Old City skyline. Water features prominently in both vistas, and indigenous flora and fruit add flashes of color. This ketubah forges a marriage of place, acknowledging the couple's love of their home state and their close connection with the Jewish homeland.

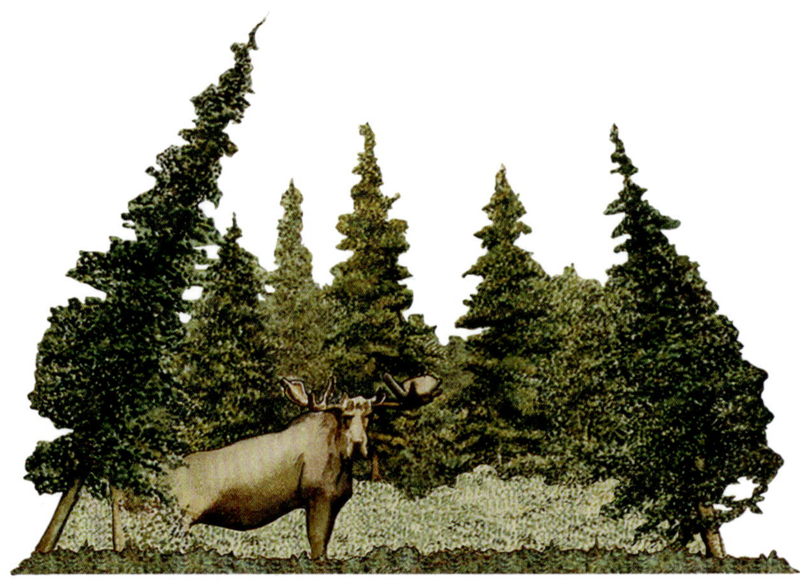

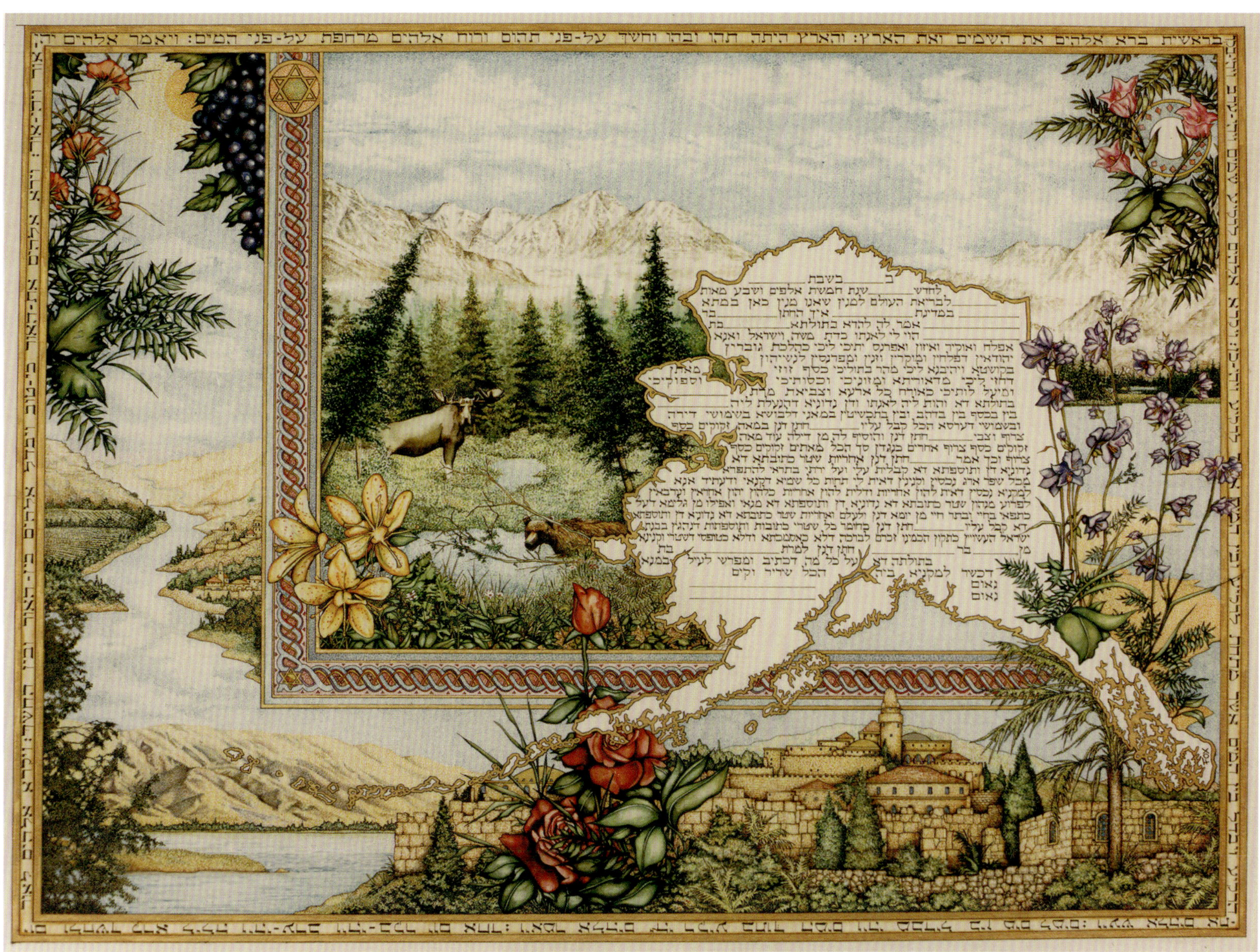

Courtesy of Howard Fox.

Ze'ev Newman

"Acqui"

1987

A graduate of The Marsha Stern Talmudical Academy—Yeshiva University High School for Boys, Ze'ev Newman makes art combining surrealism with old world flair.

With this artwork inspired by a notable 1840 ketubah from the Italian town of Acqui, Newman aimed to bring back to life a vibrant hotspot of Jewish living famous for its natural thermal waters and spas. The ketubah's bottom vignette of pouring water, a reference to the town's chief attraction, is balanced by two raised hands symbolizing the Priestly Blessing (an ancient benediction once recited by priests in the Jerusalem temple, and still recited today). Multicolored flower and leaf patterns common in eighteenth- and nineteenth-century Italy embellish the two calligraphic borders.

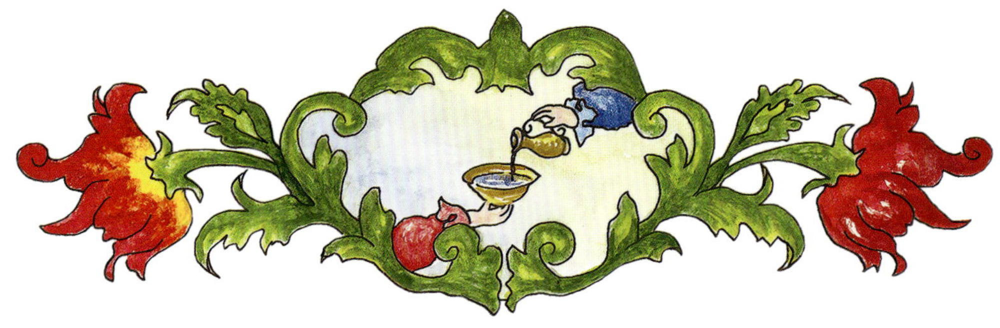

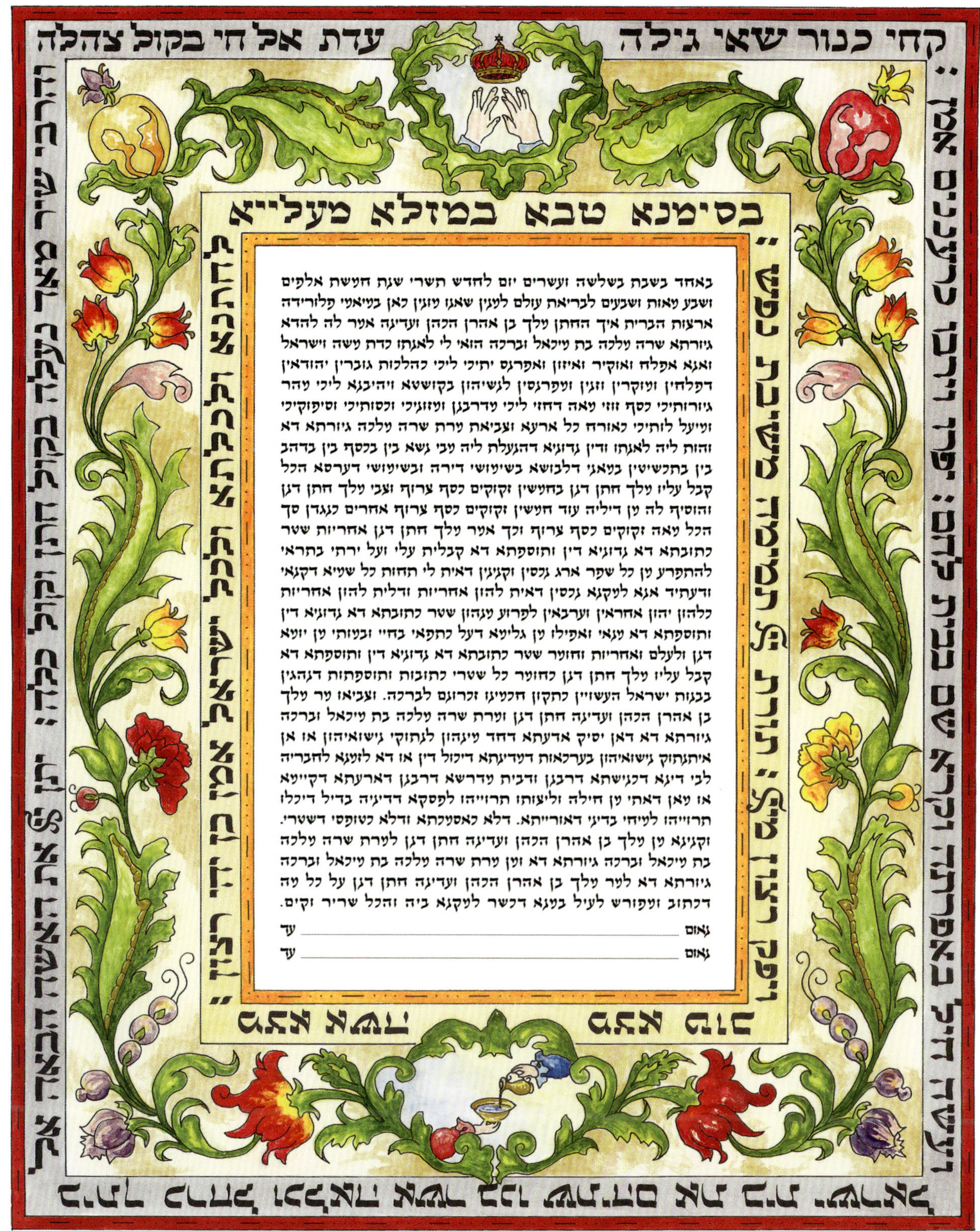

Courtesy of Ketubah.com.

Naomi Teplow

“Jerusalem Courtyard, Early Version”

1987

Born on Kibbutz Maagan Michael in Israel, Naomi Teplow came to the United States in 1979 and lives and works today in Oakland, California. Inspired by old European manuscripts and Persian miniature painting, she pairs strong, vivid colors with intricate, detailed ketubah designs to honor love, home, Jewish heritage, and the Land of Israel.

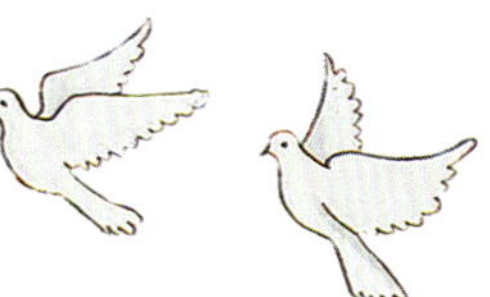

Details jump out of this carefully constructed Jerusalem courtyard: realistic snowy mountain at the top right, luscious grapes and pomegranates on the border trees, elegant blue and gold tiling. The overall impression is of a beautiful home that is also a welcoming space of love and harmony.

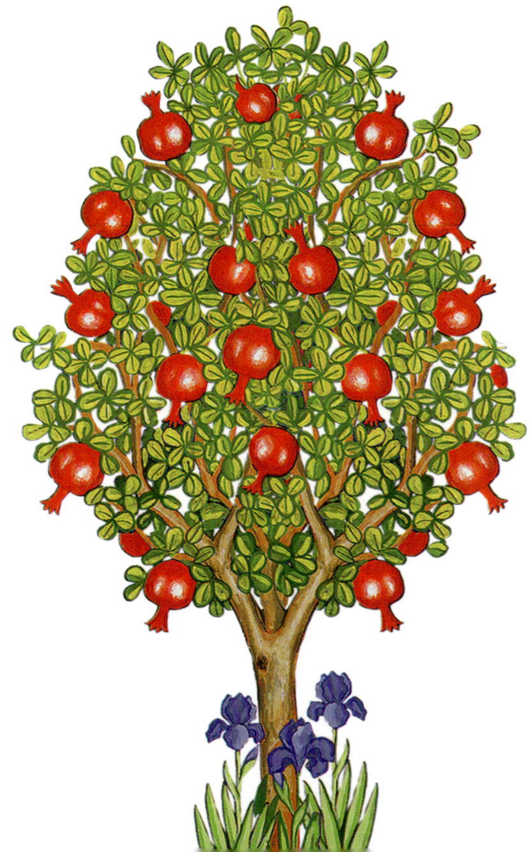

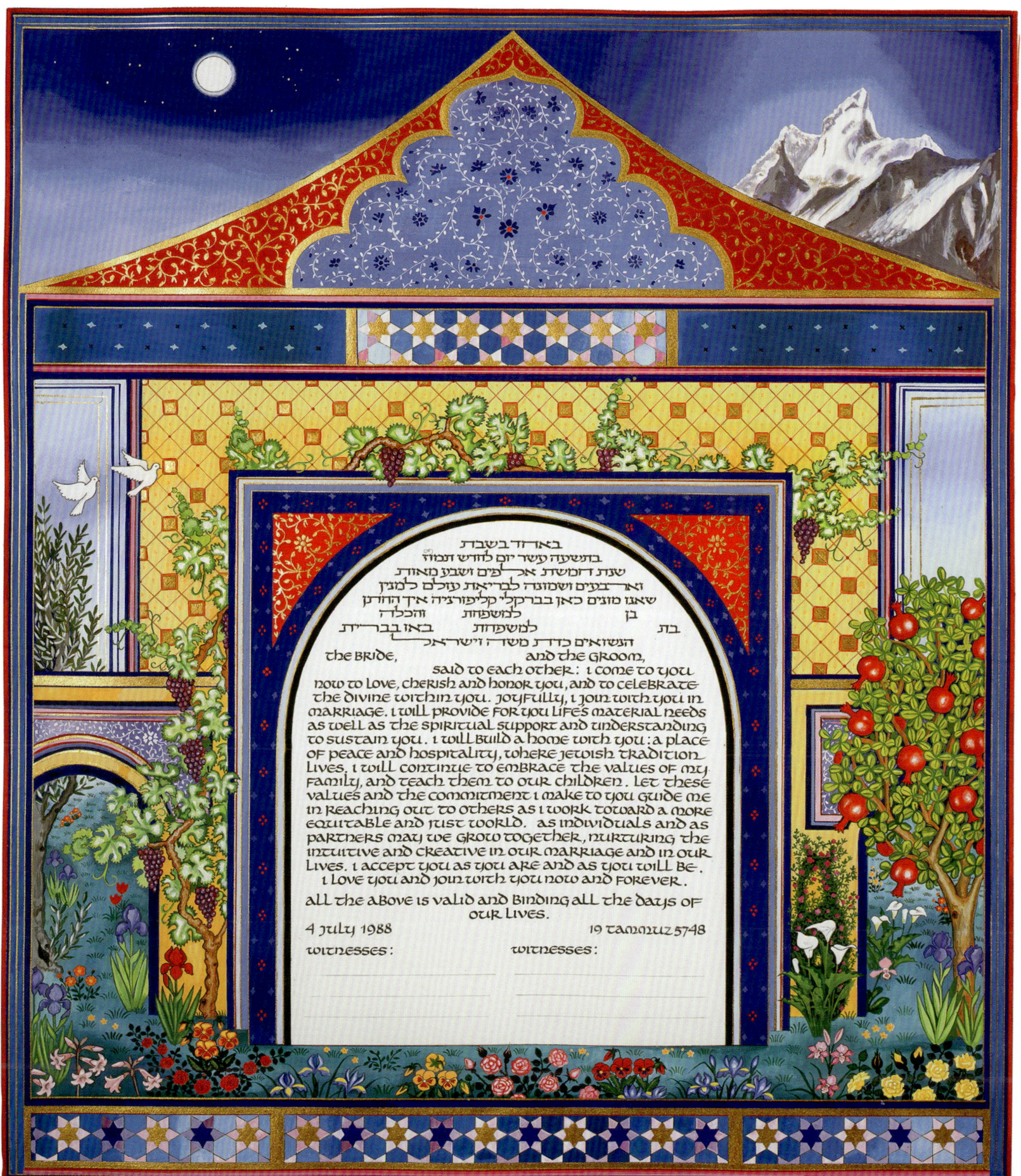

Courtesy of Naomi Teplow.

Mickie Caspi

"Jerusalem Dawn"

1988

Mickie Caspi (b. 1961) was raised in Illinois, spent several years in Israel, and now lives in Massachusetts. Her artwork combines her love of calligraphy, traditional Jewish motifs, modern art styles, and nature. She introduced the first pre-printed interfaith ketubah text as well as a gender-neutral text that could be used by same-sex couples.

This is a version of the ketubah Caspi used for her own wedding. Painted in watercolor, it draws from the Art Nouveau movement's use of soft, muted colors and stylized organic shapes. Around the semicircle of pomegranates, a glowing dawn sky offers up encircling stars. This circle symbolizes unity, wholeness, eternity, and the cycles of life and time, while the pomegranates represent fertility, wisdom, motivation, and success. Below the text lies Jerusalem, the eternal city of peace.

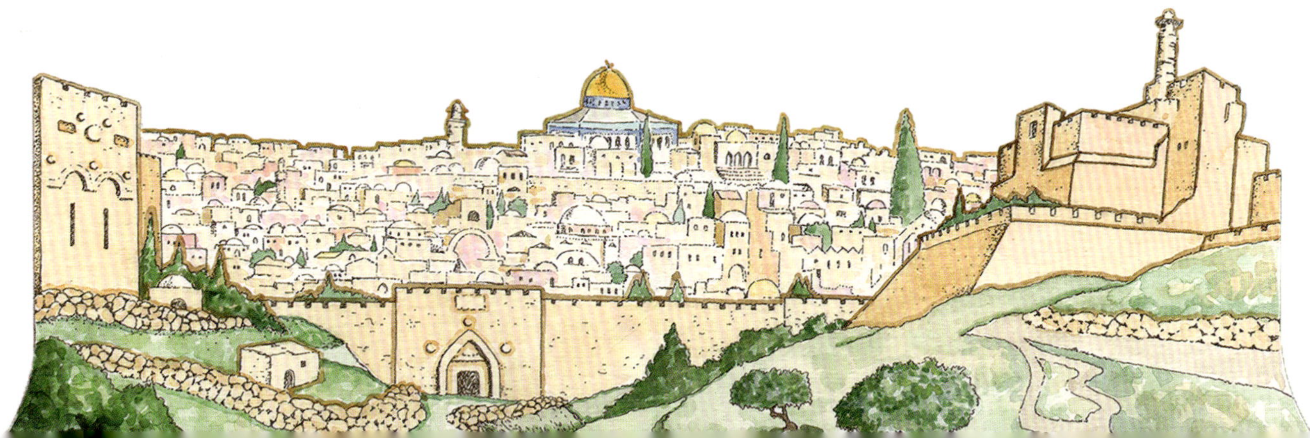

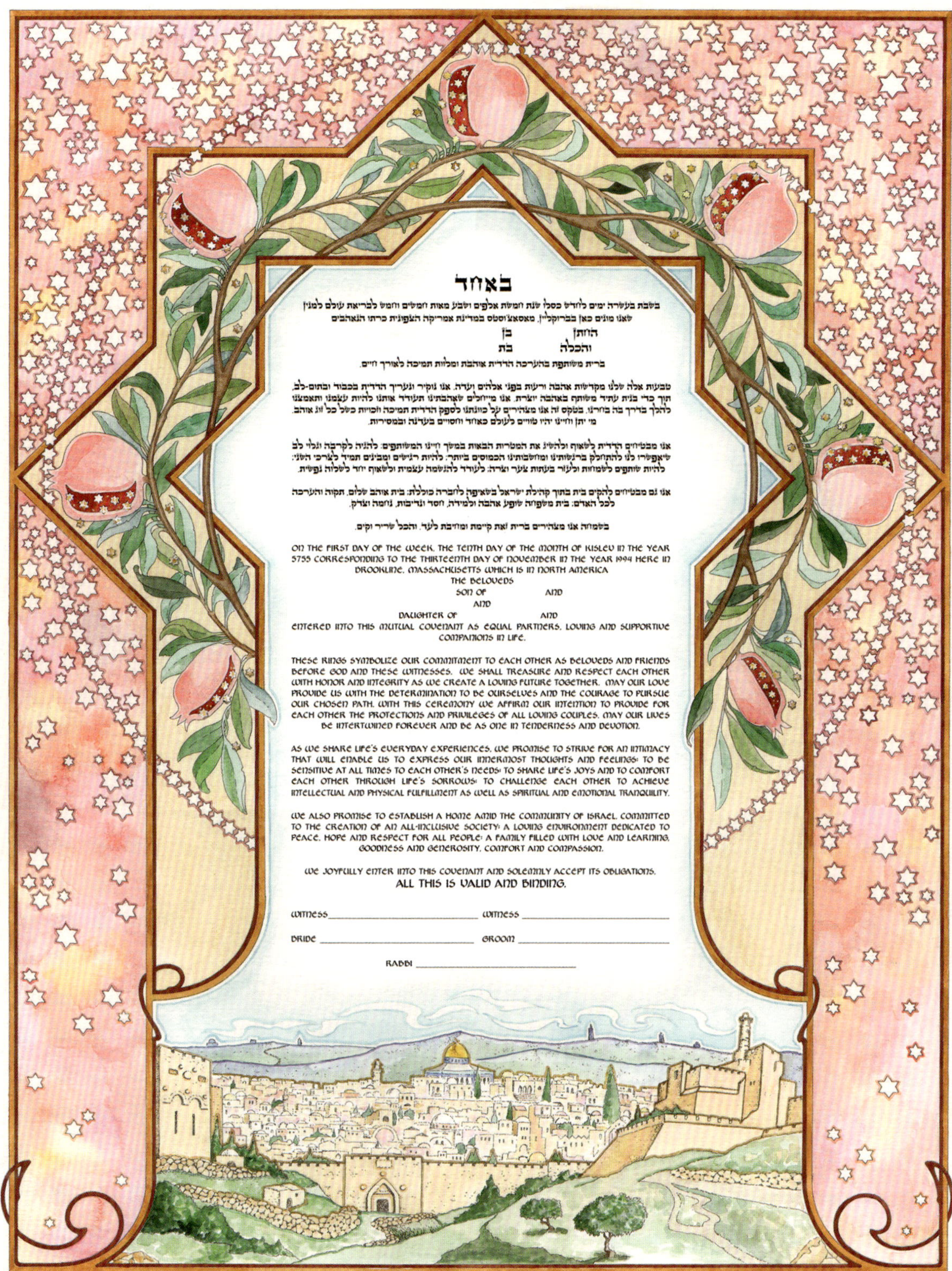

באחד

בשבת בעשרה ימים לחדש כסלו שנת חמשת אלפים ושבע מאות חמשים וחמש לבריאת עולם למנין
שאנו מונים כאן בברוקליין, מאסאצ'וסטס במדינת אמריקה הצפונית כרתו הנאהבים
החתן בן
והכלה בת
ברית משותפת בהערכה הדדית אוהבת ומלוות תמיכה לאורך חיים.

טבעות אלה שלנו מקדשות אהבה ורעות בפני אלהים ועדה. אנו נוקיר ונעריך הדדית בכבוד ובתום-לב,
תוך כדי בנית עתיד משותף באהבה יוצרת. אנו מייחלים שאהבתנו תעודד אותנו להיות עצמנו ותאמצנו
להלך בדרך בה בחרנו. בטקס זה אנו מצהירים על כוונתנו לספק הדדית תמיכה וזכויות כשל כל זוג אוהב.
מי יתן וחיינו יהיו טווים לעולם כאחד וחסויים בעדנה ובמסירות.

אנו מבטיחים הדדית לשאוף ולהשיג את המטרות הבאות במשך חיינו המשותפים: להגיה לקרבה וגלוי לב
שיאפשרו לנו להתחלק ברגשותינו ומחשבותינו הכמוסים ביותר; להיות רגישים ומבינים תמיד לצרכי השני;
להיות שותפים לשמחות ולעזר בעתות צער וצרה; לעודד להגשמה עצמית ולשאוף יחד לשלוה נפשית.

אנו גם מבטיחים להקים בית בתוך קהילת ישראל בשאיפה לחברה כוללת: בית אוהב שלום, תקוה והערכה
לכל האדם: בית משפחה שופע אהבה ולמידה, חסד ונדיבות, נחמה וצדק.

בשמחה אנו מצהירים ברית זאת קיימת ומחיבת לעד. והכל שריר וקים.

ON THE FIRST DAY OF THE WEEK, THE TENTH DAY OF THE MONTH OF KISLEV IN THE YEAR 5755 CORRESPONDING TO THE THIRTEENTH DAY OF NOVEMBER IN THE YEAR 1994 HERE IN BROOKLINE, MASSACHUSETTS WHICH IS IN NORTH AMERICA
THE BELOVEDS
SON OF AND
AND
DAUGHTER OF AND
ENTERED INTO THIS MUTUAL COVENANT AS EQUAL PARTNERS, LOVING AND SUPPORTIVE COMPANIONS IN LIFE.

THESE RINGS SYMBOLIZE OUR COMMITMENT TO EACH OTHER AS BELOVEDS AND FRIENDS BEFORE GOD AND THESE WITNESSES. WE SHALL TREASURE AND RESPECT EACH OTHER WITH HONOR AND INTEGRITY AS WE CREATE A LOVING FUTURE TOGETHER. MAY OUR LOVE PROVIDE US WITH THE DETERMINATION TO BE OURSELVES AND THE COURAGE TO PURSUE OUR CHOSEN PATH. WITH THIS CEREMONY WE AFFIRM OUR INTENTION TO PROVIDE FOR EACH OTHER THE PROTECTIONS AND PRIVILEGES OF ALL LOVING COUPLES. MAY OUR LIVES BE INTERTWINED FOREVER AND BE AS ONE IN TENDERNESS AND DEVOTION.

AS WE SHARE LIFE'S EVERYDAY EXPERIENCES, WE PROMISE TO STRIVE FOR AN INTIMACY THAT WILL ENABLE US TO EXPRESS OUR INNERMOST THOUGHTS AND FEELINGS; TO BE SENSITIVE AT ALL TIMES TO EACH OTHER'S NEEDS; TO SHARE LIFE'S JOYS AND TO COMFORT EACH OTHER THROUGH LIFE'S SORROWS; TO CHALLENGE EACH OTHER TO ACHIEVE INTELLECTUAL AND PHYSICAL FULFILLMENT AS WELL AS SPIRITUAL AND EMOTIONAL TRANQUILITY.

WE ALSO PROMISE TO ESTABLISH A HOME AMID THE COMMUNITY OF ISRAEL, COMMITTED TO THE CREATION OF AN ALL-INCLUSIVE SOCIETY; A LOVING ENVIRONMENT DEDICATED TO PEACE, HOPE AND RESPECT FOR ALL PEOPLE; A FAMILY FILLED WITH LOVE AND LEARNING, GOODNESS AND GENEROSITY, COMFORT AND COMPASSION.

WE JOYFULLY ENTER INTO THIS COVENANT AND SOLEMNLY ACCEPT ITS OBLIGATIONS.
ALL THIS IS VALID AND BINDING.

WITNESS ____________ WITNESS ____________

BRIDE ____________ GROOM ____________

RABBI ____________

Courtesy of Mickie Caspi.

Gregg Handorff

Untitled

1989

American artist Gregg Handorff (b. 1959) designed a uniquely playful ketubah: a Hebrew font printed with potato-block letters in a bold color pattern. Interestingly, this unconventional design, influenced by trends in modern art and typography, contains the handed-down Orthodox text. Still, this is a clear innovation and deviation from the traditional practice of surrounding the entire ketubah text with artwork. Here, the large block of text *is* the art.

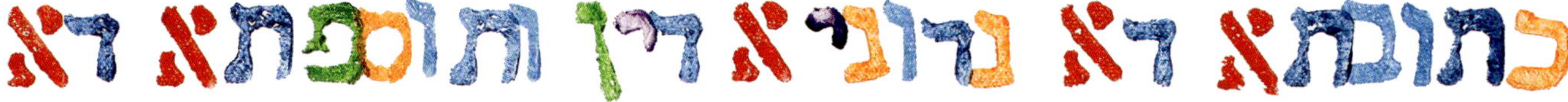

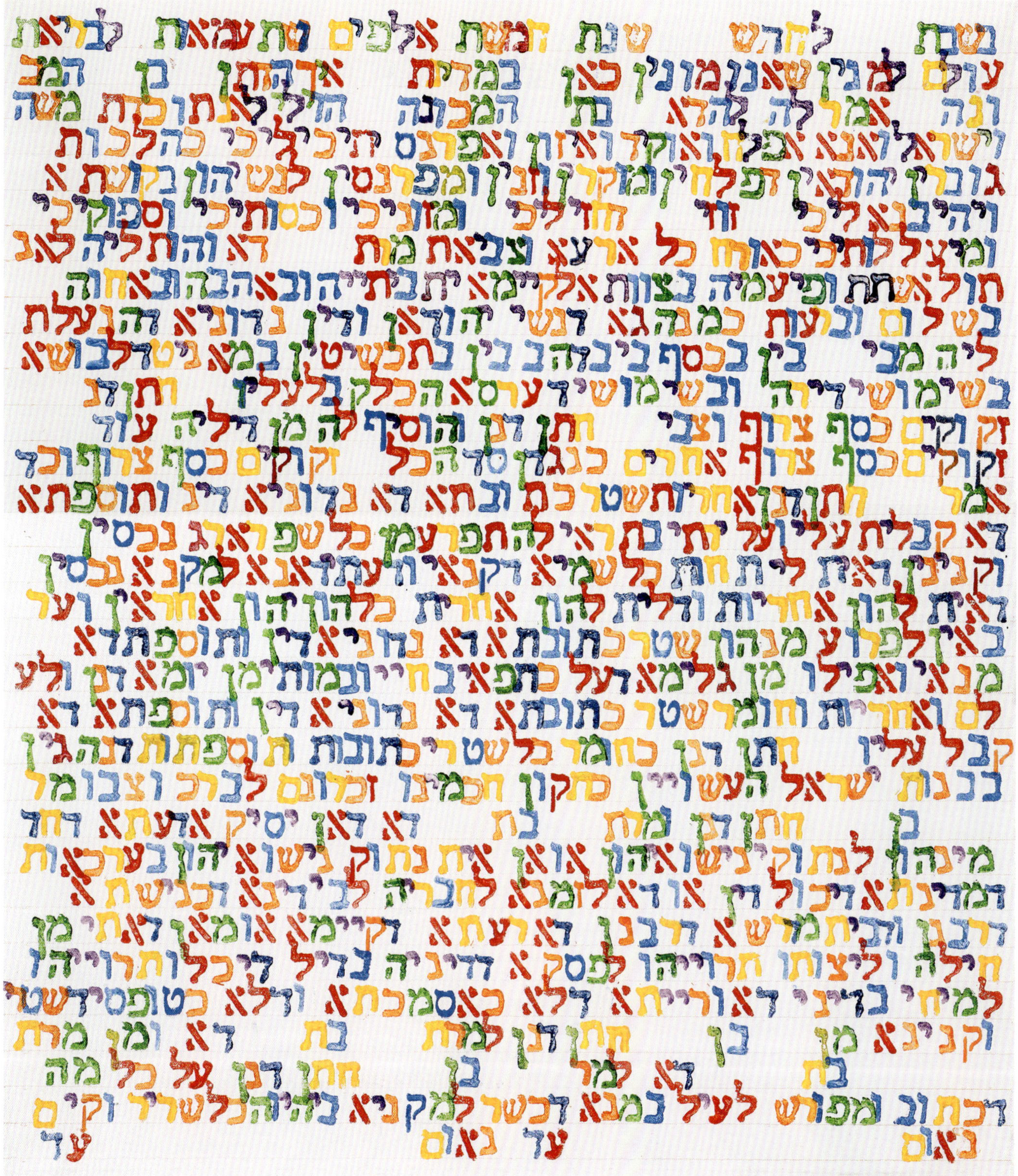

Catalog number Ket 487, courtesy of The Jewish Theological Seminary Library.

Pamela Feldman-Hill

"Amy Schottenstein Ketubah"

1989

Ohio artist Pamela Feldman-Hill is one of many ketubah artists who take inspiration from medieval illuminated manuscripts. She is interested in the culture, theology, and history of Judaism as well as women's roles in Jewish culture. Her artwork has been exhibited and collected nationally.

This two-tree design is a modern take with contemporary colors and a beautiful symmetry in the forms and border. Note that every part of the page is filled with ornament, the shape of the text is outlined multiple times, and a quotation from the Baal Shem Tov (founder of the Hasidic movement) is embedded. The artist makes a particularly skillful rinceau—the ornamental motif consisting of an undulating and branching scroll decorated with foliage and other natural forms.

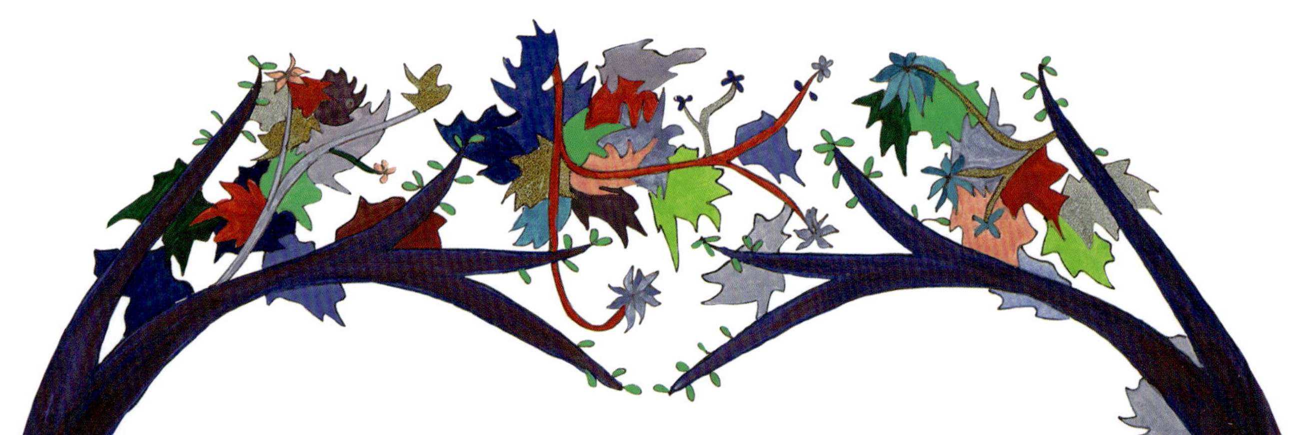

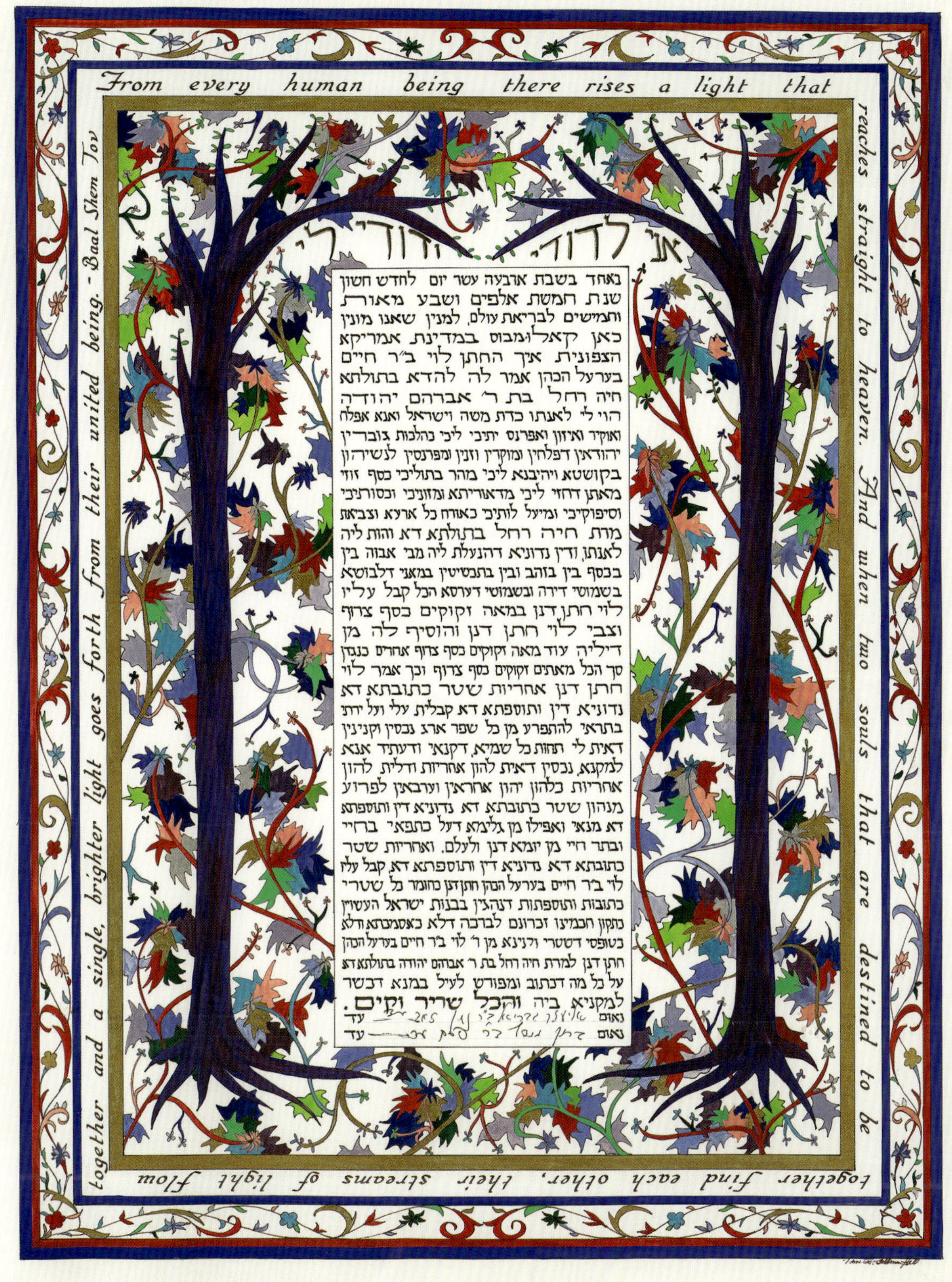

Courtesy of Pamela Feldman-Hill.

Ted Labow

“Persian Ketubah”

1989

Toronto native Ted Labow serves as cantor at Agudas Israel Congregation in North Carolina. In this artwork he takes inspiration from the carpet page of Hebrew illuminated manuscripts, presenting an eclectic mix of motifs from Persia, Spain, Asia, and the Art Deco movement.

His technique of hand-painting and hand-lettering on a printed ink template combines mass production and custom detailing.

The octagonal-shaped text alludes to the power of the number eight for new beginnings. In Jewish tradition, the eighth day is the first day of a new seven-day week, and a Jewish baby enters into God’s Covenant on the eighth day of life.

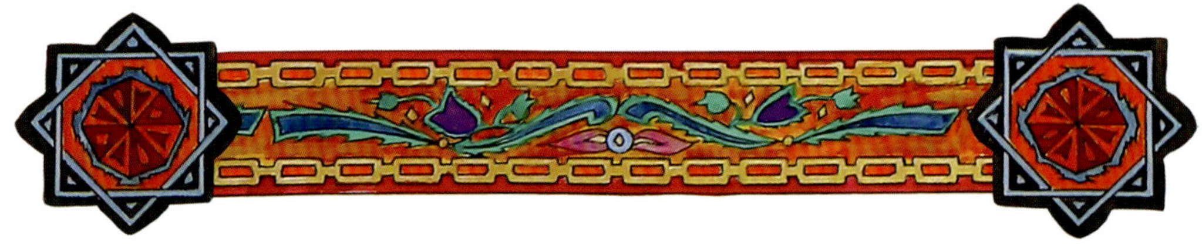

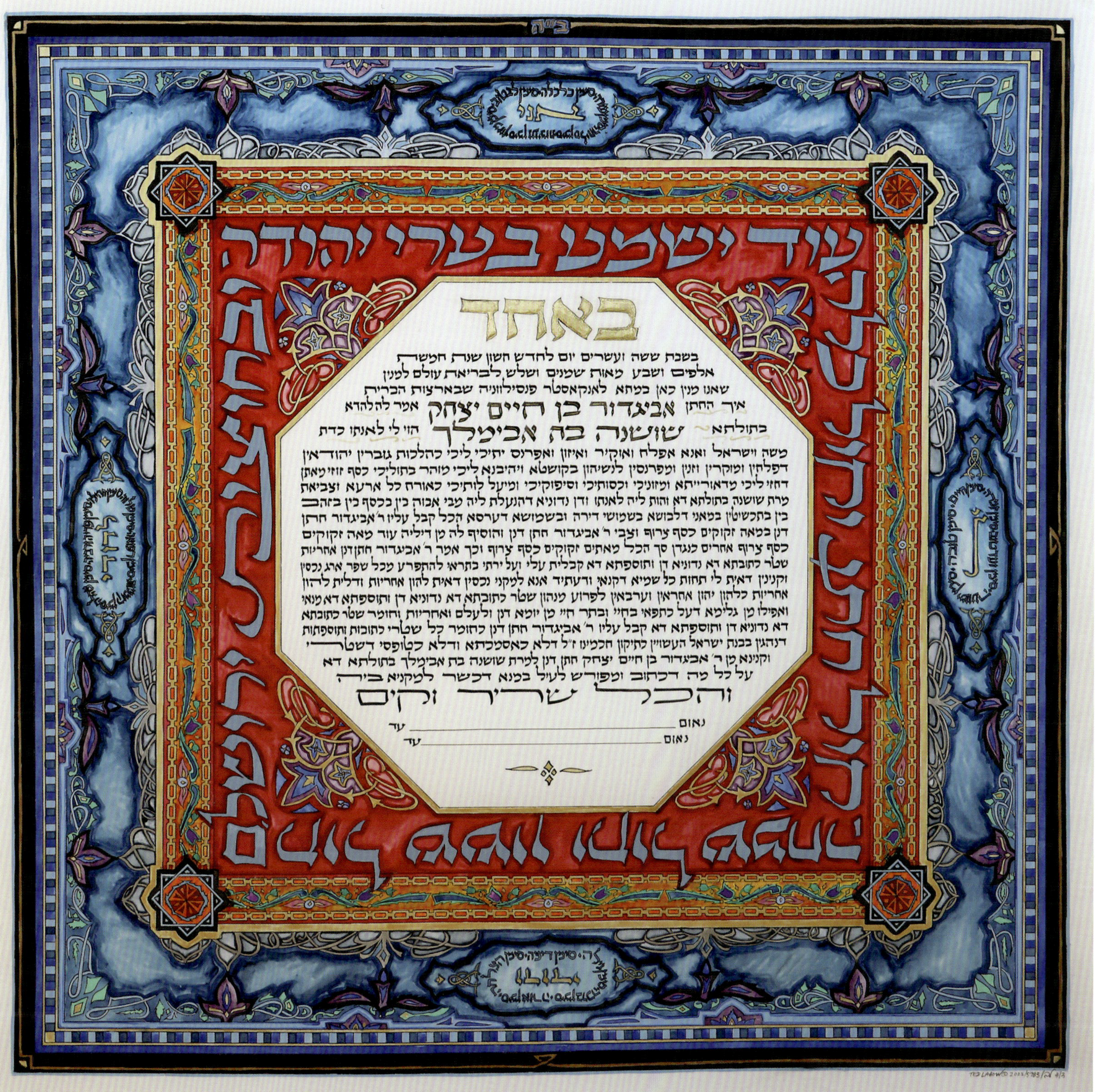

Courtesy of Ted Labow.

Orly Lauffer

“At the King’s Gate”

1990

Orly Lauffer was born in Haifa, studied in Michigan, and resides in Israel. Resonant with her Moroccan ancestry, her work is strongly influenced by Islamic and Persian motifs. She will often incorporate generous use of gold and silver and introduce intricate detail and border work reminiscent of Arabesques.

In this piece, Lauffer references the structure and ornament of Persian carpets and Muslim architecture. Pillars support the pointed, doubly rounded central arch in purples, blues, and burgundies. The highly detailed execution of multiple motifs, including eight-pointed medallions at the top and bottom, imbue a luxurious sensibility befitting for royalty.

This work demonstrates how ketubah decoration can meld with any cultural tradition: the tradition is adaptable across time and geography.

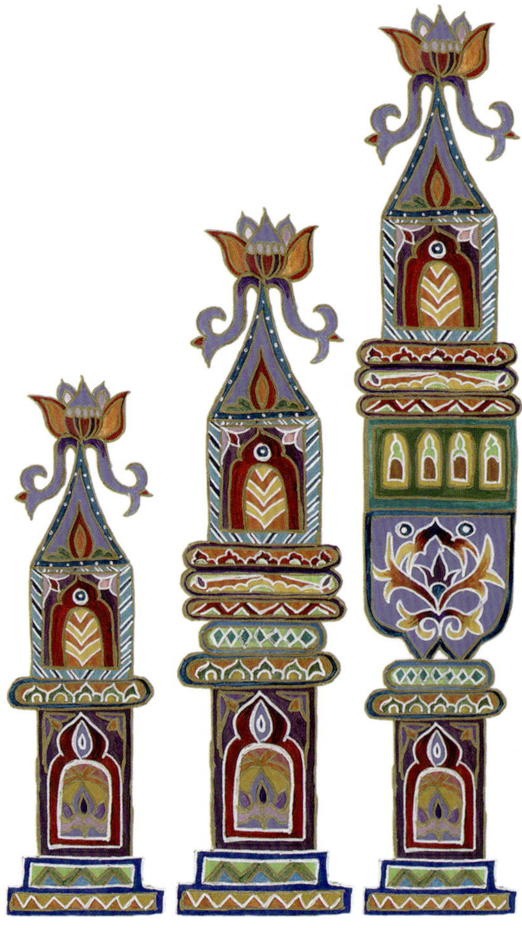

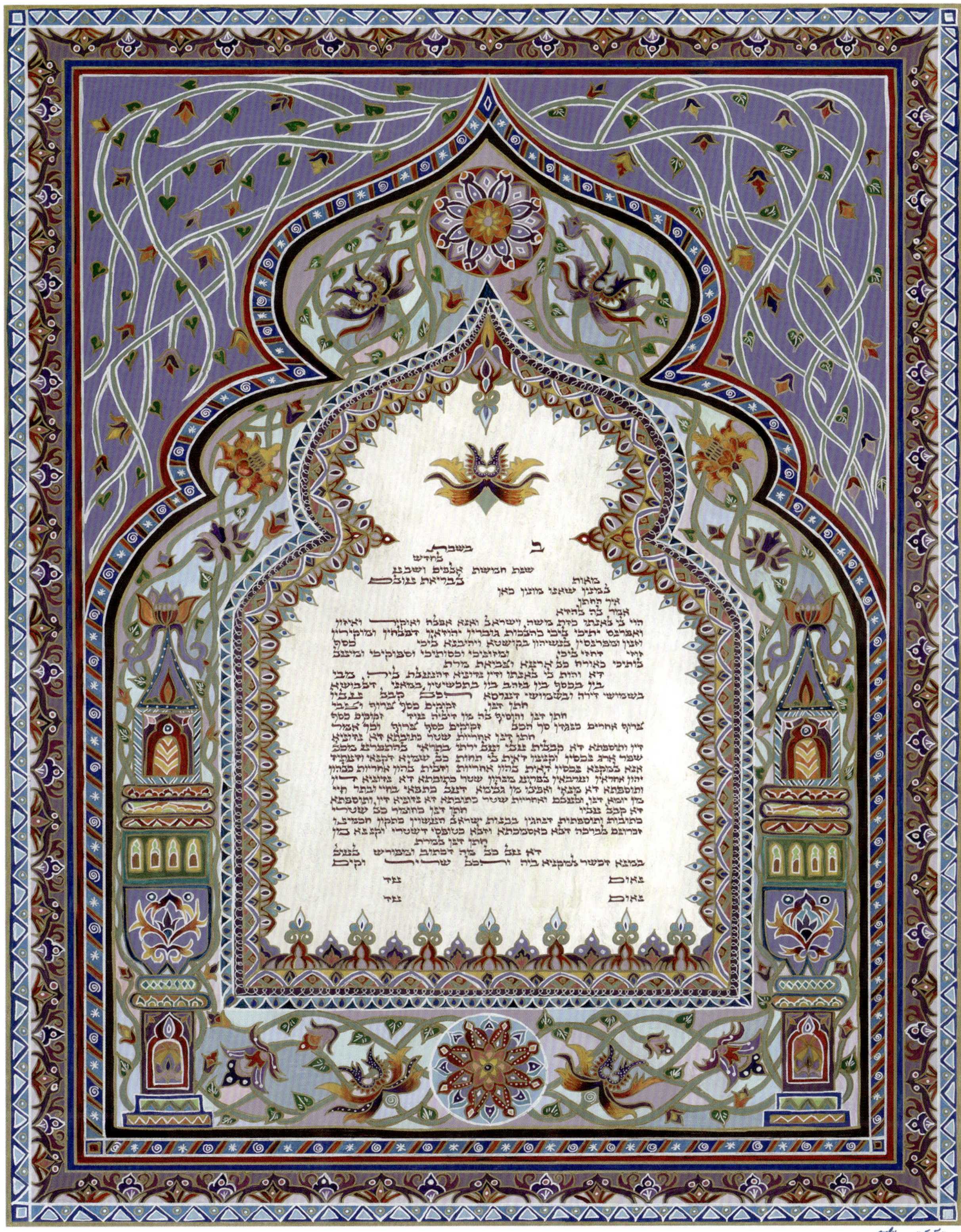

Courtesy of Orly Lauffer.

Gad Almaliah

“Pesukim”

c. 1990

Graphic designer Gad Almaliah (1939–2007) was raised in Jerusalem; worked in the United States, Mexico, and Israel; taught in Israel and the United States; and headed the Graphic Design Association of Israel.

Almaliah blended both the ancient and modern visual culture of Israel in his aesthetic. In one of his signature styles, Almaliah would add a metal, sculptural element to two-dimensional pieces. Each panel would be embossed, polished, cut by hand, and then secured to fine art paper, imbuing the work with a folk craft spirit.

This ketubah is notable for its copper panel relief design, as well as a biblical quotation from one of the seven wedding blessings, “Again there shall be heard . . . in the towns of Judah and the streets of Jerusalem . . . the sound of mirth and gladness, the voice of bridegroom and bride” (Jer. 33:10–11) emblazoned in a Zionist pioneer-era font across the top.

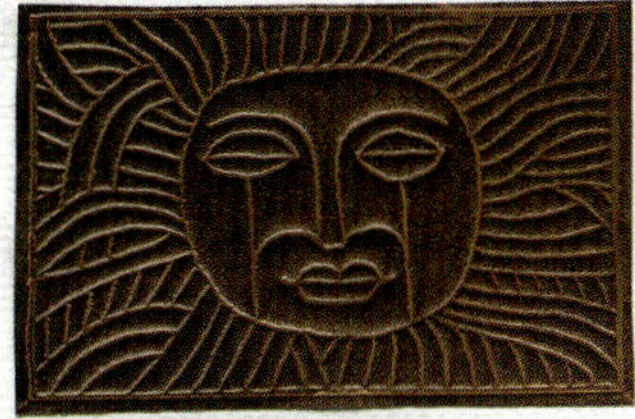

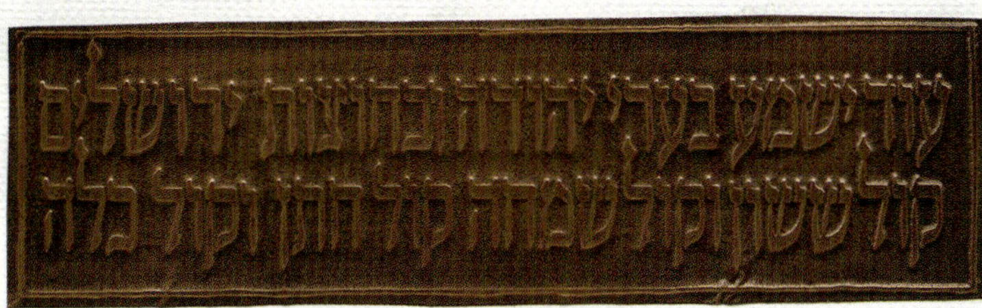

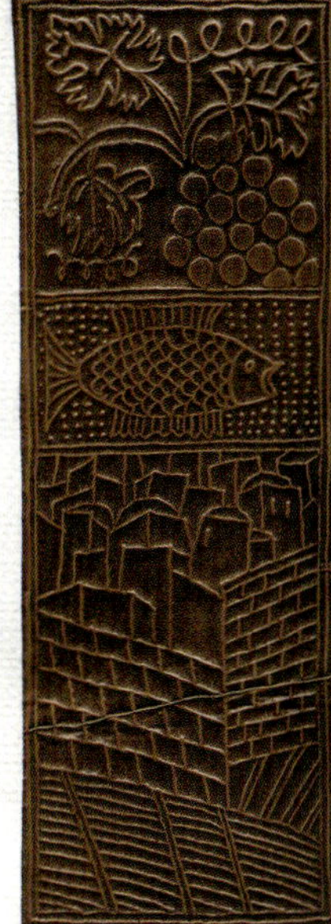

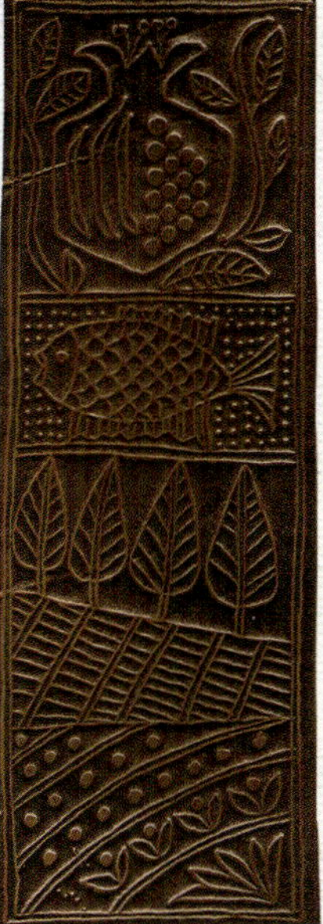

On the day of the month of in the year

ביום לחודש שנת חמשת אלפים שבע מאות

corresponding to the day of in the year

כאן

here in

אנו

we

נכנסים היום לפניכם קרובים יקרים ומבקשים להצהיר: מאוחדים באהבתנו

entered into the holy covenant of marriage and made this pledge:

ברצוננו ובנכונותנו לקבל איש את רעותו. נועד לאהוב לשמור לחזק

We unite in love to comfort and to care for one another.

לכבד ולהוקיר זה את זה. מחזקים ומאשרים אנו את מחויבותנו לתמיכה הדדית

We affirm our commitment to support each other as we meet

בעומדנו יחדיו מול אתגרי החיים. בוגרים ומנוסים נצעד אל העתיד תוך כבוד

the joys and challenges of life and we pledge to respect one

הדדי עידוד וחיזוק יכולותנו המשותפים. אנו מבטיחים לקיים בית חם

another's strengths and abilities. In our home, family and

רווי בתרבות ומסורת בית בו נארוג לתפארה אהבה שמחה רוח ומורשת אבות

friends will find laughter and warmth. "I am my beloved's and

בית בו ימצאו בעוז עונות החיים. בית בו נחגוג באורה ובשירה מועדים וחגים.

my beloved is mine." Set me as a seal upon your heart.

ביתנו בית ועד יהיה למשפחה וחברים "אני ואהובי ואהובי לי" והא החותם

With these rings we consecrate our love for one another

שעל לבנו. ובטבעות אלה נקדיש את אהבתנו ברוח מורשת אבותינו

as husband and wife.

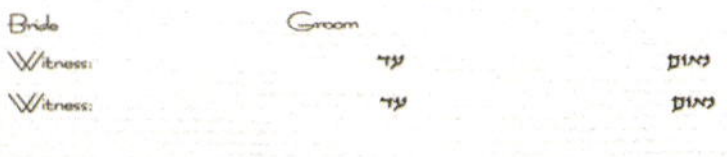

Courtesy of Gad Almaliah and Petroff Gallery.

Robin Hall and Richard Sigberman

"Synagogue Ketubah"

c. 1990

Brooklyn born Robin Hall began learning calligraphy at a young age. Now the San Francisco resident makes ketubot with handmade papers, designing modern and traditional art as well as lettering texts. Sigberman, raised in New York and now living in California's Marin County, creates art influenced by Max Fleischer's cartoons imbuing childlike joy.

This collaborative hand-painted and hand-lettered ketubah is based on an old-world synagogue. The Twelve Tribes of Israel, a Tree of Life, a peacock (representing prosperity), calla lilies (symbolizing the bride, since *kallah* is the Hebrew word for bride), and many other Jewish symbols envelop the text. One can imagine the wedding couple's promises inhabiting the sanctuary as the text floats above, reaching upward into the high arch of holy space.

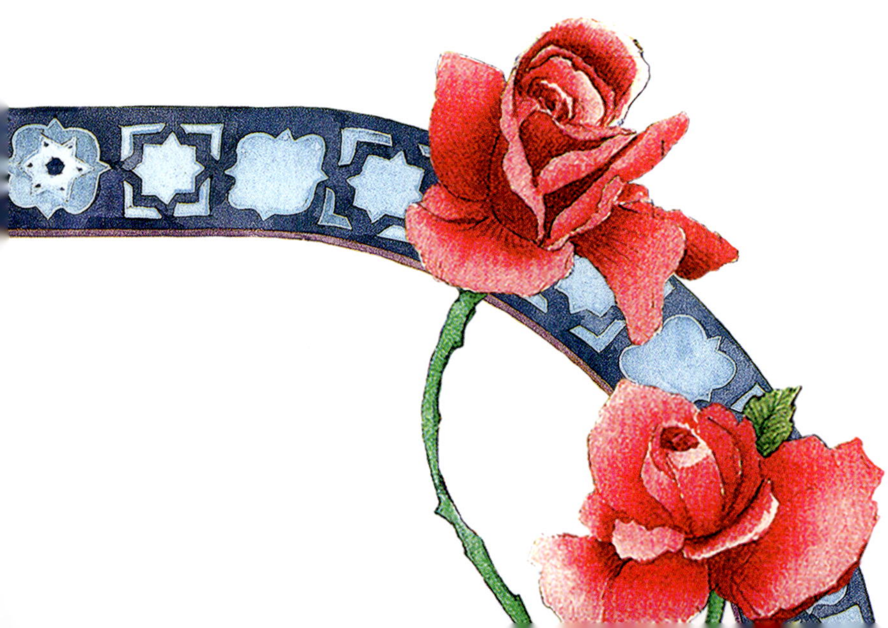

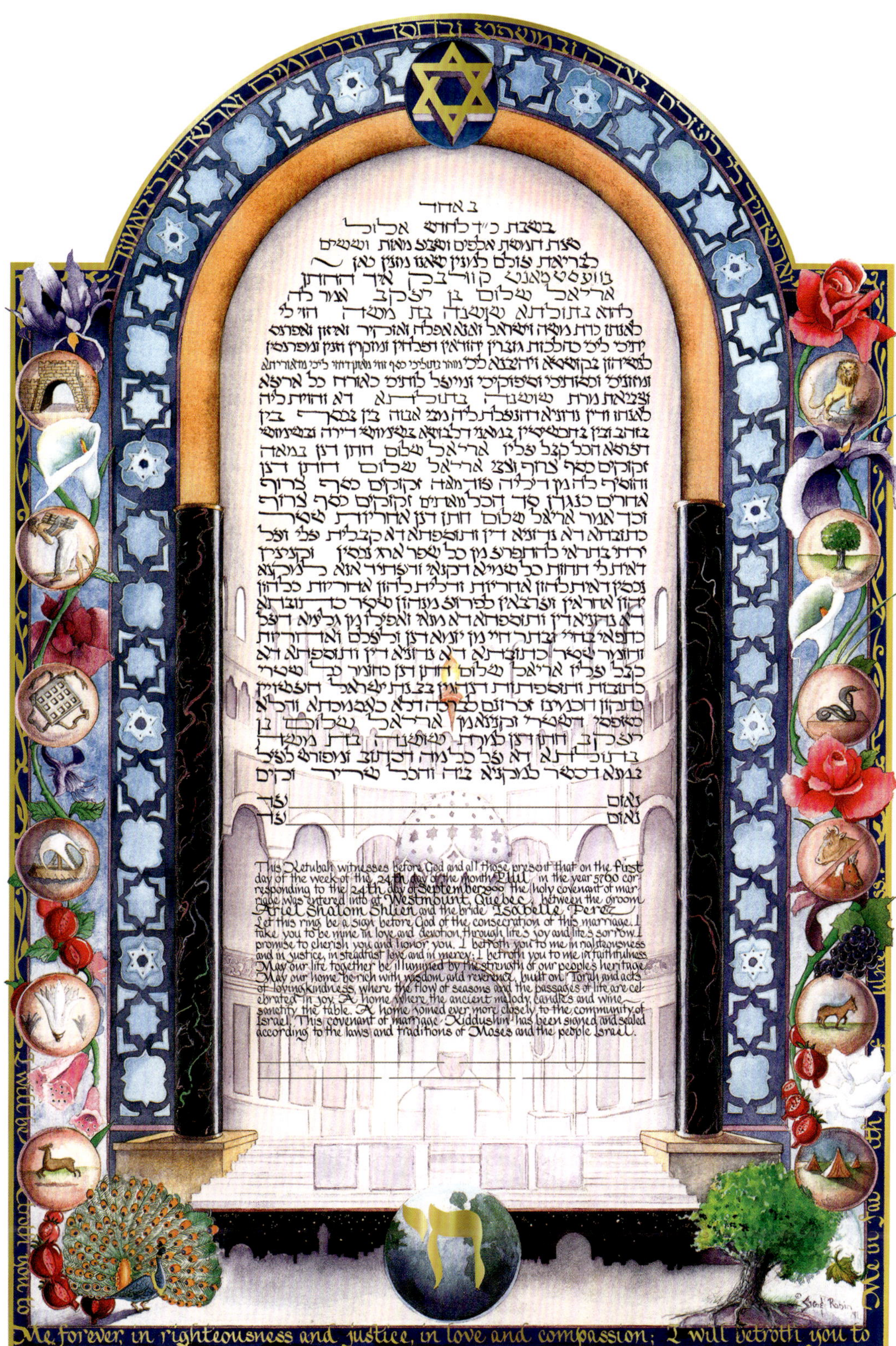

Courtesy of Robin Hall and Petroff Gallery.

Jonathan Kremer

Untitled

1991

Rabbi and artist Jonathan Kremer raised his family in Ardmore, Pennsylvania, and now lives in Ventnor, New Jersey, where he heads Congregation Shirat Hayam. His ketubot blend historical decorative motifs with refined lettering and modern aesthetics to evoke the timelessness of our Jewish heritage.

This rectangular design features a perimeter garden of jubilant spring flowers, pomegranates, figs, and dates in a rainbow of colors. Painted in a playful font is a quote from Psalms 30:12–13, part of which reads in translation: “You turned my lament into dancing, you undid my sackcloth and girded me with joy.”

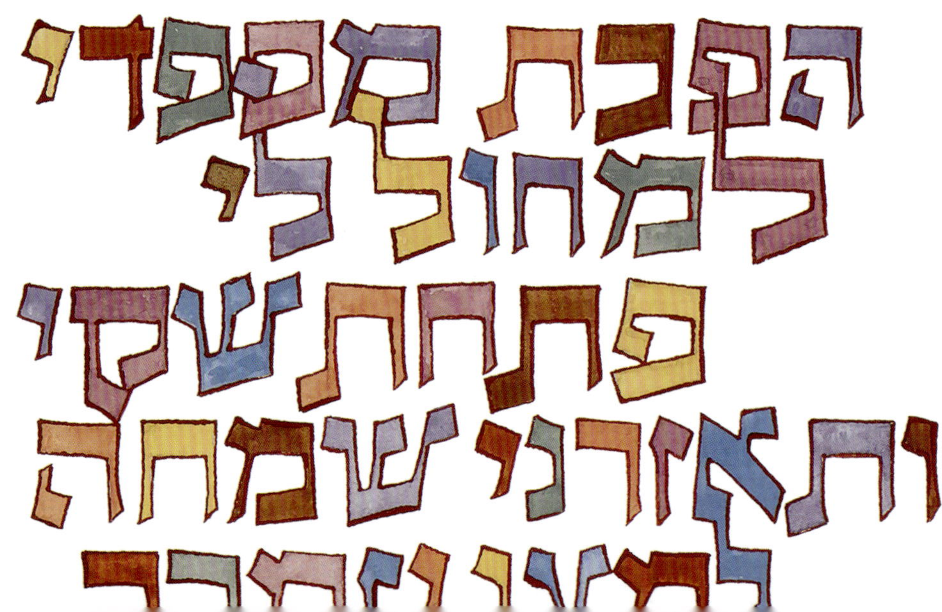

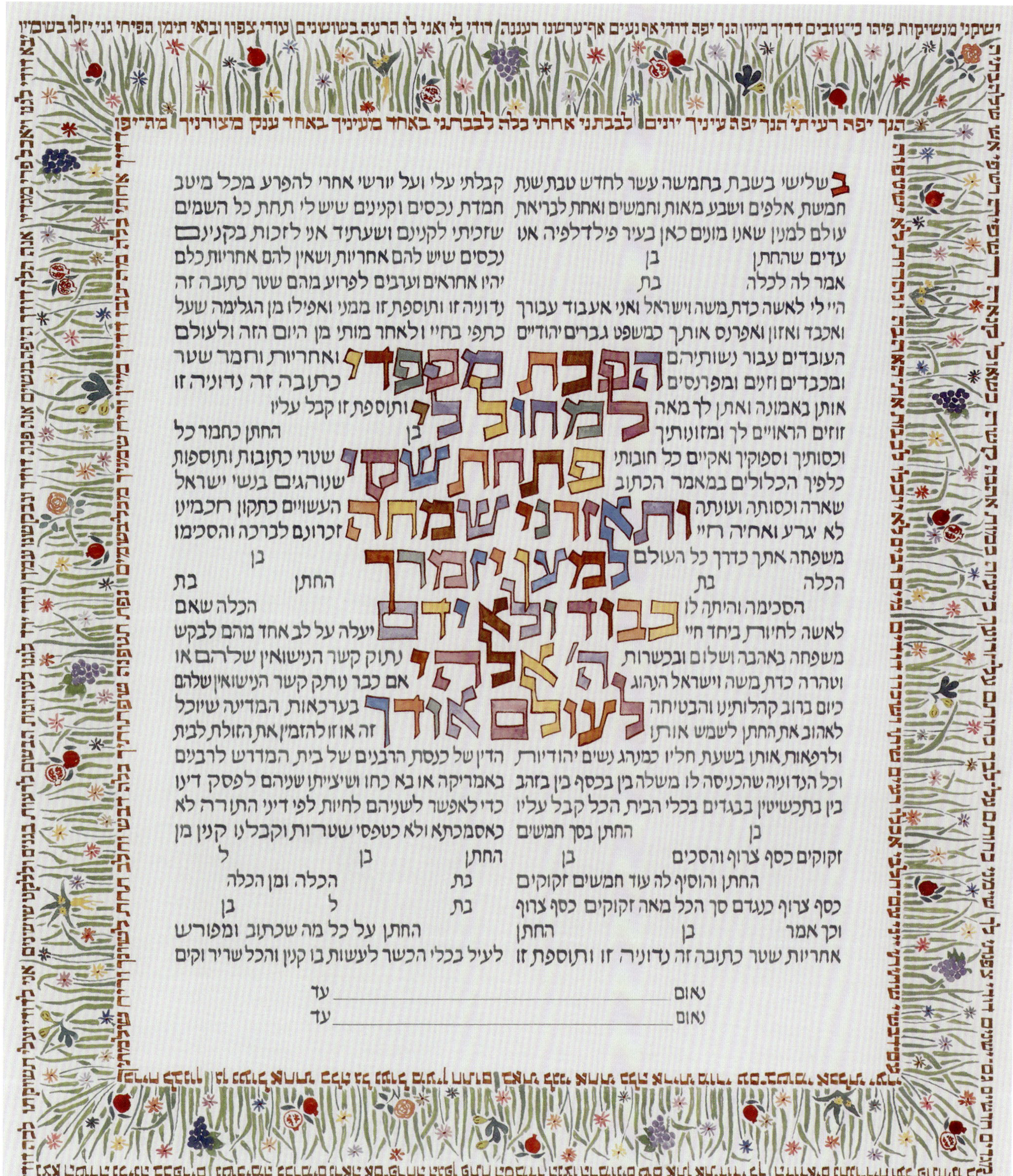

Catalog number Ket 515, courtesy of The Jewish Theological Seminary Library.

Mordechai Rosenstein

Untitled

1991

Mordechai Rosenstein (1934–2024, Philadelphia) lived in Elkins Park, Pennsylvania. Inspired by Abstract Expressionist artist Franz Kline, Rosenstein uses vibrant colors and flowing lines to elevate the art of Hebrew calligraphy. He made his first art ketubah for his own wedding in February 1961.

Rosenstein's signature fanciful style animates this ketubah. Two city skylines of significance to the couple (Hong Kong Harbour on the left, New York City on the right) bookend the work, itself framed by striking "macrography," a nearly inscrutable series of large Hebrew letters reading "Bereshit," or "In the beginning" (references to the first book and first word of the Torah). Across the top, small vignettes of biblical figures—a nod to the Hebrew names of the bride (Sarah Esther) and groom (Solomon Joseph)—are boldly depicted in a palette of predominantly primary colors.

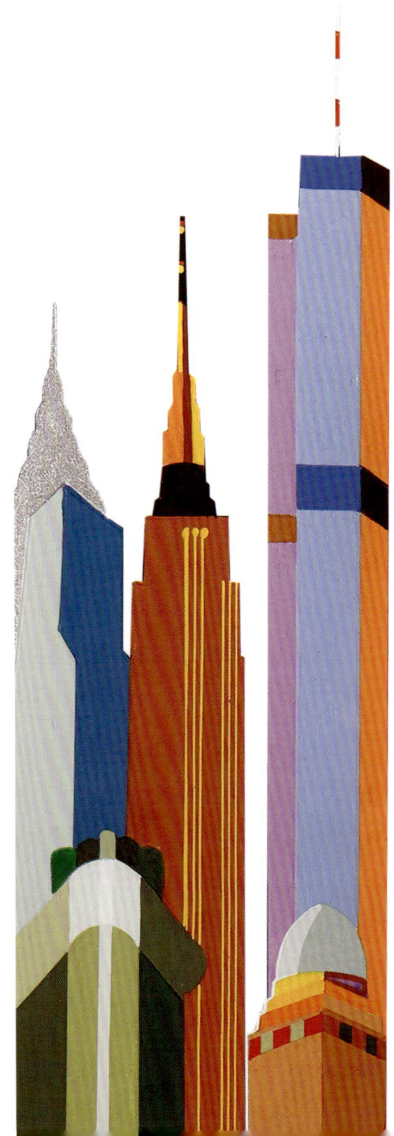

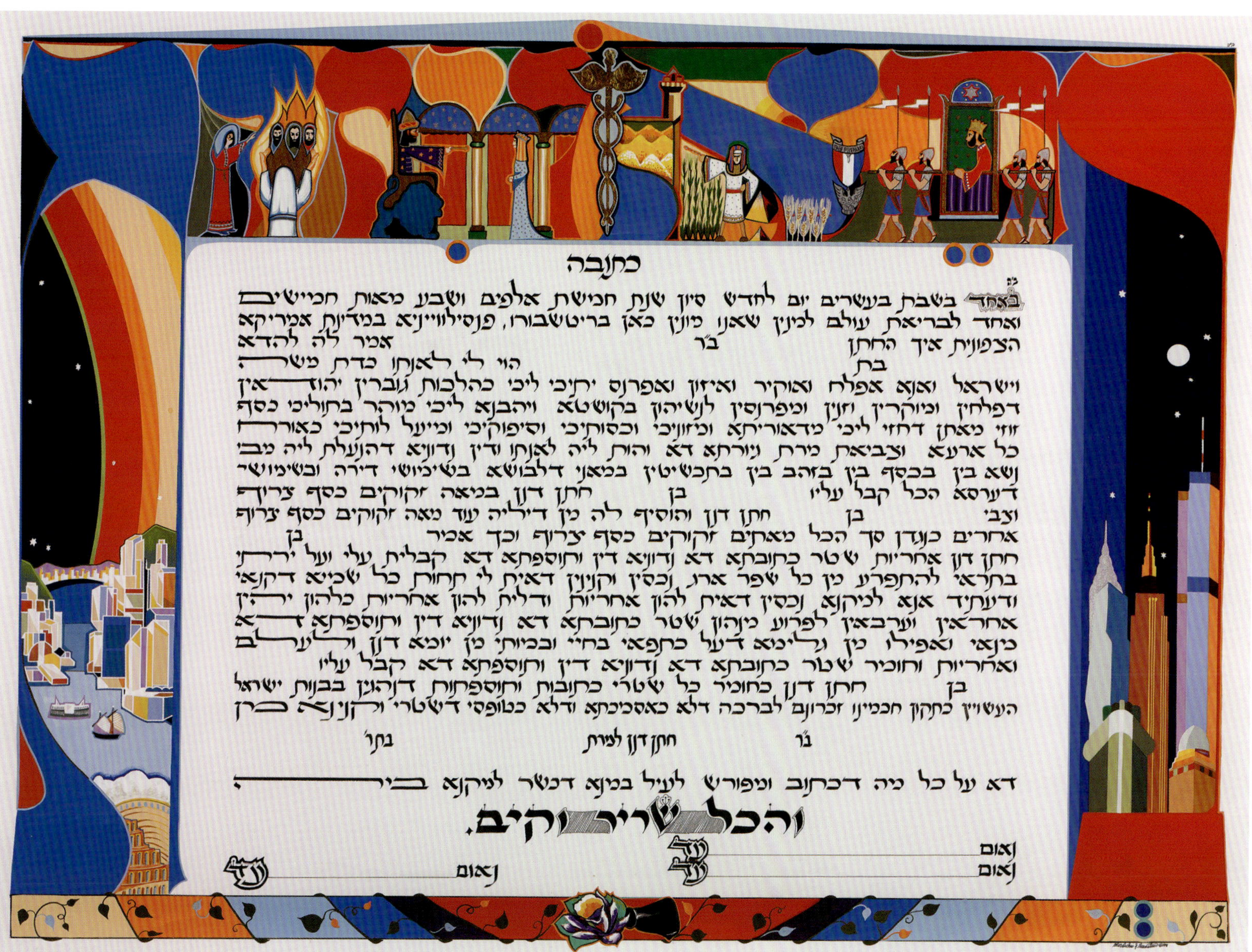

כתובה

ב״ה

באחד בשבת בעשרים יום לחדש סיון שנת חמשת אלפים ושבע מאות חמישים
ואחד לבריאת עולם למנין שאנו מונין כאן בריטשבורו, פנסילווינא במדינת אמריקא
הצפונית איך החתן בר אמר לה להדא
בת הוי לי לאנתו כדת משה
וישראל ואנא אפלח ואוקיר ואיזון ואפרנס יתיכי ליכי כהלכות גוברין יהודאין
דפלחין ומוקרין וזנין ומפרנסין לנשיהון בקושטא ויהבנא ליכי מוהר בתוליכי כסף
זוזי מאתן דחזי ליכי מדאוריתא ומזוניכי וכסותיכי וסיפוקיכי ומיעל לותיכי כאורח
כל ארעא וצביאת מרת נערתא דא והות ליה לאנתו ודין נדוניא דהנעלת ליה מבי
נשא בין בכסף בין בזהב בין בתכשיטין במאני דלבושא בשימושי דירה ובשימושי
דערסא הכל קבל עליו בן חתן דנן במאה זקוקים כסף צרוף
וצבי בן חתן דנן והוסיף לה מן דיליה עוד מאה זקוקים כסף צרוף
אחרים כנגדן סך הכל מאתים זקוקים כסף צרוף וכך אמר בן
חתן דנן אחריות שטר כתובתא דא נדוניא דין ותוספתא דא קבלית עלי ועל ירתי
בתראי להתפרע מן כל שפר ארג נכסין וקנינין דאית לי תחות כל שמיא דקנאי
ודעתיד אנא למיקנא נכסין דאית להון אחריות ודלית להון אחריות כלהון יהיו
אחראין וערבאין לפרוע מנהון שטר כתובתא דא נדוניא דין ותוספתא דא
מנאי ואפילו מן גלימא דעל כתפאי בחיי ובמותי מן יומא דנן ולעלם
ואחריות וחומר שטר כתובתא דא נדוניא דין ותוספתא דא קבל עליו
בן חתן דנן כחומר כל שטרי כתובות ותוספתות דנהגין בבנות ישראל
העשויין כתקון חכמינו זכרונם לברכה דלא כאסמכתא ודלא כטופסי דשטרי וקנינא מן

בר חתן דנן למרת בתו

דא על כל מה דכתוב ומפורש לעיל במנא דכשר למיקנא ביה

והכל שריר וקים.

נאום עד
נאום עד
נאום עד

Catalog number Ket 536, courtesy of The Jewish Theological Seminary Library.

Ardyn Halter

"Seven Species"

1991

Ardyn Halter was born in London in 1956 to Holocaust survivors, and lives in England and Israel. Together with his father, Roman Halter, he designed Yad Layeled Children's Educational Museum in the Ghetto Fighters' House Museum in Israel. He works in multiple mediums including oil painting, silkscreen, and stained glass. His work has been exhibited and collected worldwide, including at the Victoria and Albert Museum in London and The Israel Museum in Jerusalem.

Here he depicts the seven species of the Land of Israel as if in stained glass. Deep blue background panels set off the colorful produce. Repeating Stars of David form the text border, and the symmetrical tablet design is pleasantly balanced by the organic flow of foliage, fruits, and grains.

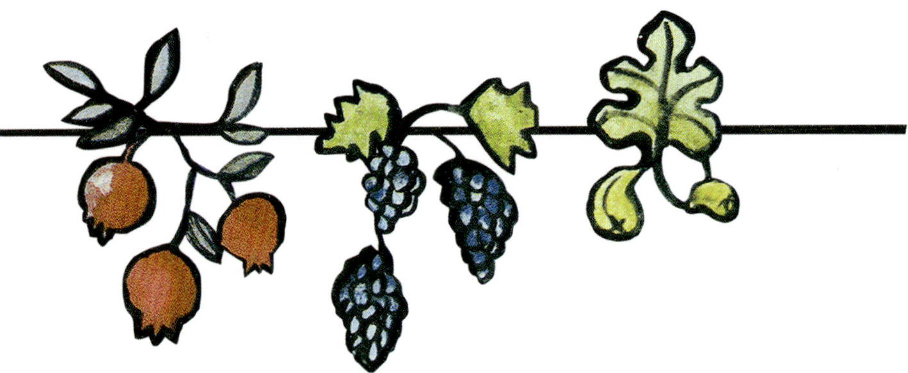

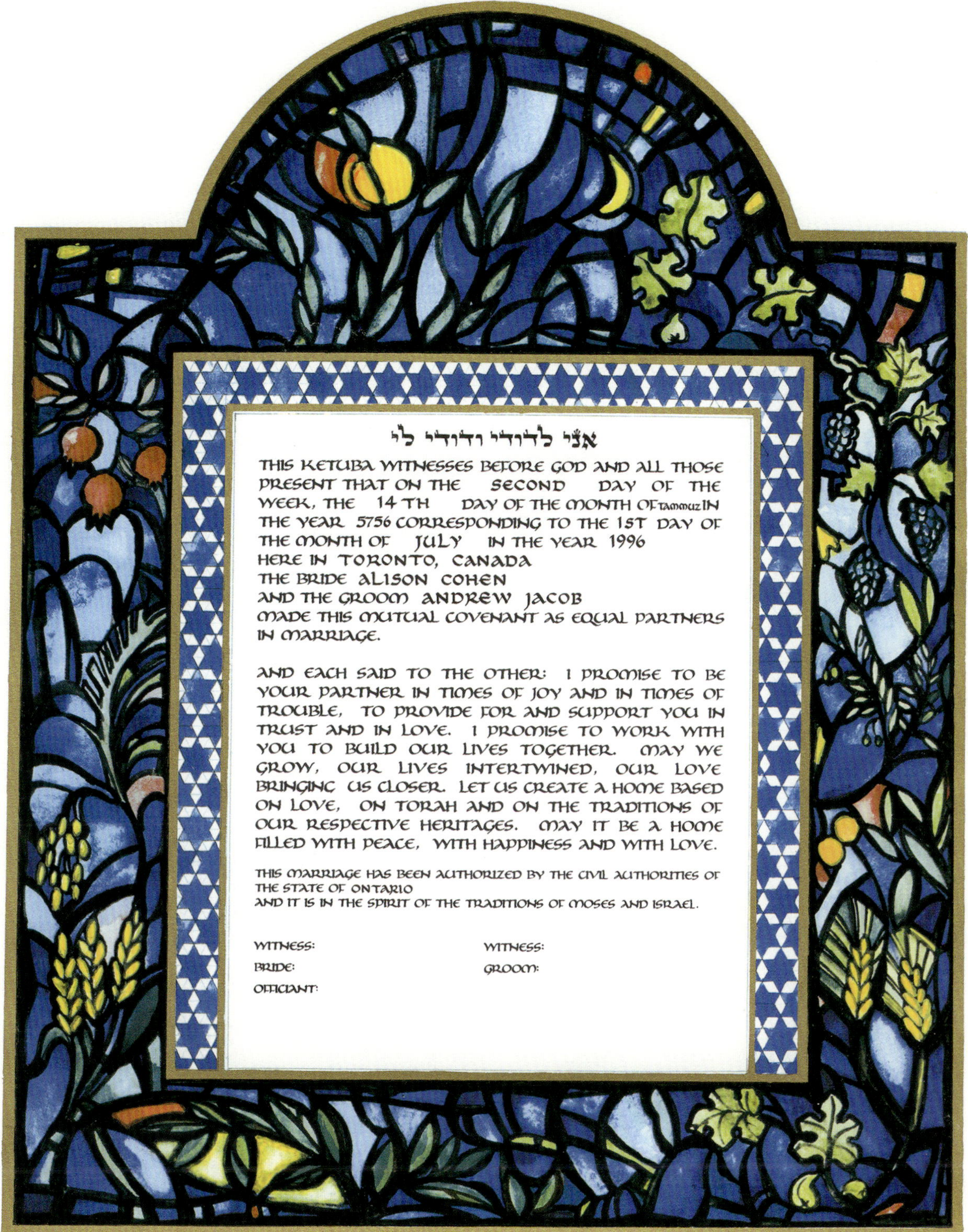

אני לדודי ודודי לי

THIS KETUBA WITNESSES BEFORE GOD AND ALL THOSE PRESENT THAT ON THE SECOND DAY OF THE WEEK, THE 14 TH DAY OF THE MONTH OF TAMMUZ IN THE YEAR 5756 CORRESPONDING TO THE 1ST DAY OF THE MONTH OF JULY IN THE YEAR 1996
HERE IN TORONTO, CANADA
THE BRIDE ALISON COHEN
AND THE GROOM ANDREW JACOB
MADE THIS MUTUAL COVENANT AS EQUAL PARTNERS IN MARRIAGE.

AND EACH SAID TO THE OTHER: I PROMISE TO BE YOUR PARTNER IN TIMES OF JOY AND IN TIMES OF TROUBLE, TO PROVIDE FOR AND SUPPORT YOU IN TRUST AND IN LOVE. I PROMISE TO WORK WITH YOU TO BUILD OUR LIVES TOGETHER. MAY WE GROW, OUR LIVES INTERTWINED, OUR LOVE BRINGING US CLOSER. LET US CREATE A HOME BASED ON LOVE, ON TORAH AND ON THE TRADITIONS OF OUR RESPECTIVE HERITAGES. MAY IT BE A HOME FILLED WITH PEACE, WITH HAPPINESS AND WITH LOVE.

THIS MARRIAGE HAS BEEN AUTHORIZED BY THE CIVIL AUTHORITIES OF THE STATE OF ONTARIO
AND IT IS IN THE SPIRIT OF THE TRADITIONS OF MOSES AND ISRAEL.

WITNESS: WITNESS:
BRIDE: GROOM:
OFFICIANT:

Courtesy of Ardyn Halter.

Avraham Cohen

"Flowers at Sunset"

1993

Illustrator and calligrapher Avraham Cohen (b. 1950) was raised in New Jersey and lives in Baltimore. He aims to represent the diversity of forms in nature and the beauty of the natural world with clean lines and clear contrast.

In this ketubah Cohen updates the perennial flower motif, symbolizing new life. The realistic style calls to mind the artist Henri Rousseau, as both artists simplify tropical foliage and botanical forms to perfection. Revealing the beauty of irises, roses, birds of paradise, and a single lily, Cohen's floral arrangement foregrounds a peaceful night landscape and even pokes out beyond the Moorish-style decorative frame, adding to the realist effect.

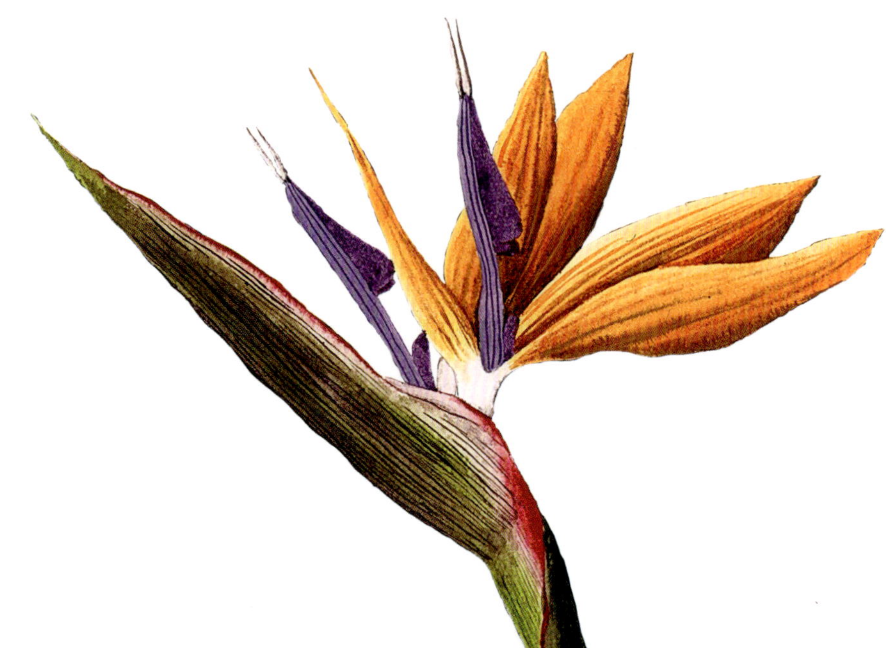

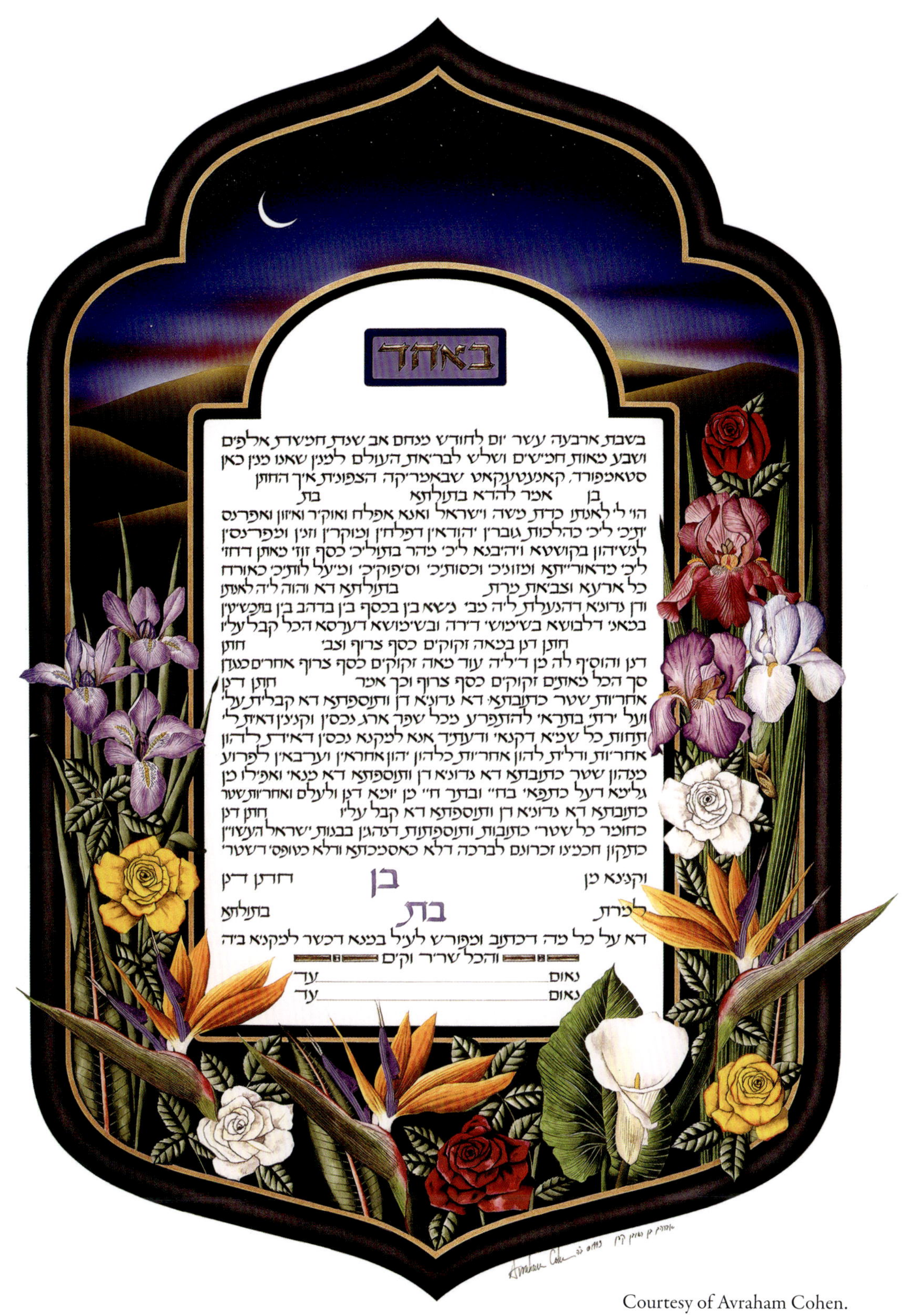

Courtesy of Avraham Cohen.

LSA (Artist Unknown)

Untitled

1995

Every effort was made to identify the artist, simply noted as LSA, but like many historical ketubot, this modern creator may never be known.

In the circular ketubah, concentric rings contain phrases in elongated Hebrew letters, detailed and abstracted Jerusalem building facades, and other festive elements. A notable innovation is the precise arching of the English text around the inner Hebrew text circle. Additionally, the design has been painted straight to the deckled edge of the paper, giving the appearance of an ancient document that has been unearthed and preserved.

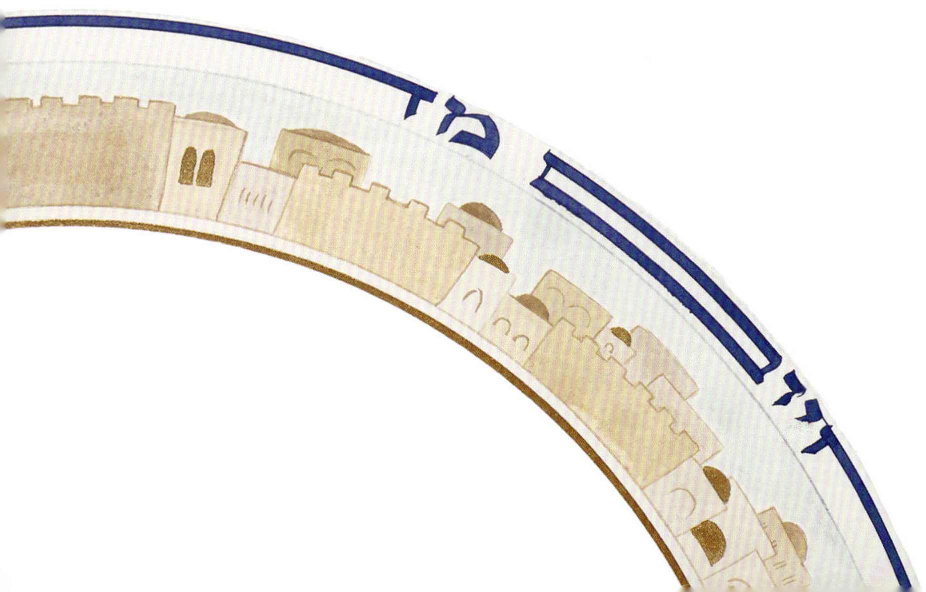

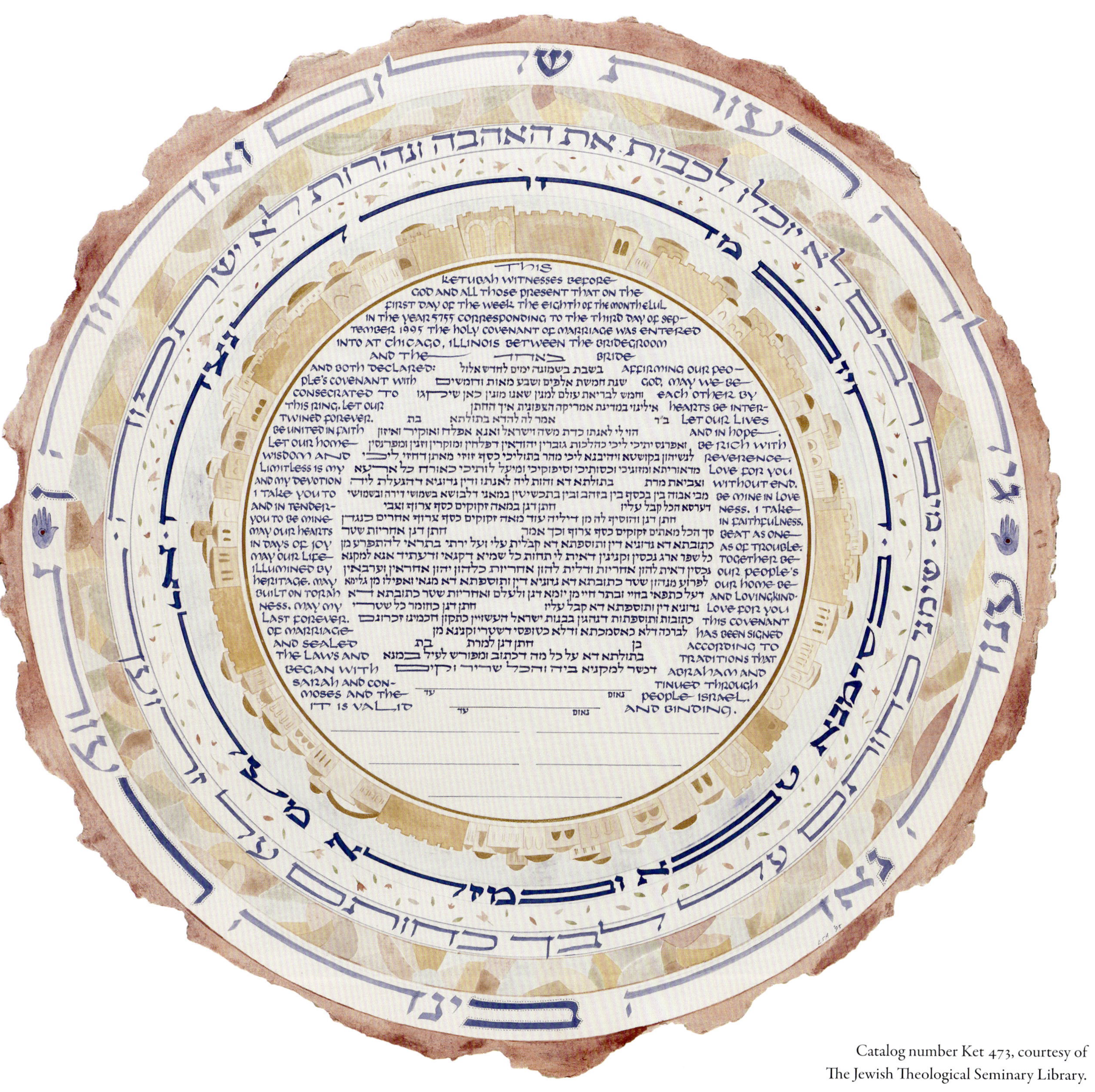

Catalog number Ket 473, courtesy of The Jewish Theological Seminary Library.

Lee Loebman

"For Susan and Stephen's Rededication Ceremony"

1995

Lee Loebman was born in Chicago and works in Grayslake, Illinois. Combining paper-cutting and painting, he designs custom works in vibrant primary colors that integrate symbols from the personal history of the bride and groom.

In this fanciful temple of love and commitment, a Jerusalem stone pattern on the ceiling and floor forms a foundation for a jigsaw-puzzle piece made of the extraordinary text shapes of an embracing couple. Postage stamps and items of Judaica float in the side panels in patterns reminiscent of stained-glass windows.

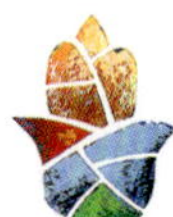

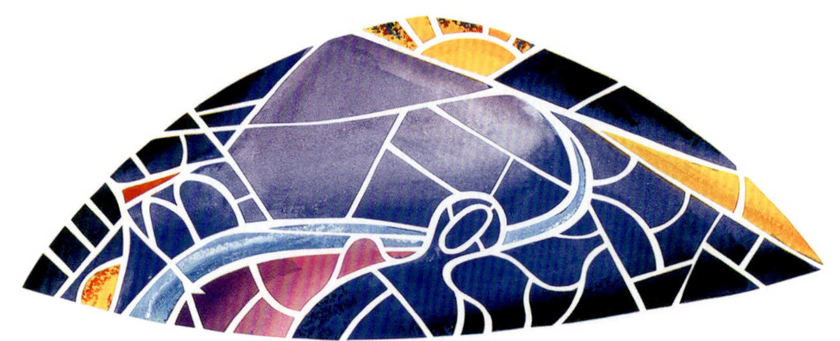

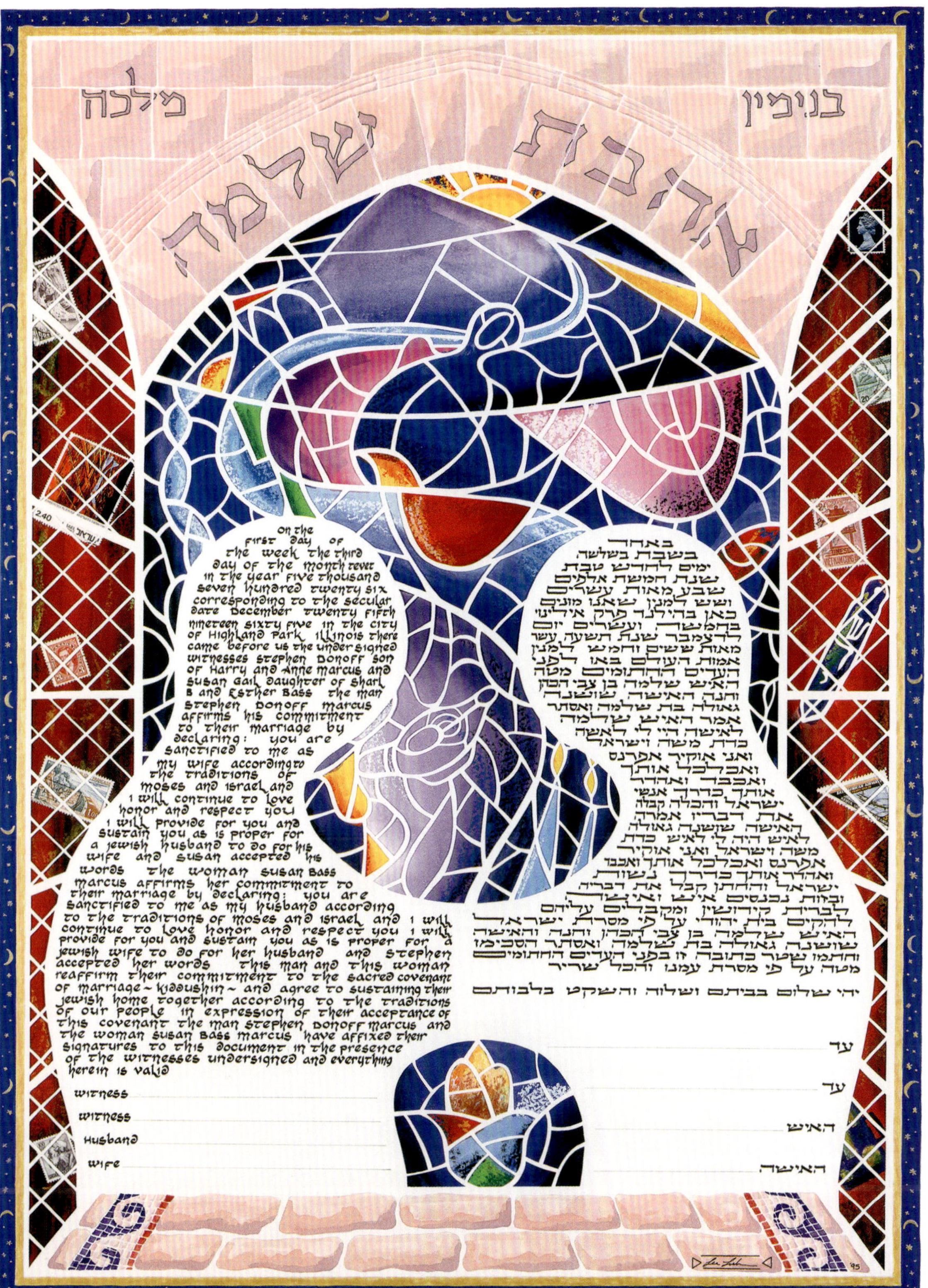

Courtesy of Lee Loebman.

Betsy Platkin Teutsch

"Trees of Life"

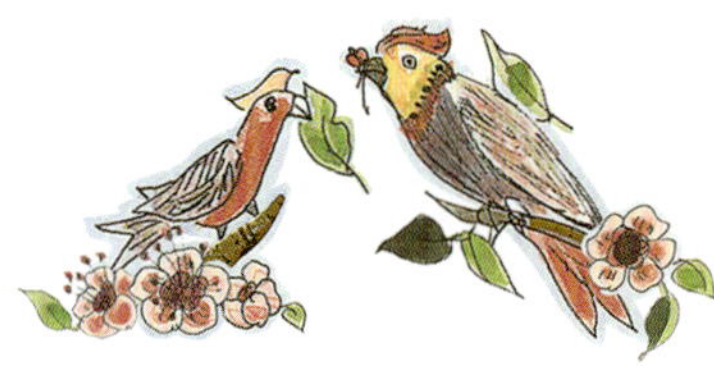

1997

A Fargo, North Dakota, native who now lives in Philadelphia, Betsy Platkin Teutsch brings strong lettering and design sense and Judaic knowledge to her craft. Coauthor of *The Encyclopedia of Jewish Symbols* (1995), she served as art editor and illustrator for the Reconstructionist movement's *Kol Haneshamah* prayerbook series.

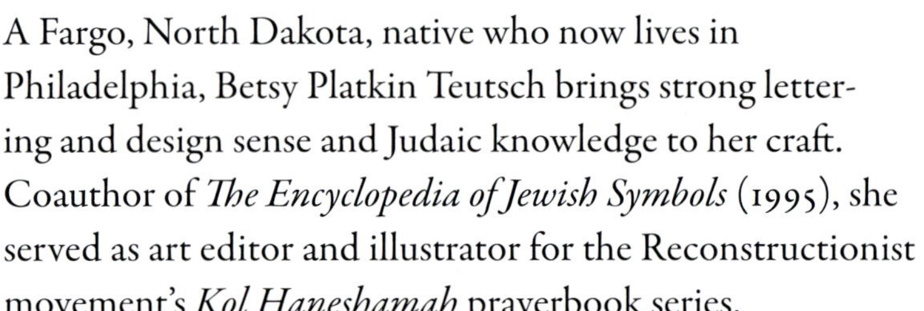

This two tree design blends foliage and exuberant flowers in a delightful tangle around the text border. Two intertwined wedding bands meet at the top. Scattered throughout are notable phrases about love and peace, in Hebrew and English, including a quotation from the daily evening Shema prayer, "Spread over us the shelter of Your peace."

When mounted on the wall, the ketubah's circular shape reflects—like a mirror—the couple's commitment to one another.

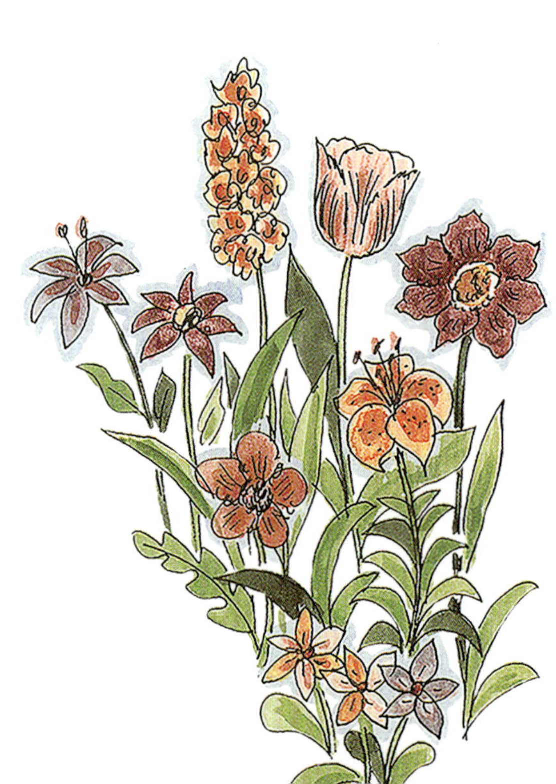

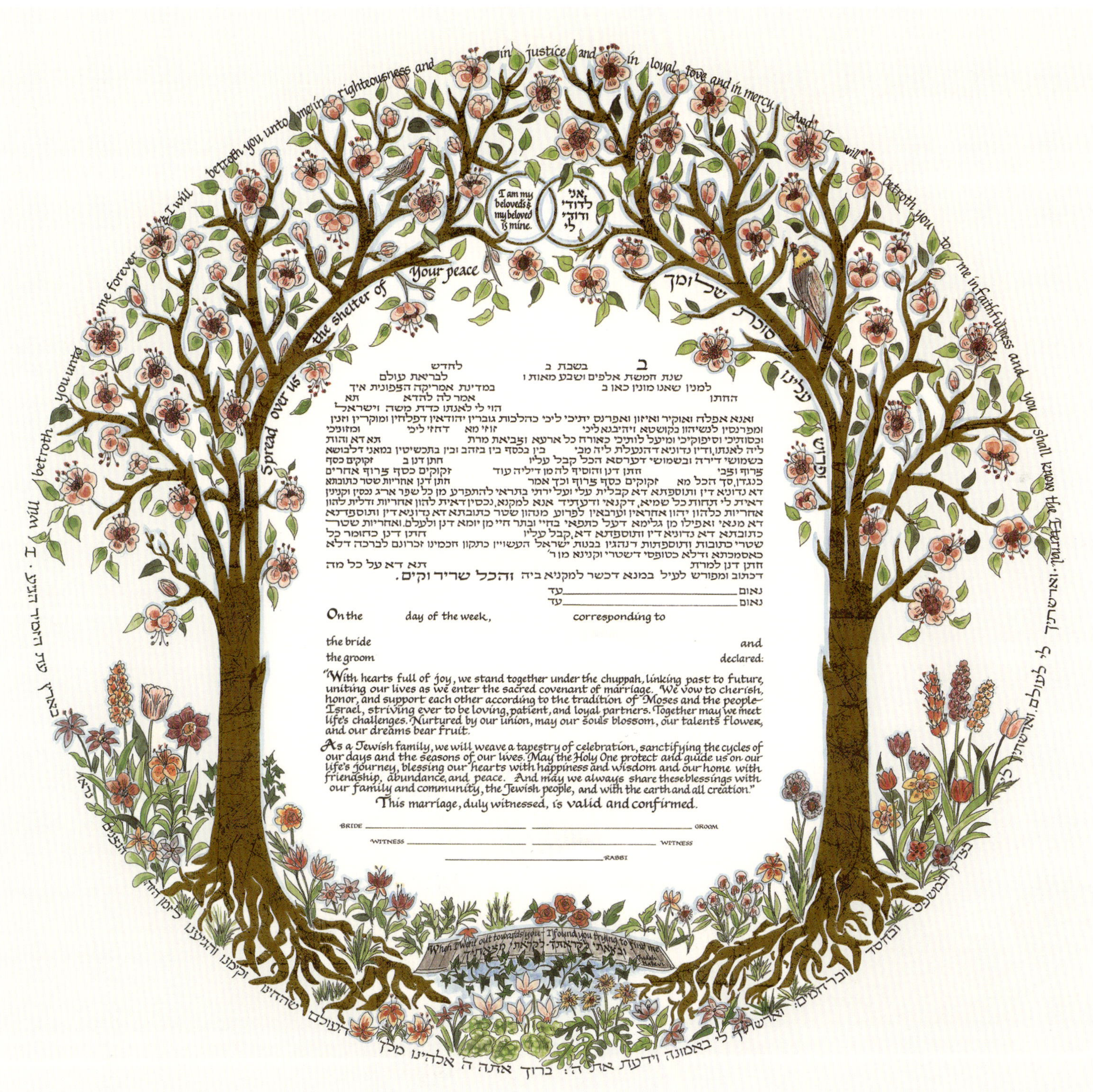

Courtesy of Betsy Platkin Teutsch and Petroff Gallery.

Stephanie Caplan

"Pomegranate"

1998

Artist and calligrapher Stephanie Caplan grew up in Montreal and Newton, Massachusetts, and resides today in New York's East Village. She treasures being in the same neighborhood where Yiddish culture once flourished and feels she can bring it back in small ways. Her artistic style gravitates toward the simple and quiet, combined with color and movement. Japanese textiles, Eames chairs, New York architecture, the ocean and trees all influence her work.

Inspired by the English Arts and Crafts movement, a design style from the turn of the twentieth century that emphasized natural elements, this ketubah features pomegranates—the biblical fruit symbolizing fertility and a traditional Jewish wedding motif. Caplan's watercolor technique brings out the rich hue of fruit and foliage with luxurious color and texture. The beautiful balance of a markedly rounded, unique Hebrew script with interlined English text is a feat by this master calligrapher.

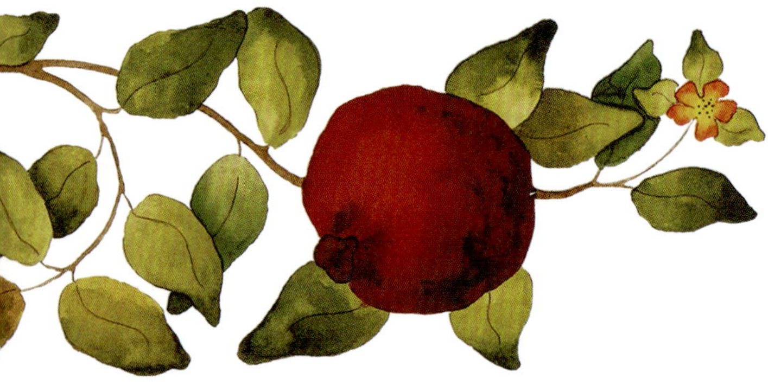

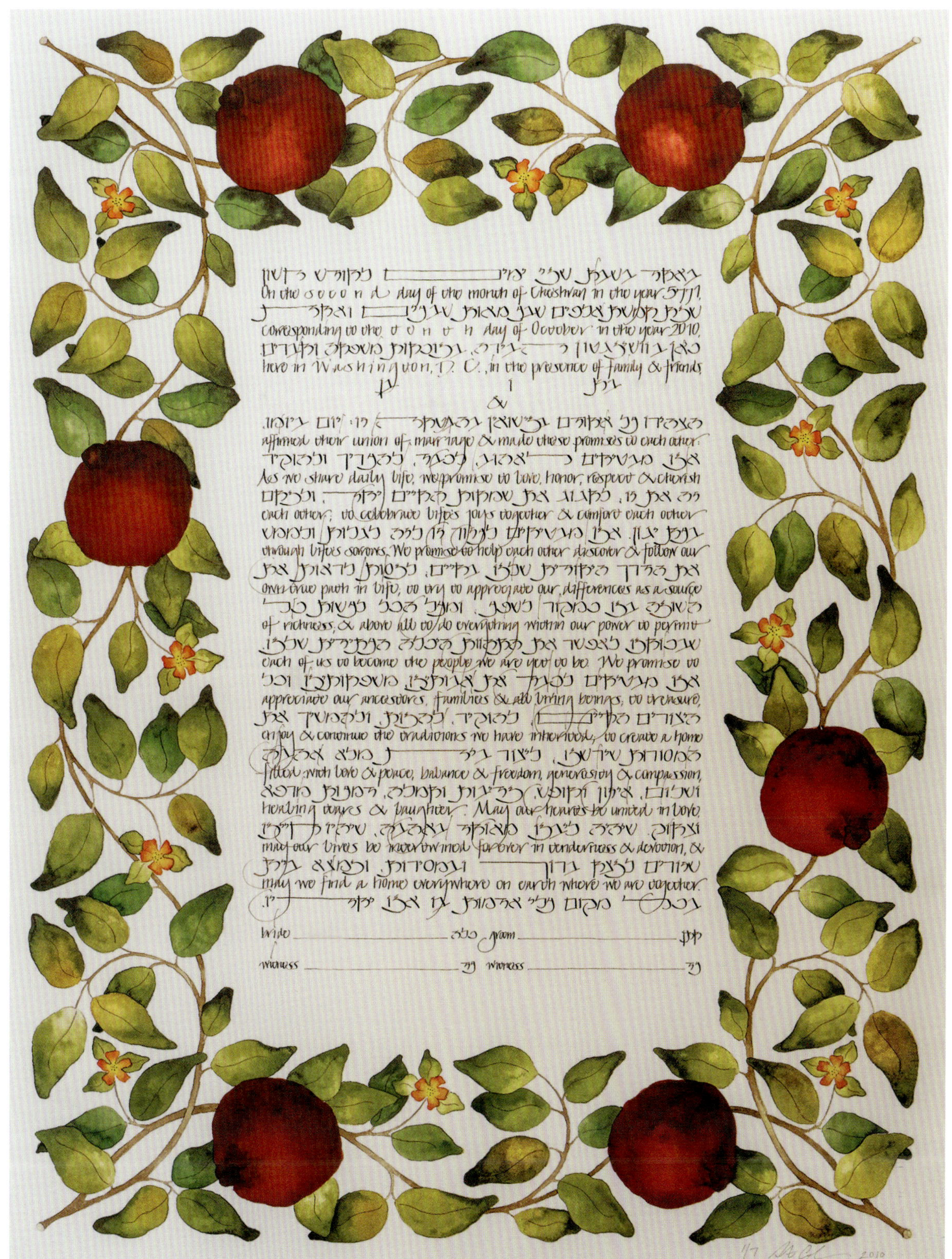

Courtesy of Stephanie Caplan.

Archie Granot

“Jerusalem Ketubah”

1999

Archie Granot (b. 1946) was born in the United Kingdom and resides in Jerusalem. His artwork integrates multiple layers of paper, each one hand cut with a surgical scalpel. He also hand cuts fine calligraphic letters to form Hebrew inscriptions and often includes mentions or representations of Jerusalem.

Granot built this abstract design with fourteen layers of paper. The depiction of the River Jordan and Dead Sea in the famous Madaba mosaic from sixth-century Jordan inspired his shape of the surrounding design, and the city’s stones and greenery inform his color palette. Two modern Hebrew poems exalt the Holy City. One of the poems “I Flourished in a Stone House” (1967) by poet Zelda Schneurson Mishkovsky (widely known as Zelda), reads in part, “Jerusalem captured my roaming soul, I drowned in light, I forgot my name.”

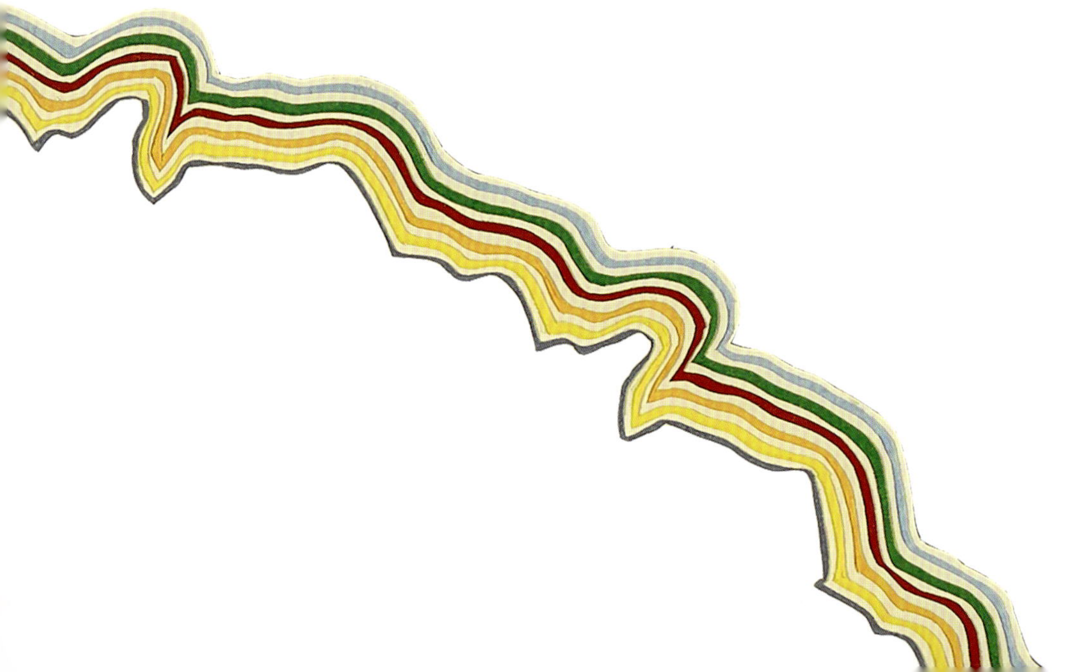

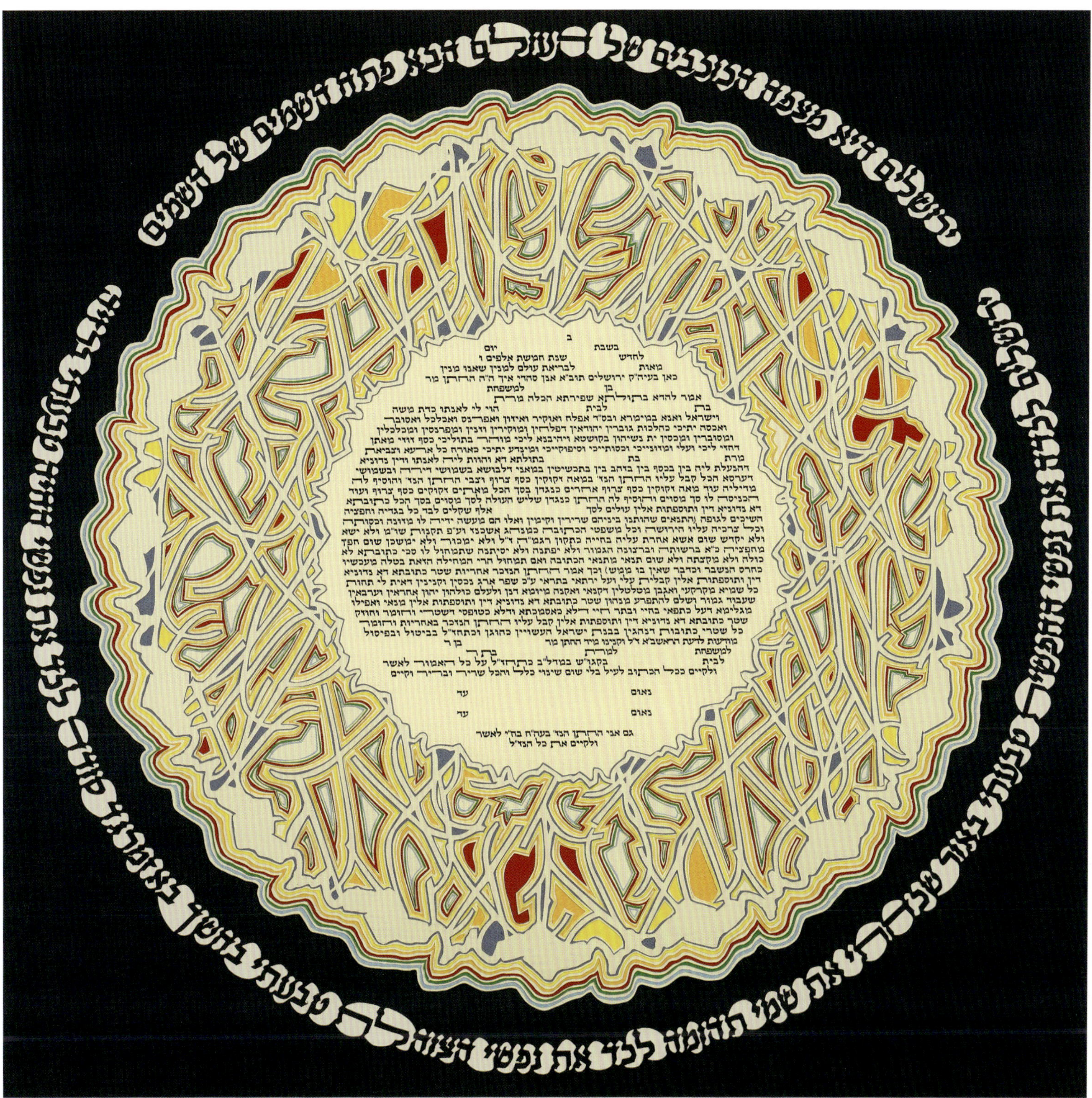

Catalog number Ket 451, courtesy of The Jewish Theological Seminary Library.

Amram Ebgi

Untitled

2000

Amram Ebgi was born in Morocco in 1939, immigrated to Israel in 1950, and resides in Florida. Symbols radiating from his work include vineyards, menorahs, men in religious garb, Noah's Ark, doves, and flora. Almost every piece incorporates the cherished symbol of the bird, symbolizing Israel's freedom. His art has been exhibited and collected worldwide.

This lithograph print combines architectural scenes of Jerusalem at top and bottom linked by vertical columns filled with a riot of Jewish and Israeli symbols, including what might be a wedding klezmer band. Ebgi's carefully etched overlaying pattern of tiles or pebble mosaic pieces adds to its old-world charm.

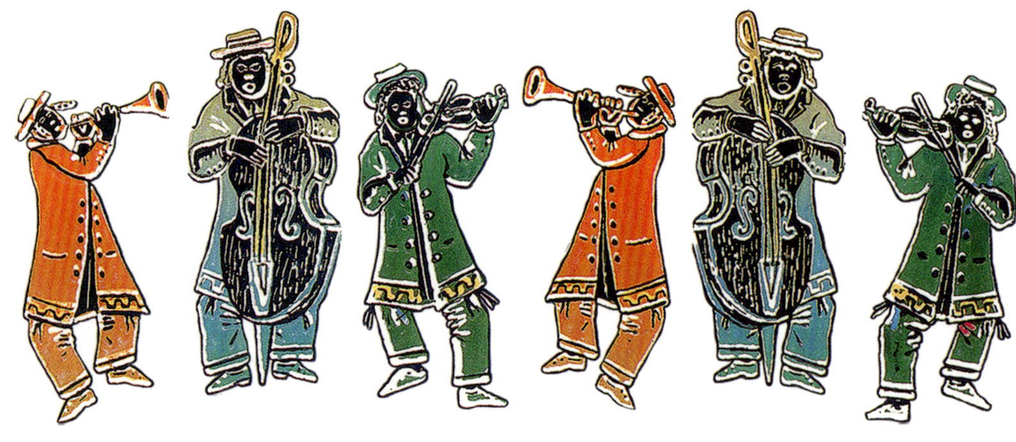

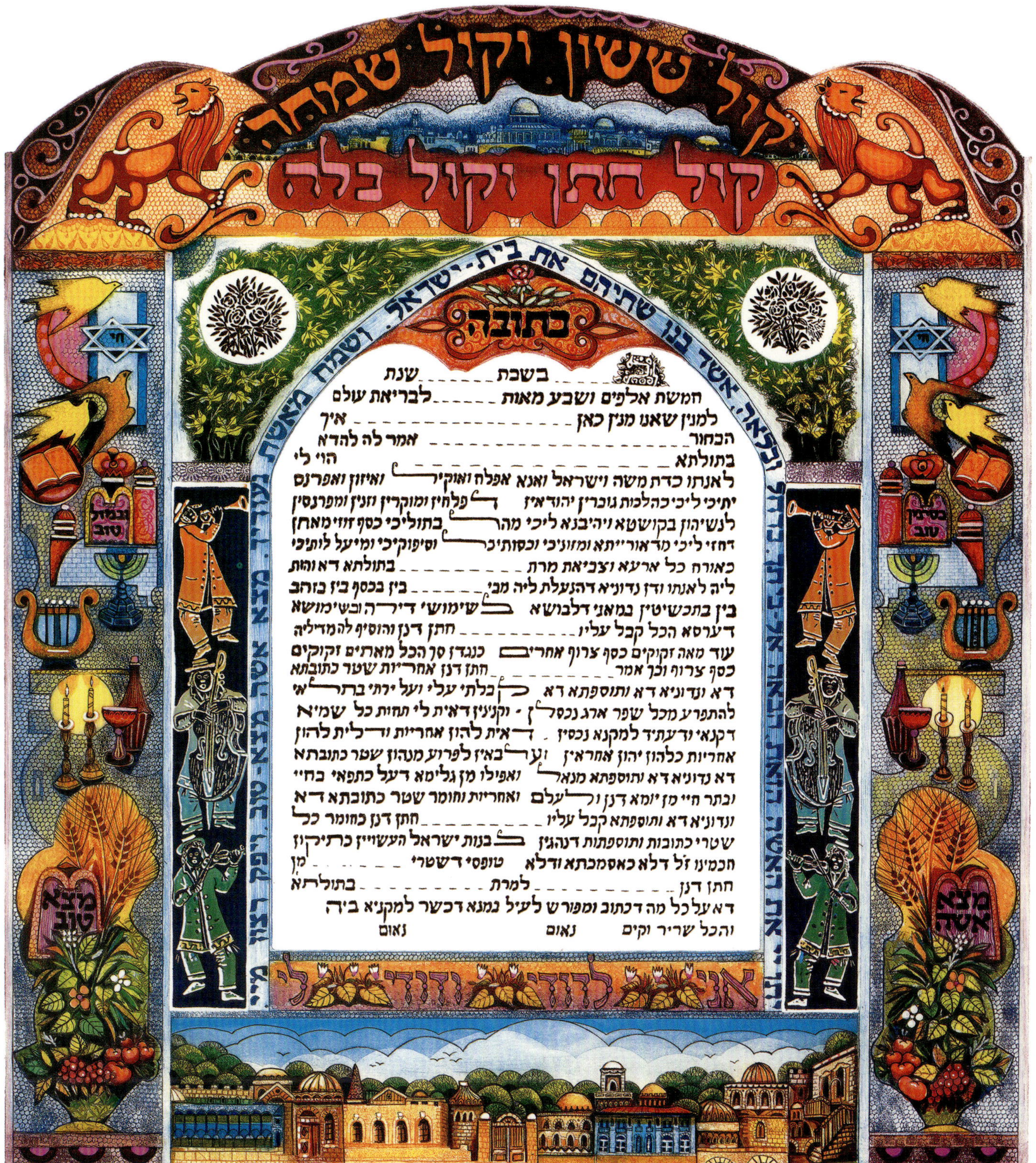

Courtesy of Amram Ebgi.

Tamar Messer

“Many Waters”

2001

Tamar Messer (b. 1962) was born and resides in Haifa. Working in a naïve illustrative style, she interprets traditional texts from a modern Israeli point of view. For example, Messer’s illustrations of biblical stories reflect the fauna and flora of Israel today. Her limited-edition books and prints can be found in various collections around the world.

In this vivid silkscreen print, a bride and groom rejoice at a river oasis between two waterfalls guarded by a lion. This is a twenty-first-century rendering of Song of Songs 8:7, which reads in part: “Vast floods cannot quench love, nor rivers drown it.”

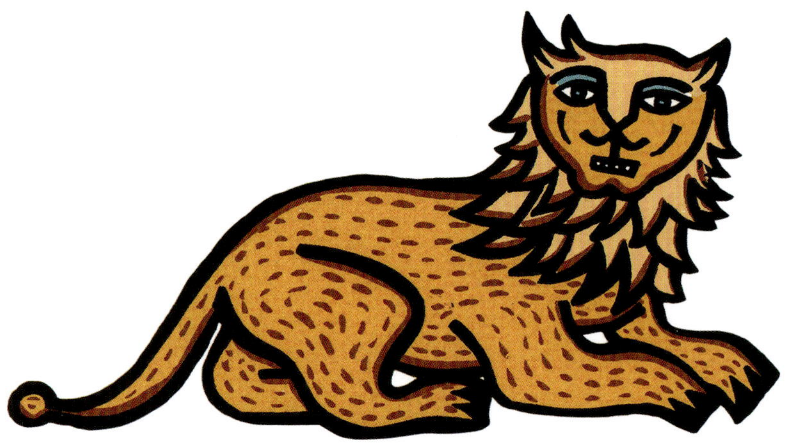

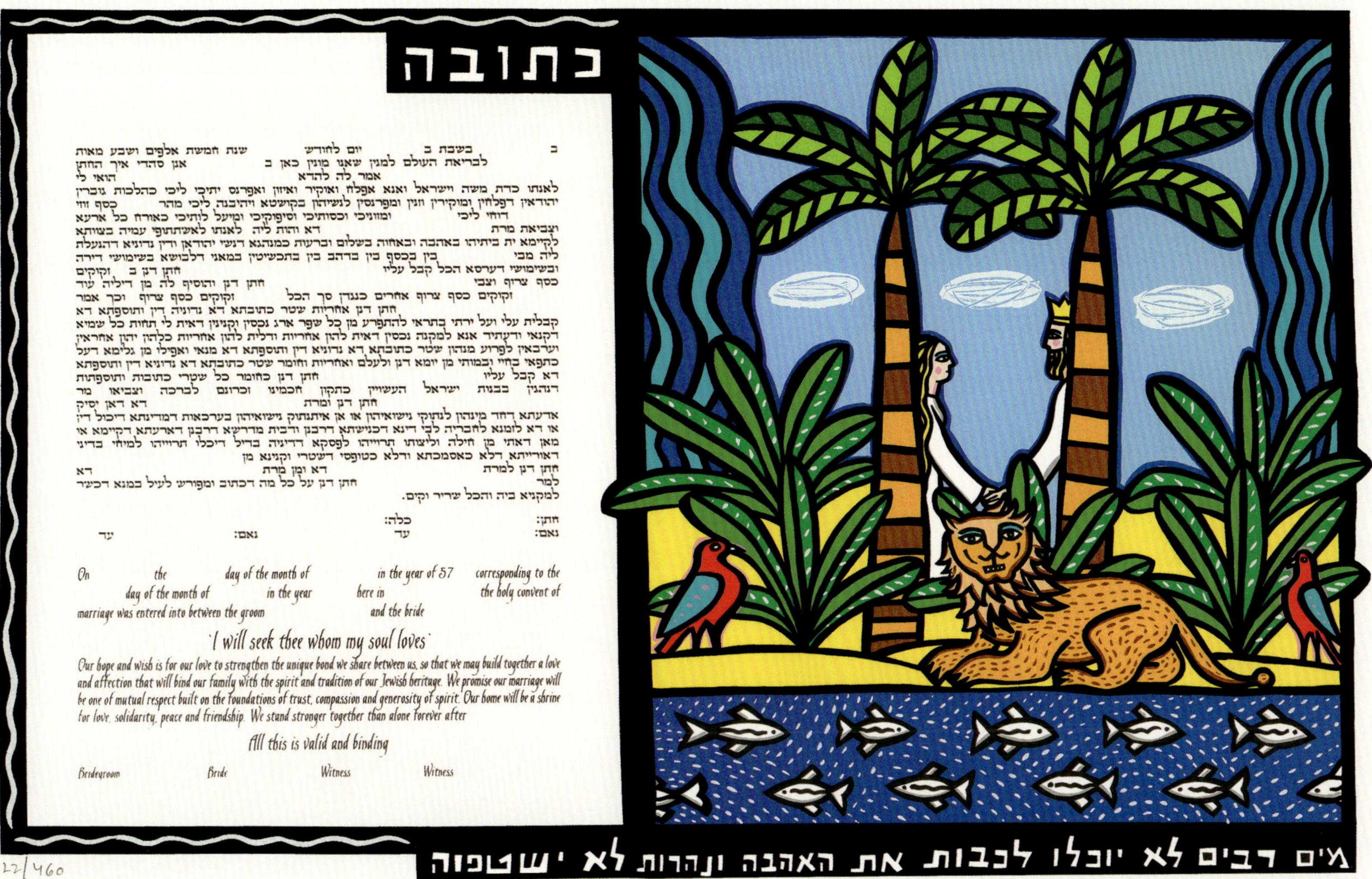

Courtesy of Tamar Messer and Petroff Gallery.

Izzy Pludwinski

“Wildscript Roundel”

2002

Born in Brooklyn in 1954, Izzy Pludwinski is now a prominent calligrapher in Israel who creates ketubot solely from textual design elements. His books, *Mastering Hebrew Calligraphy* and *The Beauty of the Hebrew Letter*, were published in 2014 and 2023, respectively; the latter was a National Jewish Book Award finalist.

On display here is his playful, innovative use of unique cursive Hebrew letter forms. The border features freely written quotations from Jeremiah 33:11 and Song of Songs 6:3, reading respectively: “The sound of mirth and gladness, the voice of bridegroom and bride,” “I am my beloved’s And my beloved is mine.”

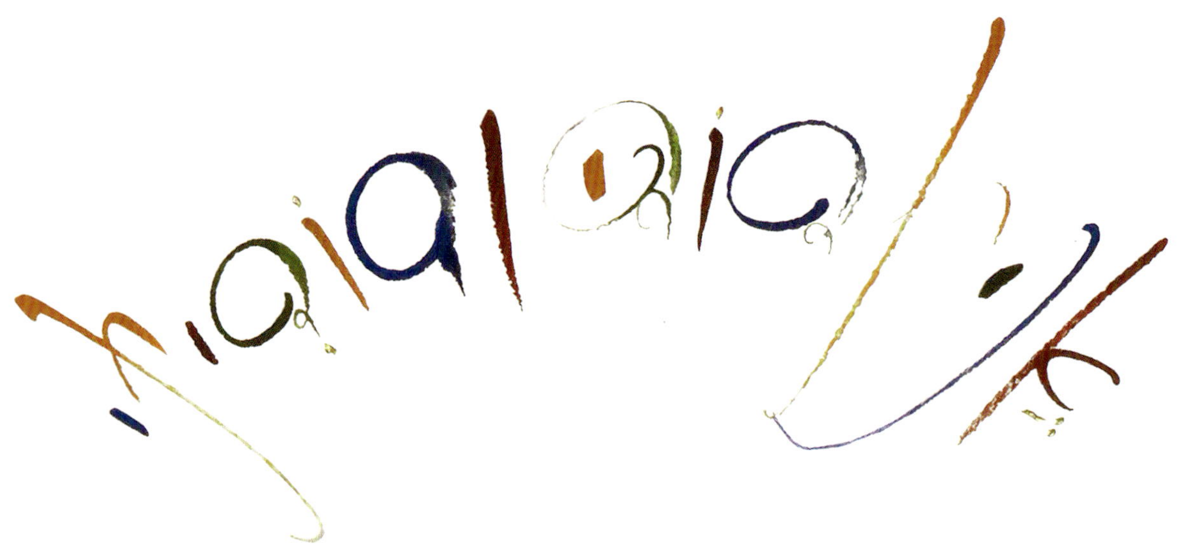

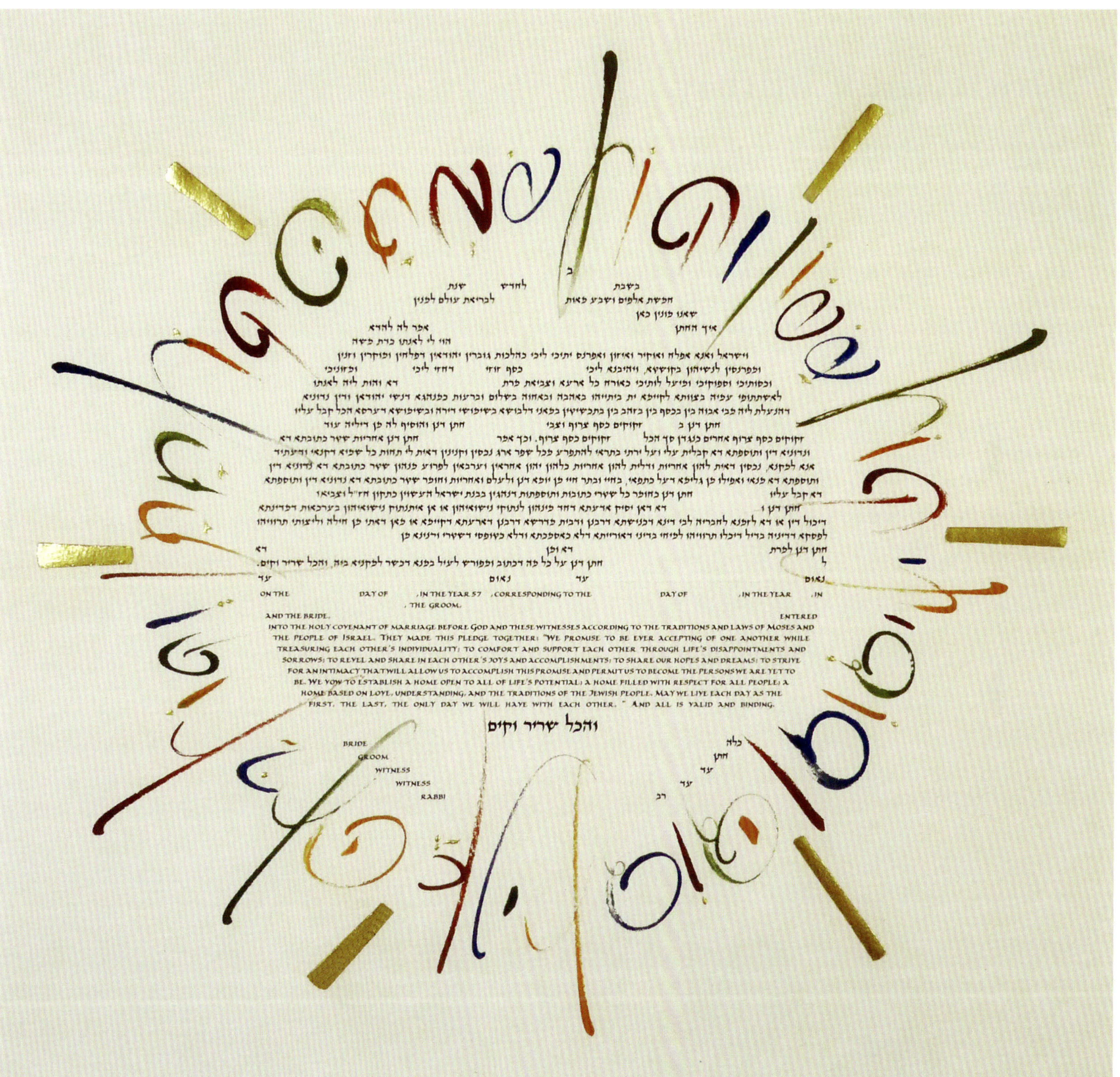

Catalog number Ket 538, courtesy of The Jewish Theological Seminary Library.

Sandi Knell Tamny

"Ortman Gardberg Ketubah"

2002

Canton, Ohio, native Sandi Knell Tamny now resides in North Hollywood, California. Her artwork is an extension of her spiritual and religious curiosity. She works intuitively, creating art by how it "feels."

In this arresting design of concentric circles, a palette of royal blue, pink, gold, and gray embellishes a festive cornucopia of intricately painted symbols including depictions of Jewish rituals and objects, zodiac signs, butterflies, Celtic knots, flowers, fruits, and even a bicycle rotating around the central text. The central interlinear text alternates lines of Hebrew and English.

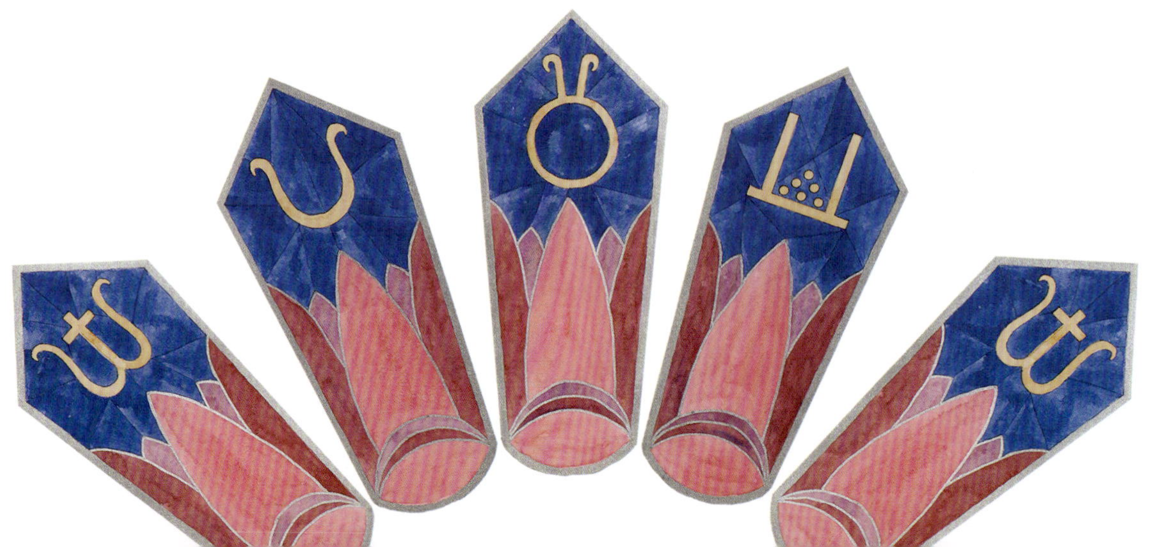

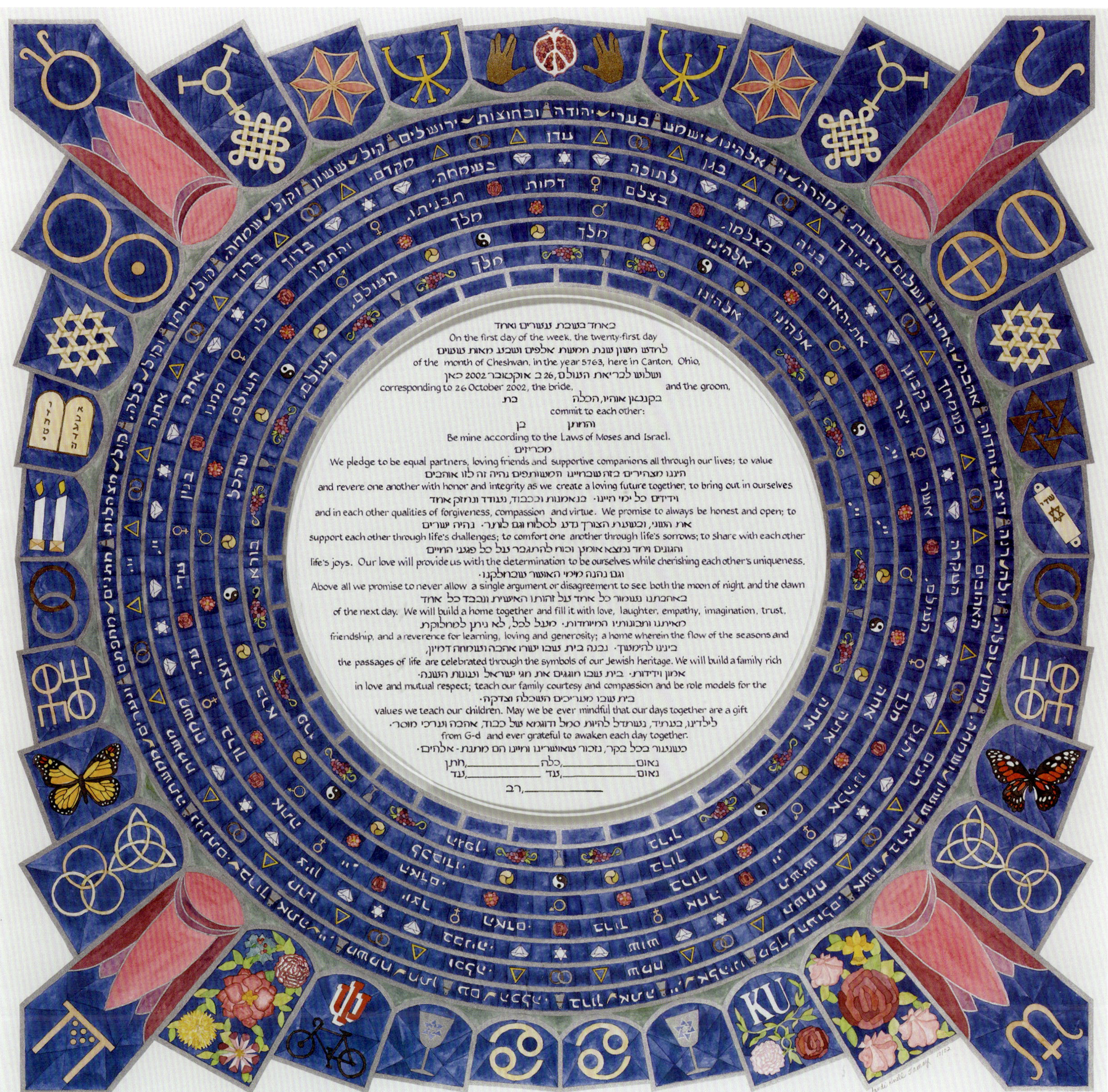

Catalog number Ket-508, courtesy of The Jewish Theological Seminary Library.

Rachel Deitsch

"Trees Ketubah"

2004

Pattern designer and illustrator Rachel Deitsch lives in California. Her "Modern Traditionalist" style of ketubot fuses folk imagery with contemporary watercolor techniques in unusual palettes.

In this ketubah, two separate trunks growing together shelter two long-tailed songbirds, pomegranates (a traditional fertility symbol), and lotus blossoms. The trees merge into a single forest canopy—a symbol of the marriage. Variegated greens in the tree leaves contrast with the lush orange and deep red figures nestled in the foliage, accented by rectangular patterns at the top and bottom that evoke an intricately sewn quilt.

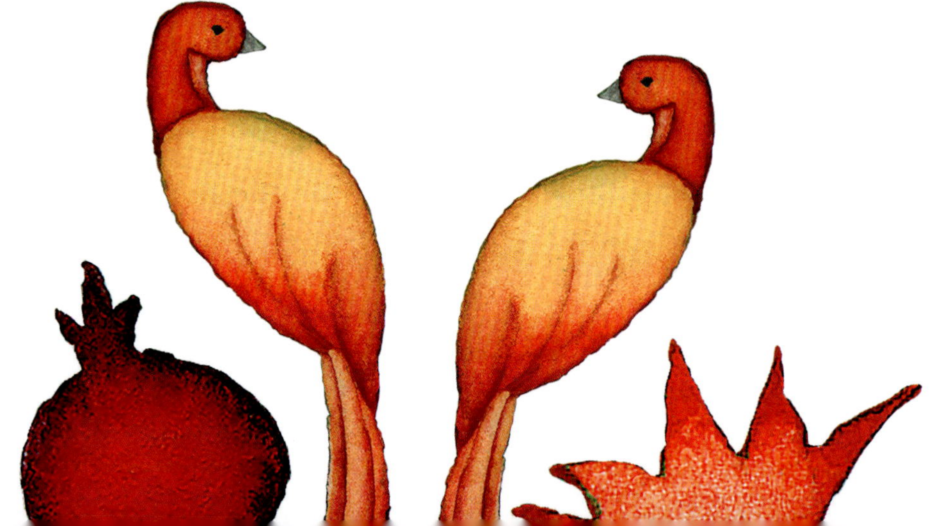

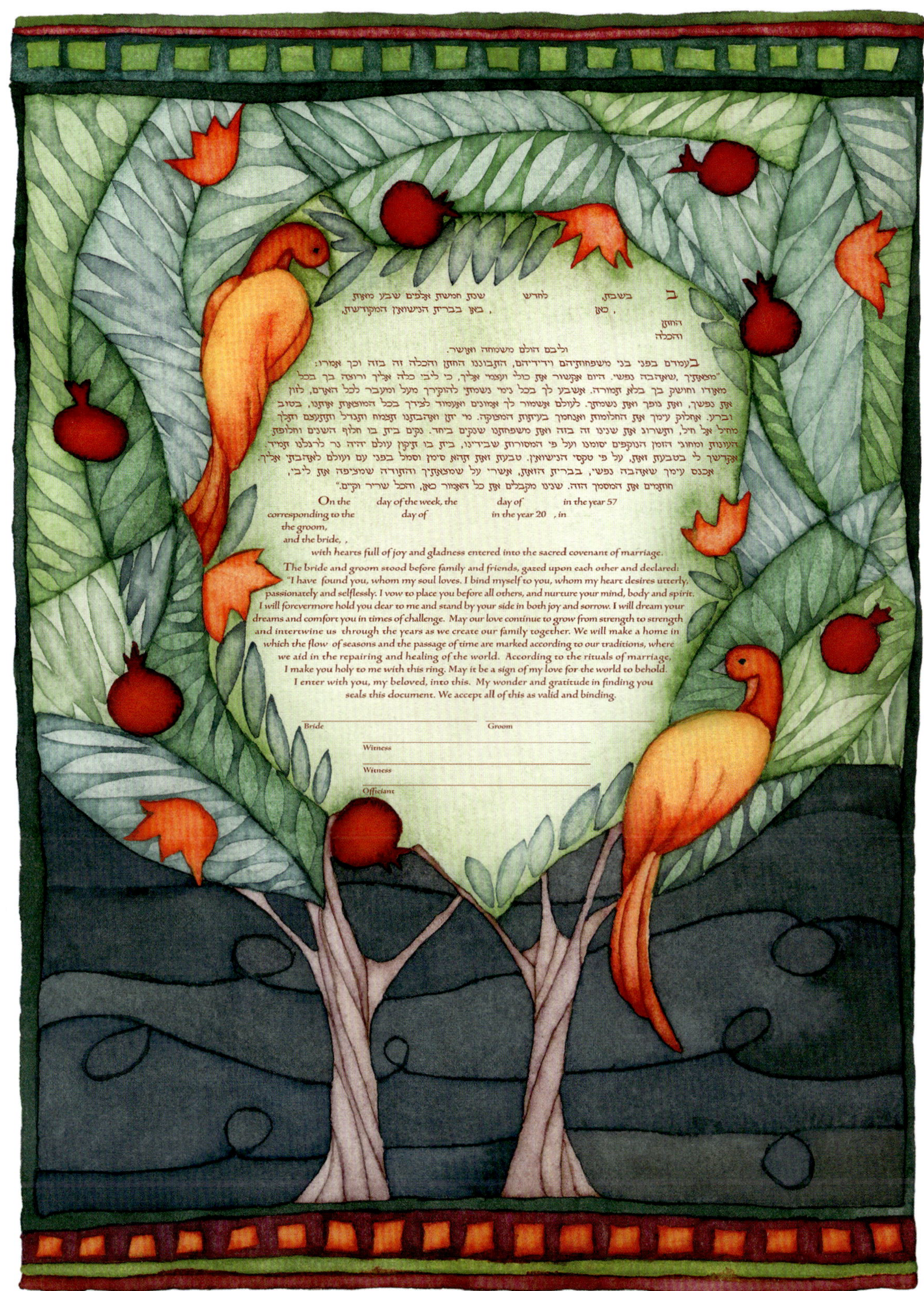

Courtesy of Rachel Deitsch.

Ian Kochberg

"Above All"

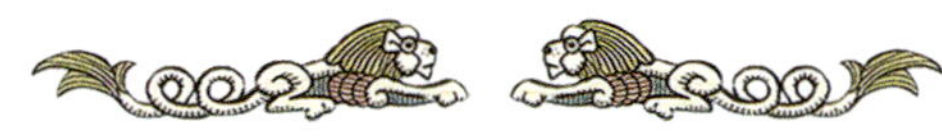

2004

Ian Kochberg is a Canadian artist whose work is a throwback to a time when craftsmanship using pre-Renaissance methods and materials was the norm. His artwork can be found in private and corporate collections worldwide.

This ketubah inspired by Celtic and medieval forms interweaves elaborate silkscreening and embossing techniques performed by hand. At the base of this design, two Lions of Judah represent the bride and groom, their tails intertwined to create a Tree of Life. On each side symbols from Jewish tradition and folklore abound, and a variety of fish appear to swim through the ketubah text, providing a unique whimsical flourish. A medieval-styled musical notation of a tune, an excerpted accompaniment from the *Sheva Brachot* (seven wedding blessings), graces the top of the frame.

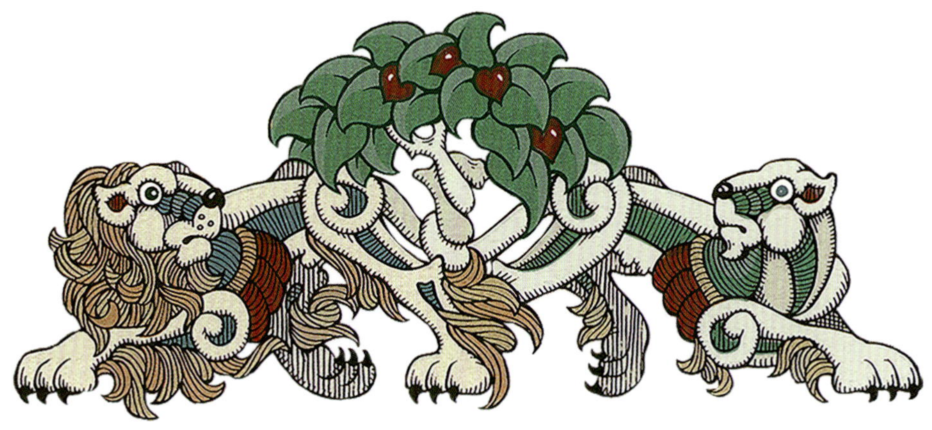

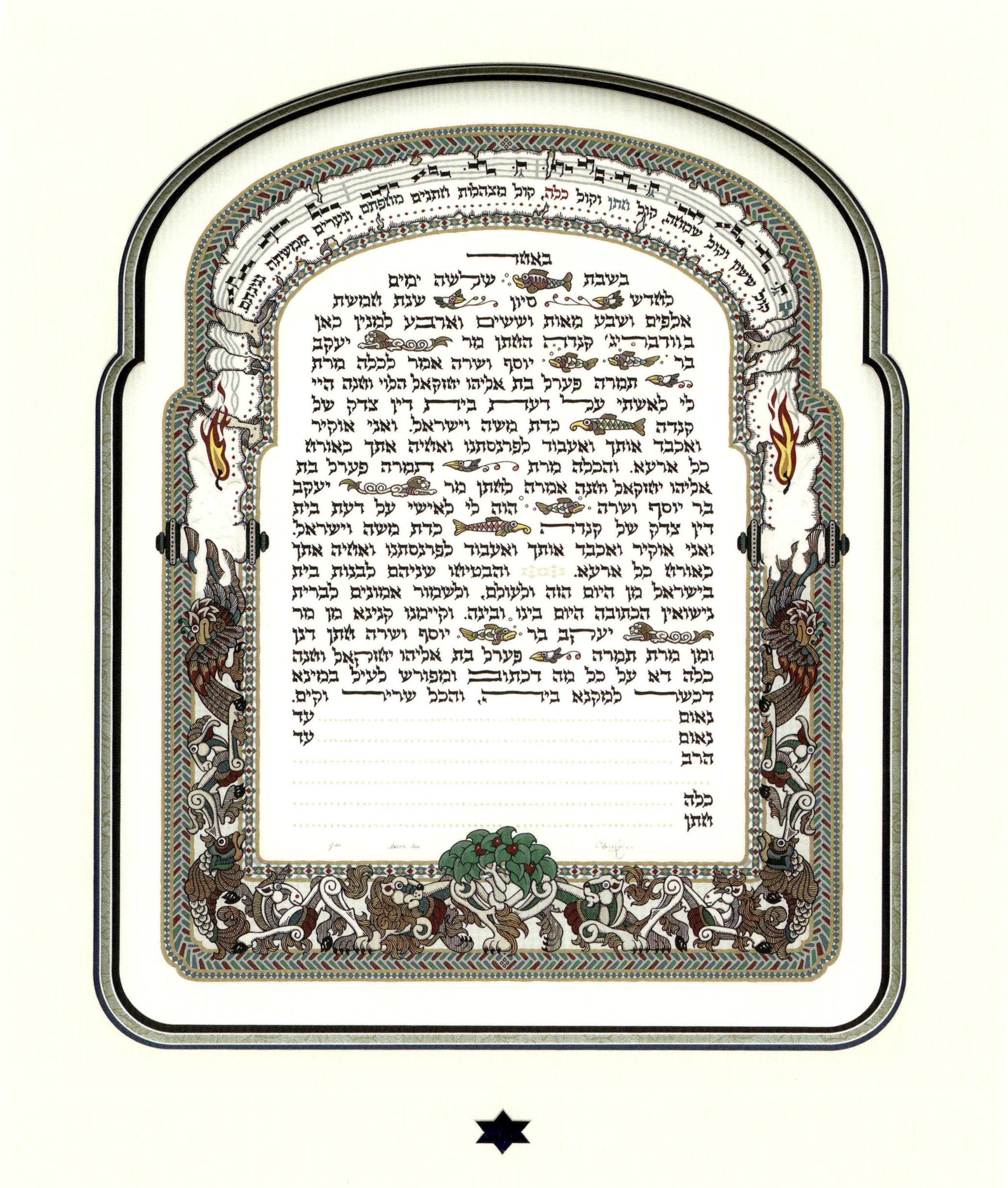

קול ששון וקול שמחה, קול חתן וקול כלה, קול מצהלות חתנים מחופתם, ונערים ממשתה נגינתם.

באחד בשבת שלשה ימים
לחדש סיון שנת חמשת
אלפים ושבע מאות וששים וארבע למנין כאן
בוודברידג' קנדה החתן מר יעקב
בר יוסף ושרה אמר לכלה מרת
תמרה פערל בת אליהו יחזקאל הלוי וחנה הוי
לי לאשתי על דעת בית דין צדק של
קנדה כדת משה וישראל. ואני אוקיר
ואכבד אותך ואעבוד לפרנסתנו ואחיה אתך כאורח
כל ארעא. והכלה מרת תמרה פערל בת
אליהו יחזקאל וחנה אמרה לחתן מר יעקב
בר יוסף ושרה הוה לי לאישי על דעת בית
דין צדק של קנדה כדת משה וישראל.
ואני אוקיר ואכבד אותך ואעבוד לפרנסתנו ואחיה אתך
כאורח כל ארעא. והבטיחו שניהם לבנות בית
בישראל מן היום הזה ולעולם. ולשמור אמונים לברית
נישואין הכתובה היום בינו ובינה. וקיימנו קנינא מן מר
יעקב בר יוסף ושרה חתן דנן
ומן מרת תמרה פערל בת אליהו יחזקאל וחנה
כלה דא על כל מה דכתוב ומפורש לעיל במנא
דכשר למקנא ביה, והכל שריר וקים.

נאום .... עד
נאום .... עד
הרב ....
....
כלה ....
חתן ....

Courtesy of Ian Kochberg.

Oded Ezer

Untitled

2007

Oded Ezer (b. 1972) is a Tel Aviv–based type designer, conceptual typographer, and design educator. He developed the type foundry Ezer Type House in 2001 and designed and illustrated Jonathan Safran Foer's *New American Haggadah*, published in 2012. His work has been exhibited worldwide.

This striking, monochromatic, text-only design is an audacious riff on the traditionally enlarged first word of illuminated Hebrew manuscripts. Ezer also boldly showcases the ketubah text in five languages. In the center is a Hebrew-language text adapted from the traditional Aramaic text, with translations in English, French, Spanish, and Yiddish.

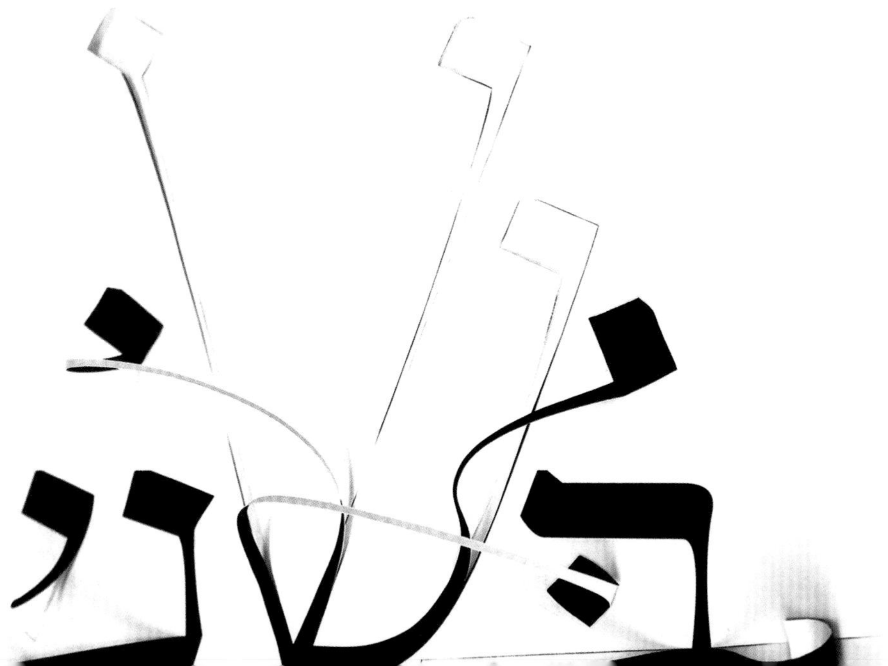

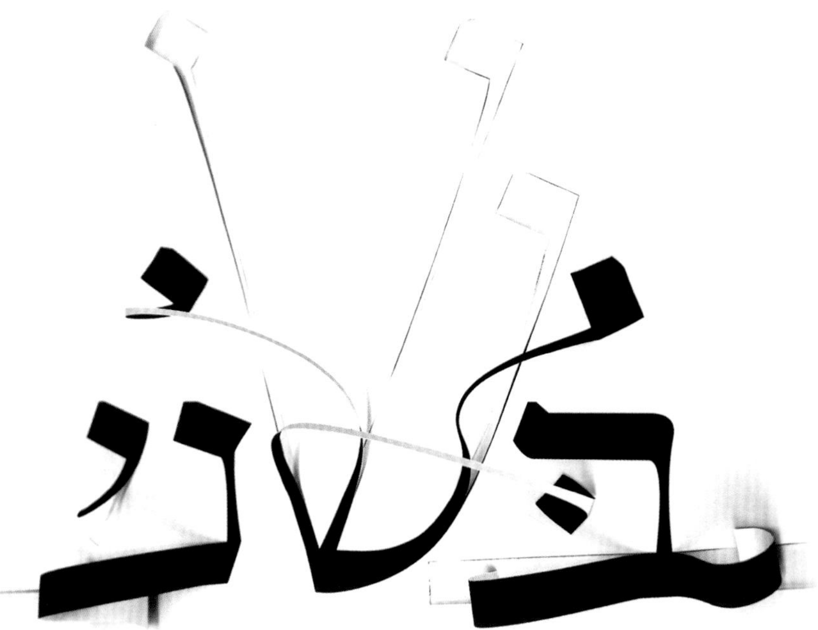

בשבת שני ימים לחדש כסלו שנת חמשת אלפים
ושבע מאות וחמשים ושמונה לבריאת העולם למנין
שאנו מונים כאן בניו־יארק במדינת ארצות הברית
באמריקה אנו עדים איך החתן בן
למשפחת אמר
לכלה שרה בת שעיה שמחה ושושנה למשפחת כפור
הרי את מקודשת לי בטבעת זו כדת משה וישראל
ואיך הכלה בת למשפחת
אמרה לחתן בן
למשפחת הרי אתה
מקודש לי בטבעת זו כדת משה וישראל. החתן
והכלה קבלו על עצמם כל תנאי קידושין
ונישואין המוטלים עליהם מן התורה ומכח בתי דין
של חכמינו זכרונם לברכה. ועוד הסכימו החתן
והכלה מרצונם לעבוד אחד עבור השני ולכבד
ולפרנס ולזון זה את זו וזו את זה ולחיות חיי משפחה
ולבנות יחד בית נאמן כמקובל לבני ולבנות ישראל.
והכלה קבלה טבעת מבחיר לבה והחתן
קבל טבעת מבחירת לבו לשם קידושין
ולסמל אהבתם. החתן והכלה גם קבלו
על עצמם אחריות לתנאי כתובה זו ולכסף ולכלי
הבית הבאים עמם מבתיהם ומבתי משפחותיהם.
וקבלנו קנין מהחתן בן
למשפחת לטובת
הכלה בת למשפחת
ומהכלה בת
למשפחת לטובת החתן בן
למשפחת
בכלי הכשר לקנין והכל שריר וקים.

נאום ______________ עד

נאום ______________ עד

הרב

On the second day after the Sabbath, on the second day of the month of Kislev, in the Jewish year of 5768, in New York, USA, we witness how the groom, said to the bride, "Behold, you are consecrated unto me through this ring according to the laws of Moses and the people Israel," and how the bride, said to the groom, as is the custom of Jewish women in our times, "Behold, you are consecrated unto me through this ring according to the laws of Moses and the people Israel." and accepted upon themselves all the conditions of the Jewish marriage commanded to them by the Torah and the Courts of Law of our rabbis, may their memories be for a blessing. and both agree, of their own will, to accept responsibility for each other, to honor, and to cherish each other, to provide for and to sustain each other. and resolve to live a Jewish life and to build a home faithful to the Jewish tradition. The bride and the groom have each received a ring of their own choice, representing the dimension of holiness brought into their marriage by the Jewish ceremony. This ring also symbolizes their mutual love. The bride and the groom together accept responsibility for this ketubah and for all the belongings they brought into this marriage, from their own homes and their families. This document was signed by the bride and the groom and their appointed witnesses.

Au deuxième jour de la semaine, le deuxième jour de Kislev, en l'an 5768, à New York, aux Etats-Unis, nous nous proclamons témoins que le fiancé a dit à la fiancée , "par cet anneau tu deviens ma femme selon la loi de Moïse et d'Israël," et que la fiancée a dit au fiancé, selon les coutumes actuelles des femmes juives, "par cet anneau tu deviens mon mari selon la loi de Moïse et d'Israël." et ont accepté toutes les conditions du mariage juif exigées par la Thora et les cours de justice de nos rabbins; que leur mémoire soit bénie. et consentent, selon leur propre volonté, de se chérir l'un l'autre, de pourvoir à leurs besoins respectifs, de se soutenir l'un l'autre avec fidélité et intégrité. et engagent à vivre une vie juive et à construire un foyer fidèle à la tradition juive. La fiancée et le fiancé ont tous deux reçu une alliance qu'ils ont choisie et qui représente la sanctification de leur mariage par la cérémonie juive. Cette alliance symbolise également leur amour réciproque. La fiancée et le fiancé acceptent ensemble la responsabilité de cette kétouba et de toutes les possessions qu'ils ont placées au sein de cette union, qu'elles soient les leurs ou celles de leurs parents. Le présent acte a été signé par les époux et les témoins pour valoir comme attestation authentique de l'union ainsi consacrée devant la communauté d'Israël.

En el segundo día de la semana, el segundo día del mes de Kislev del año 5768 según el calendario judío, en la ciudad de Nueva York, somos testigos que el novio declaró a la novia "Tú me eres consagrada por medio de este anillo de acuerdo con la ley de Moisés y el pueblo de Israel," y que la novia declaró al novio tal como es costumbre de las mujeres de nuestra época, "Tú me eres consagrado por medio de este anillo de acuerdo con la ley de Moisés y el pueblo de Israel." y aceptaron todas las condiciones del matrimonio judío que emanan de la Tora y de los tribunales de nuestros rabinos de bendita memoria. y se comprometen por voluntad propia a ser responsables el uno por el otro, a respetarse y amarse, a proveerse y apoyarse mutuamente. y se comprometen a vivir una vida judía y a construir un hogar leal a la tradición judía. Ambos novios han recibido un anillo por elección propia, el cual representa la dimensión sagrada que trae al matrimonio la ceremonia judía. Este anillo simboliza también su mutuo amor. Los novios aceptan conjuntamente la responsabilidad de esta ketubá y de todas las posesiones que han traído a este matrimonio de sus propios hogares y de sus familias. Este documento ha sido firmado por el novio, la novia y por los testigos que han designado.

צווי טעג נאָך שבת, דעם צווייטן טאָג כסלו, אין דעם ייִדישן יאָר 5768, אין שטאָט ניו־יאָרק, אין די פֿאַראייניקטע שטאַטן, זײַנען מיר עדות ווי דער חתן האָט געזאָגט דער כלה , "אָט ביסטו מיר מקודש מיט דעם פֿינגערל לויט די דינים פֿון משה און עם ישראל," און ווי די כלה שרה האָט געזאָגט דעם חתן לויט דעם מינהג פֿון ייִדישע טעכטער אין אונדזער צײַט, "אָט ביסטו מיר מקודש מיט דעם פֿינגערל לויט די דינים פֿון משה און עם ישראל." און האָבן אָנגענומען אויף זיך אַלע תנאי קידושין ונישואין וואָס די תורה און דינים פֿון אונדזערע רבנים, געבענטשט זאָלן זיי זײַן, באַפֿעלן. און זײַנען מסכים צו טראָגן אַחריות איינער פֿאַרן אַנדערן, אָפּצוגעבן כבוד, צו האַלטן זיך נאָענט, צו באַזאָרגן, צו שאַנעווען איינעם דעם צווייטן. און באַשליסן צו לעבן אַ ייִדיש לעבן און צו בויען אַ היים וואָס איז געטרײַ צו דער ייִדישע מסורה. סײַ דער חתן און סײַ די כלה האָבן באַקומען אַ פֿינגערל וואָס זיי האָבן אויסגעקליבן, וואָס איז אַ סימן פֿון דער הייליקייט וואָס זיי האָבן אַרײַנגעבראַכט אין זייער חתונה לויט די ייִדישע דינים און מינהגים. דאָס פֿינגערל סימבאָליזירט אויך זייער גרויס ליבע איינער פֿאַרן אַנדערן. דער חתן און די כלה ביידע נעמען אויף זיך די אַחריות פֿאַר דער כתובה און פֿאַר אַלע זאַכן וואָס זיי האָבן געבראַכט צו דער חתונה, פֿון זייערע היימען און זייערע משפּחות. דעם דאָקומענט האָבן געחתמעט דער חתן און די כלה און זייערע עדות.

Courtesy of Oded Ezer.

Amy Fagin

"Embrace"

2007

Influenced by world art history, Massachusetts artist Amy Fagin (b. 1959) reimagines the principles of manuscript illumination in contemporary art form.

In this design, a hallmark of Fagin's signature style, multiple swirling patterns and scrolls in multicolor vibrance frame two unusual text block shapes. Arrangements of color, pattern symbolism, and geometric composition coalesce in a joyful celebration of life, love, and marriage.

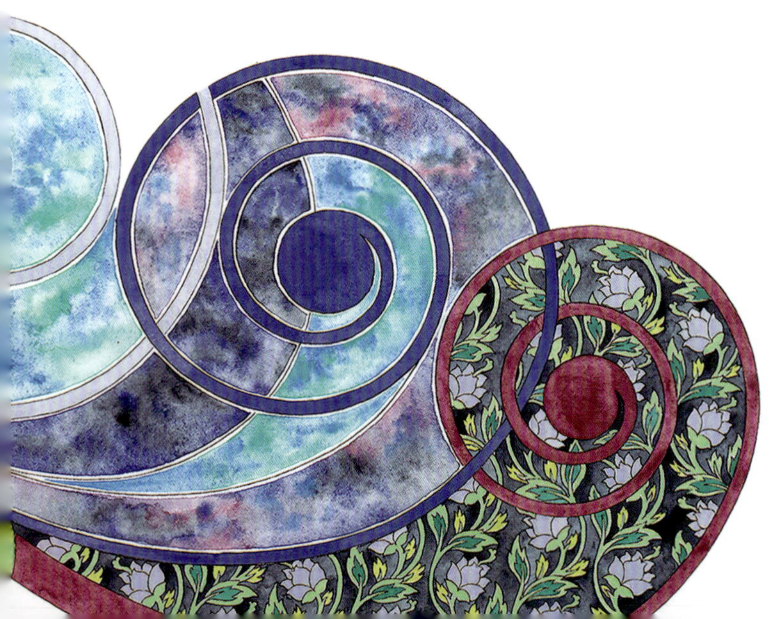

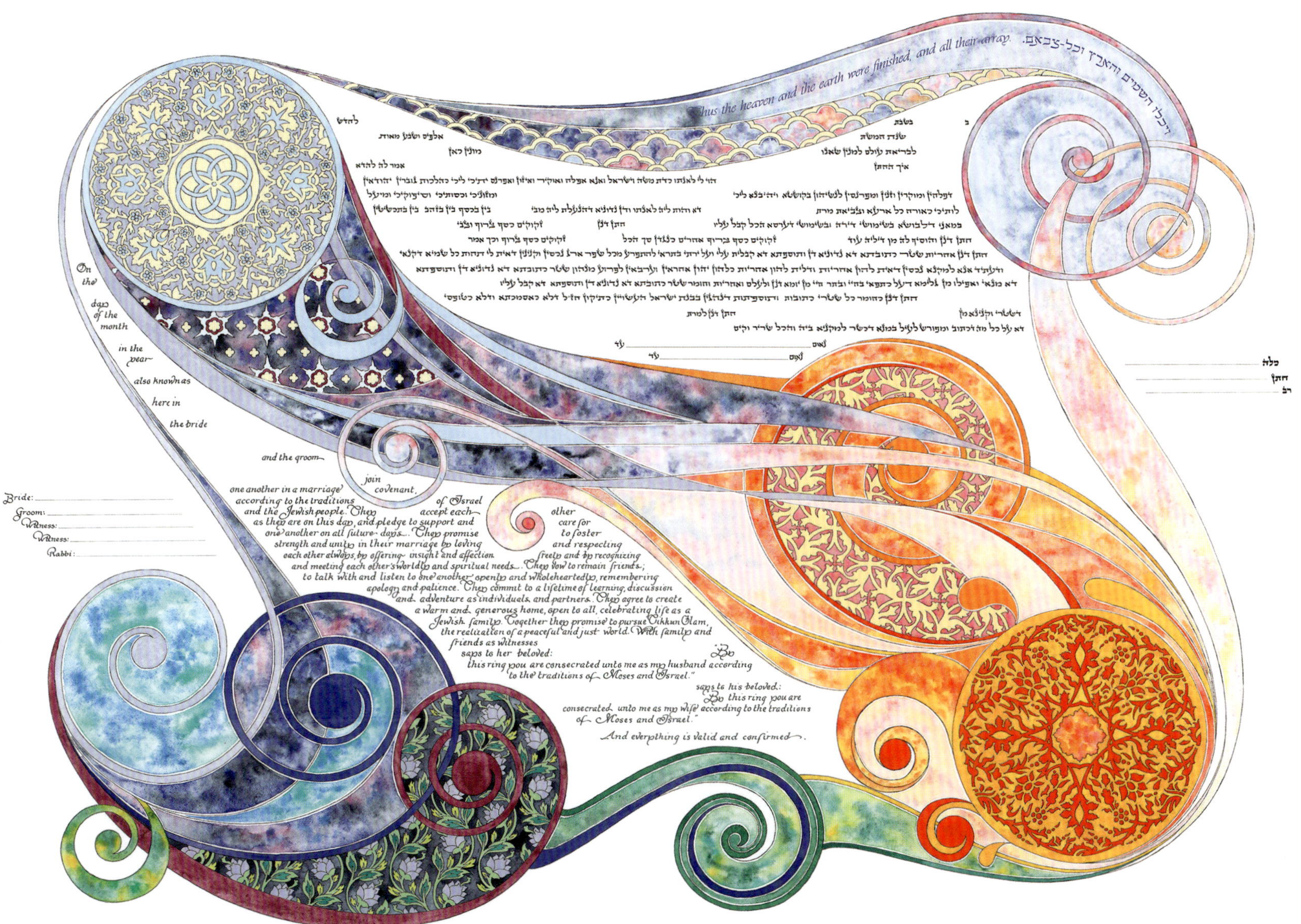

Courtesy of Amy Fagin.

Diane Palley

"Hamsa Ketubah"

2007

New Jersey–born artist Diane Palley (b. 1949) works today in New Mexico in multiple media, including papercutting, printmaking, illustration, ceramics, and fabrics. Her ketubot feature playfully precise symbols and integrate imagery from a wide variety of cultural traditions.

Framed in the image of the *hamsa* that symbolizes protection in Jewish and Islamic cultures, this design displays a menagerie of flora and fauna, as well as the cycles of the moon, candlesticks, and architectural monuments. Looking closely, one can identify the species of the trees, and spot an endangered tree frog, a reminder of the interconnection of all life.

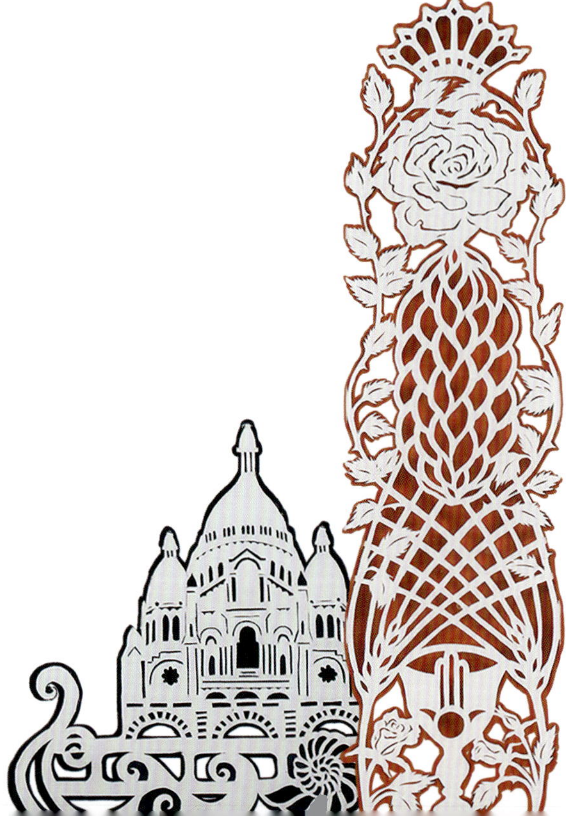

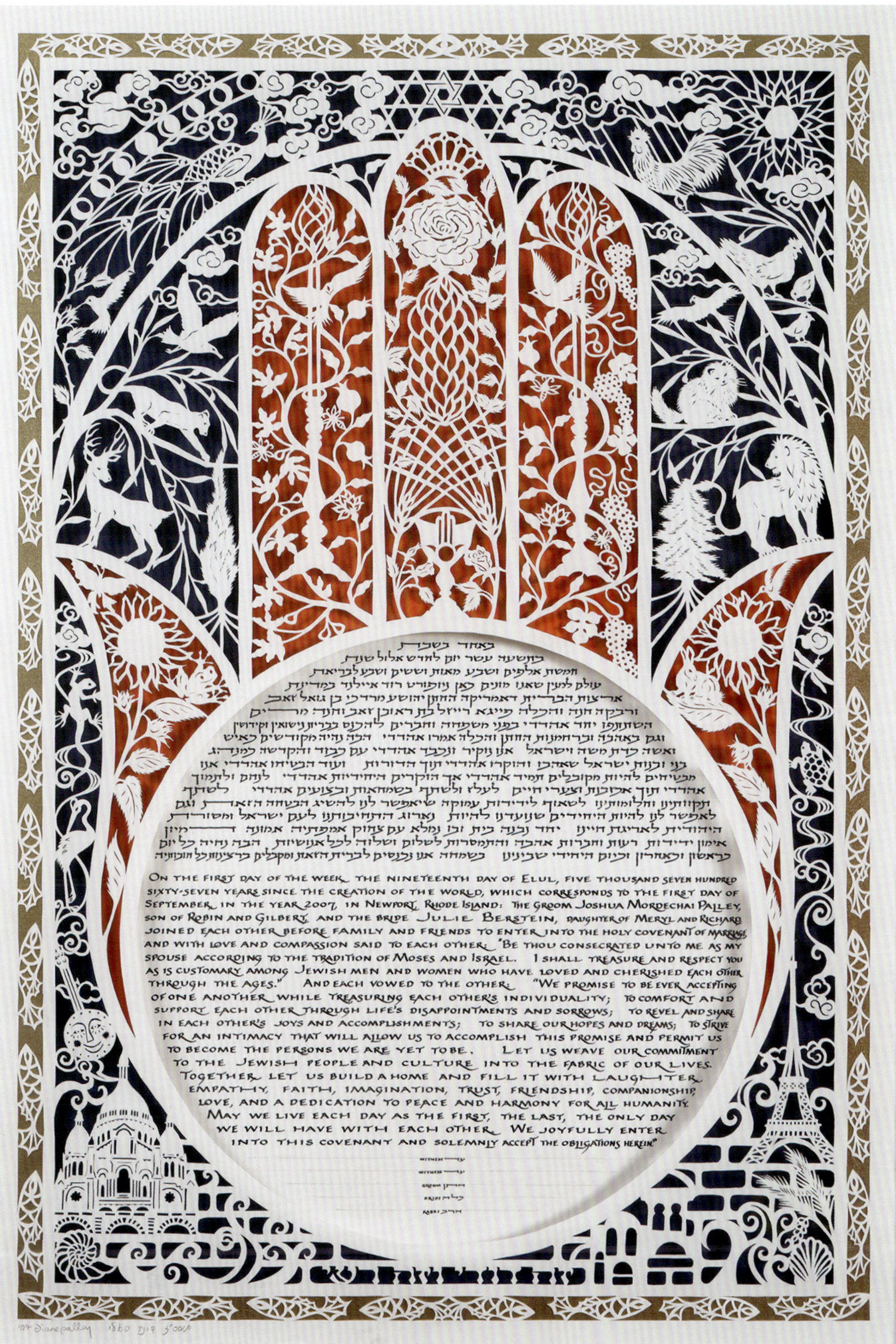

Courtesy of Diane Palley.

Ruth Stern Warzecha

"Gefen Papercut—Charcoal"

2008

Jerusalem resident Ruth Stern Warzecha was born in Toronto into a family of religious scribes, and her art is often inspired by poignant biblical phrases. She specializes in calligraphy, papercutting, glass, and needlepoint design. For her, creating ketubot is a natural fusion of these art forms.

Papercutting is enjoying a resurgence in ketubah design in the current period, and many artists are pushing the boundaries of this traditional Jewish art form. In Warzecha's intricate design, the circular ketubah text sits within a square of meandering grapevines, anchored by four delicate cornices. Running around the border in Hebrew and English is a verse from Jeremiah 25:10 traditionally sung at weddings: "the voice of joy and gladness, the voice of the groom and the voice of the bride."

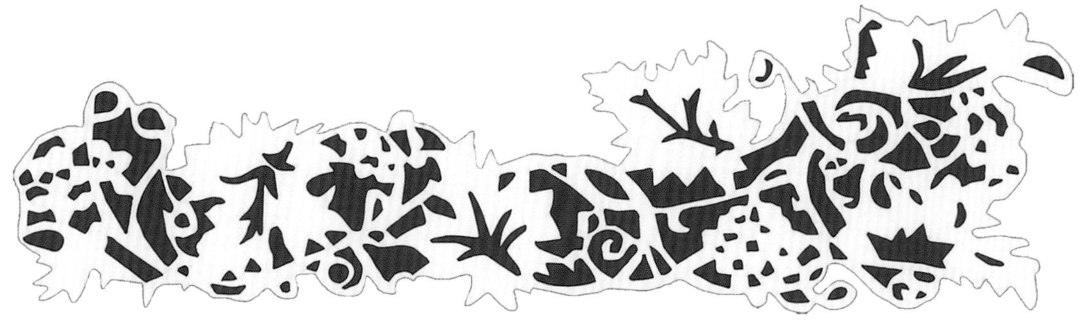

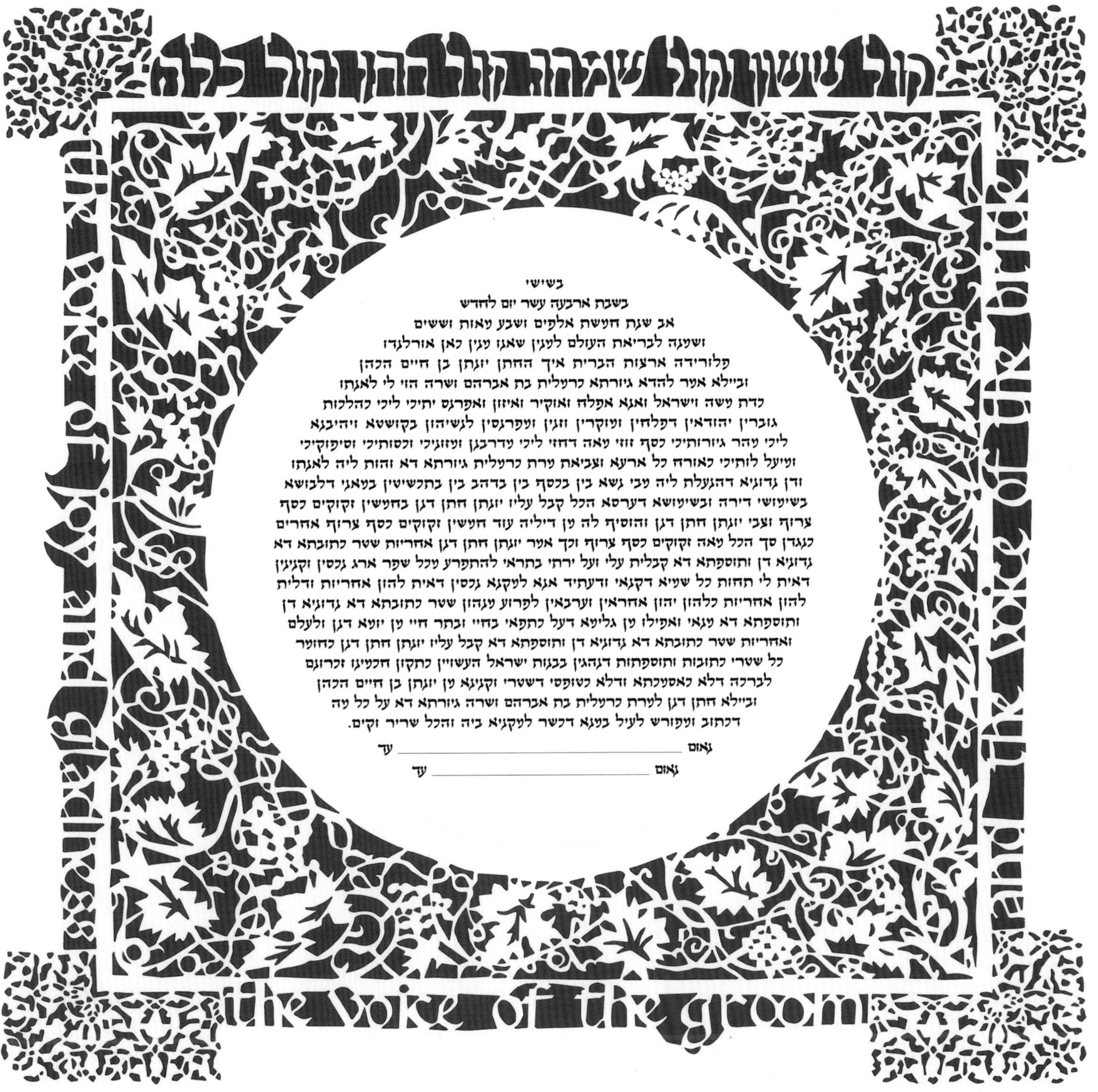

בשישי
בשבת ארבעה עשר יום לחדש
אב שנת חמשת אלפים ושבע מאות וששים
ושמנה לבריאת העולם למנין שאנו מנין כאן אורלנדו
פלורידה ארצות הברית איך החתן יונתן בן חיים הכהן
וביילא אמר להדא גיורתא כרמלית בת אברהם ושרה הוי לי לאנתו
כדת משה וישראל ואנא אפלח ואוקיר ואיזון ואפרנס יתיכי ליכי כהלכות
גוברין יהודאין דפלחין ומוקרין וזנין ומפרנסין לנשיהון בקושטא ויהיבנא
ליכי מהר גיורותיכי כסף זוזי מאה דחזי ליכי מדרבנן ומזוניכי וכסותיכי וסיפוקיכי
ומיעל לותיכי כאורח כל ארעא וצביאת מרת כרמלית גיורתא דא והות ליה לאנתו
ודן נדוניא דהנעלת ליה מבי נשא בין בכסף בין בדהב בין בתכשיטין במאני דלבושא
בשימושי דירה ובשימושא דערסא הכל קבל עליו יונתן חתן דנן בחמשין זקוקים כסף
צרוף וצבי יונתן חתן דנן והוסיף לה מן דיליה עוד חמשין זקוקים כסף צרוף אחרים
כנגדן סך הכל מאה זקוקים כסף צרוף וכך אמר יונתן חתן דנן אחריות שטר כתובתא דא
נדוניא דן ותוספתא דא קבלית עלי ועל ירתי בתראי להתפרע מכל שפר ארג נכסין וקנינין
דאית לי תחות כל שמיא דקנאי ודעתיד אנא למקנא נכסין דאית להון אחריות ודלית
להון אחריות כלהון יהון אחראין וערבאין לפרוע מנהון שטר כתובתא דא נדוניא דן
ותוספתא דא מנאי ואפילו מן גלימא דעל כתפאי בחיי ובתר חיי מן יומא דנן ולעלם
ואחריות שטר כתובתא דא נדוניא דן ותוספתא דא קבל עליו יונתן חתן דנן כחומר
כל שטרי כתובות ותוספתות דנהגין בבנות ישראל העשויין כתקון חכמינו זכרונם
לברכה דלא כאסמכתא ודלא כטופסי דשטרי וקנינא מן יונתן בן חיים הכהן
וביילא חתן דנן למרת כרמלית בת אברהם ושרה גיורתא דא על כל מה
דכתוב ומפורש לעיל במנא דכשר למקניא ביה והכל שריר וקים.

נאום ______________________ עד

נאום ______________________ עד

Courtesy of Ketubah.com.

Dafna Jalon

"Growing Together"

2009

Toronto-based artist Dafna Jalon is animated by modern stained-glass motifs. Her mixed media art showcasing nature and biblical themes is notable for its bright colors and dynamic feel.

For this multilayered contemporary ketubah Jalon created a new twist on the classic two trees motif. Here, the overlapping trunks support elegantly sweeping tree boughs unfurling stylized leaves that flow in the wind. The undulating lavender sky is patterned and translucent looking, like stained glass. Remarkably, this effect is achieved using digital tools. Light seems to shine through this hand-cut layered version, an illusion made possible by Jalon's superlative graphic design.

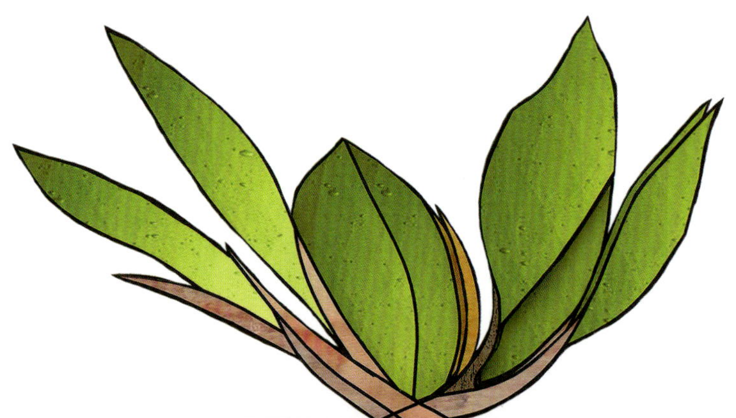

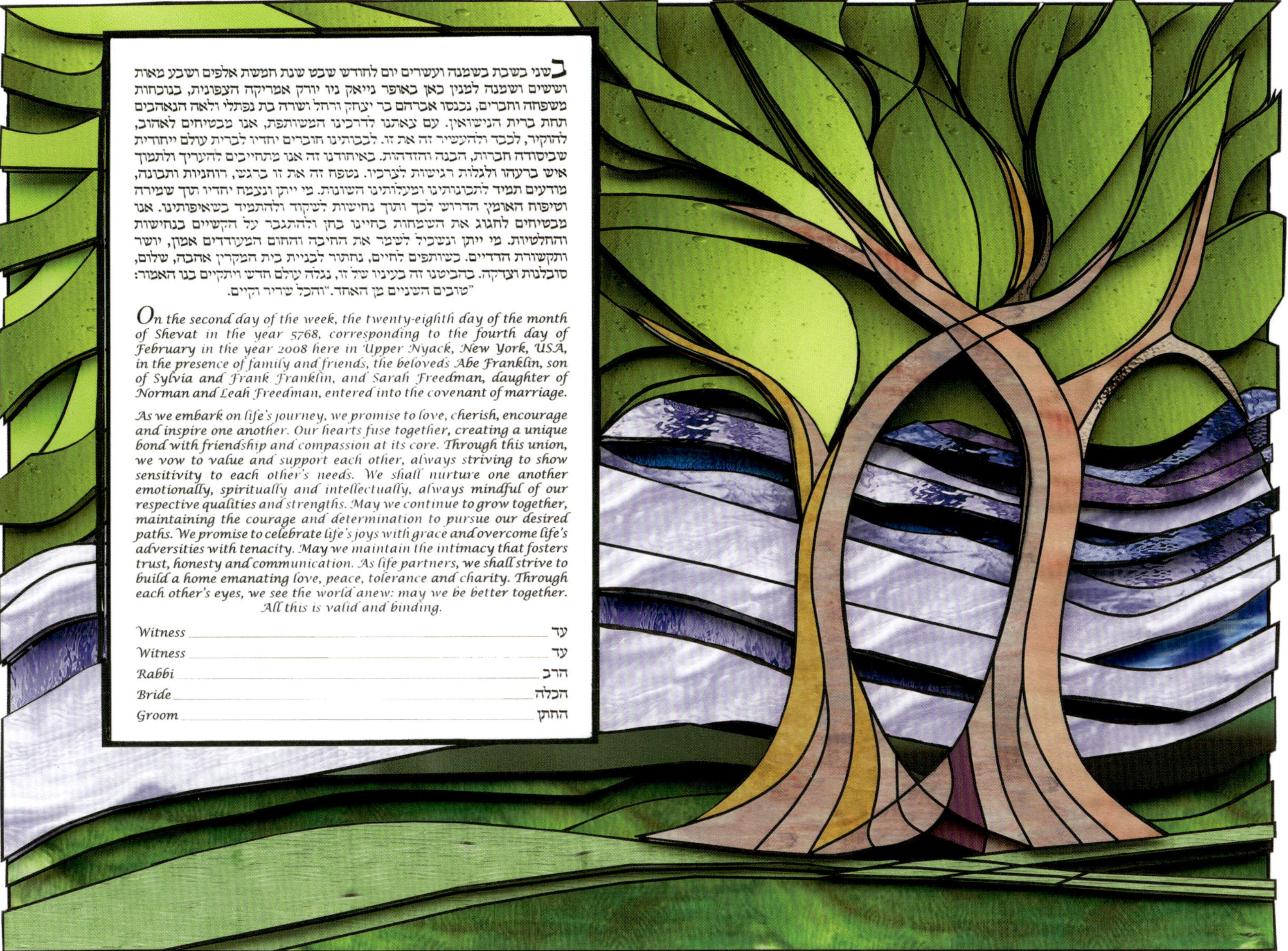

בשני בשבת בשמנה ועשרים יום לחודש שבט שנת חמשת אלפים ושבע מאות
וששים ושמנה למנין כאן באופר נייאק ניו יורק אמריקה הצפונית, בנוכחות
משפחה וחברים, נכנסו אברהם בר יצחק ורחל ושרה בת נפתלי ולאה הנאהבים
תחת ברית הנישואין. עם צאתנו לדרכינו המשותפת, אנו מבטיחים לאהוב,
להוקיר, לכבד ולהעשיר זה את זו. לבבותינו חוברים יחדיו לברית עולם ייחודית
שביסודה חברות, הבנה והזדהות. באיחודנו זה אנו מתחייבים להעריך ולתמוך
איש ברעהו ולגלות רגישות לצרכיו. נטפח זה את זו ברגש, רוחניות ותבונה,
מודעים תמיד לתכונותינו ומעלותינו השונות. מי ייתן ונצמח יחדיו תוך שמירה
וטיפוח האומץ הדרוש לכך ותוך נחישות לשקוד ולהתמיד בשאיפותינו. אנו
מבטיחים לחגוג את השמחות בחיינו בחן ולהתגבר על הקשיים בנחישות
והחלטיות. מי ייתן ונשכיל לשמר את החיבה והחום המעודדים אמון, יושר
ותקשורת הדדיים. כשותפים לחיים, נחתור לבניית בית המקרין אהבה, שלום,
סובלנות וצדקה. בהביטנו זה בעיניו של זו, נגלה עולם חדש ויתקיים בנו האמור:
"טובים השניים מן האחד." והכל שריר וקיים.

On the second day of the week, the twenty-eighth day of the month of Shevat in the year 5768, corresponding to the fourth day of February in the year 2008 here in Upper Nyack, New York, USA, in the presence of family and friends, the beloveds Abe Franklin, son of Sylvia and Frank Franklin, and Sarah Freedman, daughter of Norman and Leah Freedman, entered into the covenant of marriage.

As we embark on life's journey, we promise to love, cherish, encourage and inspire one another. Our hearts fuse together, creating a unique bond with friendship and compassion at its core. Through this union, we vow to value and support each other, always striving to show sensitivity to each other's needs. We shall nurture one another emotionally, spiritually and intellectually, always mindful of our respective qualities and strengths. May we continue to grow together, maintaining the courage and determination to pursue our desired paths. We promise to celebrate life's joys with grace and overcome life's adversities with tenacity. May we maintain the intimacy that fosters trust, honesty and communication. As life partners, we shall strive to build a home emanating love, peace, tolerance and charity. Through each other's eyes, we see the world anew: may we be better together. All this is valid and binding.

Witness ______ עד
Witness ______ עד
Rabbi ______ הרב
Bride ______ הכלה
Groom ______ החתן

Courtesy of Ketubah.com.

Judith Joseph

“Blue Forest”

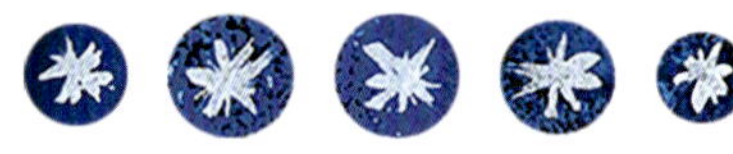

2009

Chicago-based artist Judith Joseph creates woodblock prints, paintings, and installations. Her conceptual art practice is paired with her work as a calligrapher and illustrator, and her specialty is ketubah art. In many of her ketubot, she practices sumi-e, a highly intentional Japanese style of brushwork in which each stroke of paint conveys a sense of vitality and beauty. Her artwork has been exhibited and collected internationally.

The calming, embracing blue of this double tree design calls to mind the ancient Tree of Life and the Tree of Knowledge coming together in union, forging a chuppah in a forest clearing. The color blue plays a prominent role in Jewish tradition. The term *tekhelet*, which refers to a range of blue hues, was used to construct the Tabernacle and the Holy Temple in Jerusalem, and now is used in individual ritual practice. Here it also represents equilibrium, as a shade midway between white and black, day and evening.

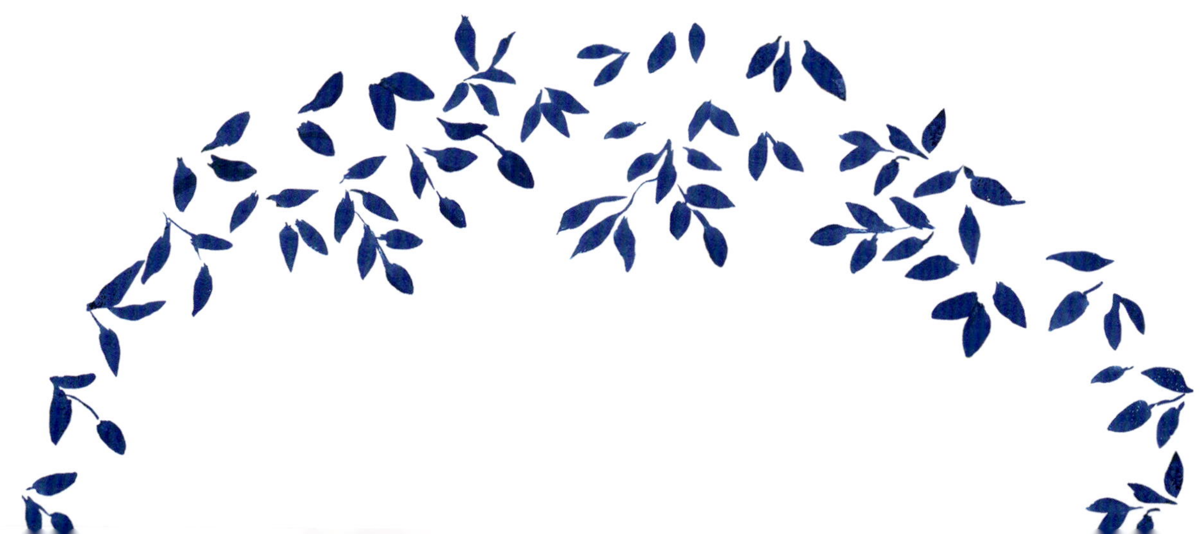

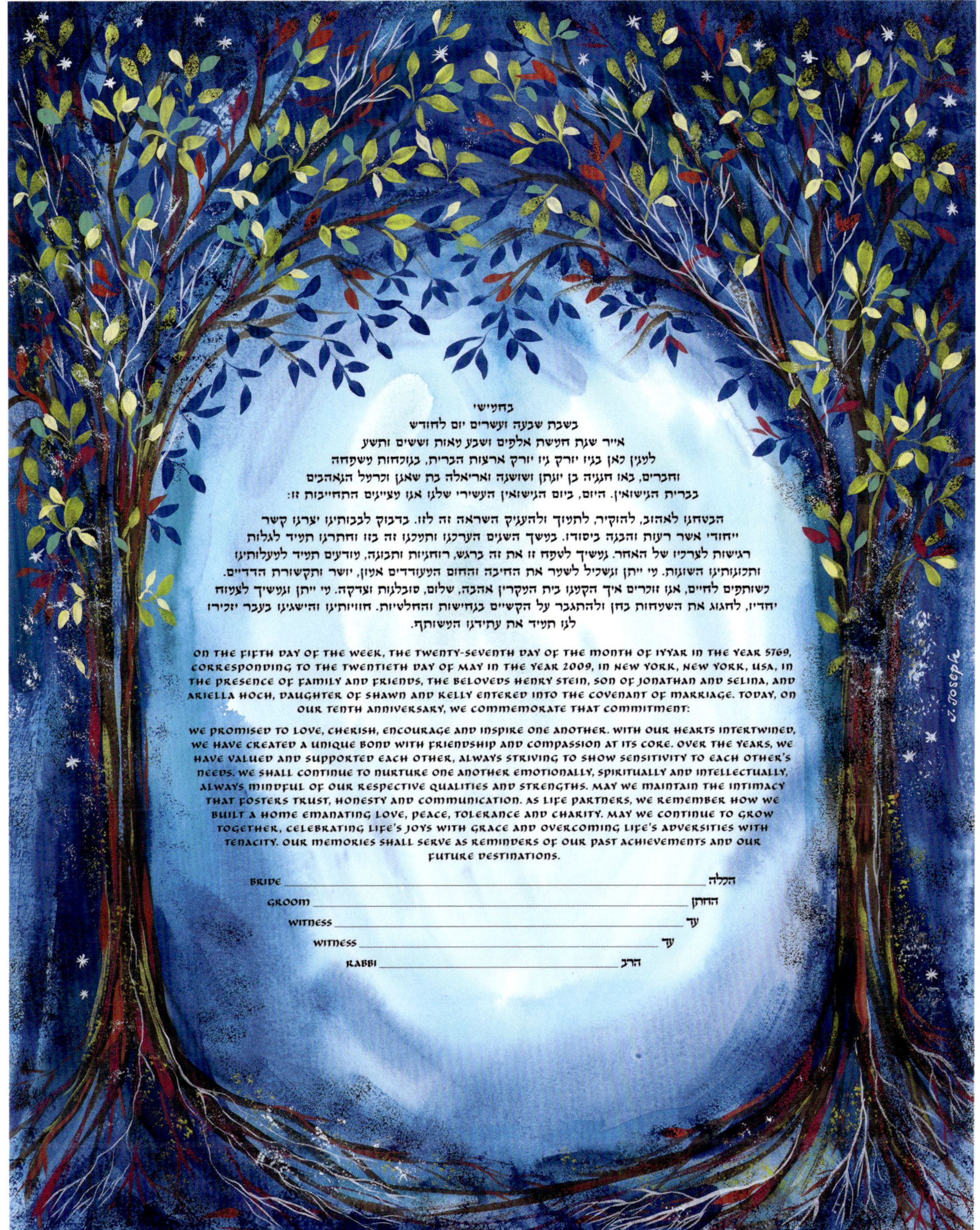

בחמישי
בשבת שבעה ועשרים יום לחודש
אייר שנת חמשת אלפים ושבע מאות וששים ותשע
למנין כאן בניו יורק ניו יורק ארצות הברית, בנוכחות משפחה
וחברים, באו הנריה בן יונתן ושושנה ואריאלה בת שאון וכרמל הנאהבים
בברית הנישואין. היום, ביום הנישואין העשירי שלנו אנו מציינים התחייבות זו:

הבטחנו לאהוב, להוקיר, לתמוך ולהעניק השראה זה לזו. בדבוק לבבותינו יצרנו קשר
ייחודי אשר רעות והבנה ביסודו. במשך השנים הערכנו ותמכנו זה בזו וחתרנו תמיד לגלות
רגישות לצרכיו של האחר. נמשיך לטפח זו את זה ברגש, רוחניות ותבונה, מודעים תמיד למעלותינו
ותכונותינו השונות. מי ייתן ונשכיל לשמר את החיבה והחום המעודדים אמון, יושר ותקשורת הדדיים.
כשותפים לחיים, אנו זוכרים איך הקמנו בית המקרין אהבה, שלום, סובלנות וצדקה. מי ייתן ונמשיך לצמוח
יחדיו, לחגוג את השמחות בחן ולהתגבר על הקשיים בנחישות והחלטיות. חוויותינו והישגינו בעבר יזכירו
לנו תמיד את עתידנו המשותף.

ON THE FIFTH DAY OF THE WEEK, THE TWENTY-SEVENTH DAY OF THE MONTH OF IYYAR IN THE YEAR 5769, CORRESPONDING TO THE TWENTIETH DAY OF MAY IN THE YEAR 2009, IN NEW YORK, NEW YORK, USA, IN THE PRESENCE OF FAMILY AND FRIENDS, THE BELOVEDS HENRY STEIN, SON OF JONATHAN AND SELINA, AND ARIELLA HOCH, DAUGHTER OF SHAWN AND KELLY ENTERED INTO THE COVENANT OF MARRIAGE. TODAY, ON OUR TENTH ANNIVERSARY, WE COMMEMORATE THAT COMMITMENT:

WE PROMISED TO LOVE, CHERISH, ENCOURAGE AND INSPIRE ONE ANOTHER. WITH OUR HEARTS INTERTWINED, WE HAVE CREATED A UNIQUE BOND WITH FRIENDSHIP AND COMPASSION AT ITS CORE. OVER THE YEARS, WE HAVE VALUED AND SUPPORTED EACH OTHER, ALWAYS STRIVING TO SHOW SENSITIVITY TO EACH OTHER'S NEEDS. WE SHALL CONTINUE TO NURTURE ONE ANOTHER EMOTIONALLY, SPIRITUALLY AND INTELLECTUALLY, ALWAYS MINDFUL OF OUR RESPECTIVE QUALITIES AND STRENGTHS. MAY WE MAINTAIN THE INTIMACY THAT FOSTERS TRUST, HONESTY AND COMMUNICATION. AS LIFE PARTNERS, WE REMEMBER HOW WE BUILT A HOME EMANATING LOVE, PEACE, TOLERANCE AND CHARITY. MAY WE CONTINUE TO GROW TOGETHER, CELEBRATING LIFE'S JOYS WITH GRACE AND OVERCOMING LIFE'S ADVERSITIES WITH TENACITY. OUR MEMORIES SHALL SERVE AS REMINDERS OF OUR PAST ACHIEVEMENTS AND OUR FUTURE DESTINATIONS.

BRIDE ____________________ הכלה
GROOM ____________________ החתן
WITNESS ____________________ עד
WITNESS ____________________ עד
RABBI ____________________ הרב

Courtesy of Ketubah.com.

Jessica Carew Kraft

“Four Seasons”

2009

Jessica Carew Kraft resides in the Sierra Foothills. The author of *Why We Need to Be Wild: One Woman’s Quest for Ancient Answers to 21st Century Problems* (2023), she constructs ketubot rooted in her deep immersion in nature. Her portrayal of seasons in ketubot speaks to the steadfast persistence of time and the blessing of the marrying couple’s enduring love through the coming years.

In this impressionist and Fauvist-inspired work, Winter, Spring, Summer, and Fall trees glimmer with vivid color while dots of paint rise and scatter like confetti, framing seamless color transitions around the commitment text.

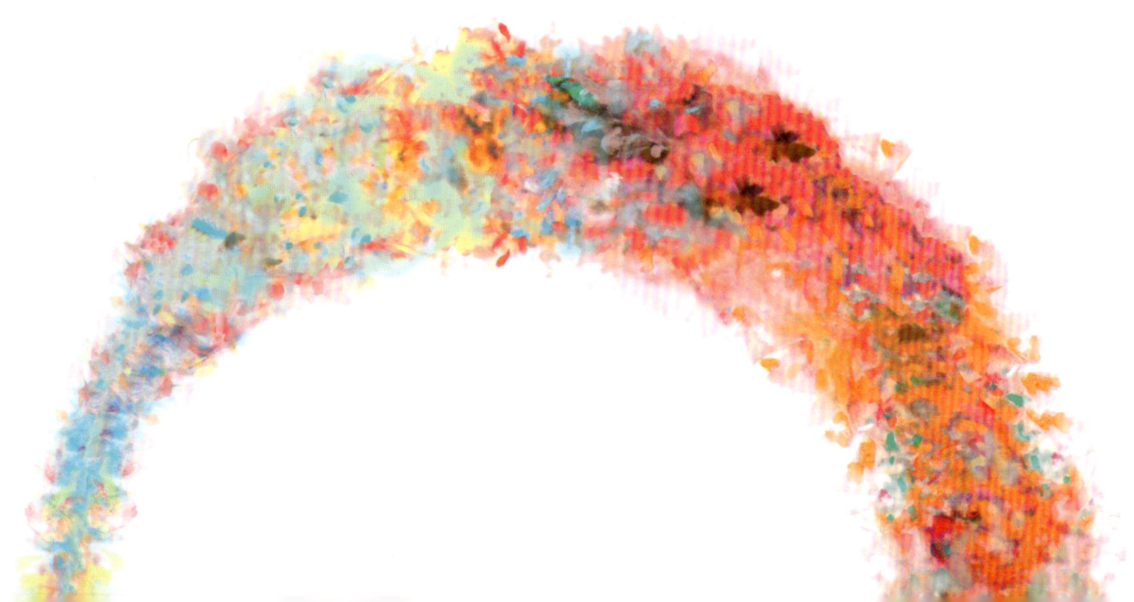

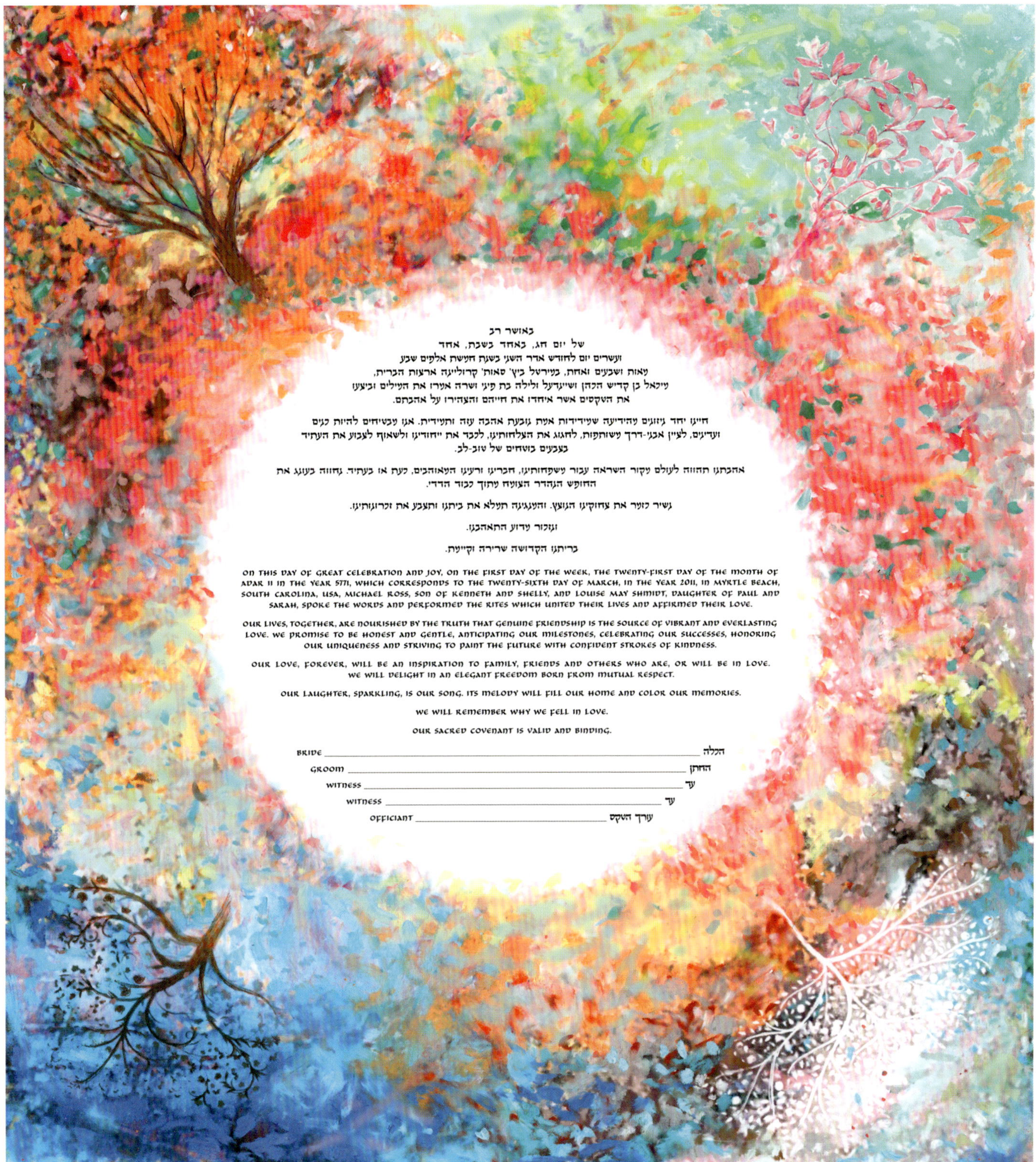

באושר רב
של יום חג, באחד בשבת, אחד
ועשרים יום לחודש אדר השני בשנת חמשת אלפים שבע
מאות ושבעים ואחת, במירטל ביץ' סאות' קרולינה ארצות הברית,
מיכאל בן קדיש הכהן ושיינדעל ולילה בת פינ' ושרה אמרו את המילים וביצעו
את הטקסים אשר איחדו את חייהם והצהירו על אהבתם.

חיינו יחד ניזונים מהידיעה שמידידות אמת נובעת אהבה עזה ותמידית. אנו מבטיחים להיות כנים ועדינים, לציין אבני-דרך משותפות, לחגוג את הצלחותינו, לכבד את ייחודינו ולשאוף לצבוע את העתיד בצבעים בוטחים של טוב-לב.

אהבתנו תהווה לעולם מקור השראה עבור משפחותינו, חברינו ורעינו המאוהבים, כעת או בעתיד. נחווה בעונג את החופש הנהדר הצומח מתוך כבוד הדדי.

נשיר כזמר את צחוקינו הנוצץ. והמנגינה תמלא את ביתנו ותצבע את זכרונותינו.

ונזכור מדוע התאהבנו.

בריתנו הקדושה שרירה וקיימת.

On this day of great celebration and joy, on the first day of the week, the twenty-first day of the month of Adar II in the year 5771, which corresponds to the twenty-sixth day of March, in the year 2011, in Myrtle Beach, South Carolina, USA, Michael Ross, son of Kenneth and Shelly, and Louise May Shmidt, daughter of Paul and Sarah, spoke the words and performed the rites which united their lives and affirmed their love.

Our lives, together, are nourished by the truth that genuine friendship is the source of vibrant and everlasting love. We promise to be honest and gentle, anticipating our milestones, celebrating our successes, honoring our uniqueness and striving to paint the future with confident strokes of kindness.

Our love, forever, will be an inspiration to family, friends and others who are, or will be in love. We will delight in an elegant freedom born from mutual respect.

Our laughter, sparkling, is our song. Its melody will fill our home and color our memories.

We will remember why we fell in love.

Our sacred covenant is valid and binding.

Bride ______________________ הכלה

Groom ______________________ החתן

Witness ______________________ עד

Witness ______________________ עד

Officiant ______________________ עורך הטקס

Courtesy of Ketubah.com.

Jeanette Kuvin Oren

"Fabric Ketubah"

2009

Jeanette Kuvin Oren (b. 1961) grew up in Florida and works in Connecticut and Jerusalem. Her large installations of fiber art, mosaic, metal, glass, papercutting, painting, and calligraphy have enriched hundreds of houses of worship, schools, community centers, and camps worldwide. She also fabricates a variety of ritual items, such as Torah covers, Torah ark curtains, ketubot, and wall hangings, that express the shared values of the couple or community.

This unusual, quilt-stitched ketubah combines a circle papercut border around the text with an unfurling design made of eclectic fabrics—metallic gold, luminous red, hand-dyed purple silk, and small scraps set into stripes—streaming out from the center. Folk art, precision ornamentation, flowing patterns, and bursts of color and texture are joined in stunning effect.

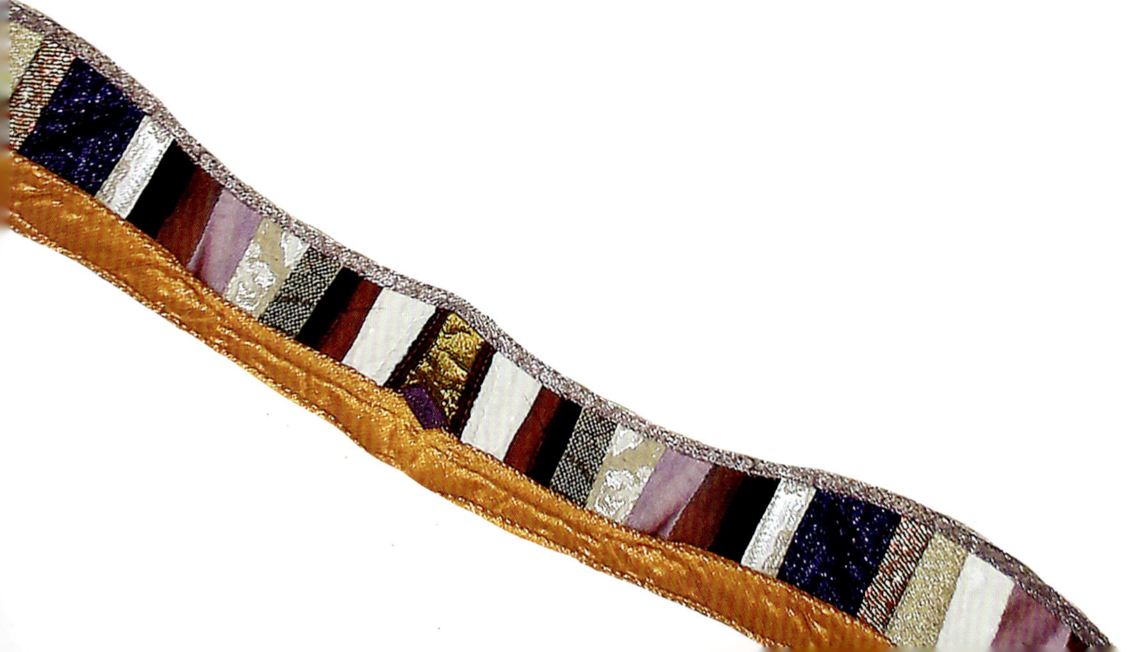

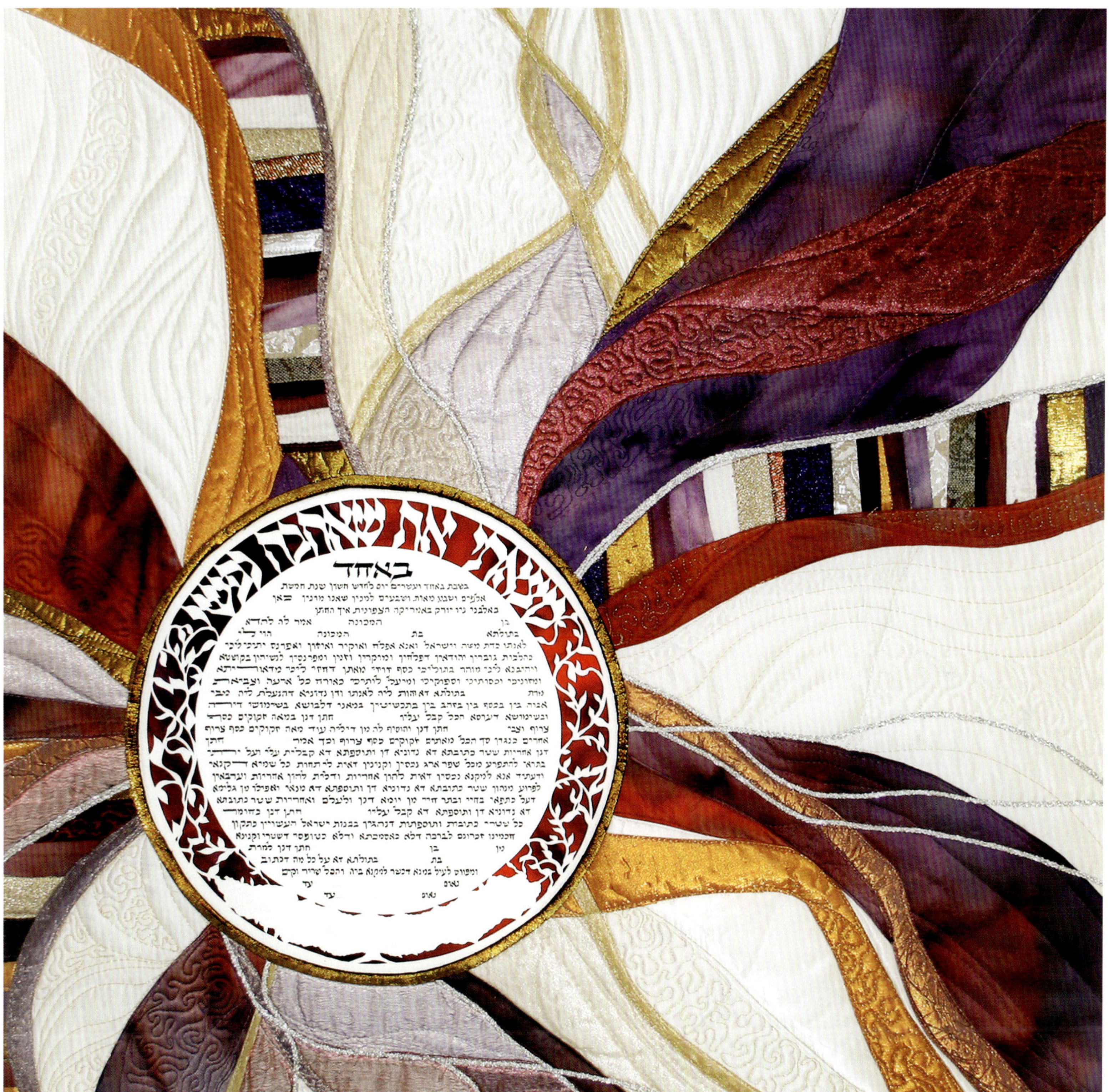

Courtesy of Jeanette Kuvin Oren.

Ruth Becker

"Revelry 18-Layer"

2010

Ruth Becker grew up in Washington DC, lived for more than fifteen years in Israel, and now resides in Chevy Chase, Maryland. She is best-known for her papercut ketubahs, created for thousands of clients and also held in private collections worldwide. Her clean, contemporary, and sophisticated work balances intricacy and structure. Precise geometries and spontaneous, organic forms coalesce in timeless patterns and designs.

This ketubah is notable for its sculptural quality and geometrical complexity. Eighteen layers of laser-cut paper, each one shifted slightly, creates the three-dimensional effect of a circular wave receding and cresting to the surface. No dye or paint has been applied. The marks from the laser cut form a sort of topographic map, perhaps of the hollows of ancient caves, like those in the Judean Hills.

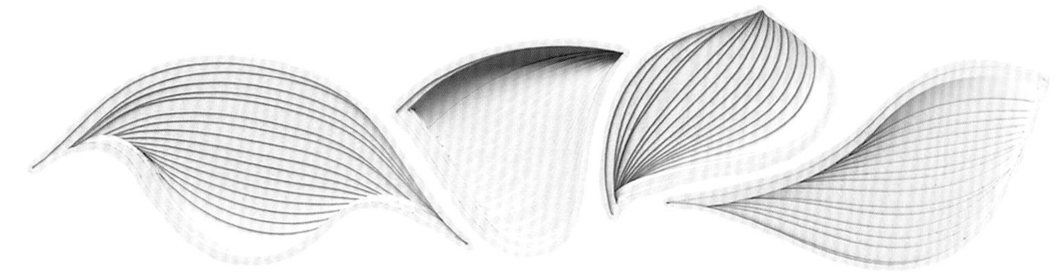

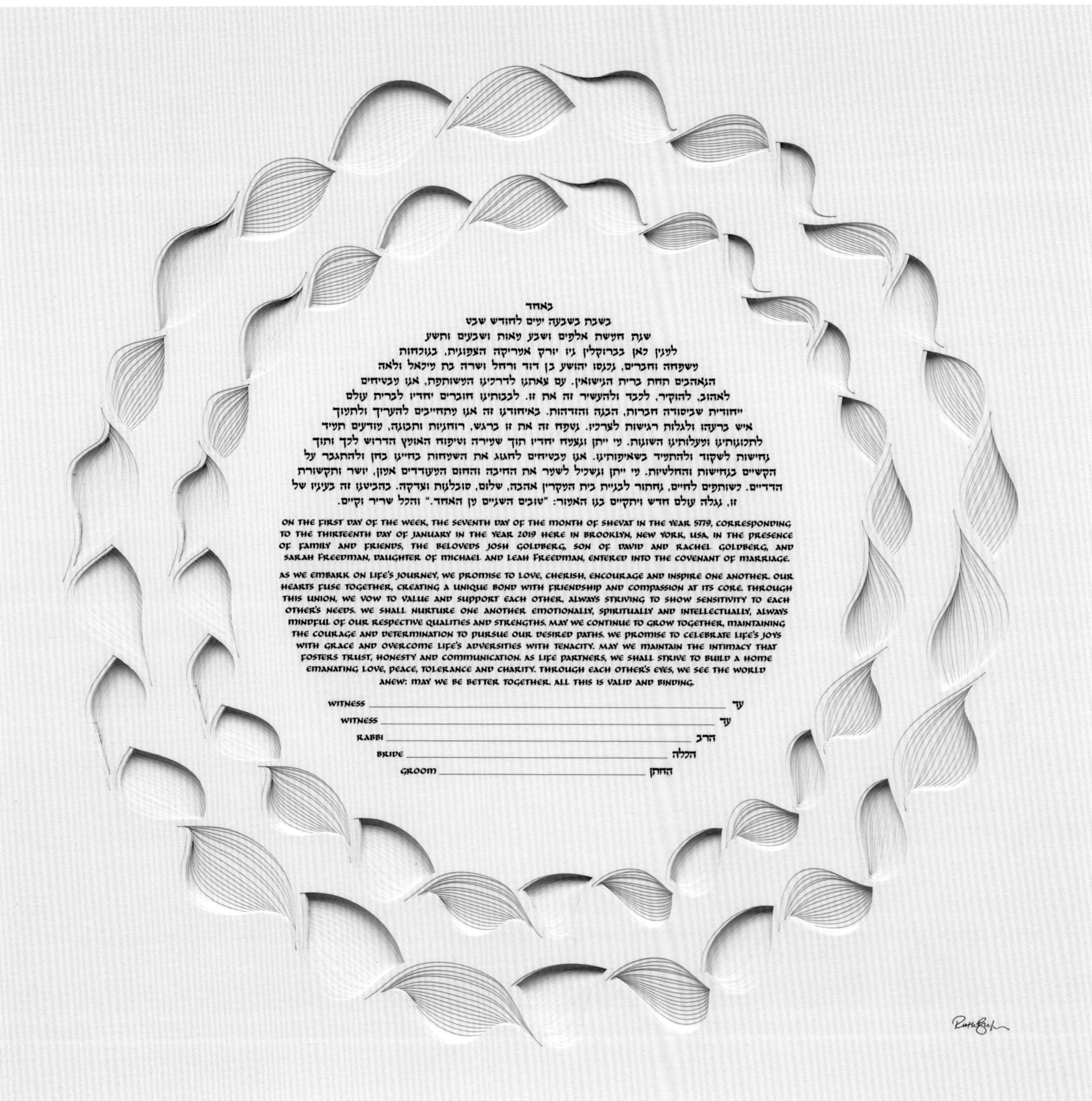

Courtesy of Ketubah.com.

Baruch Sienna

"Love, Period"

2010

Ottawa born Baruch Sienna (b. 1956) resides in Toronto. A Jewish educator as well as digital artist and graphic designer, he was the first person to create Hebrew fonts on a Mac. His ketubah work is notable for its use of fonts as the main decorative element.

Here, the word "love" is printed in the ubiquitous and iconic Helvetica font commonly found on public signage and brand logos throughout the English-speaking world. The bold, modern, and minimalist design elegantly captures the most enduring sentiment of Jewish marriage.

love.

בשביעי בשבת בשני ימים לחודש טבת שנת
חמשת אלפים ושבע מאות ושבעים ושלש
למנין שאנו מונימות כאן באורלנדו פלורידה
ארצות הברית, בנוכחות משפחה וחברימות,
נכנסו אריאל בן שמואל הכהן ורבקה וכרמיה
בת שלום ומלכה הנאהבימות תחת
ברית הנישואין.

עם צאתנו לדרכנו המשותפת, אנו מבטיחימות
לאהוב, להוקיר, לכבד ולהעשיר זה את זת.
לבבותינו חוברים יחד לברית עולם ייחודית
שביסודה חברות, הבנה והזדהות. באיחודנו זה
אנו מתחייבימות להעריך ולתמוך איש ברעהו
ולגלות רגישות לצרכיו. נטפח זה את זת ברגש,
רוחניות ותבונה, מודעימות תמיד לתכונותינו
ומעלותינו השונות. מי ייתן ונצמח יחדיו
תוך שמירה וטיפוח האומץ הדרוש לכך ותוך
נחישות לשקוד ולהתמיד בשאיפותינו. אנו
מבטיחימות לחגוג את השמחות בחיינו בחן
ולהתגבר על הקשיים בנחישות והחלטיות.
מי ייתן ונשכיל לשמר את החיבה והחום
המעודדים אמון, יושר ותקשורת הדדיים.
כשותפימות לחיים, נחתור לבניית בית המקרין
אהבה, שלום, סובלנות וצדקה. בהביטנו זה
בעיני זת, נגלה עולם חדש ויתקיים בנו האמור
"טובים השניים מן האחד."

והכל שריר וקיים.

Witness ____________________ עד

Witness ____________________ עד

On the seventh day of the week, the second day of the month of Tevet in the year 5773, corresponding to the fourteenth day of December in the year 2012 here in Orlando, Florida, USA, in the presence of family and friends, the beloveds Ariel Cantor, son of Samuel and Rikki, and Kelsey Smith, child of Shawn and Melanie, entered into the covenant of marriage.

As we embark on life's journey, we promise to love, cherish, encourage and inspire one another. Our hearts fuse together, creating a unique bond with friendship and compassion at its core. Through this union, we vow to value and support each other, always striving to show sensitivity to each other's needs. We shall nurture one another emotionally, spiritually and intellectually, always mindful of our respective qualities and strengths. May we continue to grow together, maintaining the courage and determination to pursue our desired paths.
We promise to celebrate life's joys with grace and overcome life's adversities with tenacity. May we maintain the intimacy that fosters trust, honesty and communication. As life partners, we shall strive to build a home emanating love, peace, tolerance and charity. Through each other's eyes, we see the world anew: may we be better together.
All this is valid and binding.

Bride ____________________ הכלה

Groom ____________________ החתן

Officiant ____________________ עורך הטקס

Courtesy of Ketubah.com.

Robert Saslow

“Love’s Mosaic—Sapphire and Amethyst”

2011

Robert Saslow is a ketubah designer and the official calligrapher for Los Angeles County. Monochromatic symmetry and simplicity have gained appeal in twenty-first-century ketubah design. Saslow’s mosaic rings are composed of detailed squares that subtly shift color.

Fading from dark to light to illuminate the text, this abstract design hinting of sapphires and amethysts—which he also created in a variety of other colorways inspired by additional precious and semiprecious stones—leaves room for many interpretations. It is a contemplative pathway of gems spiraling inward toward the light and bubbling upward in an infinitely circulating fountain of love.

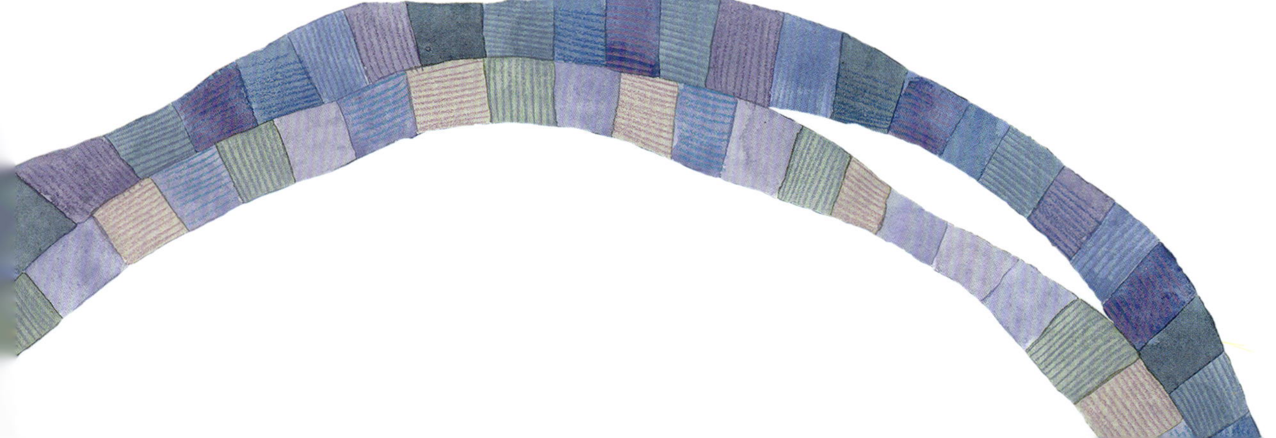

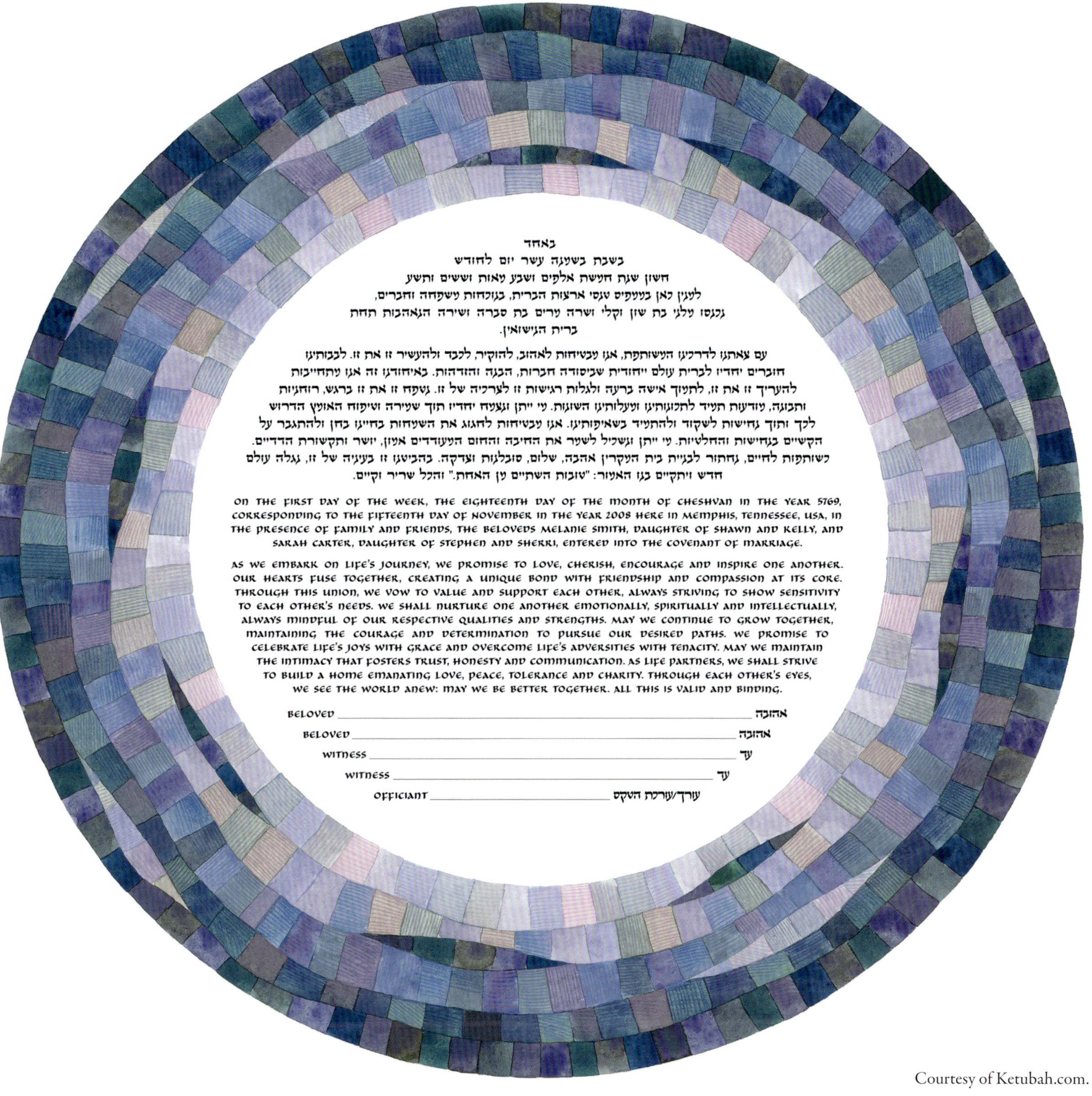

באחד
בשבת בשמונה עשר יום לחודש
חשון שנת חמשת אלפים ושבע מאות וששים ותשע
למנין כאן בממפיס טנסי ארצות הברית, בנוכחות משפחה וחברים,
נכנסו מלני בת שון וקלי ושרה מרים בת סברה ושירה הנאהבות תחת
ברית הנישואין.

עם צאתנו לדרכינו המשותפת, אנו מבטיחות לאהוב, להוקיר, לכבד ולהעשיר זו את זו. לבבותינו חוברים יחדיו לברית עולם ייחודית שביסודה חברות, הבנה והזדהות. באיחודנו זה אנו מתחייבות להעריך זו את זו, לתמוך אישה ברעה ולגלות רגישות זו לצרכיה של זו. נטפח זו את זו ברגש, רוחניות ותבונה, מודעות תמיד לתכונותינו ומעלותינו השונות. מי ייתן ונצמח יחדיו תוך שמירה וטיפוח האומץ הדרוש לכך ותוך נחישות לשקוד ולהתמיד בשאיפותינו. אנו מבטיחות לחגוג את השמחות בחיינו בחן ולהתגבר על הקשיים בנחישות והחלטיות. מי ייתן ונשכיל לשמר את החיבה והחום המעודדים אמון, יושר ותקשורת הדדיים. כשותפות לחיים, נחתור לבניית בית המקרין אהבה, שלום, סובלנות וצדקה. בהביטנו זו בעיניה של זו, נגלה עולם חדש ויתקיים בנו האמור: "טובות השתיים מן האחת." והכל שריר וקיים.

On the first day of the week, the eighteenth day of the month of Cheshvan in the year 5769, corresponding to the fifteenth day of November in the year 2008 here in Memphis, Tennessee, USA, in the presence of family and friends, the beloveds Melanie Smith, daughter of Shawn and Kelly, and Sarah Carter, daughter of Stephen and Sherri, entered into the covenant of marriage.

As we embark on life's journey, we promise to love, cherish, encourage and inspire one another. Our hearts fuse together, creating a unique bond with friendship and compassion at its core. Through this union, we vow to value and support each other, always striving to show sensitivity to each other's needs. We shall nurture one another emotionally, spiritually and intellectually, always mindful of our respective qualities and strengths. May we continue to grow together, maintaining the courage and determination to pursue our desired paths. We promise to celebrate life's joys with grace and overcome life's adversities with tenacity. May we maintain the intimacy that fosters trust, honesty and communication. As life partners, we shall strive to build a home emanating love, peace, tolerance and charity. Through each other's eyes, we see the world anew: may we be better together. All this is valid and binding.

Beloved ______________________ אהובה

Beloved ______________________ אהובה

Witness ______________________ עד

Witness ______________________ עד

Officiant ______________________ עורך/עורכת הטקס

Courtesy of Ketubah.com.

Debra Band

“Intertwined”

2012

Potomac, Maryland–based artist Debra Band creates illuminated and papercut books and *ketubot* among other works, and has written several books, including *Qohelet: Searching for a Life Worth Living* (2023), coauthored with the philosopher Menachem Fisch. Jewish texts and medieval European and Middle Eastern painting and manuscripts influence her work, which is held in private collections, community institutions, and galleries across the English-speaking world.

In this custom design, two papercut layers are intertwined in a twelve-pointed star composed of Stars of David that calls to mind the Twelve Tribes of Israel and the symbol of modern Israel. A tiny Star of David at the core of the design contains a miniature landscape of Jerusalem, while the floral border of white roses and orchids symbolize various qualities in biblical texts and midrash, from humility to beauty. Around the ketubah, a passage from Song of Songs 2:9–13, inscribed in gold, reads in part: “My beloved spoke thus to me, ‘Arise, my darling; My fair one, come away!’”

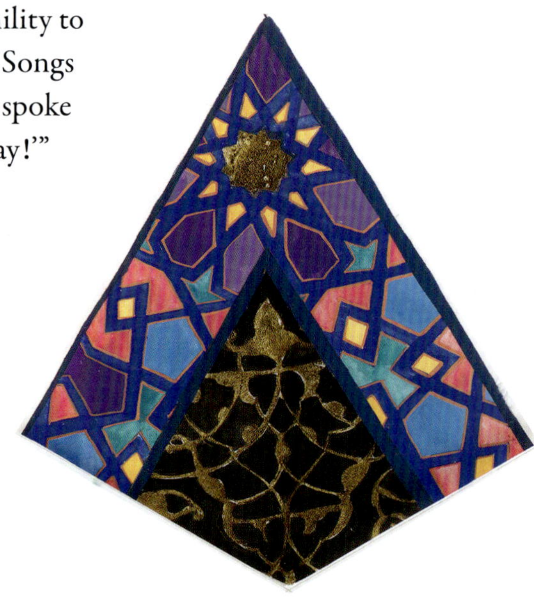

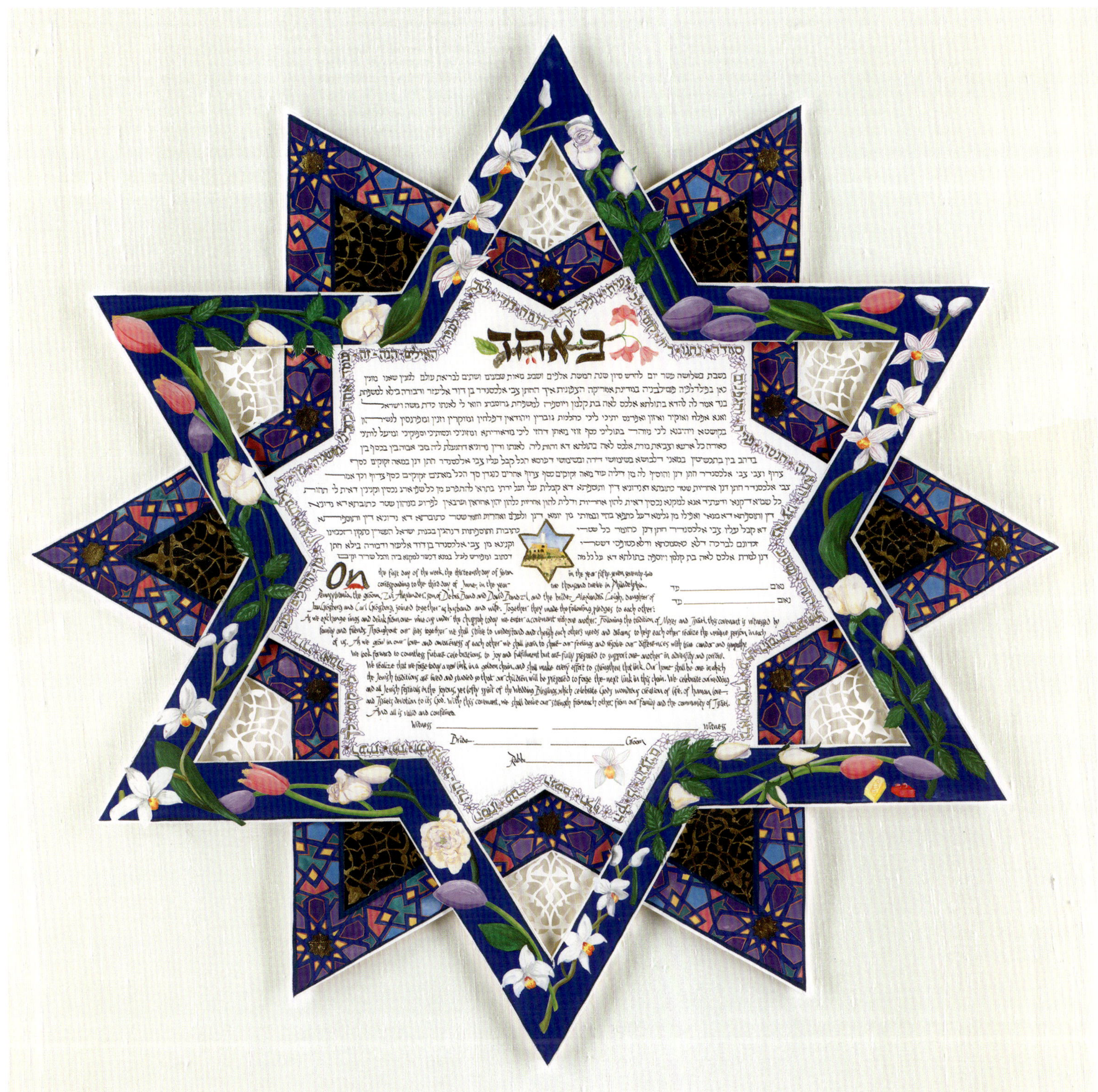

Courtesy of Debra Band.

Aliza Boyer

"Canopy"

2012

New York City–based artist and arts educator Aliza Boyer creates hand-lettered ketubot often driven by calligraphic brushwork and accented with lines of luminous colored pencil. Combining strict minimalism—paring down her designs to the barest elements—with the traditionally ornate papercut medium, she aspires to capture a lyrical essence and strike an emotional chord. Boyer often integrates words and phrases important to the themes of love and marriage.

In this work, slim papercut strokes signifying the marital chuppah frame the beautifully calligraphed interlinear text that alternates between Hebrew and English. A passage from Song of Songs 3:4 adorning the vertical poles reads in translation: "I found the one I love."

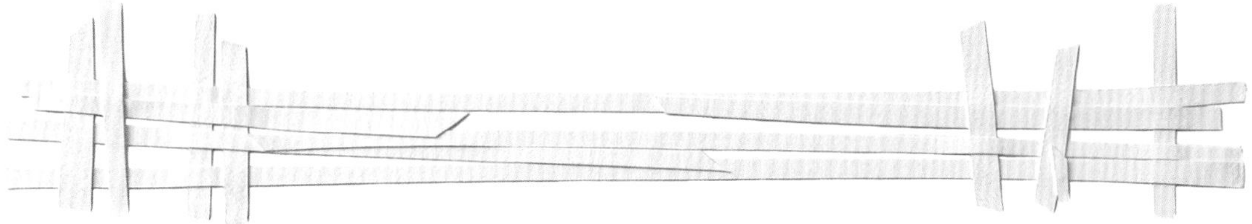

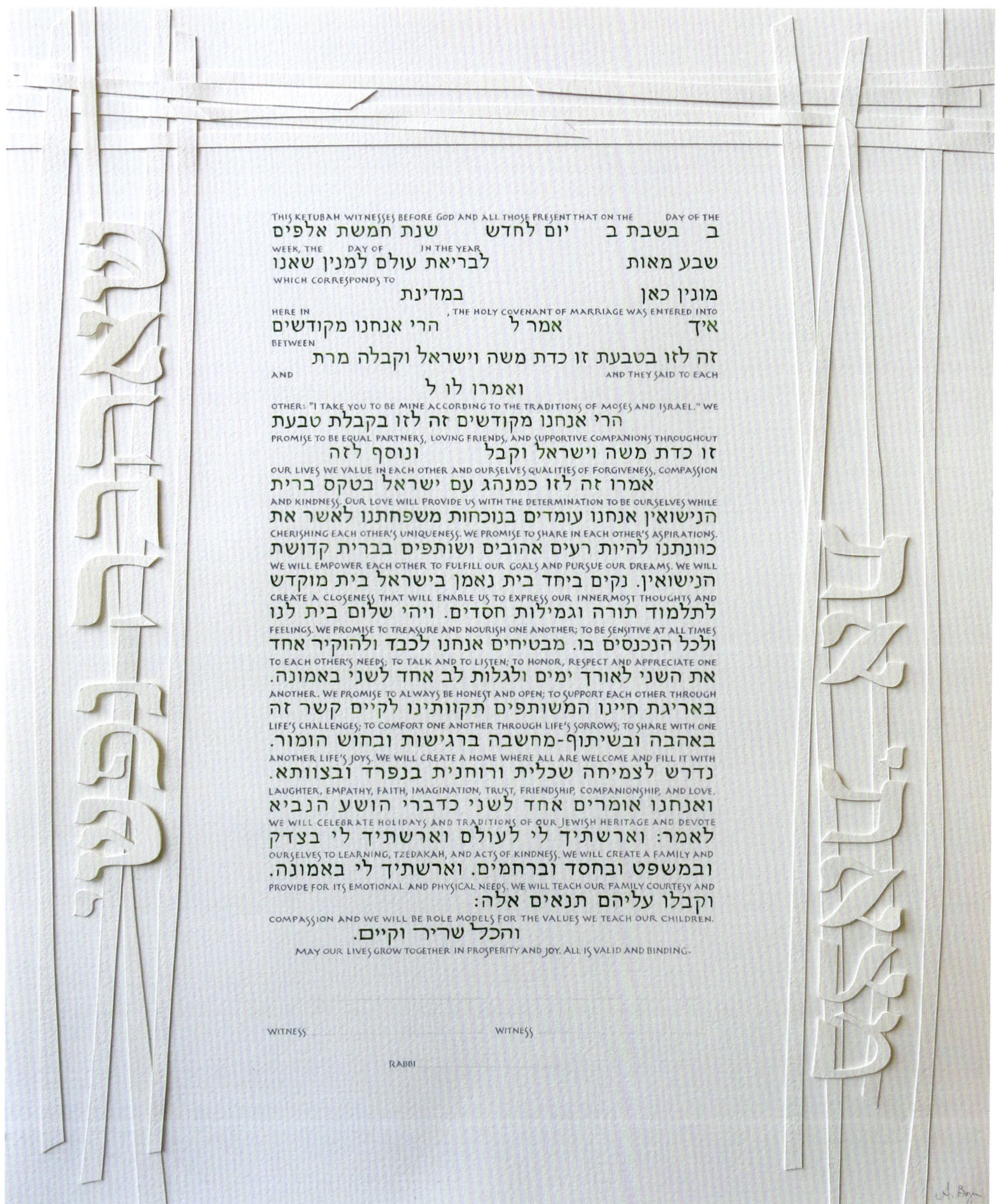

THIS KETUBAH WITNESSES BEFORE GOD AND ALL THOSE PRESENT THAT ON THE DAY OF THE
ב בשבת ב יום לחדש שנת חמשת אלפים
WEEK, THE DAY OF IN THE YEAR
שבע מאות לבריאת עולם למנין שאנו
WHICH CORRESPONDS TO
מונין כאן במדינת
HERE IN , THE HOLY COVENANT OF MARRIAGE WAS ENTERED INTO
איך אמר ל הרי אנחנו מקודשים
BETWEEN
זה לזו בטבעת זו כדת משה וישראל וקבלה מרת
AND AND THEY SAID TO EACH
ואמרו לו ל
OTHER: "I TAKE YOU TO BE MINE ACCORDING TO THE TRADITIONS OF MOSES AND ISRAEL." WE
הרי אנחנו מקודשים זה לזו בקבלת טבעת
PROMISE TO BE EQUAL PARTNERS, LOVING FRIENDS, AND SUPPORTIVE COMPANIONS THROUGHOUT
זו כדת משה וישראל וקבל ונוסף לזה
OUR LIVES WE VALUE IN EACH OTHER AND OURSELVES QUALITIES OF FORGIVENESS, COMPASSION
אמרו זה לזו כמנהג עם ישראל בטקס ברית
AND KINDNESS. OUR LOVE WILL PROVIDE US WITH THE DETERMINATION TO BE OURSELVES WHILE
הנישואין אנחנו עומדים בנוכחות משפחתנו לאשר את
CHERISHING EACH OTHER'S UNIQUENESS. WE PROMISE TO SHARE IN EACH OTHER'S ASPIRATIONS.
כוונתנו להיות רעים אהובים ושותפים בברית קדושת
WE WILL EMPOWER EACH OTHER TO FULFILL OUR GOALS AND PURSUE OUR DREAMS. WE WILL
הנישואין. נקים ביחד בית נאמן בישראל בית מוקדש
CREATE A CLOSENESS THAT WILL ENABLE US TO EXPRESS OUR INNERMOST THOUGHTS AND
לתלמוד תורה וגמילות חסדים. ויהי שלום בית לנו
FEELINGS. WE PROMISE TO TREASURE AND NOURISH ONE ANOTHER; TO BE SENSITIVE AT ALL TIMES
ולכל הנכנסים בו. מבטיחים אנחנו לכבד ולהוקיר אחד
TO EACH OTHER'S NEEDS; TO TALK AND TO LISTEN; TO HONOR, RESPECT AND APPRECIATE ONE
את השני לאורך ימים ולגלות לב אחד לשני באמונה.
ANOTHER. WE PROMISE TO ALWAYS BE HONEST AND OPEN; TO SUPPORT EACH OTHER THROUGH
באריגת חיינו המשותפים תקוותינו לקיים קשר זה
LIFE'S CHALLENGES; TO COMFORT ONE ANOTHER THROUGH LIFE'S SORROWS; TO SHARE WITH ONE
באהבה ובשיתוף-מחשבה ברגישות ובחוש הומור.
ANOTHER LIFE'S JOYS. WE WILL CREATE A HOME WHERE ALL ARE WELCOME AND FILL IT WITH
נדרש לצמיחה שכלית ורוחנית בנפרד ובצוותא.
LAUGHTER, EMPATHY, FAITH, IMAGINATION, TRUST, FRIENDSHIP, COMPANIONSHIP, AND LOVE.
ואנחנו אומרים אחד לשני כדברי הושע הנביא
WE WILL CELEBRATE HOLIDAYS AND TRADITIONS OF OUR JEWISH HERITAGE AND DEVOTE
לאמר: וארשתיך לי לעולם וארשתיך לי בצדק
OURSELVES TO LEARNING, TZEDAKAH, AND ACTS OF KINDNESS. WE WILL CREATE A FAMILY AND
ובמשפט ובחסד וברחמים. וארשתיך לי באמונה.
PROVIDE FOR ITS EMOTIONAL AND PHYSICAL NEEDS. WE WILL TEACH OUR FAMILY COURTESY AND
וקבלו עליהם תנאים אלה:
COMPASSION AND WE WILL BE ROLE MODELS FOR THE VALUES WE TEACH OUR CHILDREN.
והכל שריר וקיים.
MAY OUR LIVES GROW TOGETHER IN PROSPERITY AND JOY. ALL IS VALID AND BINDING.

WITNESS WITNESS

RABBI

Courtesy of Aliza Boyer.

Celia Lemonik

"Betrothed"

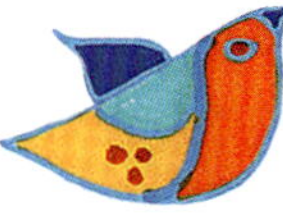

2012

Long Island, New York, graphic designer and calligrapher Celia Lemonik takes inspiration from the decorative essence of the Hebrew alphabet. Ornamental decorative patterns common across the Middle East as well as historical folk-art traditions inform her strong colors, symmetry, and accents.

Unusual in this ketubah are the bordering floral elements, reminiscent of Uzbek suzani tapestries. These embroidered textiles from Central Asia, traditionally made for brides as part of their dowry, draw from an ancient iconography, are embellished with motifs—often including botanicals—representing luck and good fortune, and signify the binding together of two families.

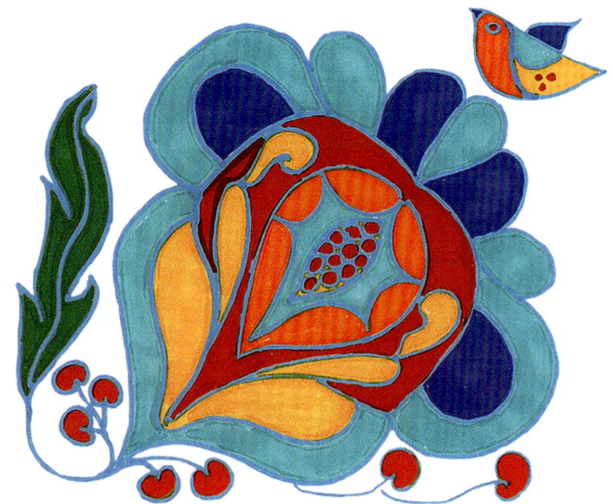

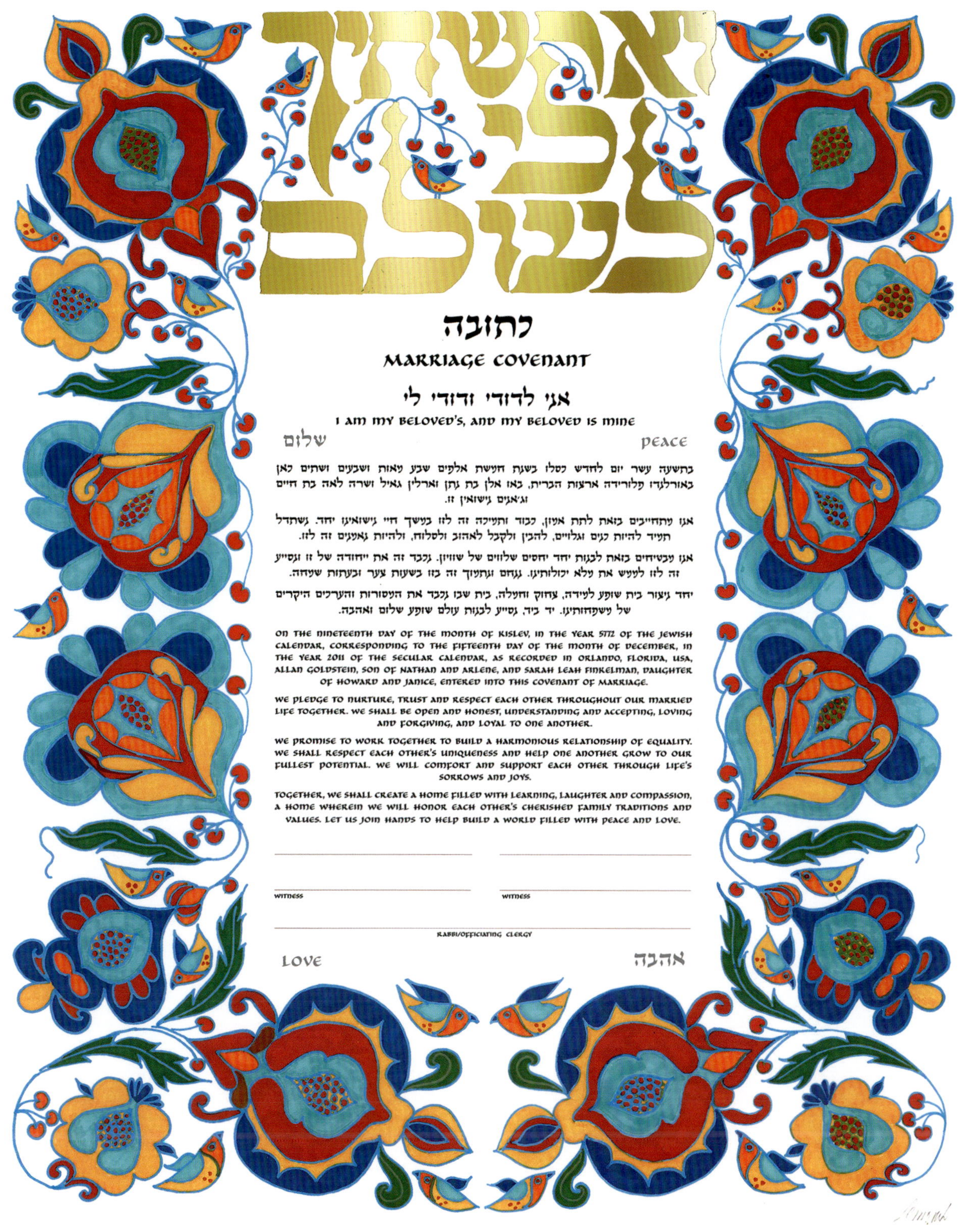

וארשתיך לי לעולם

כתובה

MARRIAGE COVENANT

אני לדודי ודודי לי

I AM MY BELOVED'S, AND MY BELOVED IS MINE

שלום PEACE

בתשעה עשר יום לחדש כסלו בשנת חמשת אלפים שבע מאות ושבעים ושתים כאן באורלנדו פלורידה ארצות הברית, באו אלן בן נתן וארלין גאיל ושרה לאה בת חיים וג'אניס נישואין זו.

אנו מתחייבים בזאת לתת אמון, כבוד ותמיכה זה לזו במשך חיי נישואינו יחד. נשתדל תמיד להיות כנים וגלויים, להבין ולקבל לאהוב ולסלוח, ולהיות נאמנים זה לזו.

אנו מבטיחים בזאת לבנות יחד יחסים שלווים של שוויון. נכבד זה את ייחודה של זו ונסייע זה לזו לממש את מלא יכולותינו. ננחם ונתמוך זה בזו בשעות צער ובעתות שמחה.

יחד ניצור בית שופע למידה, צחוק וחמלה, בית שבו נכבד את המסורות והערכים היקרים של משפחותינו. יד ביד, נסייע לבנות עולם שופע שלום ואהבה.

ON THE NINETEENTH DAY OF THE MONTH OF KISLEV, IN THE YEAR 5772 OF THE JEWISH CALENDAR, CORRESPONDING TO THE FIFTEENTH DAY OF THE MONTH OF DECEMBER, IN THE YEAR 2011 OF THE SECULAR CALENDAR, AS RECORDED IN ORLANDO, FLORIDA, USA, ALLAN GOLDSTEIN, SON OF NATHAN AND ARLENE, AND SARAH LEAH FINKELMAN, DAUGHTER OF HOWARD AND JANICE, ENTERED INTO THIS COVENANT OF MARRIAGE.

WE PLEDGE TO NURTURE, TRUST AND RESPECT EACH OTHER THROUGHOUT OUR MARRIED LIFE TOGETHER. WE SHALL BE OPEN AND HONEST, UNDERSTANDING AND ACCEPTING, LOVING AND FORGIVING, AND LOYAL TO ONE ANOTHER.

WE PROMISE TO WORK TOGETHER TO BUILD A HARMONIOUS RELATIONSHIP OF EQUALITY. WE SHALL RESPECT EACH OTHER'S UNIQUENESS AND HELP ONE ANOTHER GROW TO OUR FULLEST POTENTIAL. WE WILL COMFORT AND SUPPORT EACH OTHER THROUGH LIFE'S SORROWS AND JOYS.

TOGETHER, WE SHALL CREATE A HOME FILLED WITH LEARNING, LAUGHTER AND COMPASSION, A HOME WHEREIN WE WILL HONOR EACH OTHER'S CHERISHED FAMILY TRADITIONS AND VALUES. LET US JOIN HANDS TO HELP BUILD A WORLD FILLED WITH PEACE AND LOVE.

WITNESS WITNESS

RABBI/OFFICIATING CLERGY

LOVE אהבה

Courtesy of Ketubah.com.

Daniel Sroka

“Twin Tulips”

2013

Daniel Sroka is a fine art photographer based in Morristown, New Jersey. His art is a meditation on how humans experience nature. Intimate portraits of leaves, sticks, flowers, and seeds speak to our most common connections to the natural world. His artwork is in private collections as well as on display in resorts, corporate offices, and wellness centers worldwide.

Interfaith ketubot are a specialty, and he employs close-up nature photography to convey the vitality of marriage and love. This emblematic work hones in on a pair of beautiful pink tulips to symbolize two individuals becoming one. A unique choice is a quote from French Romantic author and poet Victor Hugo: “Life is the flower for which love is the honey.”

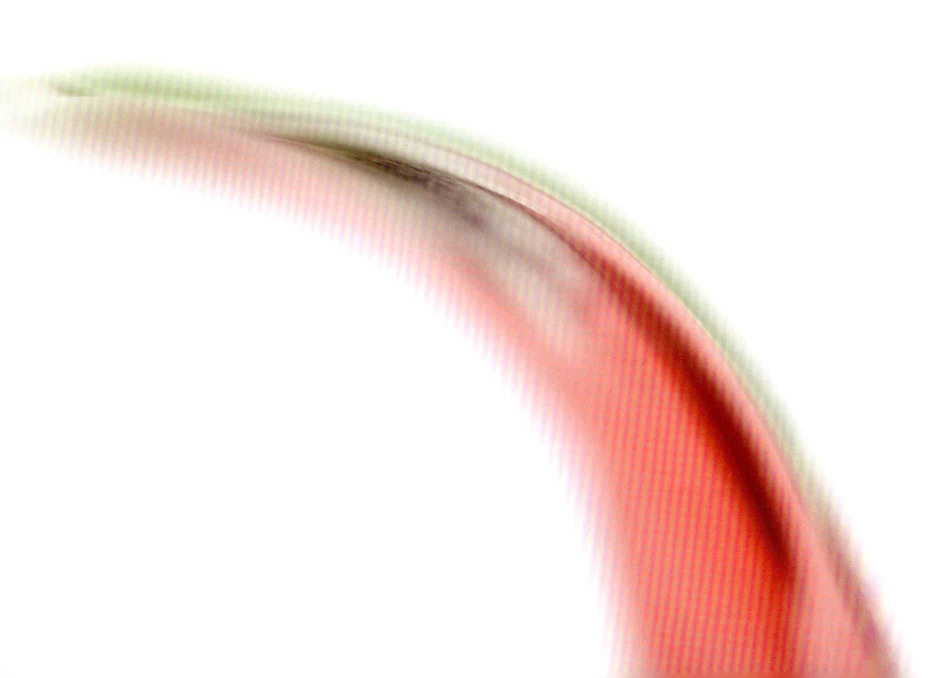

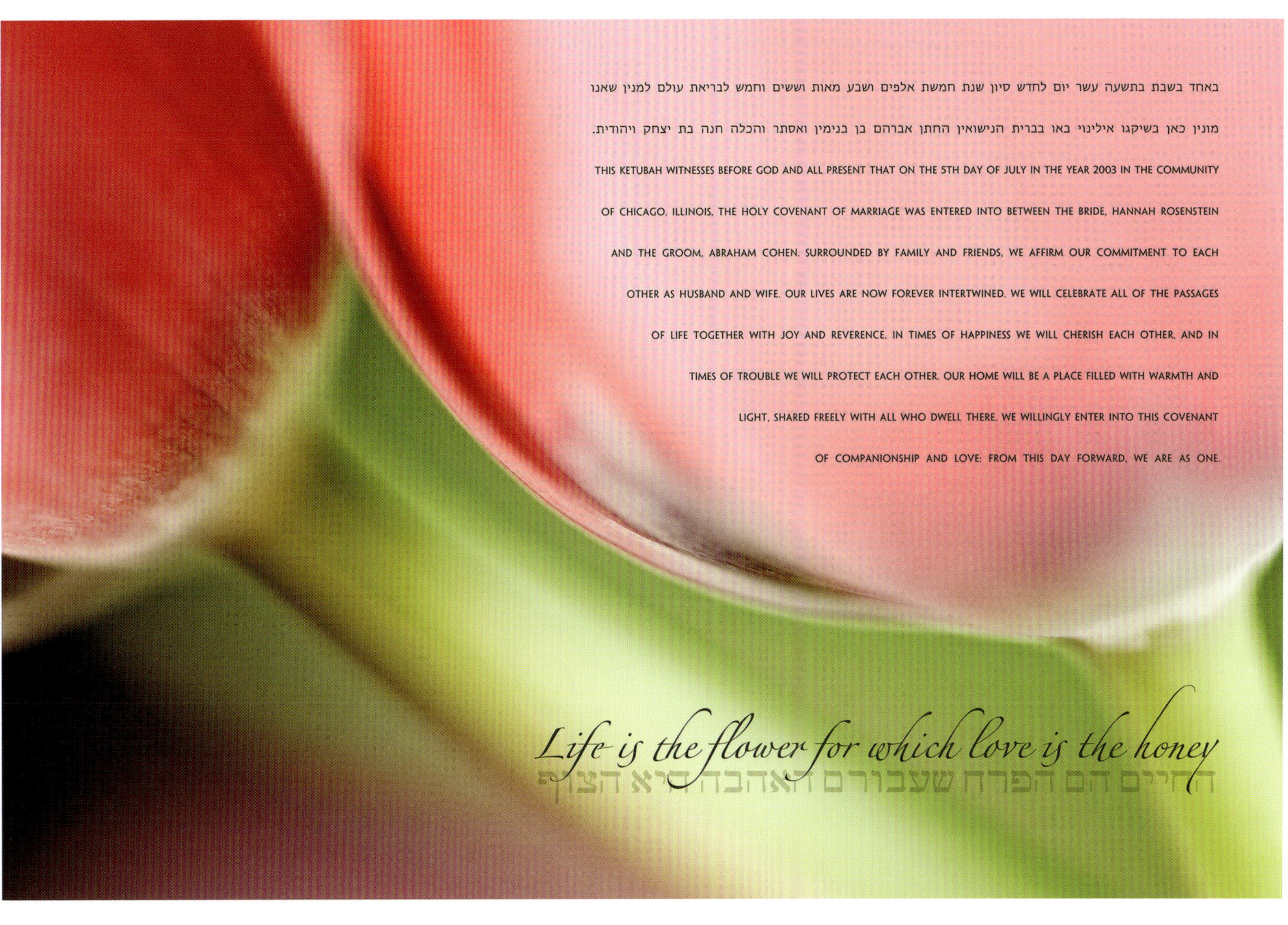

באחד בשבת בתשעה עשר יום לחדש סיון שנת חמשת אלפים ושבע מאות וששים וחמש לבריאת עולם למנין שאנו מונין כאן בשיקגו אילינוי באו בברית הנישואין החתן אברהם בן בנימין ואסתר והכלה חנה בת יצחק ויהודית.

THIS KETUBAH WITNESSES BEFORE GOD AND ALL PRESENT THAT ON THE 5TH DAY OF JULY IN THE YEAR 2003 IN THE COMMUNITY OF CHICAGO, ILLINOIS, THE HOLY COVENANT OF MARRIAGE WAS ENTERED INTO BETWEEN THE BRIDE, HANNAH ROSENSTEIN AND THE GROOM, ABRAHAM COHEN. SURROUNDED BY FAMILY AND FRIENDS, WE AFFIRM OUR COMMITMENT TO EACH OTHER AS HUSBAND AND WIFE. OUR LIVES ARE NOW FOREVER INTERTWINED. WE WILL CELEBRATE ALL OF THE PASSAGES OF LIFE TOGETHER WITH JOY AND REVERENCE. IN TIMES OF HAPPINESS WE WILL CHERISH EACH OTHER, AND IN TIMES OF TROUBLE WE WILL PROTECT EACH OTHER. OUR HOME WILL BE A PLACE FILLED WITH WARMTH AND LIGHT, SHARED FREELY WITH ALL WHO DWELL THERE. WE WILLINGLY ENTER INTO THIS COVENANT OF COMPANIONSHIP AND LOVE: FROM THIS DAY FORWARD, WE ARE AS ONE.

Life is the flower for which love is the honey

החיים הם הפרח שעבורם האהבה היא הצוף

BRIDE GROOM RABBI WITNESS WITNESS

Courtesy of Daniel Sroka.

Sivia Katz

“Creation in Three Languages”

2014

Sivia Katz is a Philadelphia-based artist whose works have been presented to former presidents and exhibited in museums and galleries throughout the United States and Israel.

One of the earliest contemporary ketubah designers still working, Katz has been creating original watercolors that integrate playful calligraphy since 1972. Her paintings, based on Hebrew texts, seek to integrate the hues of the natural world, modern tonalities, and the lyricism of the Hebrew alphabet.

This joyful, exuberant design interweaves four seasons on a central tree overlaid with a trilingual text in German, English, and Hebrew. Geometric and organic forms create a quilt of rainbow colors that meld contrasting scenes of night and day, and land, sea, and sky.

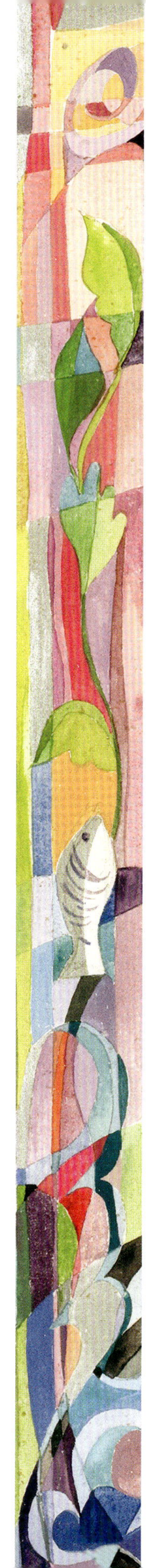

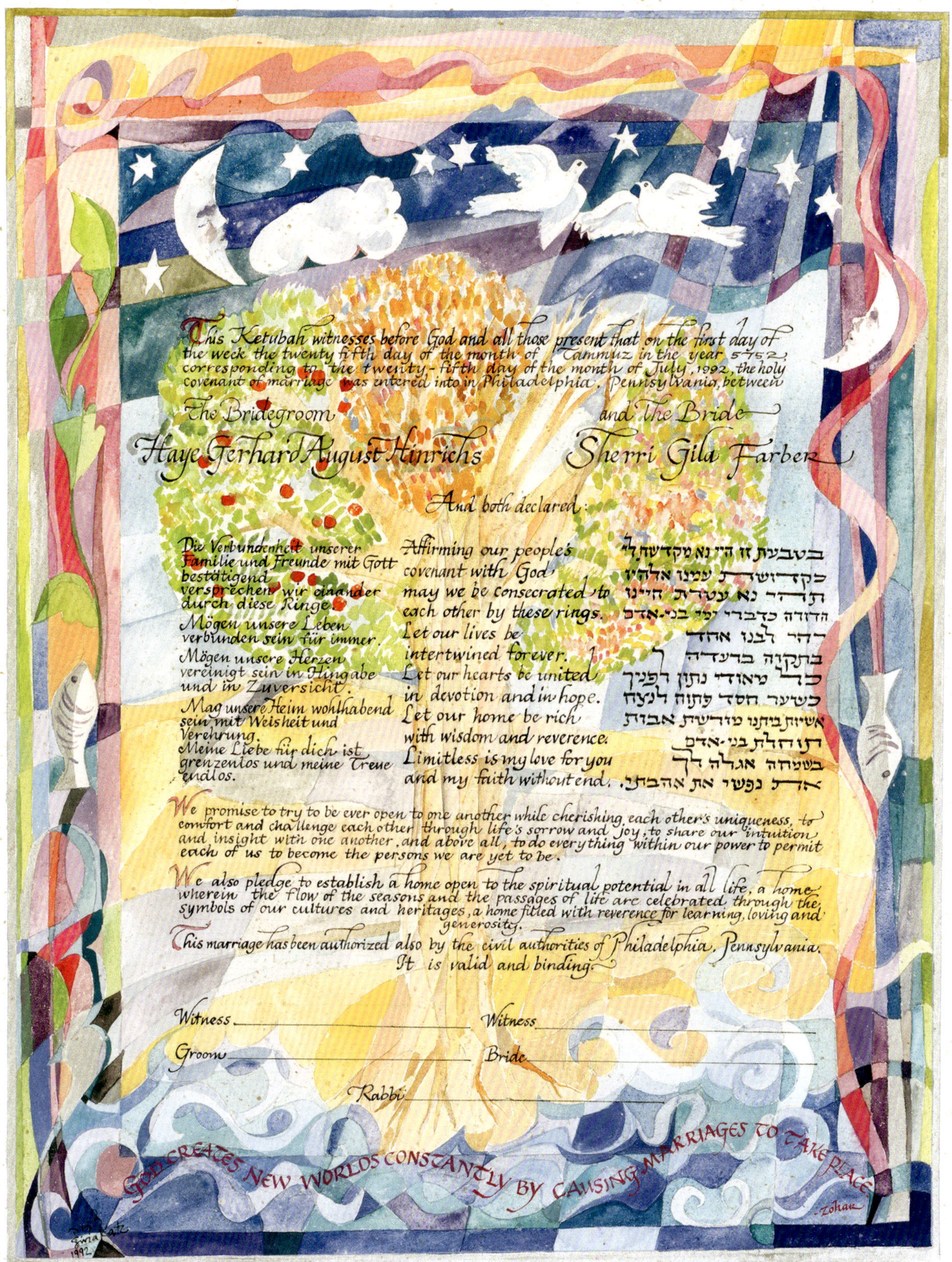

This Ketubah witnesses before God and all those present that on the first day of the week the twenty fifth day of the month of Tammuz in the year 5752, corresponding to the twenty-fifth day of the month of July, 1992, the holy covenant of marriage was entered into in Philadelphia, Pennsylvania, between

The Bridegroom	and The Bride
Haye Gerhard August Hinrichs	Sherri Gila Farber

And both declared:

Die Verbundenheit unserer Familie und Freunde mit Gott bestätigend versprechen wir einander durch diese Ringe. Mögen unsere Leben verbunden sein für immer. Mögen unsere Herzen vereinigt sein in Hingabe und in Zuversicht. Mag unsere Heim wohlhabend sein mit Weisheit und Verehrung. Meine Liebe für dich ist grenzenlos und meine Treue endlos.	Affirming our people's covenant with God, may we be consecrated to each other by these rings. Let our lives be intertwined forever. Let our hearts be united in devotion and in hope. Let our home be rich with wisdom and reverence. Limitless is my love for you and my faith without end.	בטבעת זו הרי נא מקדשת לי בקדושת עמנו אלהינו תהי נא עטרת חיינו הדורה כדברי ימי בני-אדם יהי לבנו אחד בתקוה ברעדה בכל מאודי נתון לפניך כשער חסד פתוח לנצח אשיות ביתנו מודשת אבות תוחלת בני-אדם בשמחה אגלה לך את נפשי את אהבתי.

We promise to try to be ever open to one another while cherishing each other's uniqueness, to comfort and challenge each other through life's sorrow and joy, to share our intuition and insight with one another, and above all, to do everything within our power to permit each of us to become the persons we are yet to be.

We also pledge to establish a home open to the spiritual potential in all life, a home wherein the flow of the seasons and the passages of life are celebrated through the symbols of our cultures and heritages, a home filled with reverence for learning, loving and generosity.

This marriage has been authorized also by the civil authorities of Philadelphia, Pennsylvania. It is valid and binding.

Witness ____________ Witness ____________

Groom ____________ Bride ____________

Rabbi ____________

God creates new worlds constantly by causing marriages to take place. —Zohar

Sivia Katz 1992

Courtesy of Sivia Katz.

Nava Shoham

“Infinite Love”

2014

Nava Shoham was born and raised in Israel. Her artwork, reflective of a colorful, soulful journey to integrate tradition and modernity, is showcased by museums and galleries and held in private collections around the world.

With the energy of pop artists like Roy Lichtenstein, Shoham’s design infuses a graphic of a heart shape atop an infinity symbol with a rainbow of bold colors pouring out of the page like a gushing fire hydrant. She painted the entire work with one fluid brushstroke to convey the infinitely dynamic opportunities in a long-lasting love union. Speaking likewise to unity in a different context, the design was also chosen to represent the city-wide civic initiative “Compassionate Fort Worth” promoting unity and volunteerism in Fort Worth, Texas.

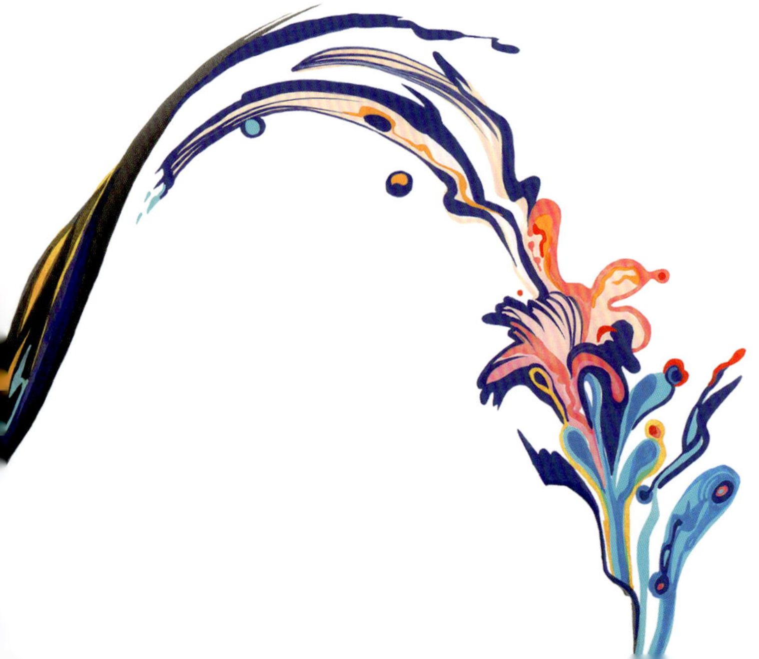

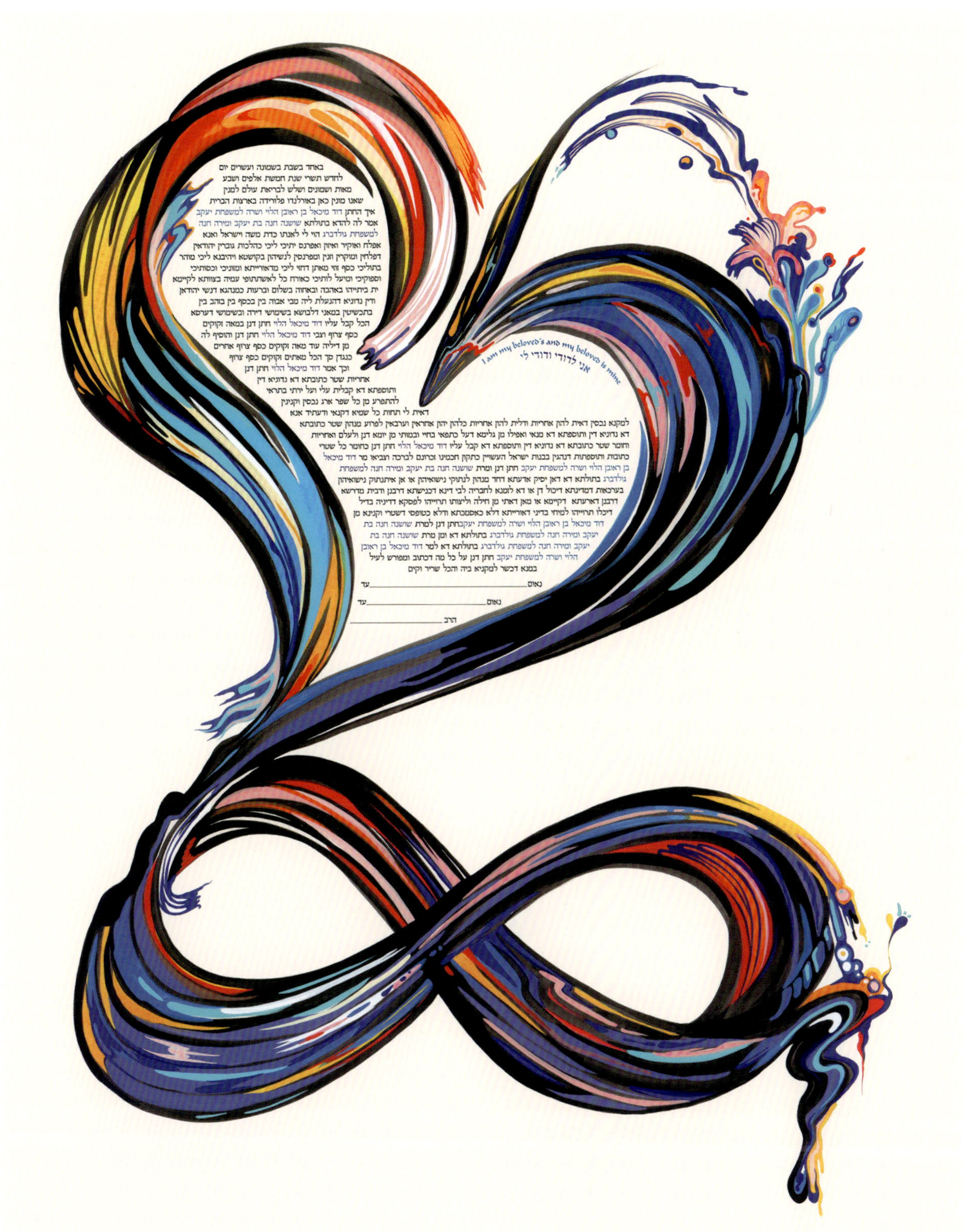

Courtesy of Nava Shoham.

Danny Azoulay

“Azure”

2016

Danny Azoulay was born in Morocco, grew up in Qiryat Shmona, and resides in the village of Tzur Hadassah in the Jerusalem hills. He draws from the richness of Jewish traditions and folklore to create papercuts enhanced with giclée printed artwork and hand-embellished with 24K gold leaf. Believing that art ought to echo one’s origins, he melds the landscapes of his childhood with Jewish symbolism, and artistic and architectural motifs from Europe, Morocco, and Israel.

This papercut depicting two gentle deer resting in the shade of an olive tree is accentuated by an ombre of celestial blue and embellished with gold leaf. A beautiful declaration from Hosea 2:21, “And I will espouse you forever: I will espouse you with righteousness and justice, And with goodness and mercy,” attests to the couple’s aspirations and love for one another.

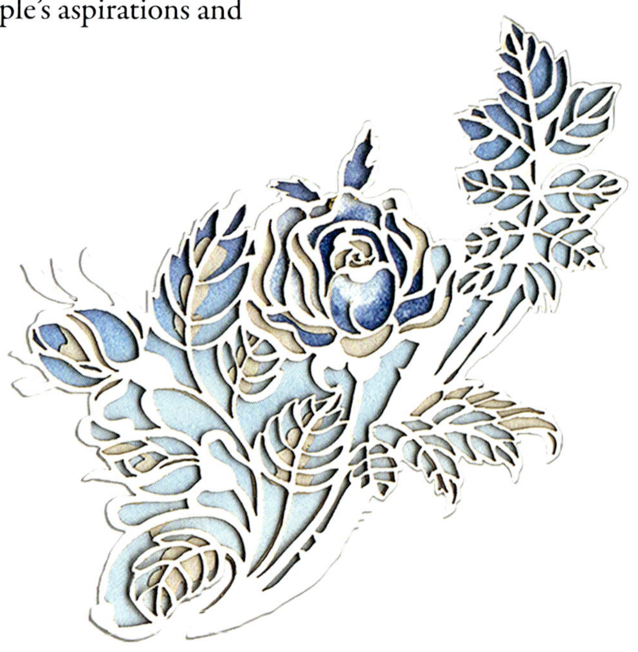

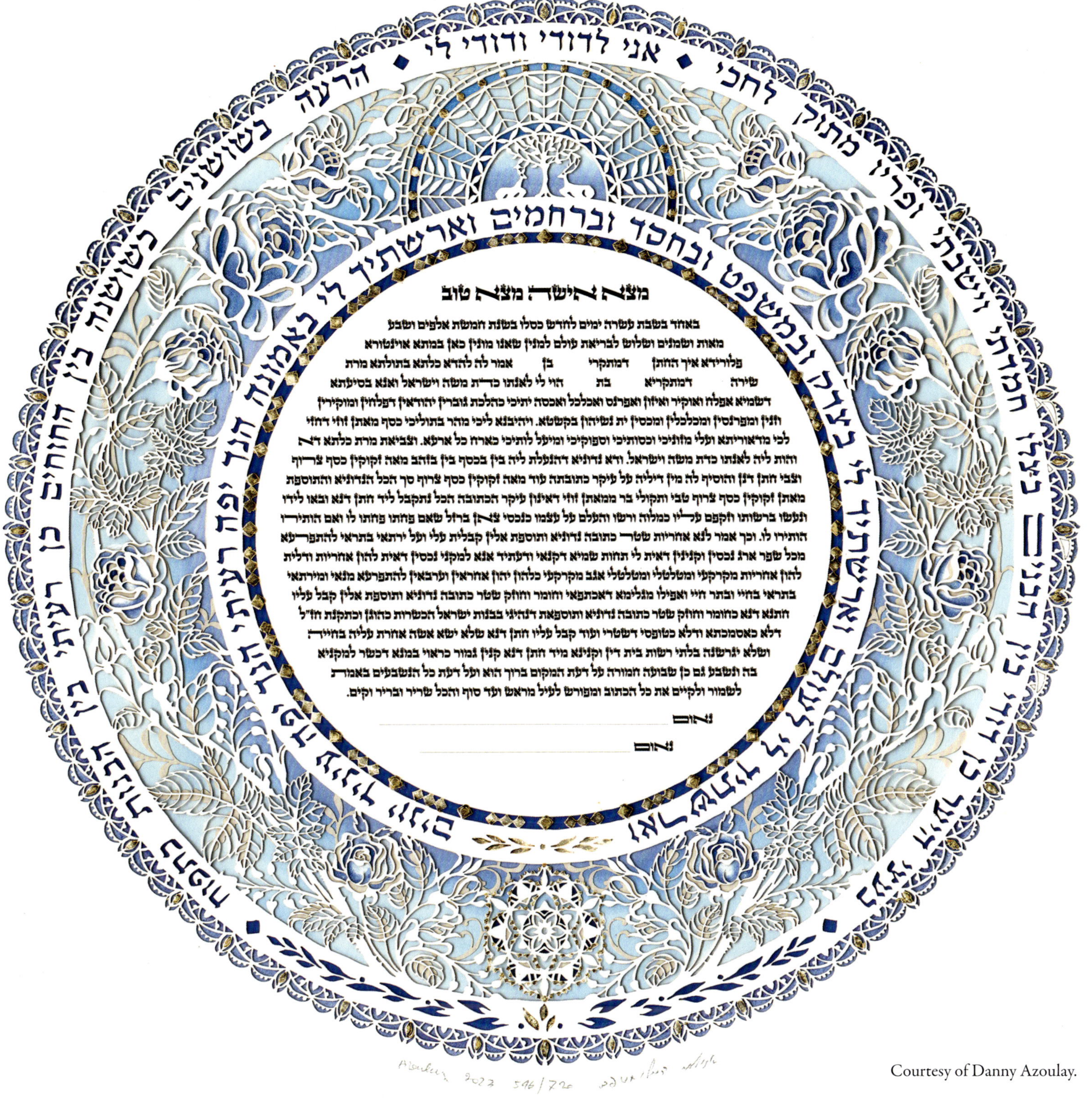

Courtesy of Danny Azoulay.

Amalya Nini

“Garden of Eden”

2017

Born into a Yemenite family who arrived in the Land of Israel early in the twentieth century, Amalya Nini (b. 1948) now lives in Tzur Hadassah in the Jerusalem hills. Her intricate papercuts infused with Jewish motifs resemble illuminated manuscripts. A deep love of nature, the flowers of her garden, and the Jerusalem hills landscape near her home inspire her work, exhibited in both the United States and Israel.

This elaborately painted circular papercut displays a rainbow of irises, often a potent symbol of wisdom, hope, and protection. Smaller flowers, perching multicolored birds, and ornamental flourishes additionally weave into a tapestry of love overflowing with nature’s miraculous delights.

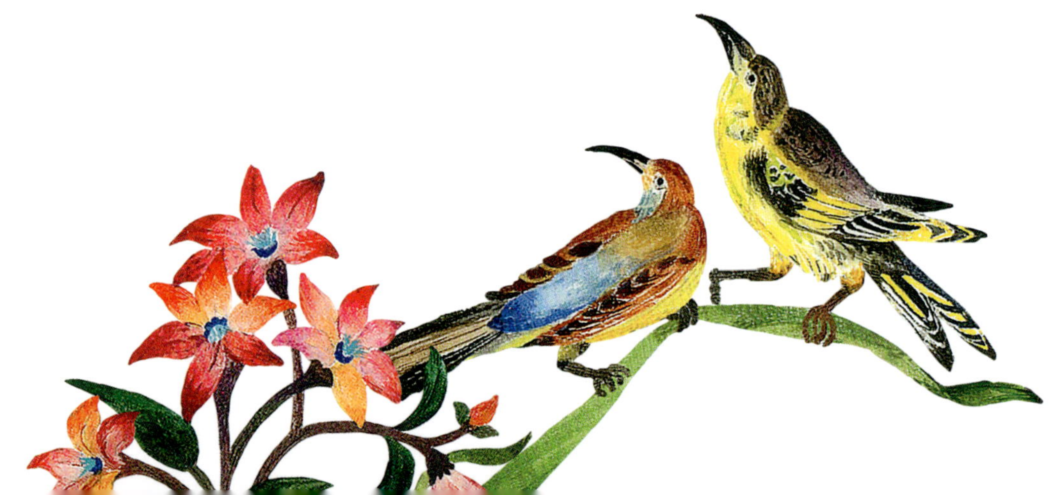

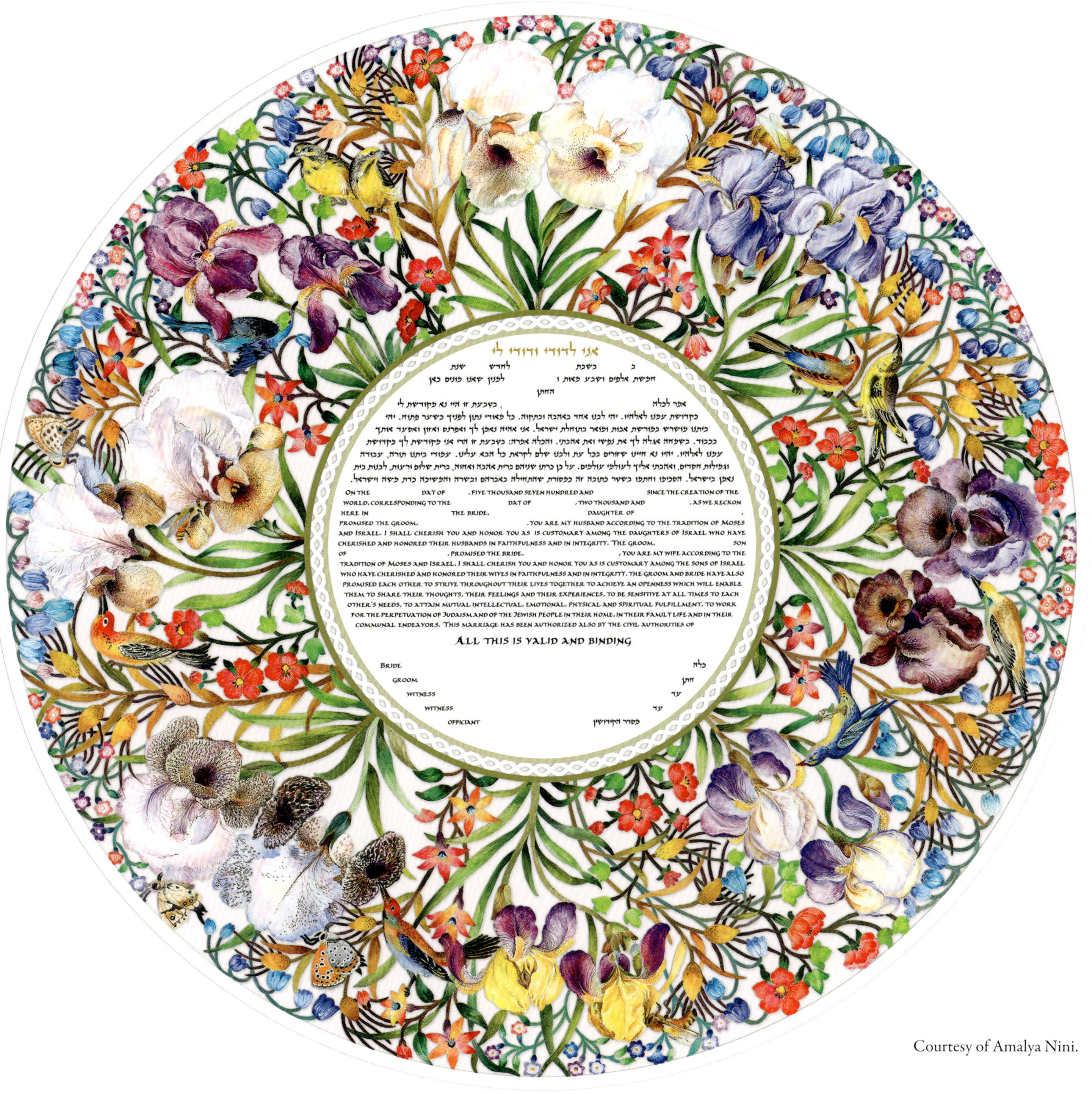

Courtesy of Amalya Nini.

Shell Rummel

“Adventure of a Lifetime II”

2017

Artist and interior designer Shell Rummel splits her time between the west coast of Florida and the outskirts of Washington DC. She is drawn to organic lines, authentic materials, and textures that allow for juxtaposing perfect and imperfect details in nature. Symbolic imagery, gorgeous watercolor washes, and textural papercuts are interwoven to effect a modern, fresh, and timeless feel. Her work has been collected by private and corporate art patrons throughout the globe.

This metaphoric outdoor scene symbolically depicts raw beauty and hints at the journey a couple may take through dark passages, fiery sunsets, mountain vistas, and luxurious rolling clouds. Rummel’s unique wet-on-wet watercolor technique incorporating alcohol inks gives rise to variegated areas of concentrated color and translucency.

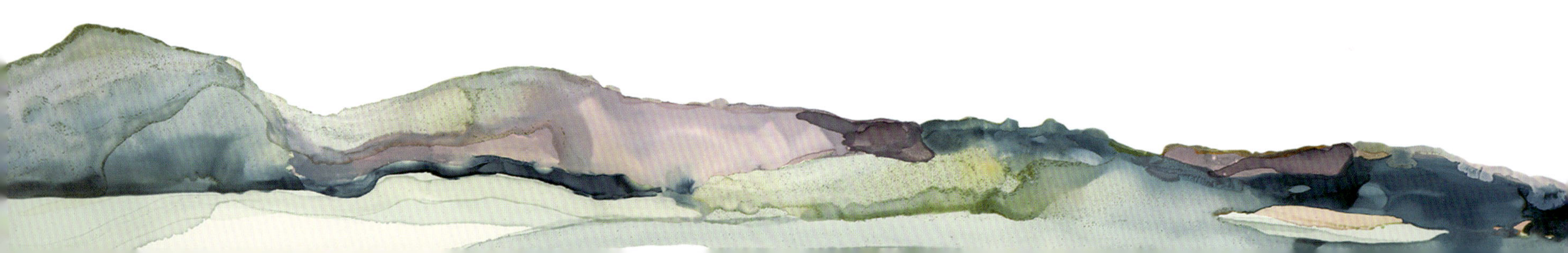

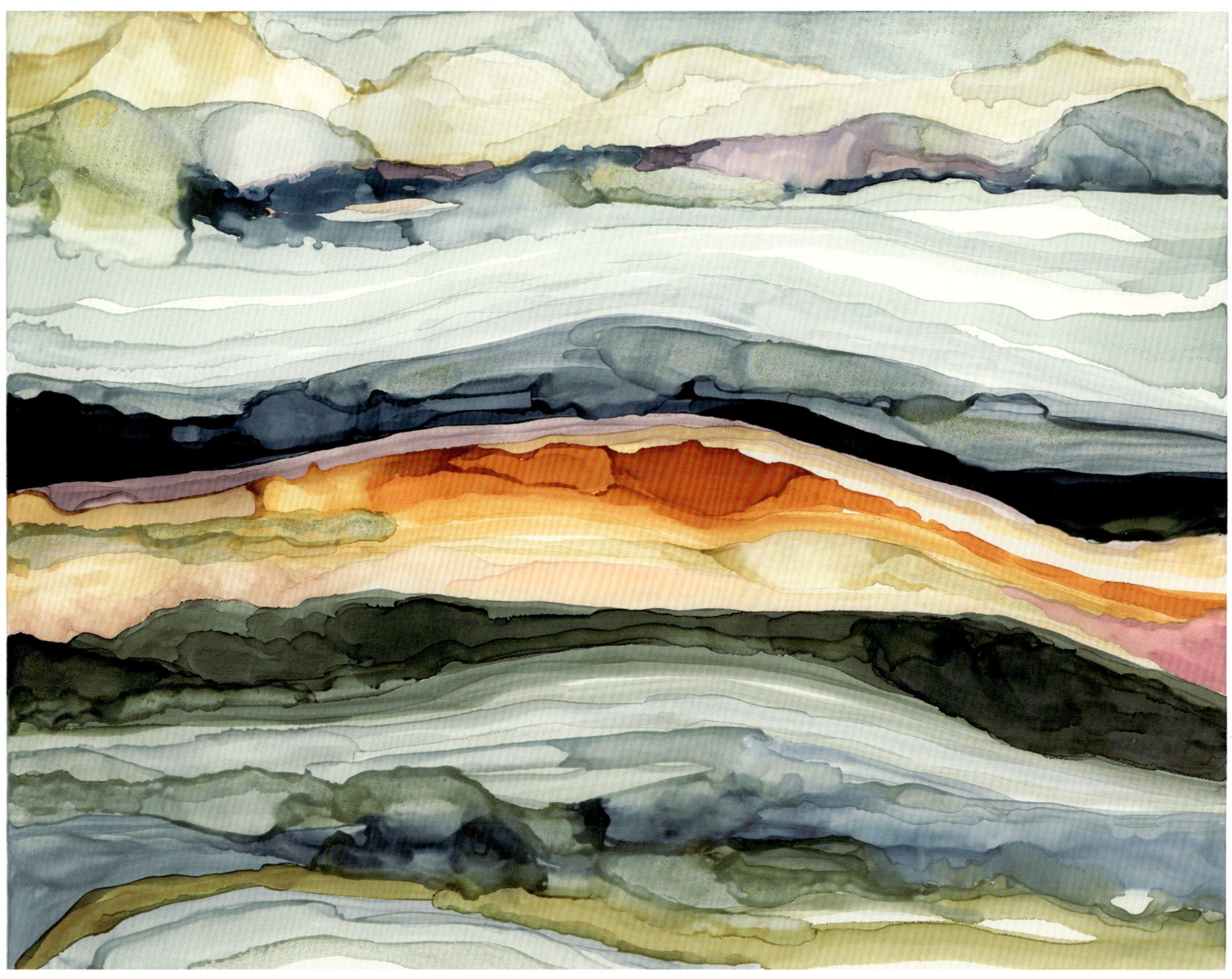

באושר רב של יום חג, בשביעי בשבת, שני ימים לחודש כסלו בשנת חמשת אלפים שבע מאות ושבעים ותשע, בסבנה ג׳ורג׳יה ארצות הברית, מרדכי בן טביה וספירה וקרמית בת שמואל ובײלא אמרו את המילים וביצעו את הטקסים אשר איחדו את חייהם והצהירו על אהבתם, בנוכחות ברכות אלוהים וכדת משה וישראל.

החברות שבינינו חזקה מכל. אנו התקוות והעתיד זה של זו. אנו ידידים בנפש, ונותנים זה לזו כוחות. בעומדי לידך בגאווה, בעינך אני רואה אהבה, ובלבך אני רואה את חלומותיי, ובהבטחתנו אני רואה איחוד אמיתי ואיתן, מוקדש כולו לחמלה, לחסד ולכנות. לא היתה בשום מקום ובשום זמן אהבה כמו שלנו, וסיפורנו יסופר ביופי, בחן ועם משמעות.

אנו מתחייבים לעזור ולסעוד זה את זו, להיענות לאתגרי החיים בכוח שליו ובאומץ-לב, ולאמץ את ברכות החיים בהשתאות, שמחה וצחוק. נגדל כל אחד בדרכו ונתענג על החופש הנהדר הצומח מתוך כבוד הדדי. בשום מקום ובשום זמן לא יהיה עוד סיפור כמו שלנו.

בריתנו הקדושה שרירה וקיימת.

ON THIS DAY OF GREAT CELEBRATION AND JOY, ON THE SEVENTH DAY OF THE WEEK, THE SECOND DAY OF THE MONTH OF KISLEV IN THE YEAR 5779, WHICH CORRESPONDS TO THE NINTH DAY OF NOVEMBER, IN THE YEAR 2018, IN SAVANNAH, GEORGIA, USA, MATTHEW ROSS, SON OF THOMAS AND SYLVIA, AND KIMBERLY STONE, DAUGHTER OF SAM AND BARBARA, SPOKE THE WORDS AND PERFORMED THE RITES WHICH UNITED THEIR LIVES AND AFFIRMED THEIR LOVE IN THE PRESENCE OF GOD'S BLESSINGS AND IN ACCORDANCE WITH THE LAWS OF MOSES AND ISRAEL.

YOU ARE MY BEST FRIEND, MY HOPES AND FUTURE, MY STRENGTH, MY SOULMATE. STANDING PROUDLY BESIDE YOU, IN YOUR EYES I SEE MY LOVE, AND IN YOUR HEART I SEE MY DREAMS, AND IN OUR PROMISE I SEE A UNION, TRUE AND STEADFAST, UNIQUELY DEVOTED TO COMPASSION, KINDNESS AND SINCERITY. THROUGH ALL TIME AND SPACE, THERE HAS BEEN NO LOVE LIKE OURS, AND OUR STORY WILL UNFOLD WITH BEAUTY, GRACE AND MEANING.

WE PLEDGE TO CHERISH AND SUSTAIN EACH OTHER, MEETING LIFE'S TRIALS WITH QUIET STRENGTH AND COURAGE, AND MEETING LIFE'S BLESSINGS WITH WONDER, JOY AND LAUGHTER. WE WILL GROW AS INDIVIDUALS AND DELIGHT IN AN ELEGANT FREEDOM BORN FROM MUTUAL RESPECT.

THROUGH ALL TIME AND SPACE, THERE WILL BE NO STORY LIKE OURS.

OUR SACRED COVENANT IS VALID AND BINDING.

BRIDE ______________________ הכלה GROOM ______________________ החתן RABBI ______________________ הרב

WITNESS ______________________ עד WITNESS ______________________ עד

Courtesy of Ketubah.com.

Linda Frimer

“Summit Vista”

2019

Born in the wilderness town of Wells in British Columbia and now living in Vancouver, Linda Frimer draws inspiration from experiencing the awe of creation in Western Canada. The author of *Luminous: An Artist’s Story as a Guide to Radical Creativity* (2022), she creates works of art that honor the sanctity of life. Her paintings are part of the collections of UBC Hospital, Richmond General Hospital, and Beth Tikvah Synagogue, among other venues.

Her gestural brushstrokes and inventive coloring here recall the nineteenth-century art innovations of the Impressionists and post-Impressionists who guided a new vision of light on the land. From the vantage point of a colorfully blooming meadow, the eye is invited to follow the river beyond the center circular text to the alpine lake and into the mountains beyond.

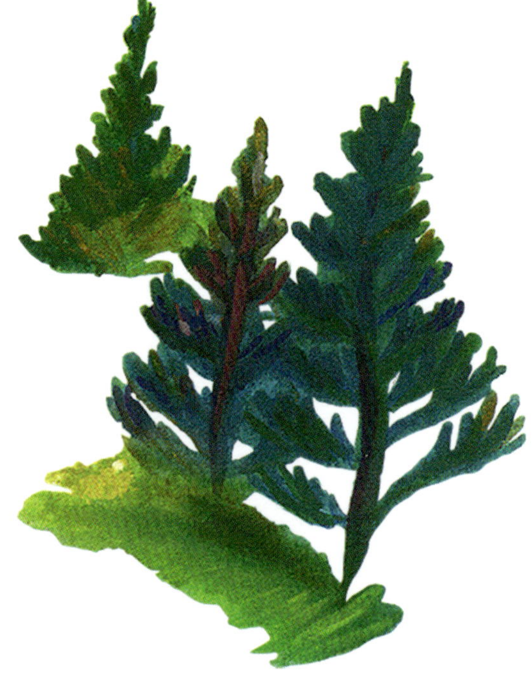

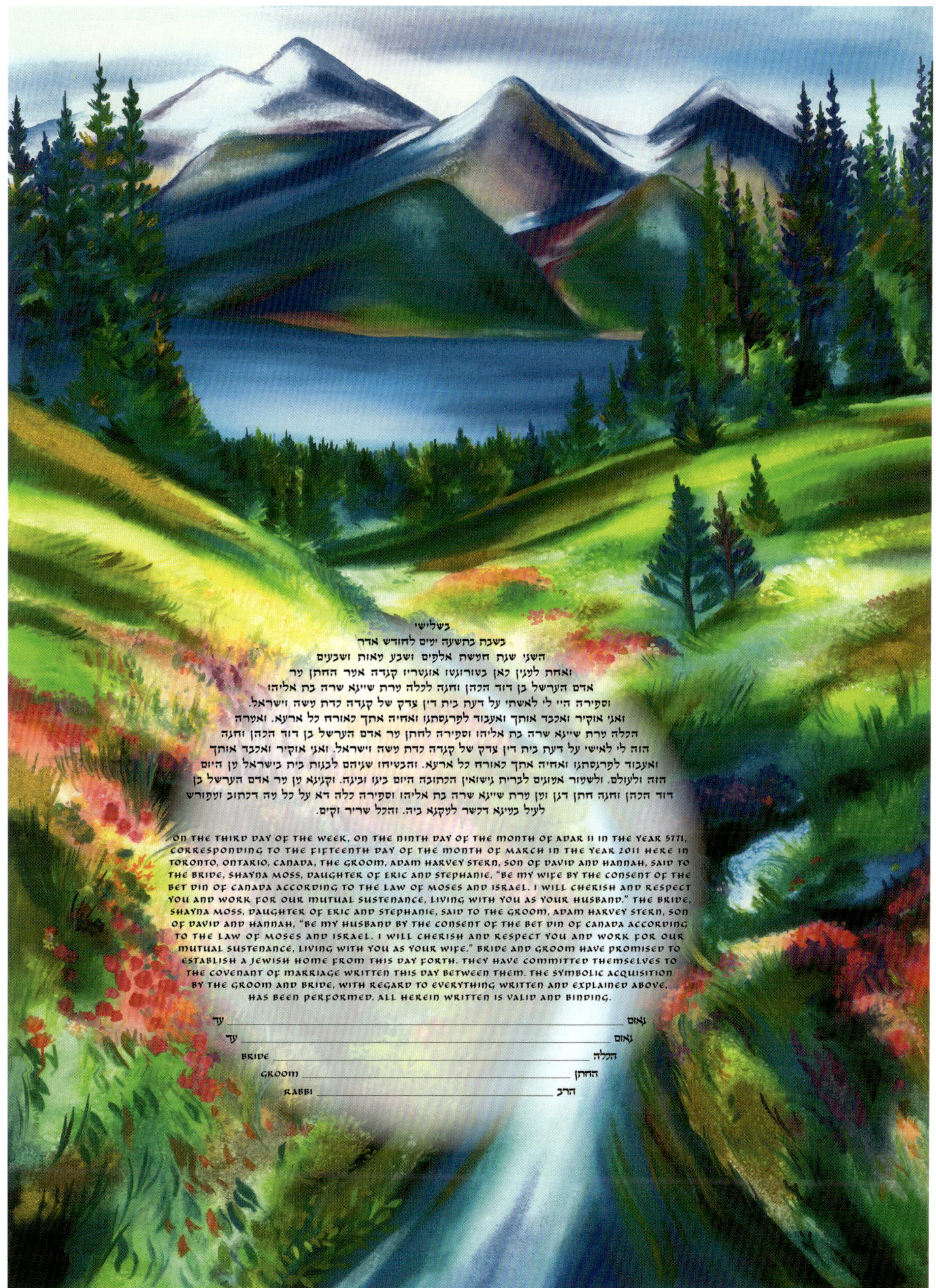
בשלישי
בשבת בתשעה ימים לחודש אדר
השני שנת חמשת אלפים ושבע מאות ושבעים
ואחת למנין כאן בטורונטו אונטריו קנדה אמר החתן מר
אדם הערשל בן דוד הכהן וחנה לכלה מרת שיינא שרה בת אליהו
וספירה הוי לי לאשתי על דעת בית דין צדק של קנדה כדת משה וישראל.
ואני אוקיר ואכבד אותך ואעבוד לפרנסתנו ואחיה אתך כאורח כל ארעא. ואמרה
הכלה מרת שיינא שרה בת אליהו וספירה לחתן מר אדם הערשל בן דוד הכהן וחנה
הוה לי לאישי על דעת בית דין צדק של קנדה כדת משה וישראל. ואני אוקיר ואכבד אותך
ואעבוד לפרנסתנו ואחיה אתך כאורח כל ארעא. והבטיחו שניהם לבנות בית בישראל מן היום
הזה ולעולם. ולשמור אמונים לברית נישואין הכתובה היום בינו וביניה. וקנינא מן מר אדם הערשל בן
דוד הכהן וחנה חתן דנן ומן מרת שיינא שרה בת אליהו וספירה כלה דא על כל מה דכתוב ומפורש
לעיל במנא דכשר למקנא ביה. והכל שריר וקים.

On the third day of the week, on the ninth day of the month of Adar II in the year 5771, corresponding to the fifteenth day of the month of March in the year 2011 here in Toronto, Ontario, Canada, the groom, Adam Harvey Stern, son of David and Hannah, said to the bride, Shayna Moss, daughter of Eric and Stephanie, "Be my wife by the consent of the Bet Din of Canada according to the law of Moses and Israel. I will cherish and respect you and work for our mutual sustenance, living with you as your husband." The bride, Shayna Moss, daughter of Eric and Stephanie, said to the groom, Adam Harvey Stern, son of David and Hannah, "Be my husband by the consent of the Bet Din of Canada according to the law of Moses and Israel. I will cherish and respect you and work for our mutual sustenance, living with you as your wife." Bride and groom have promised to establish a Jewish home from this day forth. They have committed themselves to the covenant of marriage written this day between them. The symbolic acquisition by the groom and bride, with regard to everything written and explained above, has been performed. All herein written is valid and binding.

נאום ______ עד
נאום ______ עד
הכלה ______ BRIDE
החתן ______ GROOM
הרב ______ RABBI

Courtesy of Ketubah.com.

Enya Keshet

“Sasson Papercut Luxe”

2019

Enya Keshet is based in Pardes Hanna, Israel. Her work preserves the style of the Lisbon manuscript workshop, which flourished in Portugal at the end of the fifteenth century. In keeping with this tradition, she accentuates her papercuts with calligraphy, color illumination, and gold leaf. Decorative writing, in both large and small letters, is enjoined with delicate, fantastic florals.

Opulent visual harmony is on display in this papercut design. Geometrical and nature-inspired patterns generate delicate, delightful movement, and Swarovski crystals and 23K gold leaf, masterly applied by hand, accentuate the vibrant, radiating energy. In the square corners, one heart positioned upside-down atop another is reminiscent of a Star of David, softened by love. The inscription from the sixth wedding blessing reads: “Loving companions will surely gladden, as You gladdened Your creations in the Garden of Eden in the East.”

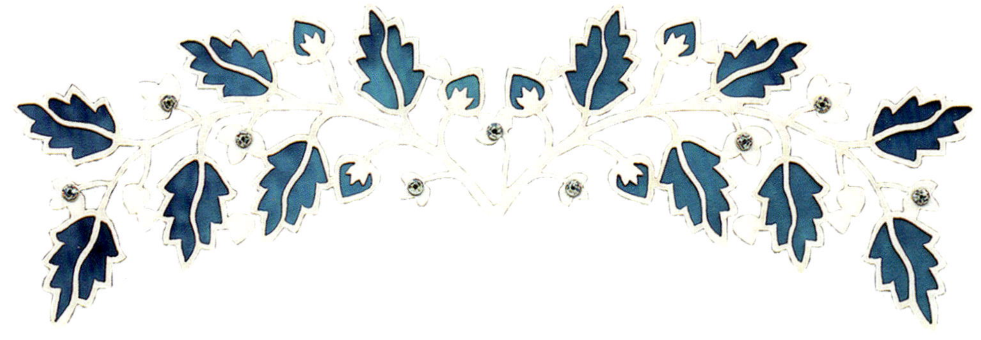

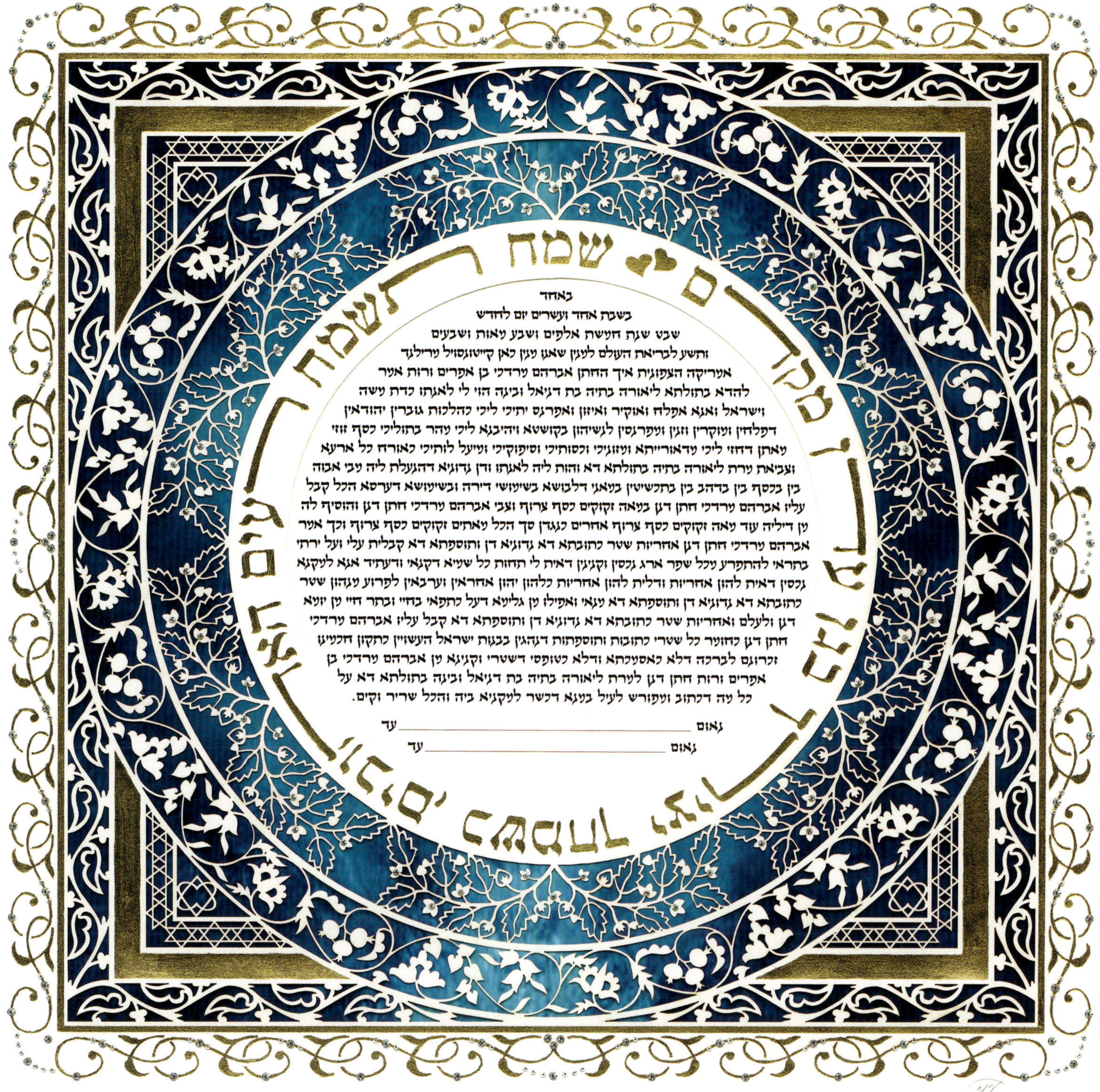

Courtesy of Ketubah.com.

Britt Yudell

“White & Gold Garden Embroidery”

2020

Britt Yudell was born in Jerusalem, lived in Brooklyn, and now resides in Tel Aviv. Her ketubot combine a unique fusion of rare watercolor styles, bright colors, and traditional embroidery.

This circular, symmetrical work exemplifies the couple’s infinitely growing love and connection. Its border is entirely embroidered. Delicate white details that evoke a sense of purity intertwine with the richness of royal gold thread. The aesthetic recalls the sanctity of Yom Kippur, and especially the sacred covenant the bride and groom enter with each other on their wedding day.

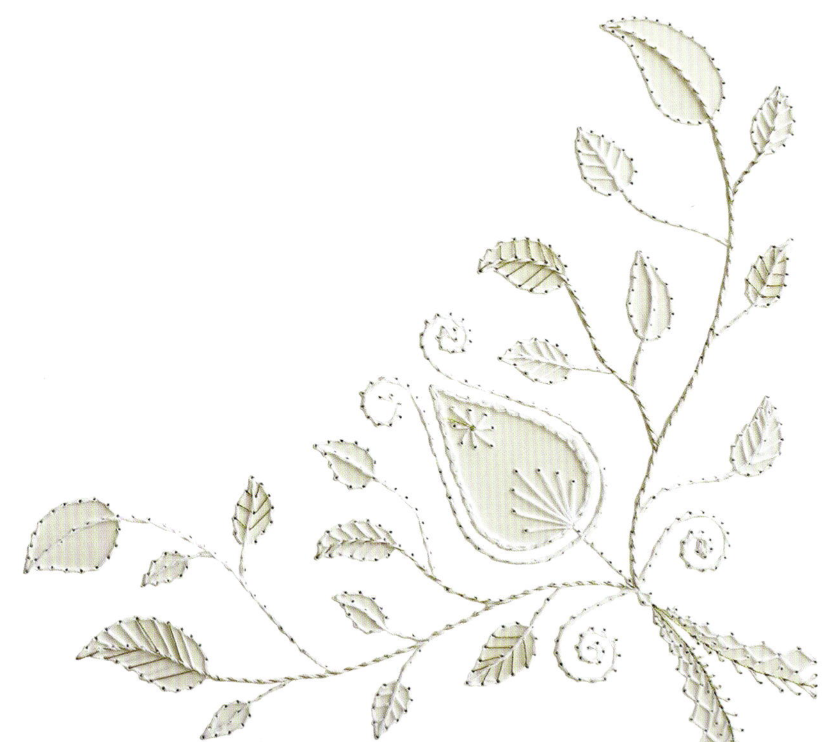

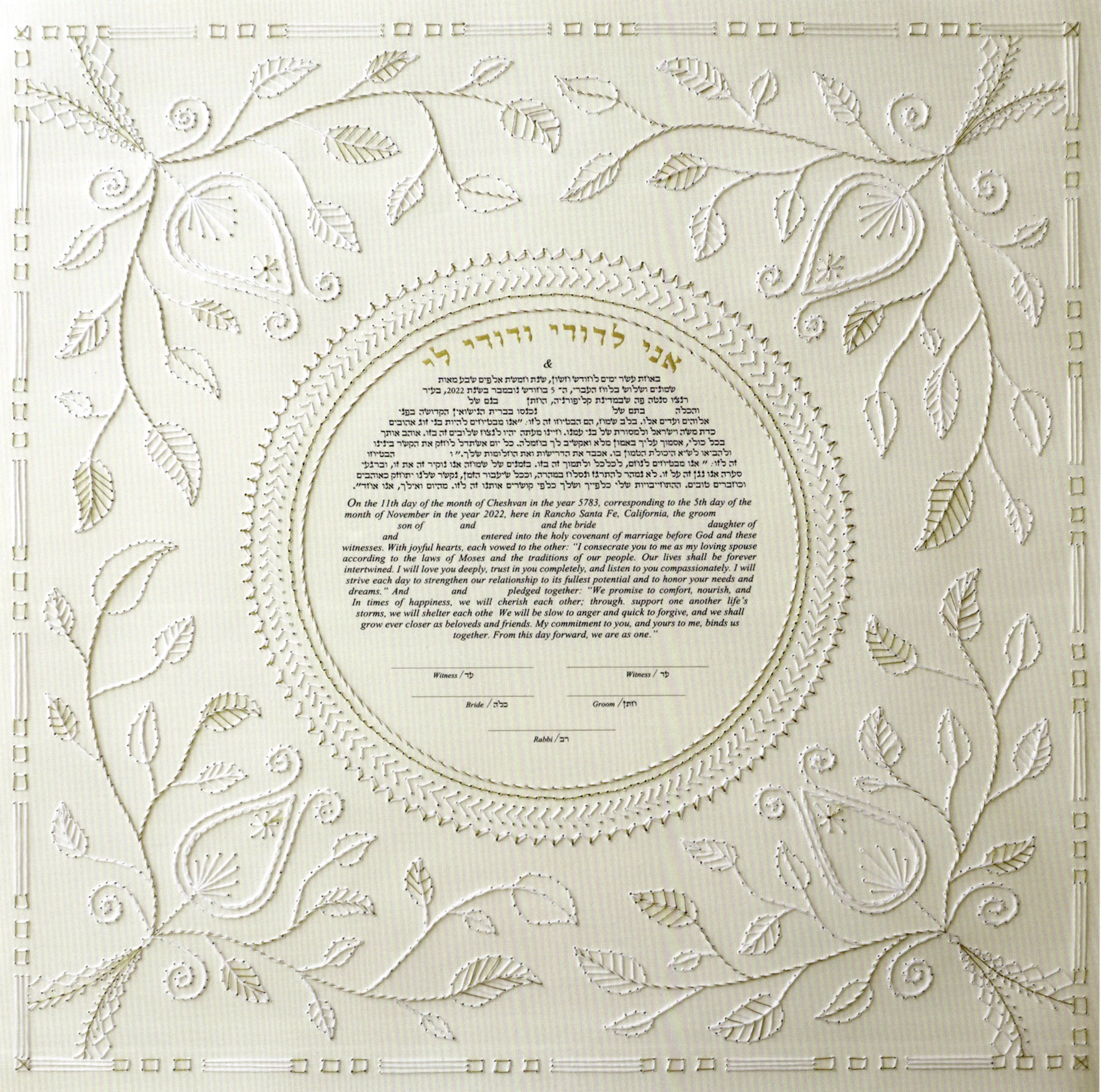

אני לדודי ודודי לי

&

באחד עשר ימים לחודש חשון, שנת חמשת אלפים שבע מאות
שמונים ושלוש בלוח העברי, ה־ 5 בחודש נובמבר בשנת 2022, בעיר
רנצ'ו סנטה פה שבמדינת קליפורניה, החתן בנם של
והכלה בתם של נכנסו בברית הנישואין הקדושה בפני
אלוהים ועדים אלו. בלב שמח, הם הבטיחו זה לזו: "אנו מבטיחים להיות בני זוג אהובים
כדת משה וישראל ולמסורת של בני עמנו. חיינו מעתה יהיו לנצח שלובים זה בזו. אוהב אותך
בכל כולי, אסמוך עליך באמון מלא ואקשיב לך בחמלה. כל יום אשתדל לחזק את הקשר בינינו
ולהביאו לשיא היכולת הטמון בו. אכבד את הדרישות ואת החלומות שלך." ו הבטיחו
זה לזו: " אנו מבטיחים לנחם, לכלכל ולתמוך זה בזו. בזמנים של שמחה אנו נוקיר זה את זו, וברגעי
סערה אנו נגן זה על זו. לא נמהר להתרגז ונסלח במהרה, וככל שיעבור הזמן, נקשר שלנו יתחזק כאוהבים
וכחברים טובים. ההתחייבויות שלי כלפיך ושלך כלפי קושרים אותנו זה לזו. מהיום ואילך, אנו אחד".

On the 11th day of the month of Cheshvan in the year 5783, corresponding to the 5th day of the month of November in the year 2022, here in Rancho Santa Fe, California, the groom son of and and the bride daughter of and entered into the holy covenant of marriage before God and these witnesses. With joyful hearts, each vowed to the other: "I consecrate you to me as my loving spouse according to the laws of Moses and the traditions of our people. Our lives shall be forever intertwined. I will love you deeply, trust in you completely, and listen to you compassionately. I will strive each day to strengthen our relationship to its fullest potential and to honor your needs and dreams." And and pledged together: "We promise to comfort, nourish, and In times of happiness, we will cherish each other; through. support one another life's storms, we will shelter each othe We will be slow to anger and quick to forgive, and we shall grow ever closer as beloveds and friends. My commitment to you, and yours to me, binds us together. From this day forward, we are as one."

Witness / עד | Witness / עד

Bride / כלה | Groom / חתן

Rabbi / רב

Courtesy of Britt Yudell.

Jessica Tamar Deutsch

“Forest at Night”

2020

Jessica Tamar Deutsch grew up in New Rochelle, New York, and resides in Brooklyn. Deeply inspired by the Jewish Renewal movement, she often explores the pulse of ancient tradition within contemporary culture. She has authored and illustrated several books, including *The Illustrated Pirkei Avot: A Graphic Novel of Jewish Ethics* (2017) and *Rebbe Nachman's The Lost Princess* (2024).

Here, Deutsch calls upon imagery in nature to inspire feelings of awe and commitment. She links the circular ketubah, a common feature of the contemporary ketubah renaissance, to the cycle of the moon underpinning the months of the Hebrew calendar. Her illustrative style, reminiscent of classic books such as Maurice Sendak's *Where the Wild Things Are*, adds an element of childlike wonder.

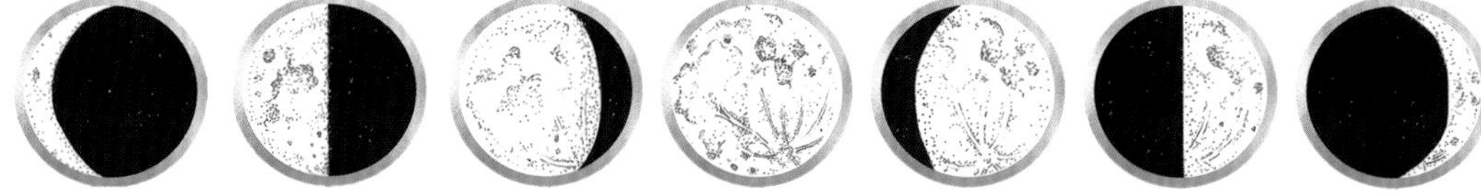

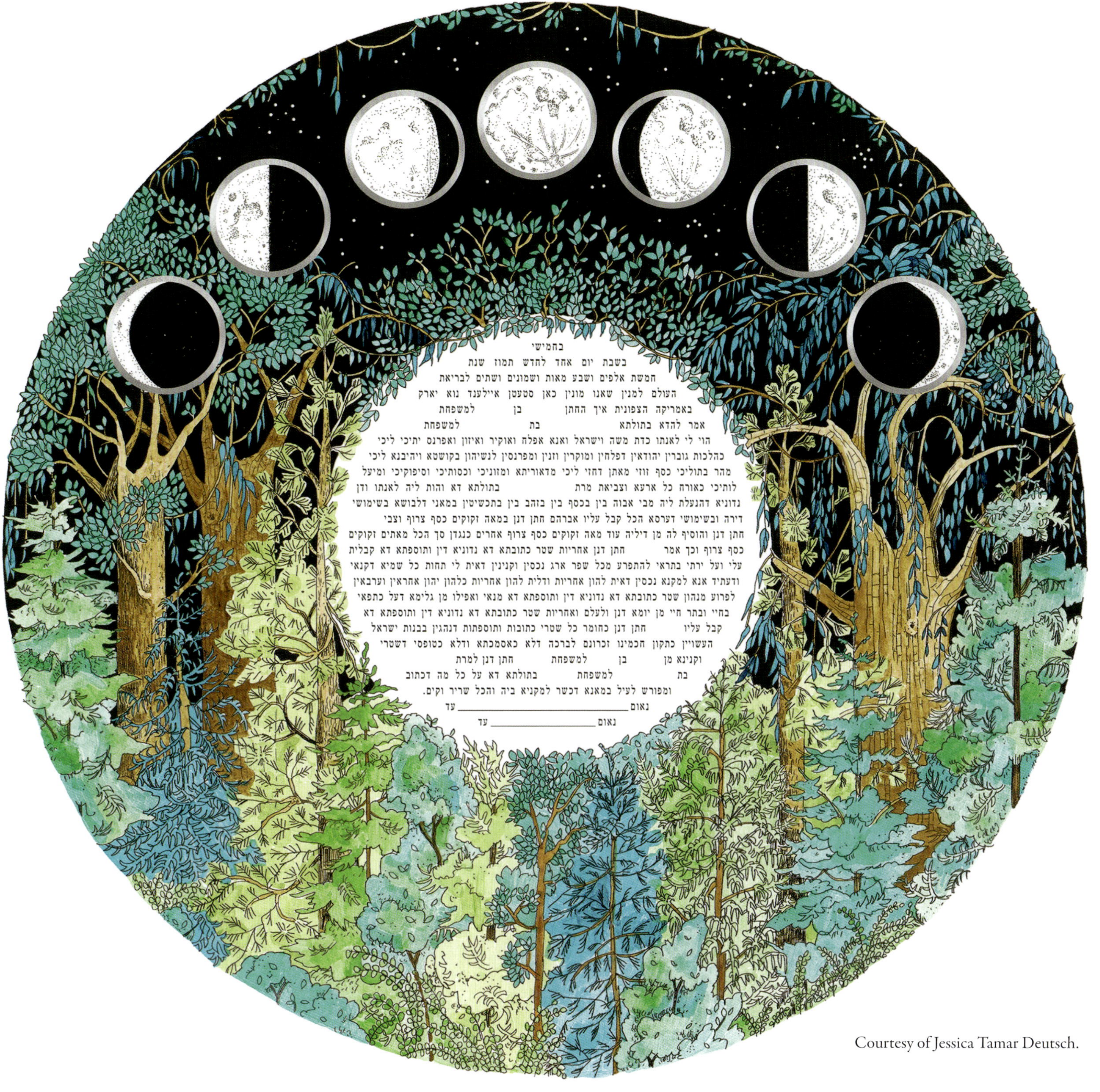

Courtesy of Jessica Tamar Deutsch.

Rachel Ellison

“The Old Will Be Made New; The New Will Be Made Holy. The Phoenix Will Rise”

2020

Rachel Ellison grew up near Cincinnati and resides in Chicago. Her work highlights the diversity of contemporary Jewish life. She is inspired by how rituals mark communal time and how art can serve as connective tissue across time, space, and people. By creating ketubot, she adds her own voice to the rich history of Jewish ritual art—a polyphony of multigenerational traditions.

Here, Ellison’s blend of Native American symbols with traditional Jewish motifs forges a uniquely old-and-new American Jewish aesthetic. The natural cycle of the moon shown at the top is central to the Jewish lunar-based calendar. The Moorish-inspired shield framing the text is guarded by the Eye of Providence, a possible allusion to God’s compassionate watchfulness over humanity. At the bottom, a rising phoenix taking flight from below symbolizes the couple’s grandparents, who were Holocaust survivors. For this Jewish bride and groom marrying in America, the fruit and vines encircling the text additionally invoke reconnecting to this land and its abundance.

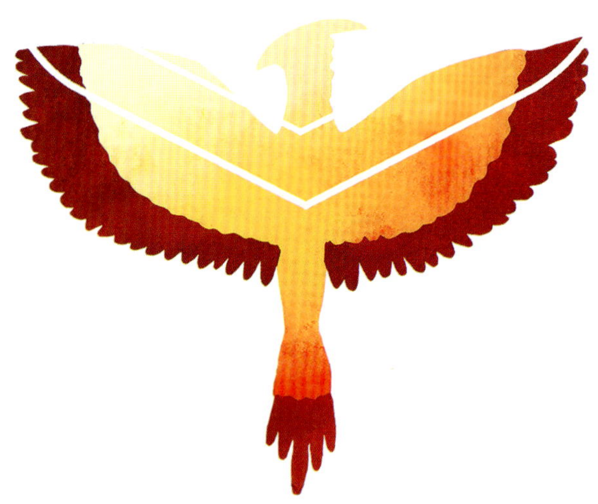

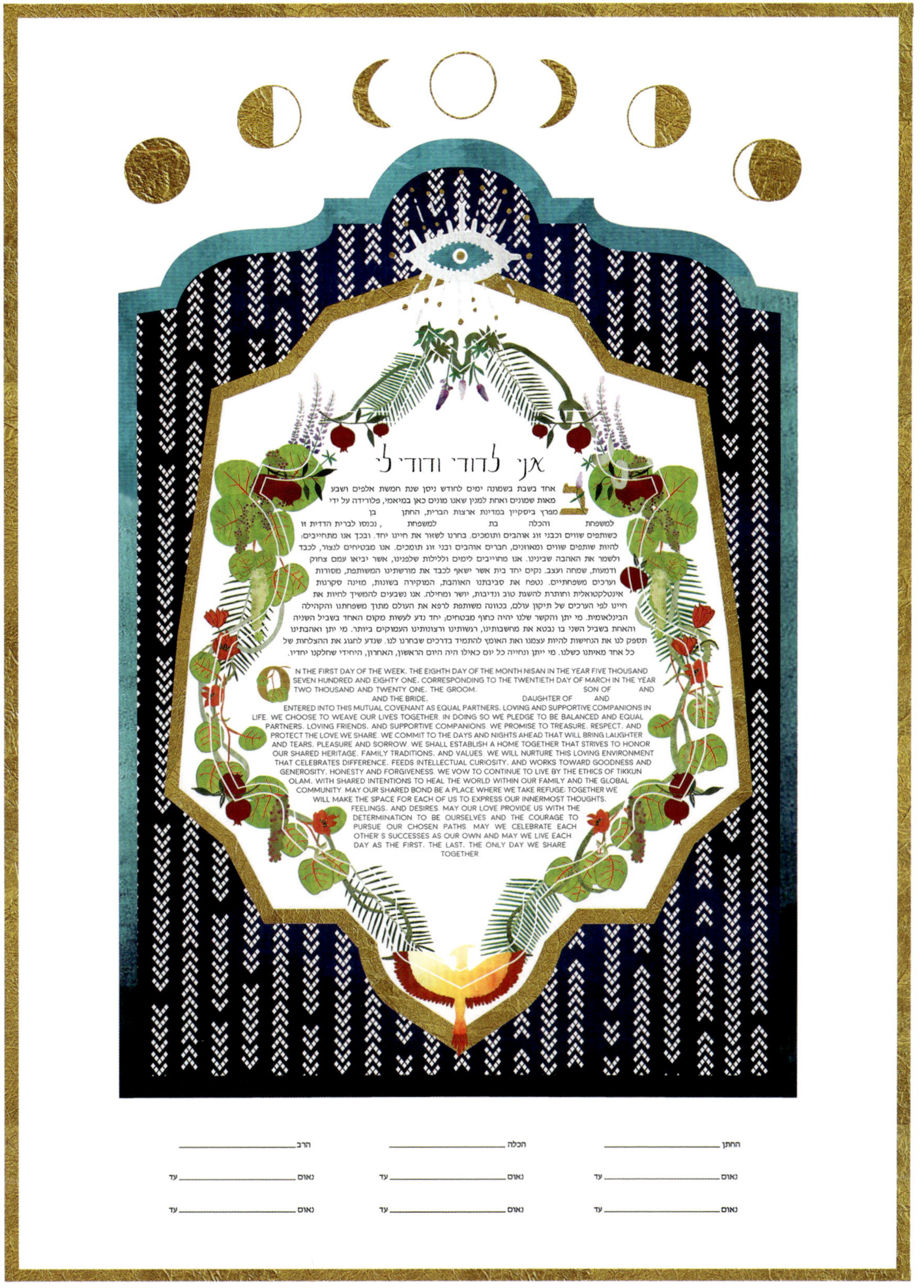

אני לדודי ודודי לי

באחד בשבת בשמונה ימים לחודש ניסן שנת חמשת אלפים ושבע מאות שמונים ואחת למנין שאנו מונים כאן במיאמי, פלורידה על ידי מפרץ ביסקיין במדינת ארצות הברית, החתן בן למשפחת והכלה בת למשפחת , נכנסו לברית הדדית זו כשותפים שווים וכבני זוג אוהבים ותומכים. בחרנו לשזור את חיינו יחד. ובכך אנו מתחייבים: להיות שותפים שווים ומאוזנים, חברים אוהבים ובני זוג תומכים. אנו מבטיחים לנצור, לכבד ולשמר את האהבה שבינינו. אנו מחוייבים לימים וללילות שלפנינו, אשר יביאו עמם צחוק ודמעות, שמחה ועצב. נקים יחד בית אשר ישאף לכבד את מורשתינו המשותפת, מסורות וערכים משפחתיים. נטפח את סביבתנו האוהבת, המוקירה בשונות, מזינה סקרנות אינטלקטואלית וחותרת להשגת טוב ונדיבות, יושר ומחילה. אנו נשבעים להמשיך לחיות את חיינו לפי הערכים של תיקון עולם, בכוונה משותפת לרפא את העולם מתוך משפחתנו והקהילה הבינלאומית. מי יתן והקשר שלנו יהיה כחוף מבטחים; יחד נדע לעשות מקום האחד בשביל השניה והאחת בשביל השני בו נבטא את מחשבותינו, רגשותינו ורצונותינו העמוקים ביותר. מי יתן ואהבתינו תספק לנו את הנחישות להיות עצמנו ואת האומץ להתמיד בדרכים שבחרנו לנו. שנדע לחגוג את ההצלחות של כל אחד מאיתנו כשלנו. מי ייתן ונחייה כל יום כאילו היה היום הראשון, האחרון, היחידי שחלקנו יחדיו.

ON THE FIRST DAY OF THE WEEK. THE EIGHTH DAY OF THE MONTH NISAN IN THE YEAR FIVE THOUSAND SEVEN HUNDRED AND EIGHTY ONE. CORRESPONDING TO THE TWENTIETH DAY OF MARCH IN THE YEAR TWO THOUSAND AND TWENTY ONE. THE GROOM. SON OF AND AND THE BRIDE. DAUGHTER OF AND ENTERED INTO THIS MUTUAL COVENANT AS EQUAL PARTNERS. LOVING AND SUPPORTIVE COMPANIONS IN LIFE. WE CHOOSE TO WEAVE OUR LIVES TOGETHER. IN DOING SO WE PLEDGE TO BE BALANCED AND EQUAL PARTNERS. LOVING FRIENDS. AND SUPPORTIVE COMPANIONS. WE PROMISE TO TREASURE. RESPECT. AND PROTECT THE LOVE WE SHARE. WE COMMIT TO THE DAYS AND NIGHTS AHEAD THAT WILL BRING LAUGHTER AND TEARS. PLEASURE AND SORROW. WE SHALL ESTABLISH A HOME TOGETHER THAT STRIVES TO HONOR OUR SHARED HERITAGE. FAMILY TRADITIONS. AND VALUES. WE WILL NURTURE THIS LOVING ENVIRONMENT THAT CELEBRATES DIFFERENCE. FEEDS INTELLECTUAL CURIOSITY. AND WORKS TOWARD GOODNESS AND GENEROSITY. HONESTY AND FORGIVENESS. WE VOW TO CONTINUE TO LIVE BY THE ETHICS OF TIKKUN OLAM. WITH SHARED INTENTIONS TO HEAL THE WORLD WITHIN OUR FAMILY AND THE GLOBAL COMMUNITY. MAY OUR SHARED BOND BE A PLACE WHERE WE TAKE REFUGE: TOGETHER WE WILL MAKE THE SPACE FOR EACH OF US TO EXPRESS OUR INNERMOST THOUGHTS. FEELINGS. AND DESIRES. MAY OUR LOVE PROVIDE US WITH THE DETERMINATION TO BE OURSELVES AND THE COURAGE TO PURSUE OUR CHOSEN PATHS. MAY WE CELEBRATE EACH OTHER'S SUCCESSES AS OUR OWN AND MAY WE LIVE EACH DAY AS THE FIRST. THE LAST. THE ONLY DAY WE SHARE TOGETHER.

החתן ______	הכלה ______	הרב ______
נאום ______ עד	נאום ______ עד	נאום ______ עד
נאום ______ עד	נאום ______ עד	נאום ______ עד

Courtesy of Rachel Ellison.

Ayala Ophir

"Modern Nature"

2021

Ayala Ophir was born in Tel Aviv and resides in Ofra. Her papercut ketubot draw from Jewish spiritual sources and the landscapes of Israel. Painting in watercolor over her papercuts gives her designs an illuminated vibrancy.

In this papercut ketubah handpainted in blue, green, and brown watercolors, two thirsty deer encountering one another by the waters represent two lovers yearning to fill their hearts with pure love.

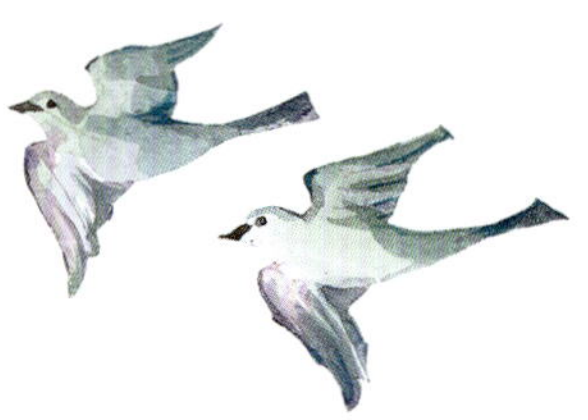

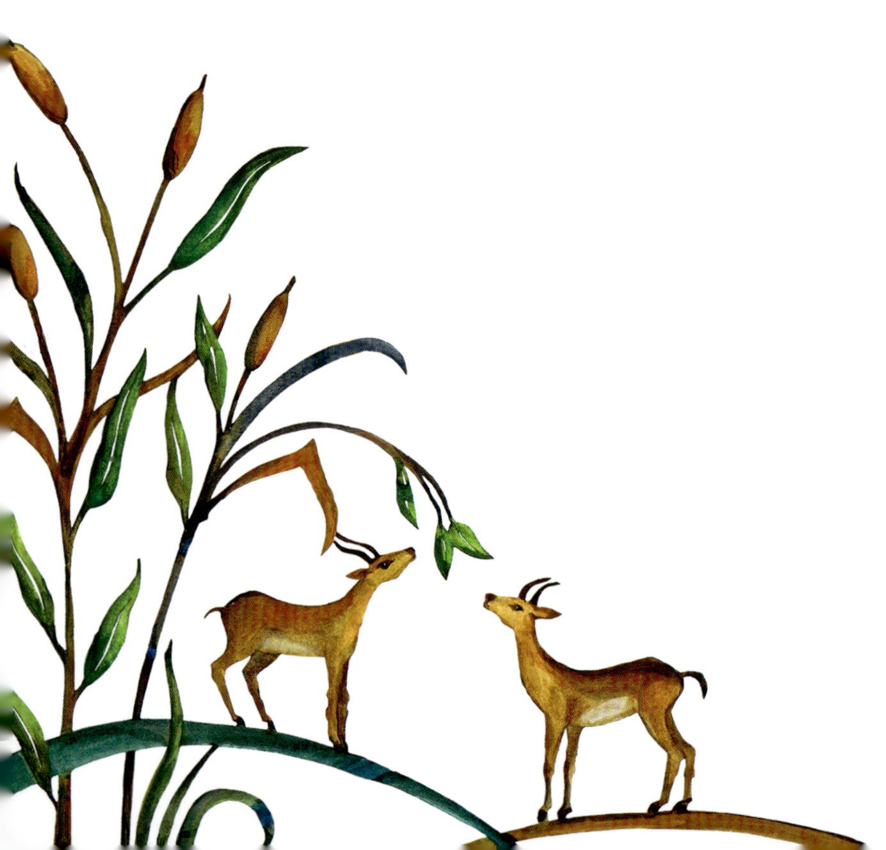

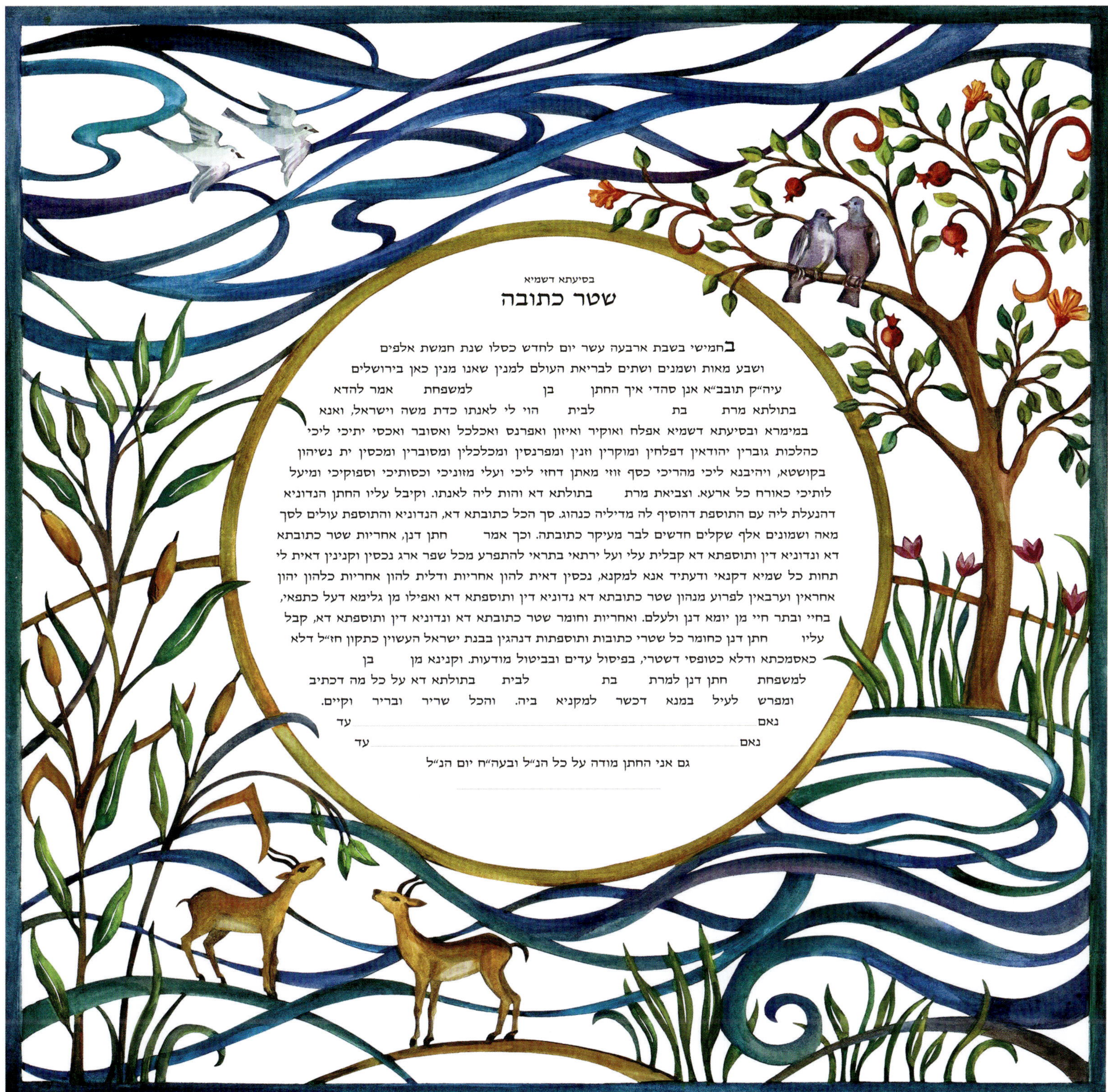

בסיעתא דשמיא

שטר כתובה

בחמישי בשבת ארבעה עשר יום לחדש כסלו שנת חמשת אלפים
ושבע מאות ושמנים ושתים לבריאת העולם למנין שאנו מנין כאן בירושלים
עיה״ק תובב״א אנן סהדי איך החתן בן למשפחת אמר להדא
בתולתא מרת בת לבית הוי לי לאנתו כדת משה וישראל, ואנא
במימרא ובסיעתא דשמיא אפלח ואוקיר ואיזון ואפרנס ואכלכל ואסובר ואכסי יתיכי ליכי
כהלכות גוברין יהודאין דפלחין ומוקרין וזנין ומפרנסין ומכלכלין ומסוברין ומכסין ית נשיהון
בקושטא, ויהיבנא ליכי מהריכי כסף זוזי מאתן דחזי ליכי ועלי מזוניכי וכסותיכי וספוקיכי ומיעל
לותיכי כאורח כל ארעא. וצביאת מרת בתולתא דא והות ליה לאנתו. וקיבל עליו החתן הנדוניא
דהנעלת ליה עם התוספת דהוסיף לה מדיליה כנהוג. סך הכל כתובתא דא, הנדוניא והתוספת עולים לסך
מאה ושמונים אלף שקלים חדשים לבר מעיקר כתובתה. וכך אמר חתן דנן, אחריות שטר כתובתא
דא ונדוניא דין ותוספתא דא קבלית עלי ועל ירתאי בתראי להתפרע מכל שפר ארג נכסין וקנינין דאית לי
תחות כל שמיא דקנאי ודעתיד אנא למקנא, נכסין דאית להון אחריות ודלית להון אחריות כלהון יהון
אחראין וערבאין לפרוע מנהון שטר כתובתא דא נדוניא דין ותוספתא דא ואפילו מן גלימא דעל כתפאי,
בחיי ובתר חיי מן יומא דנן ולעלם. ואחריות וחומר שטר כתובתא דא ונדוניא דין ותוספתא דא, קבל
עליו חתן דנן כחומר כל שטרי כתובות ותוספתות דנהגין בבנת ישראל העשוין כתקון חז״ל דלא
כאסמכתא ודלא כטופסי דשטרי, בפיסול עדים ובביטול מודעות. וקנינא מן בן
למשפחת חתן דנן למרת בת לבית בתולתא דא על כל מה דכתיב
ומפרש לעיל במנא דכשר למקניא ביה. והכל שריר ובריר וקיים.
נאם ________ עד
נאם ________ עד
גם אני החתן מודה על כל הנ״ל ובעה״ח יום הנ״ל

Courtesy of Ayala Ophir.

Hadass Mor Gerson

"Camp Harlam 60th Anniversary Ketubah"

2021

Baltimore native Hadass Mor Gerson explores the timeless beauty and harmony of nature in her ketubah designs. Her watercolor paintings imbue Jewish wedding traditions with modern love stories. Her artwork has been exhibited in galleries throughout America and is held in private collections worldwide.

This ketubah was commissioned for the sixtieth anniversary of Camp Harlam, a Union for Reform Judaism summer camp nestled in the Pocono Mountain foothills, to celebrate all the couples who first met at camp and eventually married, transforming their summer loves into forever loves. The imagery draws from the Pennsylvania camp's scenic landscape, and the original text (Gerson's collaboration with Rabbi Benjamin David and Dan Slipakoff) expresses the camp's foundational role in forging friendships as well as the hope that the couples continue to brighten one another's lives and illuminate the larger world as well. Gerson's transcendent watercolors uplift this unconventional commitment document now permanently installed at Camp Harlam.

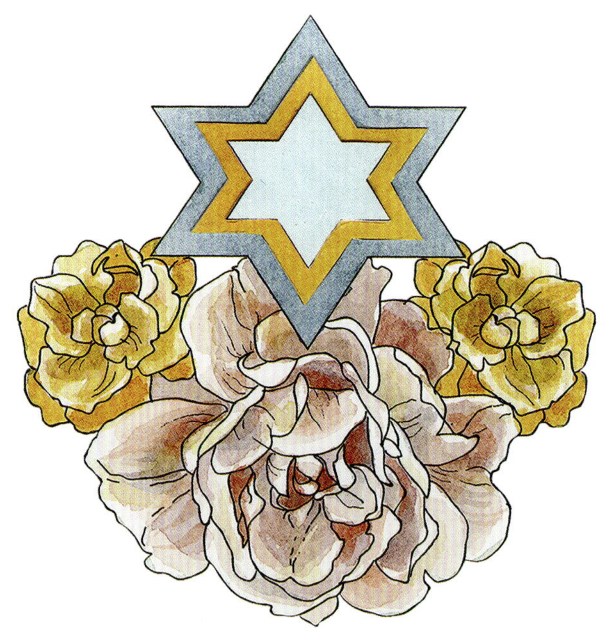

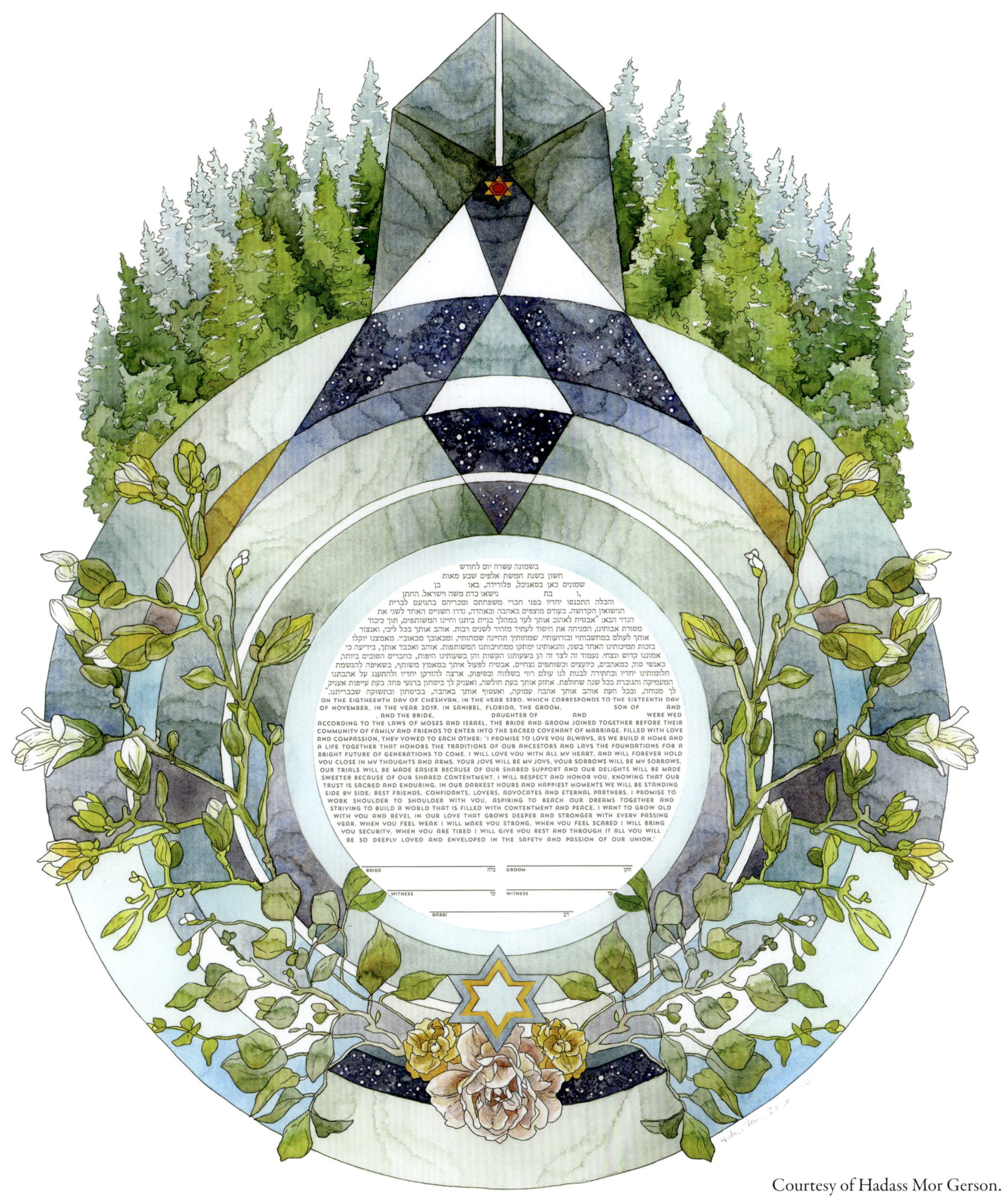

בשמונה עשרה יום לחודש
חשון בשנת חמשת אלפים שבע מאות
שמונים כאן בסאניבל, פלורידה, באו בן
ו, בת נישאו כדת משה וישראל. החתן
והכלה התכנסו יחדיו בפני חברי משפחתם ומכריהם בהגיעם לברית
הנישואין הקדושה. בעודם מוצפים באהבה ובאהדה, נדרו השניים האחד לשני את
הנדר הבא: "אבטיח לאהוב אותך לעד במהלך בניית ביתנו וחיינו המשותפים, תוך כיבוד
מסורת אבותינו, המניחה את היסוד לעתיד מזהיר לשנים רבות. אוהב אותך בכל ליבי, ואנצור
אותך לעולם במחשבותיי ובזרועותיי. שמחותיך תהיינה שמחותיי, ומכאובך מכאוביי. מאמצנו יוקלו
בזכות תמיכותינו האחד בשני, והנאותינו ימתקו ממחויבותנו המשותפות. אוהב ואכבד אותך, בידיעה כי
אמוננו קדוש ונצחי. נעמוד זה לצד זה הן בשעותנו הקשות והן בשעותינו היפות, כחברים הטובים ביותר,
כאנשי סוד, כמאהבים, כיועצים וכשותפים נצחיים. אבטיח לפעול איתך במאמץ משותף, בשאיפה להגשמת
חלומותינו יחדיו ובחתירה לבנות לנו עולם רווי בשלווה ובסיפוק. ארצה להזדקן יחדיו ולהתענג על אהבתנו
המעמיקה והגוברת בכל שנה שחולפת. אחזק אותך בעת חולשה, ואעניק לך ביטחון ברגעי פחד. בעת עייפות אעניק
לך מנוחה, ובכל העת אוהב אותך אהבה עמוקה, ואעטוף אותך באהבה, בביטחון ובתשוקה שבבריתנו."

ON THE EIGTHEENTH DAY OF CHESHVAN, IN THE YEAR 5780, WHICH CORRESPONDS TO THE SIXTEENTH DAY OF NOVEMBER, IN THE YEAR 2019, IN SANIBEL, FLORIDA, THE GROOM, SON OF AND , AND THE BRIDE, DAUGHTER OF AND WERE WED ACCORDING TO THE LAWS OF MOSES AND ISRAEL. THE BRIDE AND GROOM JOINED TOGETHER BEFORE THEIR COMMUNITY OF FAMILY AND FRIENDS TO ENTER INTO THE SACRED COVENANT OF MARRIAGE. FILLED WITH LOVE AND COMPASSION, THEY VOWED TO EACH OTHER: "I PROMISE TO LOVE YOU ALWAYS, AS WE BUILD A HOME AND A LIFE TOGETHER THAT HONORS THE TRADITIONS OF OUR ANCESTORS AND LAYS THE FOUNDATIONS FOR A BRIGHT FUTURE OF GENERATIONS TO COME. I WILL LOVE YOU WITH ALL MY HEART, AND WILL FOREVER HOLD YOU CLOSE IN MY THOUGHTS AND ARMS. YOUR JOYS WILL BE MY JOYS, YOUR SORROWS WILL BE MY SORROWS, OUR TRIALS WILL BE MADE EASIER BECAUSE OF OUR SHARED SUPPORT AND OUR DELIGHTS WILL BE MADE SWEETER BECAUSE OF OUR SHARED CONTENTMENT. I WILL RESPECT AND HONOR YOU, KNOWING THAT OUR TRUST IS SACRED AND ENDURING. IN OUR DARKEST HOURS AND HAPPIEST MOMENTS WE WILL BE STANDING SIDE BY SIDE; BEST FRIENDS, CONFIDANTS, LOVERS, ADVOCATES AND ETERNAL PARTNERS. I PROMISE TO WORK SHOULDER TO SHOULDER WITH YOU, ASPIRING TO REACH OUR DREAMS TOGETHER AND STRIVING TO BUILD A WORLD THAT IS FILLED WITH CONTENTMENT AND PEACE. I WANT TO GROW OLD WITH YOU AND REVEL IN OUR LOVE THAT GROWS DEEPER AND STRONGER WITH EVERY PASSING YEAR. WHEN YOU FEEL WEAK I WILL MAKE YOU STRONG, WHEN YOU FEEL SCARED I WILL BRING YOU SECURITY, WHEN YOU ARE TIRED I WILL GIVE YOU REST AND THROUGH IT ALL YOU WILL BE SO DEEPLY LOVED AND ENVELOPED IN THE SAFETY AND PASSION OF OUR UNION."

BRIDE כלה GROOM חתן

WITNESS עד WITNESS עד

RABBI רב

Courtesy of Hadass Mor Gerson.

Appendix

Common Ketubah Symbols

Bride and Groom—Depictions of the marrying couple, common on ketubot after the Middle Ages, were generally not portraits, but depictions of biblical characters whose names were shared by one or both of the couple, such as Sarah and Abraham, Jacob and Rachel, or Rebecca and Isaac. Nowadays, interlocking wedding rings are more commonly used to symbolize the bride and groom. *See* Ring.

Chuppah—(Heb. "canopy"), today a portable canopy resting on four poles carried by four people under which the wedding ceremony takes place. Open on all four sides, the chuppah can symbolize wholehearted hospitality (akin to the biblical Abraham and Sarah's welcoming tent, also open on all sides), and as such, a Jewish home embodied by acts of kindness and love.

Cypress Trees—One of the most widespread symbols of Jerusalem in Sephardic ketubot, cypress trees can also symbolize the Land of Israel, although the trees are not indigenous to Israel but typically grown either as ornamentals or as windbreaks in orchards. Some scholars postulate the symbol appeared on ketubot because cypress trees were growing on the Temple Mount. Others believe that Jews couldn't see which trees were growing on the Temple Mount from their vantage point on the narrow plaza in front of the Western Wall, and mistakenly identified the cypress trees with the similar looking cedars comprising the building material of the ancient Temple.

Flowers—A symbol of weddings since time immemorial, as they signify the flourishing of new life, flowers have been popular decorations for ritual objects and monuments throughout Jewish history. For many centuries Jewish brides and grooms wore wreaths of flowers and foliage on their heads during the wedding ceremony.

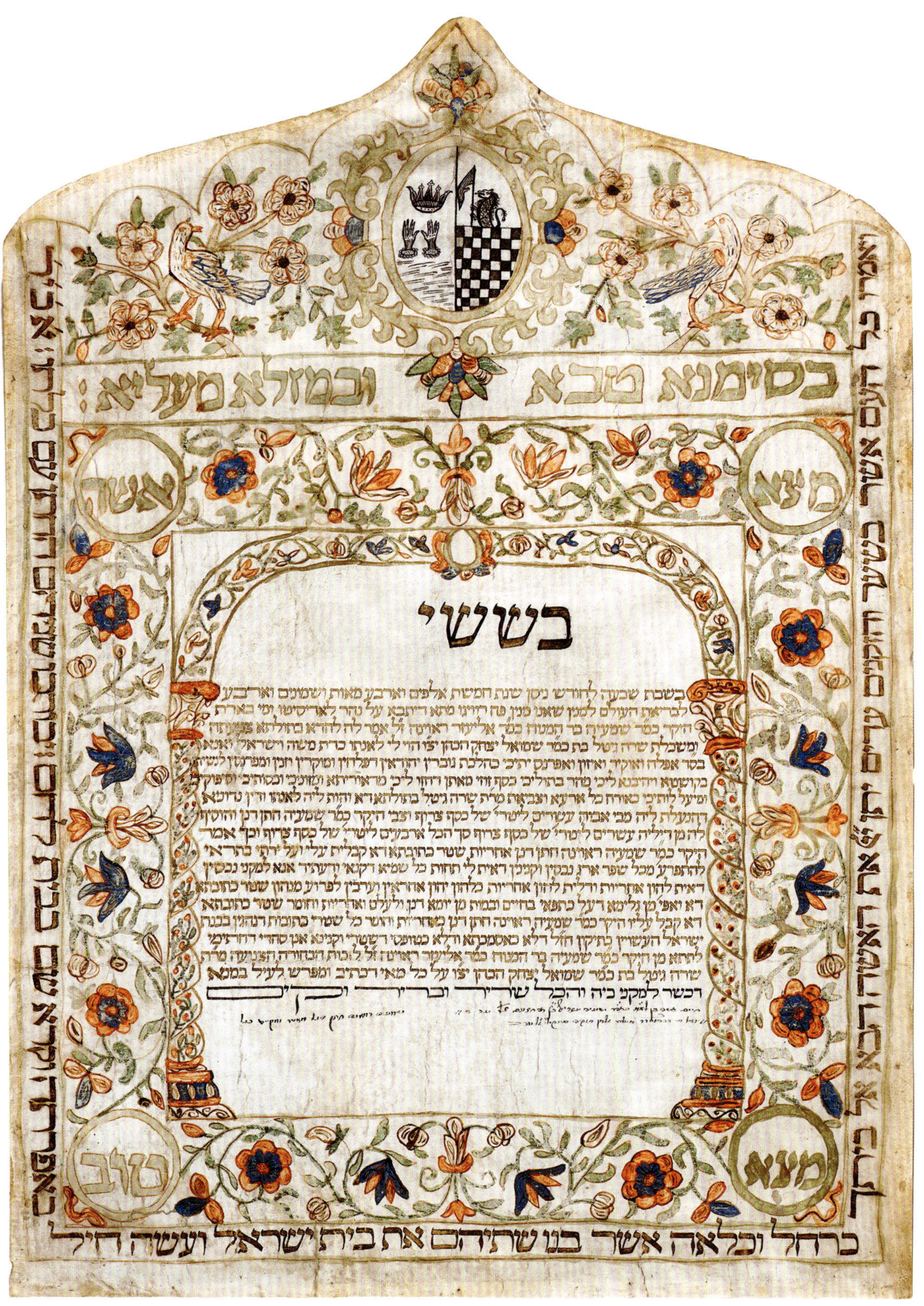

Fig. 16. Ketubah from Rovigo (outside of Venice), 1724. Courtesy of The Jewish Theological Seminary Library.

Gateways—The most popular motif used on artistic ketubot throughout history, going back to the earliest extant ketubot, gateways represent the gates of heaven through which the righteous shall pass, and may also allude to the Temple gates. Gateways also symbolize the newlyweds' transition from one stage of life to the next, as well as their future home that they enter through the sacred ceremony of the wedding. Some gateways have double arches and draw a visual reference to the Tablets of the Law, the holy document that embodies the covenant between the Almighty and the people of Israel.

Hamsa—The downturned stylized hand, often with an eye at the center or with a second thumb replacing the fourth finger, has long been believed to ward off bad luck and invoke the hand of God. Islamic, Christian, and Jewish cultures all adopted the symbol, which has been called the hand of Fatima, the hand of Mary, and the hand of Miriam respectively. On an artistic ketubah, it conveys wishes for good fortune offered to the marrying couple on their wedding day.

Jerusalem and Its Temple—Since 70 CE, when the Romans destroyed the Jerusalem Temple, Jews held the hope alive that the Temple would be restored in the holy city of Jerusalem. Images such as the city skyline, cypress trees (one of two types of trees used in the Temple's construction; see above), and Temple architecture and fixtures became perennial themes of Jewish art, and feature prominently on early ketubot. After the Muslim conquest of the Temple Mount in 637 CE, some ketubah illustrations include the Al-Aqsa Mosque in the Jerusalem skyline. Facades of vernacular Jewish homes in Jerusalem are also a popular visual motif.

Lion—A symbol of justice, strength, and divine protection, the lion is also the emblem of the Tribe of Judah; from his deathbed, the biblical Jacob foretells Judah's future strength, symbolized by "a lion's whelp" (Gen. 49:9). Balaam speaks of the Israelites, "Lo, a people that rises like a lioness, Leaps up like a lion" (Num. 23:24); 2 Samuel describes David's heart "as the heart of a lion" (17:10); and 1 Kings reports on carvings of "lions, oxen, and cherubim" in Solomon's Temple (7:29). Additionally, lions appear to have roamed in the Land of Israel in mishnaic, talmudic, and crusader times. Depictions of lions are particularly common on Persian ketubot: the Jews of Isfahan (capital of Persia 1590–) demonstrated their loyalty to the regime by displaying this early symbol of Persian rule. However, lions also appear on ketubot in some forty nations where "the king of beasts" is a national symbol (from Czechia to Morocco to the UK) as well as in other countries without lions as national symbols (for example, the Ottoman Empire, Italy, and the United States).

Menorah—(Heb., "candelabrum"), a seven-branched candelabrum featured on the Tabernacle the Israelites build in the wilderness and, later, in the First and Second Temples. God is said to show Moses a pattern of this menorah at Mount Sinai, and one of the Tabernacle's vessels is a gold menorah whose lamps burned from evening to morning. Ten gold *menorot* also stood in the Jerusalem Temple built by Solomon. After Antiochus Epiphanes IV removed the golden menorah standing in the Second Temple in 169 BCE, Judah Maccabee made a new one, whose oil burned for eight nights in the miracle of Chanukah. The menorah became an—if not the most—important Jewish visual motif after the Second Temple's destruction, a symbol of Israel as a "light unto the nations" and of the continuity of Jewish tradition.[1]

Ring—A circular band symbolizing the cycle of life and the hope for an everlasting marriage. Jewish weddings traditionally involved one ring, which according to halakhah only the groom gave to the bride. Today, "double ring" imagery is common on contemporary ketubot for weddings where there is an exchange of rings.

Seven Species—The seven agricultural products referenced in the Torah to describe the victual abundance of the Land of Israel: wheat, barley, grapes, figs, pomegranates, olive (oil), and dates (honey). Symbolizing nobility, fruitfulness, and peace in biblical texts, the seven species can also connote longevity and immortality. Other ketubot reference the number seven itself, which figures prominently in and around the wedding ceremony, *Sheva Brachot* (Heb. "seven benedictions" or "seven blessings"). These blessings, recited over a goblet of wine, celebrate the marriage, love, harmony, and creation. Traditional newlyweds partake in a weeklong *Sheva Brachot* celebration, with a different family or friend hosting them each day for their first seven days of marriage. In the Ashkenazic tradition the bride circles the groom seven times (presumably to ward off evil spirits); and in some Oriental communities, the bride is fed seven times as part of a women-only ceremony (likewise, designed to ward off the evil eye) the evening before the wedding.

Shofar—One of the earliest known musical instruments still in use today, the animal horn is mentioned sixty-nine times in the Bible, first in relation to God's appearance at Mount Sinai. In Temple times, the horn of one of five kosher animals—sheep, goat, mountain goat, antelope, or gazelle—fulfilled the ritual commandment to sound the *shofar*.[2] In our own day, a ram's horn is sounded on the New Year because of the ram's connection with the *Akedah* (sacrifice of Isaac), the Torah reading on the second day of the festival. Open to interpretation, a shofar on a ketubah may represent the power of age-old traditions as well as the "sound of joy and the sound of happiness, the sound of the groom and the sound of the bride" as the newlyweds celebrate their new lives together.[3]

Solomon's Temple/Temple of David—Per the Bible, King Solomon built the First Temple from the fourth to the eleventh year of his reign. Solomon's Temple is also known as the Temple of David because King David is said to have conquered the Jerusalem area, built an altar there (on the very spot tradition identifies with the binding of Isaac), and planned to build the Temple there, but instead took the prophet Nathan's counsel to let his son Solomon do the building. Fast forward to the seventeenth through nineteenth centuries, when Jews in Italy and Islamic countries sought beautifully decorated ketubot, and illustrators connected the marriage document with the dream of renewing the Temple service in a rebuilt Jerusalem. Perhaps they were abiding by the biblical proclamation "if I do not keep Jerusalem in memory even at my happiest hour" (Ps. 137:6) and, consequently, the Rabbis' requirement that Jews elevate the memory of Jerusalem over other happy occasions. In a similar vein, to this day the ceremonial "breaking of the glass" is often thought to commemorate the destruction of the Temple amidst the joyous wedding celebration.

Star of David (also Magen David, Heb., "Shield of David")—Part of Jewish cultural life for generations, the six-pointed star did not become a recognized, distinctly Jewish symbol until the Middle Ages, when the Prague Jewish community adopted it as its official emblem. In 1354, when Charles IV allowed the community to bear its own flag, the Star of David was likely chosen because it was said that King David wore the six-pointed star on his shield. The symbol then travelled to other communities, and exiled Jews continued its dispersion. In the Ottoman world, the shield displayed on ketubot was understood to symbolize protection in the name of the pious, biblical warrior king. By the nineteenth century, the Jews' quest for a visual symbol of Judaism—akin to the emblem of the cross for Christianity—led to the star's ascendancy, including on the first issue of Theodore Herzl's Zionist journal *Die Welt*. In the twentieth century, its rendering as *the* major symbol on the State of Israel flag became symbolic of Jewish pride in the newly established homeland state. Thus, a Star of David on ketubot can speak deeply to Jewish tradition, faith, and identity through the ages.

Torah Crown—Denoting power and dignity, this crown emphasizes the centrality of the Torah in Jewish life. In the Mishnah, Rabbi Shimon said, "There are three crowns: the crown of Torah, the crown of priesthood, and the crown of monarchy [kingship]—but the crown of a good name outweighs them all."[4] When used on a ketubah, the crown can signify any of these meanings.

Tower of David—An ancient citadel near the Jaffa Gate entrance to the Old City of Jerusalem, the Tower of David first acquired its name after the Byzantine rulers erroneously identified the Jerusalem hill area as Mount Zion, and then further assumed the citadel was David's palace referenced in 2 Samuel. As a distinctive, recognizable part of the Jerusalem cityscape, it is often depicted in ketubot linking the marriage document to the promise, land, and beauty of Israel.

Tree of Life—In the biblical Garden of Eden, *Etz ha-Chayim* (in Hebrew) is one of two trees planted by God. It also often refers to the Torah—"She is a tree of life to those who grasp her" (Prov. 3:18)—as well as the ten divine qualities of Kabbalah (the tradition of Jewish mysticism). A Tree of Life (or sometimes a depiction of two trees) remains a popular symbol on contemporary ketubot because of its resonance with the joining together of the first beloveds.

Western Wall—The last vestige of the Second Temple that the Romans destroyed in 70 CE, this still intact western portion of the retaining wall became a sacred site in Jewish religious and national consciousness. It is associated with (1) mourning over the Temple's destruction and Israel's exile (hence the "Wailing Wall," among the wall's other names); (2) religious meaning, given its nearness to the Western Wall of the Holy of Holies in the Temple, from which it has been said the Divine Presence has never departed, along with the Jews' longstanding hope to restore the Temple to its former glory; and (3) national meaning, particularly after the League of Nations' Mandate for Palestine, enforced in September 1923, required Britain to effectuate the Balfour Declaration's "national home for the Jewish people" in the Land of Israel. For two millennia, Jews throughout the world have prayed toward the Western Wall. Looking back, its artistic representation on ketubot addresses this rich history of yearning and hope. Looking ahead, it speaks to the vision and possibility for Israel today and tomorrow.

Wine/Grapes/Vineyard—Wine plays a vital role in Judaism, both as a religious obligation (replacing the Temple sacrifice) and as a symbol of joy ("And now that the Temple is not standing [and one cannot eat sacrificial meat], he can fulfill the mitzvah of rejoicing on a Festival only by drinking wine, as it is stated: 'And wine that gladdens the heart of man'"[5]). Winemaking itself—the time-laden, perennially developing process of growing, harvesting, pressing, fermenting, and aging grapes—is seen, too, as a metaphor for marriage: young love, like wine, can be imbued with new richness and depth over the years. Twice during the wedding ceremony, the marrying couple drink wine from the same cup—a symbol of sealing their union, which is itself blessed by the wine they share. Additionally, a fruitbearing vineyard is considered a metaphor both for a family endowed with offspring and for Israel's redemption at the End of Days. So depictions of wine, grapes, or vineyards on ketubot may connote joy, blessings, and bliss in marriage, fertility, transformative love, even messianic hope for the future.

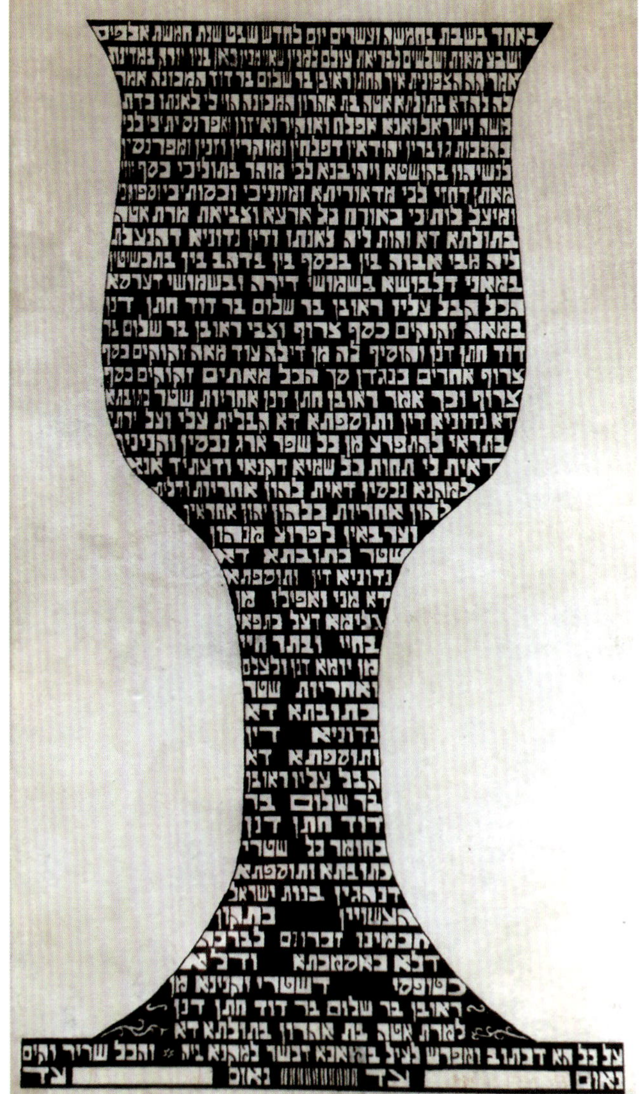

Fig. 17. David Moss, Ketubah of Eta and Ron Paransky, 1969. Courtesy of David Moss.

Notes

FOREWORD

1. For a general survey of the ketubah and its decoration, see "The Ketubbah: A Historical Overview" section of Sabar, *Ketubbah: Jewish Marriage Contracts*, 3–32.
2. For a detailed analysis of the text and decoration of ketubot in the many lands where the Jews settled from the Middle Ages to modern times, see Sabar, *Art of the Ketubbah*. For the origins and meaning of the most popular designs that decorate old ketubot (based on examples from The Israel Museum, Jerusalem), see Sabar, *Mazal Tov*.
3. Landsberger, "Illuminated Marriage Contracts," 503–42.

PREFACE

1. b. Bava Kamma 9b.
2. Exhibit catalog consulted at the Judah L. Magnes Museum in 2018.
3. Exod. 15:2, b. Shabbat 133b.
4. Ochs, *Inventing Jewish Ritual*, 89.

INTRODUCTION

1. Gaster, *Ketubah*, 54.
2. There is a long tradition of thinking of the Torah as the ketubah that God (the groom) gave to the Israelites (the bride) at Mount Sinai to signify the covenant for all time between the Almighty and the Jewish people. Some ornate Shavuot ketubot are an artful expression of this metaphor.
3. Later this tradition would spread as far west as Spain and eventually to the post-expulsion Sephardic diaspora.

4. "A Magnificently Decorated Ketubbah from Bombay, 1853," Sothebys, accessed December 2020, https://www.sothebys.com/en/buy/auction/2020/sassoon-a-golden-legacy/a-magnificently-decorated-ketubbah-from-bombay-2.
5. Abt, "Illuminated Ketubah" (1955), 20.
6. Moss, *Love Letters* (unpaginated).
7. Sabar, *Ketubbah: Art of the Jewish Marriage Contract*, 15.

1. THE KETUBAH IN ISRAEL

1. Sabar, *Ketubbah: Art of the Jewish Marriage Contract*, 21.

2. A LANDMARK ERA

1. Jenny McCommas, "Jewish American Artists in the Twentieth Century," Sidney and Lois Eskenazi Museum of Art Collections Online, Indiana University, accessed October 28, 2022, https://artmuseum.indiana.edu/collections-online/features/european-american/jewish-american-artists.php.
2. Abt, "Illuminated Ketubah" (1955), 22.
3. Abt, "Illuminated Ketubah" (1955), 22.
4. Kleeblatt, *Treasures of the Jewish Museum*, 192.
5. See https://thejewishmuseum.org/collection/20528-today-is-the-birthday-of-the-world.
6. Shahn, *Love and Joy About Letters*. See also "Some Perfect Lettering by Ben Shahn," February 14, 2014, https://www.darius-art.com/some-perfect-lettering-by-ben-shahn/.
7. See https://travel.thejewishmuseum.org/collection/553-eternal-peace.
8. Abt, "Illuminated Ketubah" (1969), 129.
9. Quoted from Gary Rosenthal's LinkedIn profile under Experience, C.E.O. Gary Rosenthal Collection, accessed November 22, 2024, https://www.linkedin.com/in/gary-rosenthal-0864a37/.
10. "About Kolbo Fine Judaica Gallery," Patch.com, accessed October 28, 2022, https://patch.com/massachusetts/brookline/directory/listing/29391/kolbo-fine-judaica-gallery.
11. Hinda Mandell, "Make Room for New," *The Boston Globe*, March 27, 2011, http://archive.boston.com/news/local/massachusetts/articles/2011/03/27/on_harvard_street_in_brookline_jewish_traditions_stand_up_to_change/.
12. "Judaica Crafts Fair," *The New York Times*, December 9, 1990, https://www.nytimes.com/1990/12/09/arts/judaica-crafts-fair.html.
13. Siegel, Strassfeld, and Strassfeld, *First Jewish Catalog*, 190.
14. "Whole Earth Catalog," Fall 1969, https://en.wikipedia.org/wiki/Whole_Earth_Catalog.
15. Siegel, Strassfeld, and Strassfeld, *First Jewish Catalog*, 190.
16. Siegel, Strassfeld, and Strassfeld, *First Jewish Catalog*, 196.
17. Siegel, Strassfeld, and Strassfeld, *First Jewish Catalog*, 195.
18. "About Us," Kol HaOt, accessed October 28, 2022, https://www.kolhaot.com/about.
19. Moss, *Love Letters* (third unnumbered page of author's introduction).
20. Moss, *Love Letters*, 4.
21. Julie Zauzmer, "'I Not Only Envisioned It. I Fought for It': The First Female Rabbi Isn't Done Yet," *Washington Post*, May 24, 2016, https://www.washingtonpost.com/news/acts-of-faith/wp/2016/05/24/i-not-only-envisioned-it-i-fought-for-it-the-first-female-rabbi-isnt-done-yet/.
22. Zauzmer, "'I Not Only Envisioned It.'"
23. "Aviel Barclay Becomes First Female Torah Scribe," Jewish Women's Archive, October 6, 2003, https://jwa.org/thisweek/oct/06/2003/aviel-barclay.
24. Michal Lando, "The First Soferet," *The Jerusalem Post*, October 2, 2007, https://www.jpost.com/jewish-world/jewish-features/the-first-soferet.
25. Darvick, *This Jewish Life*, 173.
26. Moss, *Love Letters*, 2.

3. KETUBAH TEXT TRANSFORMATIONS

1. Yevamot 89a.
2. "Mishnah," 319–20.

3. Marriage Document, Brooklyn Museum, accessed October 28, 2022, https://www.brooklynmuseum.org/opencollection/objects/3488.
4. Maimonides, *Mishneh Torah* 4:33, "Halachot Yebum vehakitza."
5. The use of the common historical term "Palestinian" here refers to the Land of Israel from 70 CE until the birth of the State of Israel in 1948 and not to contemporary concepts of this term.
6. Italics added for emphasis.
7. Gaster, *Ketubah*, 21.
8. Chief Rabbinate of Israel, "Marriage Registration Procedure," July 2019, https://www.gov.il/he/departments/policies/nohal_ishut1.
9. Rabbinical Council of America, collection of *ketubot*, accessed October 28, 2022, https://rabbis.org/ketubot/.
10. Beth Din of America, "The Prenup," accessed October 28, 2022, https://theprenup.org/.
11. Ketubbot 1:2.
12. Rabbinical Council of America, collection of *ketubot*.
13. For the Conservative ketubah text with the Lieberman clause, see https://www.rabbinicalassembly.org/sites/default/files/public/halakhah/teshuvot/19861990/newketubbah.pdf (accessed November 22, 2024).
14. For the egalitarian ketubah text by Rabbi Gordon Tucker, see https://ketubah.com/shop/product/gordon-tucker-egalitarian/ (accessed November 22, 2024).
15. Abt, "Illuminated Ketubah" (1969), 129.
16. Allen Salkin, "Wedding on the Wall," *The New York Times*, June 10, 2001.
17. For a Reform ketubah text, see option V (Reform), https://tallulahketubahs.com/pages/english-ketubah-wedding-contract-text-options (accessed November 22, 2024).
18. For Canadian Reform ketubah text, see https://ketubah.com/shop/product/canadian-reform/ (accessed November 22, 2024).
19. Chalom and Kornfeld, *Contemporary Humanistic Judaism*, 188.
20. "Secular Humanist 1," accessed November 22, 2024, https://ketubah.com/shop/product/secular-humanist-1/.
21. "Secular Humanist 2," accessed November 22, 2024, https://ketubah.com/shop/product/secular-humanist-2/.
22. Interfaith ketubah of Ezra & Isabelle, accessed October 28, 2022, https://static1.squarespace.com/static/5717e40f8259b528055ae673/t/5c963ea108522938214b7ab3/1553350313012/Interfaith.pdf.
23. Mickie and Eran Caspi, "Gender Neutral Ketubah Text" (now entitled "Same Sex Hebrew and English"), accessed November 22, 2024, https://www.caspicards.com/2018/02/gender-neutral-ketubah-text/.
24. Caspi, "Gender Neutral Ketubah Text."
25. Adler, *Engendering Judaism*, 214–18.
26. Adler, *Engendering Judaism*, 214.
27. Aliyah Guttmann, "Introducing Non-Binary Ketubah Texts," May 19, 2020, https://ketubah.com/introducing-non-binary-ketubah-texts/.

4. THE SCRIPT OF THE KETUBAH

1. Greenfield, "Aramaic in the Achaemenian Empire," 698–713.
2. Sanhedrin 21b (*Koren Talmud Bavli*).
3. "Alphabet, Hebrew," *Encyclopedia Judaica*, v. 2, 681. Also, "Writing," *Encyclopedia Judaica*, v. 16, 668.
4. "Alphabet, Hebrew," *Encyclopedia Judaica*, v. 2, 707.
5. "Alphabet, Hebrew," *Encyclopedia Judaica*, v. 2, 707.
6. "Alphabet, Hebrew," *Encyclopedia Judaica*, v. 2, 706.
7. See, for example, Menachot 29b and Tractate Soferim 9. Shabbat 89a.
8. For example, a fragment of an early ketubah from 117 CE (now housed in the Israel Department of Antiquities and Museums, Jerusalem) helped scholars identify Palestine cursive Negev script. *Encyclopedia Judaica*, v. 2, 691.

9. Gaster, *Ketubah*, 53; also Steiner, "Jewish Marriage Contract," 7.
10. Gaster, *Ketubah*, 25, 53; also Steiner, "Jewish Marriage Contract," 6–7.
11. Yardeni, *Book of Hebrew Script*, 101–3.
12. Hebrew has only five letters that take on a different form when they are the final letter of a word.
13. Leaf, *Hebrew Alphabets*, 1.
14. Greenspan, *Hebrew Calligraphy*, 142.
15. Nahson, *Ketubbot*, 14.
16. Judith Joseph, "Shelter: Re-Imagining the Ketubah," 2009 Conney Conference on Jewish Arts, Minds at UW, April 23, 2009, http://digital.library.wisc.edu/1793/76644.

5. THE ART OF KETUBAH PRODUCTION

1. See "Kedem-World Class Judaica and Israeliana Auction House," accessed November 22, 2024, Kedem-auctions.com.
2. The *tenaim* ceremony was traditionally a separate ceremony, often held a year before the wedding, in which the two families declared their intention for their children to marry each other. Later, given the stringency of this prewedding betrothal—and the financial penalty if either party backed out—this ceremony was moved to immediately precede the wedding ceremony. In some communities and time periods, these "betrothal conditions" were written into a specially designated area of the artistic ketubah border.
3. "Chieri, 1706 [Ket 260]" from Sabar, *Art of the Ketubbah*, 11n5.
4. Annie Abrams, "A Ketubah Shows the Promise That Turned a Young Printer Into a Renowned Artist," *Tablet*, November 25, 2013, https://www.tabletmag.com/sections/community/articles/julius-bien-ketubah. See https://thejewishmuseum.org/collection/20036-marriage-contract for the 1852 marriage contract produced by Julius Bien.
5. Joseph Shadur, "Jewish Papercutting," My Jewish Learning, accessed November 22, 2024, https://web.archive.org/web/20150107002727/http://www.myjewishlearning.com/culture/2/Art/History_and_Theory/Jewish_Folk_Art/Jewish_Papercuts.shtml?p=0.
6. Shadur, "Jewish Papercutting."
7. See, for example, https://ketubah.com/shop/product/cycles-of-life-personalized-papercut/.
8. See, for example, https://ketubah.com/shop/product/mandala-luxe-wood/.

6. KETUBAH IN THE TWENTY-FIRST CENTURY

1. In 1964 the intermarriage rate in the United States was 7 percent; in 2020, according to the Pew Research Study, 42 percent of all married Jews are intermarried. Moreover, since 2010, 61 percent of all weddings involving Jews—and 72 percent when excluding Orthodox Jews—are interfaith weddings. See Lawrence Goodman, "Is Intermarriage Good for the Jews?," Brandeis University—The Jewish Experience, June 15, 2022, https://www.brandeis.edu/jewish-experience/jewish-america/2022/june/intermarriage-interfaith-marriage.html; Pew Research Center, "Jewish Americans in 2020—Marriage, Families, and Children," May 11, 2021, https://www.pewresearch.org/religion/2021/05/11/marriage-families-and-children/.
2. Judith Joseph, "Artist's Statement: Shelter: Reimagining the Ketubah, A Collaboration by Chicago Artist Judith Joseph and Barcelona-based Artist Brooke Borg," Judith Joseph Studio, 2008, https://www.judithjosephart.com/installation-interactive-art.
3. According to the Pew Research Center's "Jewish Americans in 2020" study, 28 percent of children in interfaith marriages are being raised "Jewish by religion" and 29 percent are being raised "Jewish but not by religion"; yet another 12 percent are being raised with multiple religions. Pew Research Center, "Jewish Americans in 2020."
4. This author adopted the "old-new" term from *Altneuland* ("The Old New Land"), the title of Theodore Herzl's 1902 utopian novel envisioning a modern Jewish state in the Land of Israel.
5. For example, Yiddish inserts the silent (in Hebrew) letter "ayin" into a word wherever the short "e" sound is needed,

instead of placing three dots (in triangular formation) below a consonant, as is done in Hebrew.

6. Samantha Murphy Kelly, "Who Says Romance Is Dead? Couples Are Using ChatGPT to Write Their Wedding Vows," CNN, April 12, 2023, https://www.cnn.com/2023/04/12/tech/chatgpt-wedding-vows/index.html; Etsy, "Modern, AI-Generated Digital Ketubah," accessed November 22, 2024, https://www.etsy.com/ca/shop/ImagineDigiCreations?ref=return_to_search&listing_id=1555265880&from_page=listing&search_query=ai+generate.
7. I literally spotted this "ketubah" out of the corner of my eye through the front window of the restaurant,while standing across the street!
8. David Moss invents new words such as: Aramaic + magic = aramagic; and, a few lines down, pride + groom = pridegroom.
9. From the do-it-yourself article "The Lovely Art of Ketubbah-making," in Siegel, Strassfeld, and Strassfeld, *Jewish Catalog*, 195.

APPENDIX

1. See Exod. 25:40; Lev. 24:3; 1 Kings 7:49; 2 Chron. 4:7; 1 Macc. 1:21, 4:49–50; 2 Macc. 10:3.
2. RH 27a.
3. From the last blessing of the *Sheva Brachot.*
4. Pirkei Avot 4:13.
5. Pesachim 109a, quoting from Ps. 104:15.

Bibliography

Abt, Harry. "The Illuminated Ketubah." *Jewish Affairs* 10, no. 7 (July 1955): 22.

Abt, Harry. "The Illuminated Ketubah." *Jewish Affairs* 24, no. 8 (August 1969): 129.

Adler, Rachel. *Engendering Judaism: An Inclusive Theology and Ethics*. Philadelphia: The Jewish Publication Society, 1998.

Chalom, Adam, Jodi Kornfeld, and Jeremy Kridel. *Contemporary Humanistic Judaism: Beliefs, Values, Practices*. Philadelphia: The Jewish Publication Society, 2025.

Darvick, Debra. *This Jewish Life: Stories of Discovery, Connection, and Joy*. Canton MI: Read the Spirit Books, 2013.

Davidovitch, David. *The Ketuba: Jewish Marriage Contracts Through the Ages*. Tel Aviv: Lewin-Epstein Ltd., 1968.

Diamant, Anita. *The New Jewish Wedding*. New York: Summit Books, 2017.

Eis, Ruth, and David Moss. *A Tradition Reborn: Contemporary Ketubot by David Moss*. Berkeley CA: Judah L. Magnes Memorial Museum, 1974.

Encyclopedia Judaica. 16 vols. Jerusalem: Keter, 1972.

Friedman, Mordechai Akiva. "The Remains of Nine Ketubot according to the Customs of the Land of Israel from the Geniza." *Dinei Yisrael* 34 (2000): 173–238.

Gaster, Moshe. *The Ketubah*. Holon, Israel: Rimon Pub. Co., 1925.

Greenfield, Jonas. "Aramaic in the Achaemenian Empire." In *The Median and Achaemenian Periods,* edited by I. Gershevitch, 698–713. Vol. 2 of *The Cambridge History of Iran*. Cambridge: Cambridge University Press, 1985.

Greenspan, Jay. *Hebrew Calligraphy: A Step-by-Step Guide*. New York: Schocken Books, 1981.

Jewish Publication Society. *Tanakh: The Holy Scriptures: The New JPS Translation According to the Traditional Hebrew Text*. Philadelphia: The Jewish Publication Society, 1985.

Kleeblatt, Norman. *Treasures of the Jewish Museum*. New York: Universe Books, 1986.

Landsberger, Franz. "Illuminated Marriage Contracts with Special Reference to the Cincinnati Ketubbot." *Hebrew Union College Annual* 26 (1955): 503–42.

Leaf, Reuben. *Hebrew Alphabets: 400 BCE to Our Days*. New York: Bloch Publishing, 1950.

Moss, David. *Love Letters*. Berkeley CA: Bet Alpha Editions, 2004.

Nahson, Claudia. *Ketubbot: Marriage Contracts from the Jewish Museum*. New York: Jewish Museum, 1998.

Ochs, Vanessa L. *Inventing Jewish Ritual*. Philadelphia: The Jewish Publication Society, 2007.

Pludwinsḳi, Izzy. *The Beauty of the Hebrew Letter: From Sacred Scrolls to Graffiti*. Waltham MA: Brandeis University Press, 2023.

Sabar, Shalom. *The Art of the Ketubbah: Marriage Contracts from the Library of the Jewish Theological Seminary*. 2 vols. New York: Library of the Jewish Theological Seminary, 2022.

———. "The Beginnings and Flourishing of Ketubbah Illustration in Italy: A Study in Popular Imagery and Jewish Patronage During the Seventeenth and Eighteenth Centuries." PhD dissertation, University of California—Los Angeles, 1987.

———. "Illustrated Ketubbot in the Jewish Museum of Greece." In *The Jewish Museum of Greece*, edited by Zanet Battinou, 260–68. Athens: Jewish Museum of Greece, 2013.

———. *Ketubbah: The Art of the Jewish Marriage Contract*. New York: Rizzoli International and the Israel Museum, 2000.

———. *Ketubbah: Jewish Marriage Contracts of the Hebrew Union College Skirball Museum and Klau Library*. Philadelphia: The Jewish Publication Society, 1990.

———. *Mazal Tov: Illuminated Jewish Marriage Contracts from the Israel Museum Collection*. Jerusalem: The Israel Museum, 1993.

———. "The Preservation and Continuation of Sephardi Art in Morocco." *European Judaism: A Journal for the New Europe* 52, no. 2 (Autumn 2019): 59–81.

Shadur, Joseph, and Yehudit Shadur. *Traditional Jewish Papercuts: An Inner World of Art and Symbol*. Hanover NH: University Press of New England, 2002.

Shahn, Ben. *Love and Joy About Letters*. New York: Grossman Publishers, 1963.

Siegel, Richard, Michael Strassfeld, and Sharon Strassfeld, eds. *The First Jewish Catalog*. Philadelphia: The Jewish Publication Society, 1973.

Skolnik, Fred, and Michael Berenbaum, eds. *Encyclopaedia Judaica*. 2nd ed. Detroit: Macmillan Reference USA in association with the Keter Pub. House, 2007.

Steiner, Benjamin. "The Jewish Marriage Contract: A Window into Jewish Social History." PhD dissertation, Brandeis University, 2020.

Yardeni, Ada. *The Book of Hebrew Script: History, Palaeography, Script Styles, Calligraphy & Design*. Jerusalem: Carta, 1997.